Ben Franklin's Web Site:

Privacy and Curiosity from Plymouth Rock to the Internet

Other Books by Robert Ellis Smith

Privacy: How to Protect What's Left of It (1979)

Workrights (1984)

The Big Brother Book of Lists (co-author)(1984)

The Law of Privacy Explained (1993)

Our Vanishing Privacy (1993)

Compilation of State and Federal Privacy Laws (1997)

Ben Franklin's Web Site:

Privacy and Curiosity from Plymouth Rock to the Internet

By Robert Ellis Smith

Privacy Journal
Providence RI USA

Second printing, 2004
Copyright © 2000, 2004 Robert Ellis Smith
All rights reserved
Printed in the United States of America
By Sheridan Books

Library of Congress Cataloging-in-Publication Data

Smith, Robert Ellis.
Ben Franklin's web site : privacy and curiosity from Plymouth Rock
to the internet / Robert Ellis Smith.
p. cm.
Includes bibliographical references and index.
ISBN 0-930072-14-6 (alk. paper)
1. Privacy, Right of--United States--History. I. Title.
JC596.2.U5 S646 2000
323.44'8'0973--dc21
00-008511

www.privacyjournal.net
orders@privacyjournal.net

For Gregor, Benjamin, David, and Marc

All Smiths, all good guys.

CONTENTS

To the Reader

I had to remind myself continually when writing this book that there were wars and great explorations going on at the time of the events and ideas I describe. This book of history is not about wars and explorations. It's about the lives and living conditions and values of average individuals, who in their own ways contributed to the tapestry of American history.

This is a book about "the silences in traditional history." I am talking about those episodes that were not a part of traditional recorded history because they concerned not momentous public events but discrete occurrences in the lives of everyday persons – individuals who create the raw materials of history. While much of this book is about the actions and beliefs of public men and women, what really propelled the story of personal privacy in American life, of course, were the actions of average persons. Such as Abigail Roberson, Paolo Pavesich, Michael Hardwick, Edward Lawson, Stephen Roy, Estelle Griswold, Elizabeth Hill, and others who appear in this story.[1]

With regard to the public personalities in the book, it has been interesting to me that the same ones appear and then reappear in the narrative – for good or for ill. They include Benjamin Franklin, James Madison, Jay Gould, Walt Whitman, William Randolph Hearst, Anthony Comstock, Joseph Pulitzer, Louis Brandeis, J. Edgar Hoover, Richard M. Nixon, and William H. Rehnquist.

In the course of writing and publishing a monthly newsletter since 1974 about the right to privacy, I have practiced the advice attributed to the twenty-ninth First Lady of America, Eleanor Roosevelt: "Go out and see for yourself. Make others see what you've seen." This book is the product of that endeavor.

Since I have been publishing *Privacy Journal*, writing books on the subject, and advocating increased recognition of the right to privacy, I have been accumulating lots of files. In one of those folders marked "History of Privacy," I kept items like the one about J. Edgar Hoover complaining about clandestine sex in the motor courts of the 1930s. Then, through the writings of David J. Seipp, I found an intriguing observation from the French humorist

Paul Blouet late in the Nineteenth Century about the typical American, "Meeting you in a railway carriage, he will ask you point blank where you are going, what you are doing, and where you are from. By degrees, he grows bolder." At that point formed the idea for a book on the history of privacy.

But this story is about more than privacy. (Secretly, I have long felt that Americans are a little bit nervous about the subject – and probably reluctant to read a whole book about privacy.) Nearly all other books about privacy assume that this is a positive value shared by all Americans. I'm not sure that it is. Our feelings about personal privacy – our privacy and everyone else's – are ambivalent. To understand why, you have to look to all aspects of our culture. That is what this book does. It looks into the hidden niches of our history. I'll be pleased if when you read each page of this book you say to yourself, "I didn't realize that."

And so, this book offers a different way of looking at parts of our nation's history, to see how they have shaped our ideas about privacy, how they have brought us to our current situation at the beginning of the millennium – a time when we all think that our personal sense of privacy has disappeared.

My intent is to describe the events and ideas that brought us to where we are today. From that we can see that some of the debates of today have been waged before and that some of the earlier warning signs were ignored. Especially, I hope, we can see that the drift of technology is not inevitable. Instead, it is determined by corporate decisions, government actions, individuals' tastes and prejudices – some of them unwise and others of them hastily considered. The direction of technology is determined also by seemingly unrelated events occurring at the same time.

As I continued to travel the country in the course of writing this book, I kept asking myself (usually as I looked down on American cities and towns from an airplane window), "How is what I am writing about relevant to readers across this huge country?" This nation stretches across a full continent and beyond, with different ethnic and language groups that have heritages quite different from the Anglo-Saxon roots of our founders. Much of my story takes place in New England and the rest of the East Coast. It is about our Puritan roots. Is that relevant to Americans everywhere? The more I wrote, the more I understood that it is indeed relevant, because those Puritan roots affect every aspect of our nation, from Alaska to Florida and from Maine to Hawaii – our legal system, our communications with each other, our values, our governmental structure, and our relationships to large private and public organizations.

The historian David Hackett Fischer points out that every one of our elected Presidents but one has had direct blood lines from the four regional groups in England that first settled this country. (The only exception so far has been John F. Kennedy. Ironically he was the President in the Twentieth Century most identified with New England.) The government and the laws they administered and the values they tried to appeal to – all stemmed from our Puritan beginnings in the Seventeenth Century.

And so even though this saga, like so many other accounts of American history, seems to concern only a small corner of the nation, the elements of the story affect any one of us who calls himself or herself an American. "Whoever gets there first sets the tone for the culture," according to one of my colleagues, Douglass Lea.

As I wrote, I kept nearby – buried under papers on my desk, to be sure, but nearby – a warning from a critic in the journal *Foreign Affairs*:

> "Books that propound theories of history – that is, that claim to find common patterns in events widely separated in time and space – have had a deservedly dicey history among the professionals. When such books are good they can be very good: a classic like William McNeill's *Plagues and Peoples* can permanently change the way you look at human affairs."

My goal has been to avoid the pitfalls pointed out by the critic, who was reviewing a 1996 book by David Hackett Fischer, *The Great Wave: Price Revolutions and the Rhythm of History*. For me, Fischer's *Albion's Seed* is another example of a book that succeeds at this. Luckily it touches on issues of privacy in every chapter, and so I consulted it regularly. And its structure served as a model for me.

In looking at American history through the prism of personal privacy, I allow myself and the reader to take short digressions that shed light on the topic at hand. To me, each of the detours reflects on the larger story – America's tug between privacy and curiosity. Occasionally they are simply interesting on their own. The fact that George Washington as President would pack his bags and travel to country inns and stay out of touch from his own staff for days and days may not tell us anything about the theme of the book (although my wandering mind grasps the connection). The anecdote itself is interesting, however, and so I included it. I believe that it contributes to the final mosaic, in ways we don't even realize at first.

As they told me in the first-year of law school "Wait till you get to the end to see how it all fits together."

When you do get to the end, I hope that you will send me your ideas and reactions. I can be reached at *Privacy Journal*, P.O. Box 28577, Providence RI 02908 or at our World Wide Web site, www.privacyjournal.net.

For clarity, I have updated spellings and punctuation in early writings and quotations, but only occasionally. Where it was not necessary for clarity, I have not done so. I have not included in my account the legal development of searches and seizures under the Fourth Amendment to our Constitution, only because that has been written about elsewhere with great expertise. Besides, a purist might say that the history of searches and seizures belongs in a history of criminal justice more than in a history of personal privacy. All I can say is that the omission here is intentional.

This is the place in an author's preface when he or she acknowledges the legion of interns, research assistants, and grant-funded minions who hustled to make the book happen. I wish that I had such a list. To my continual regret, getting foundations to fund research, writing, and advocacy in this field has been impossible. Grants makers simply reflect the nervousness about the subject of "privacy" that I believe all Americans sense. I hope that this book persuades some of them that the field of privacy is coherent, defined, and desperate for attention. It is also filled with a cadre of extraordinarily committed and perceptive scholars and activists, most of whom are cited in the text or the footnotes. They are also a very congenial group. One of the reasons that this issue has sustained my interest over more than 25 years is that the experts in the field easily cross traditional disciplinary lines; there are scholars, lawyers, business executives, public-policy activists, politicians, computer enthusiasts, and technologists active in this field. I have relied on their work continually.

Shelley Roth, of the Roth Agency in Rehoboth, Massachusetts – within a short ride of where the events in the early part of this story took place – was passionate and persistent in her belief in this book. In that respect, as a literary agent, she has been a true partner in this endeavor. In my writing and research, I had special help from Dawud G. Alexis, Elisha S. Anderson, David A. Banisar, Bill Brown, Pam Brown, David B. Burnham, Ann Cavoukian, James X. Dempsey, David H. Flaherty, Stephen J. Fortunato, A. Michael Froomkin, Simson Garfinkel, Dana Hawkins, Ralph Keyes, Douglass Lea, Ronald B. Lewis, Douglas Parker, Stan Pottinger, Daniel Asa Rose, Marc Rotenberg, William Safire, James J. Sulanowski, Shauna Van Dongen, for fact checking and editing; Richard Ziehler – and most especially Kathryn Ritter-Smith. Each of them was ready to assist me in a second.

I have to offer acknowledgment to two tools of the 1990s: Microsoft's word processing and its Encarta multimedia encyclopedia, both of which make the writer's task a lot easier.

Join me now in an exploration from our beginnings as a nation to the new millennium, to discover why we as a people are so curious that we seem to have lost our privacy irrevocably. For me the odyssey has reaffirmed the words of the poet T.S. Eliot, which illuminated my involvement in this issue in the first place. They are a variation on Eleanor Roosevelt's advice:

> "We shall not cease from exploration
> And the end of all our exploring
> Will be to arrive where we started
> And know the place for the first time."

Illustrations by Sangram Majumdar

Introduction

Since this continent was settled from Europe, Americans have quested for personal privacy, first in our physical space and later in the use of our personal information.

At the same time, Americans have always been extremely curious. Virtually all visitors from abroad say that about us. We are too willing to intrude into the affairs of others and, by the same token, too willing to furnish strangers with personal information about ourselves. No other culture has more outlets for gathering information and disseminating it – "talk radio" and television news 24 hours a day, a gaggle of weekly magazines, ubiquitous tabloid newspapers and published memoirs with personal revelations by celebrities and non-celebrities, news and information within reach of virtually all Americans, in the car, at home, by computer modem, and even by earphones while alone in the woods. We seem to be enamored with the idea of privacy, but probably more enamored with the idea of learning more and more about our friends and neighbors – and about the celebrities among us.

By understanding this duality in the American character we can come to understand the current conflicts over protecting privacy. We Americans have institutionalized this duality in our Constitution, which protects the sanctity of each private residence at the same time that it requires each of us to report our whereabouts to the government at least once every ten years. The same Constitution that protects the right to remain silent gives unprecedented protection to authors and news reporters to find out about other people and write about them.

Just what is privacy? It is the desire by each of us for physical space where we can be free of interruption, intrusion, embarrassment, or accountability and the attempt to control the time and manner of disclosures of personal information about ourselves. In the first half of our history, Americans seemed to pursue the first, physical privacy; in the second half – after the Civil War – Americans seemed in pursuit of the second, "informational privacy."

Each time when there was renewed interest in protecting privacy it was in reaction to new technology. First, in the years before 1890, came cameras, telephones, and high-speed publishing; second, around 1970, came the development of computers; and third, in the late 1990s, the coming of personal computers and the World Wide Web brought renewed interest in this subject. In each case, the rhetoric had similar sounds to it. What worried people was not so much the technology; what worried them was that it was in the hands of large and powerful organizations.

The coming of personal computers and the Internet has changed the equation in significant ways. In this new era, individuals and small organizations have gained cyberpower that seems comparable to what large organizations can effectively manage. A solitary individual can now publish a news periodical and reach as many readers as his or her content warrants. A solitary individual now possesses the technical wherewithal to intrude into another's business, to keep information on other persons, and even to alter the content of information in the computer systems of large organizations. Individuals, like large organizations, can now snoop into the private activities of others and record them on audio or video tape. And many individuals have attempted to do just that. At the height of the Watergate scandal, a columnist for *The Washington Post*, Nicholas von Hoffman, observed, "We still know more about our government than it knows about us." But the balance is shifting.

In the end, the question of privacy throughout our history comes down to the relationship of the individual to large organizations and the method by which those large organizations foster and use new technology. The theme of the story ahead is privacy vs. curiosity, but the leitmotif is surely the impact of new technology on our individual rights and our autonomy.

Watchfulness

*Living conditions, community values, and surveillance
in the Colonies and the search for confidentiality in mailed
correspondence*

"We must all watch one another."

That was the instruction from the Rev. Robert Browne for church members in the Colonial period of our nation's history. Browne was an Anglican minister back in England whose views had great influence on the Puritans who settled in New England. In 1582, he set down on paper his guiding principles for the Congregational church. He laid out more than 125 Frequently Asked Questions, including, "How are we made Kings?" His answer was "We must all watch one another, and try out all wickedness. We must privately and openly rebuke the private and open offenders. We must also separate the willful and more grievous offenders, and withdraw ourselves from them." Browne's tenets became the basis for modern Congregationalism in America.[1]

Keeping an eye on one another was important to Puritans because good behavior in people's private lives was regarded as a prerequisite for a functioning society. For practicing Puritans in early New England, subjecting their private lives – including one's most intimate activities *and thoughts* – to public scrutiny was routinely expected. It was a tenet of their church, and the church was then the dominant force in regulating behavior.[2]

Browne's own Church of England created courts to supervise the morality of the entire population. Puritans in New England didn't go that far, because they regarded the ecclesiastical courts in England as ineffectual and corrupt. They knew in fact that the courts had aimed much of their zeal at infractions by Puritans themselves. There were no church-run courts in New England. Puritans imposed their discipline only upon volunteers who freely joined the church, not on the whole community, as the Church of England had done.

One Calvinist meeting house painted the all-seeing eye of God on the front of the pulpit from which the minister preached, lest any members of the congregation think for a moment that they were not accountable. In front of the pulpit, beneath the big eye, sat the lay leaders of the church on the "elder bench," monitoring the parishioners during the church service.

The Puritan leader Thomas Hooker took it upon himself "to prevent all taint of sin in any Member of the Society, that either be never committed; or if committed, it may speedily be removed." Hooker tried to impress upon church members that there was a duty to inform on others. This attitude was a part of the church notion of "the Relation," in which a person seeking admission to the church would subject himself or herself to scrutiny by church members, to specific questioning about his or her personal life, and to the testimony of friends and neighbors. Nothing less than dealing "nakedly and sincerely" with one's shortcomings would do, ac-

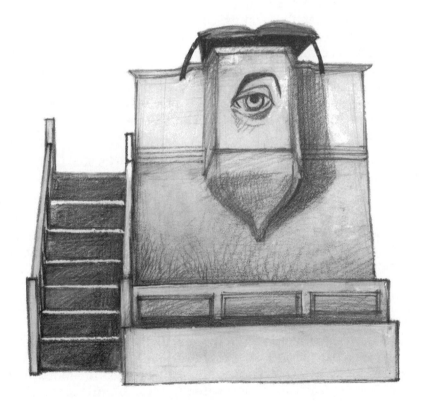

The all-seeing eye in a New England church

cording to Hooker. He knew, however, that he could not impose this discipline on non-church members.

The clergy of the late 1600s tried their best to keep track of what was going on within members' households. They banned most frivolity, including celebrations of Christmas. They required attendance at church on the Sabbath (although this usually was not onerous because going to church was a crucial social opportunity during the week, an opportunity to pick up a little gossip).

Further, "no one could settle in a New England town without permission of the inhabitants or their representatives," reported David H. Flaherty, in his original study on *Privacy in Colonial New England*. Heads of households in New England had to register with the town the names of any overnight guests. Captains of ships docking in the ports were sometimes expected to provide passenger lists to town authorities.

There were laws in nearly all communities prohibiting living alone. For the good of families and the community as a whole, the church regarded living together in a family unit as the best possible arrangement. The rule applied to widows and young persons alike. There are records in Middlesex County, Massachusetts, of the court systematically searching residences in 1668 for single persons and placing them with families. This was a requirement that the settlers had become accustomed to in their villages back in England.

William Petty, an English political economist who took a special interest in the Pennsylvania Colony, decreed that "no youth of between 18 and 58 yeares old, nor woman of between 16 and 41 yeares old, bee unmaryed."[3]

It is also true that there were good practical reasons at that time *not* to live alone. It was a waste of resources in many ways, an unnecessary risk, and in an agriculture economy – virtually impossible. A person living alone would not be able to maintain even a small farm.

These teachings stuck with the early Americans – long after Puritanism lost its influence over the majority of the population. A French writer in the 1790s observed that an American woman was eager to be married – even though a women had "unlimited freedom" when unmarried and as a wife she became "little more than a nursemaid."[4]

The authorities were empowered to enter homes without warning to enforce laws against drunkenness even in private homes. Where order in the family had broken down, the constables were expected to restore it, even removing children or servants from the home.[3] Increase Mather, the crusty pastor of the North Church in Boston and father of the equally crusty Cotton Mather, begged constables, "Especially see that you keep a vigilant eye over these private, dark alehouses."[4]

Laws based on religious beliefs prohibited certain kinds of dress, but these restrictions had disappeared in England by then and were difficult to enforce in New England.

**"Among the peculiarly English ideas
which the Colonists brought to Massachusetts,
which all the wear and tear of democracy
have not been able to obliterate, was that of family.
Family feeling, family pride, family hope and fear
and desire, were, in my early day, strongly marked traits.
'Of a very respectable family' was a sentence so often
repeated at the old fireside that its influence went
in part to make up my character."**

Nineteenth-Century novelist Harriet Beecher Stowe.[5]

And then there was the custom of the "nightwatch." Puritan authorities appointed ordinary citizens to stroll neighborhoods "in case they meet with any persons walking in the streets unseasonably . . . to examine them, and in case they cannot give a good account of their occasions" to arrest them, according to the law in Connecticut. Neighboring Massachusetts had a similar law. Boston instructed its nightwatch to lurk and listen "in order to make discovery."[6] Still, Boston was more restrictive than other port cities; its authorities monitored personal behavior more than elsewhere in the colonies. By the early 1700s this onerous custom had been curtailed even in Boston, except for surveillance of persons of color and persons suspected of misbehavior.

Not only was the church the arbiter of proper behavior, it was also the keeper of vital records about the population. Colonists had been accustomed to codes in England that required the reporting of births, deaths, and marriages in the community, and they continued to report this data back to England. (In the previous century, Governor John White of Roanoke Colony created what is probably the first birth certificate in the New World. He sent a note back to England: "The 18 [of August, 1587] Elenor, daughter to the Governor, and wife to Ananias Dare one of the Assistants, was delivered of a daughter in Roanoak, and the same was Christened there the Sunday following, and because this child was the first Christian borne in Virginia, she was named Virginia.[9])

This task of data collection fell to the clergy. They, after all, conducted the baptisms, weddings, and burials and were in the best position to record vital statistics. The church also collected information about salvations, heresies, and near heresies. Before long, clergymen like the Rev. John Eliot of First Church in Roxbury, Massachusetts, were also recording the causes of death, accidents, family size, number of houses, and other information of a civic, not ecclesiastical nature. They even collected demographic information about Indians, as best they could. The New England church was as much a vital-records office as a place of salvation. Many of the early debates about separation of church and state – which were to become crucial in the 1700s – focused in the 1600s on the propriety of the church keeping these civic records.

Of all the settlements, the Massachusetts Bay Colony developed the most sophisticated information-collection system. It was apparently the first jurisdiction to require citizens themselves to report information. In 1639, the legislature of the colony, the General Court of Massachusetts, required, "That there bee records kept of all wills, administrations & inventories, as also of the dayes of every marriage, birth & death of every person within this jurisdiction."[10] Later, the other colonies followed the practices in Massachusetts. To this day, the Commonwealth of Massachusetts is the only state to require an annual census by each town clerk, to list name, date of birth, occupation, nationality, and residence of each and every resident. By law, the police have access to the lists, and the names of all school-age children must be submitted to the school authorities.

The massive information collection by governmental agencies in the second half of the Twentieth Century had its roots in the importance the early New Englanders placed in having accurate data about illnesses, mortality, types of employment, and mobility within the colonies. Obviously they wanted the data in order to prevent or control epidemics. They wanted also to notify next-of-kin in England of settlers' whereabouts. And they wanted to attract new settlers with data about opportunities in the New World. Massachusetts Bay authorities were protective of their data – just like

Twenty-First-Century bureaucrats. They refused to disclose information on mortality rates, not so much to protect the identities of individuals, but out of fear that release of the information may have made the colony less attractive to prospective settlers back in England. And so began a 350-year tradition of government agencies trying to avoid sharing with the public the information they had gathered.

Nor was data collection any easier then than it is now. Many residents were not Puritans and did not cooperate with the church-managed nose counts; others wanted to conceal births out of wedlock; still others lived in the wilderness and did not bother or refused to be registered. Some colonies were obligated to report back to England the number of Dissenters (those Protestants who did not conform to the Church of England), but as the numbers multiplied this became impossible. Dissenters, of course, would not consent to be married or buried by the established church in the colonies, and so the church was not able to keep counts as the years went on. In the next century, after the Revolutionary War, the difficulties of the clergy in keeping tabs on everybody in the community increased to such an extent that secular leaders were pleading with church leaders to compile accurate demographic statistics.[11]

As tensions increased between the Colonies and the Crown, collecting personal data became even more difficult. Colonial governors, who reported to the British government, complained that they had no authority and no funds to act as census takers. They said that there was widespread lack of cooperation. An officious emissary from England named Edward Randolph who sought to collect personal data in New England – and collect fees in the process – wrote home in 1686, "I am called Register, but no man comes and records their Deeds at my Office."[12]

The new settlers had brought with them across the Atlantic another medieval custom for keeping order in their villages. "Tythingmen," a term based on the Old English word for ten or tenth, were responsible for supervising the moral conduct of ten families. These men seemed to be outside the recognized law enforcement cadre but could haul an offender before a magistrate after a warning. They were on the look-out for "all single persons that live from under Family Government, stubborn and disorderly children and Servants, nightwalkers, [tipplers], Sabbath breakers, [and associated other reprobates, debauchers, atheists, or other rude or non-church going characters]." As an example, Hampshire County, Massachusetts, instructed its tythingmen "to have a vigilant eye upon all persons that shall without just and necessary Cause be un-seasonably abroad in the Evenings from their parents or masters houses or familyes."[13]

Written records of the time indicate that tythingmen could inspect private homes. The records also show that the tythingmen seemed not to exercise the vague and broad authority they had been given, instead confining themselves to a few arrests for drunkenness and absences from church services. Their diligence – such as it was – seemed to wane over the years, and many of those selected chose not to serve. "What shall we do?" Cotton Mather, the great pro-tector of Puritan ethics, asked in 1704. Even he recognized that the enforcers must exercise discretion in singling out miscreants.

Indeed, there was one important privacy protection that happened to be built into the system. Tythingmen served on a rotating basis, rarely for more than one year. By the time one of the enforcers learned juicy details of the families he "supervised," he was off the job in favor of someone without benefit of the background infor-mation.

Complementing the tythingmen's work was a loose network of in-formers, who were often paid for tips about the misdeeds of their neighbors. Their job was to satisfy the church's expectation that all members had an obligation to report sins of others to the authori-ties. Beyond that, so-called Select members of the church were ever vigilant for sins by others.

This aggregation of informers, tythingmen, nightwatches, and clergy members who regularly visited homes and did not hesitate to keep tabs on drinking and socializing seems to add up to an en-vironment of oppressive and constant surveillance for the early settlers from England. But that is only half the story.

As the years went on, the church and Puritan teachings had far less influence on peoples' lives than they did at the time North America was first settled from abroad. The Relation ritual in the church was voluntary on the part of citizens who wished to join the church. Far fewer than a majority of residents – perhaps only one-fifth – con-sidered themselves among the "Elect" of church members bound by these principles. And by 1700 the practice had pretty much been phased out.[14] By 1704 Cotton Mather was complaining that New England Christians were neglecting to watch over one another adequately.

A visiting English journalist noted this inclination of New Englanders to snoop on each other but he himself, with old country values and with no fear of retaliation, disparaged one member of the Select as "Mr. Busie-Body" and seemed to believe that the man deserved a whack for his nosiness. Here is the full account by the visiting journalist, Edward Ward:

> "A good Cudgel apply'd in the Dark is an excellent Medicine for a Malignant Spirit. I know it once Experienced at Boston, with very good success, upon an Old rigged Precisian, one of their Select, who used to be more then ordinary vigilant in discovering every little Irregularity in the Neighborhood; I happened one Night to be pritty Merry with a Friend, opposite to the Zealot's dwelling, who got out of his Bed in his Wast-coat and Drawers, to listen at our Window. My Friend having oft been serv'd so, had left unbolted his Cellar Trap-door, as a Pit-fall for Mr. Busie-Body, who stepping upon it, sunk down with an Outcry like a distressed Mariner in a sinking Pinnace. My Friend having planted a Cudgel ready, run down Stairs, crying 'Thieves,' and belabour'd Old Troublesome very sevearly before he would know him. He crying out, 'I am your Neighbor.'"[15]

With settlers having real concerns about protecting themselves from Native Americans, resisting oppressive measures from England, and facing the harsh reality of establishing communities in the New World, the sanctimonious enforcers of the church, in spite of their best efforts, simply couldn't keep up with the task. What law enforcement officers there were in those times were pressured to stay out of the private affairs of residents. "Let every one meddle with his own Business" was a proverb of the time.[16]

In fact, church ministers had limits imposed on them by the need to stay in the good graces of their congregations. The great fire-and-brimstone preacher Jonathan Edwards, for instance, lost his pulpit by demanding more allegiance to church canons than his parishioners were willing to accept. Another clergyman was criticized for asking a dying woman intrusive questions in the presence of family and close friends.

Even in these times, the authorities recognized the principle from England that a person ought not be compelled to confess his own crimes, or as one legal treatise used by Colonial magistrates put it, no man should have his faults wrung out of him. From this principle, the framers of the Bill of Rights in the next century forged the Fifth Amendment protection against self-incrimination.[17]

"He that prieth into every cloud may be struck with a thunderbolt."

English Proverb brought to Colonial New England.

Puritanism was not the totality of the New England experience. The harshness of the natural environment, the constant threats to personal safety from hostile Indians, the weather, wildlife, the estrangement from family and culture back in England, the day-to-day needs to survive and to make a living, and the fear of retaliation from abroad – all of these contributed to the culture of early New England as well. And many of these factors created a cultural recognition of privacy, even if officialdom seemed to do the opposite. The clergy who led the original migration to America came in search not of liberty for everyone but the freedom to preach their chosen doctrines as they wished. But the rank and file who accompanied them were people who took the ultimate risk of leaving home precisely because of a sense of oppression – a deprivation of freedom – in their homeland. By the time the first settlers from Europe had landed off the Mayflower, surely these people had a notion of leading their own lives free of church or governmental oppression. The rhetoric in their pronouncements shows that.

The First Charter of Massachusetts, for instance, spoke of the right to "enjoy all liberties and immunities of free and natural subjects." The charters for the Colonial communities eventually recognized freedoms – some of them granted in England – of religion, of conscience, of assembly, and against unreasonable searches. Taken together, these are the precursors to an explicit right to autonomy.[18]

While it appears that the rigidities of Colonial life dictated a life of little personal privacy at all, there were other factors at work that simultaneously created some elements of privacy. One of the founders of Connecticut, the Puritan cleric the Rev. John Davenport, Sr., even used the term "privacy" in a letter in the 1630s.[19] He wrote of "my naturall desire of privacy and retiredness." Here, in a theme to be repeated continually by the leaders in America for the next 100 years, was a community leader stressing the need for solitude, reserve, and privacy as a respite from his day of engagement in public affairs.

William Penn, the Quaker who founded the Pennsylvania Colony, made a similar observation, in a collection of aphorisms called *Fruits of Solitude* that was a best seller in the Colonies. This was not a tome on the subject of solitude but instead *the product* of solitude. In it Penn wrote, "The country life is to be preferred, for there we see the works of God; but in cities, little else but the works of men; and the one makes a better subject for our contemplation than the other . . . a sweet and natural retreat from noise and talk, and allows opportunity for reflection."[20]

A Virginia farmer and prolific writer, William Byrd, wrote to a friend in England in 1726, bragging about life in America – a new world of "innocence and retirement."

> "We sit securely under our vines, and our fig trees without any danger to our property. . . . We have no such trades carried on amongst us, as that of housebreakers, highwaymen, or beggars. We can rest securely in our beds with all our doors and windows open, and yet find everything exactly in place the next morning."[21]

If there is one thing that colonists had in abundance, it was space outdoors – elbow room. (In fact, a document from 1679-80 used the term "elbow room.")[22] Finding physical privacy outdoors – in the form of solitude or serenity – was not difficult. But, in a strange new land, there were countervailing considerations. Most communities were laid out with the homes located close to each other. "The reason was that they might keep together, both for more safety and defence, and the better improvement of the general employments," wrote Nathaniel Morton, one of the prominent colonists in Plymouth, in 1669.[23]

For five years during the 1630s, the Massachusetts Colony actually forbade construction of homes beyond half a mile from the meeting house, the center of town. This was exactly the layout of the villages in England that the settlers had left.[24] The fact that the Massachusetts ordinance was repealed in 1640 showed that there was a growing desire to sprawl. Land, after all, was a cheap commodity.

David Flaherty pointed out, "After the first generations of settlement in New England, the gradual weakening of Puritan influence over the community, familiarity with life in the New World, and the disappearance of the Indian threat to most towns encouraged flexibility in town planning and the location of homes." Here is the genesis of the American belief that we need to surround ourselves with grass and greenery for a sense of privacy. Some might say that the main tangible legacy of the early New Englanders was fences – stone walls or, as New Englanders called them, "stone fences." They used the stone walls for a sense of possessiveness – of their livestock and of their land. The walls also provided nothing more than a place to put all of the stones cleared from the New England soil when preparing it for cultivation.

To be alone for contemplation or to engage in sexual relations, residents needed only to walk outside and into the woods. In fact, harvest time, in the eyes of many young people, became known as an opportunity for finding a safe haven for sex in the fields. Cotton Mather called the autumn a time of rudeness and lewdness. In early America, the woods became a refuge for privacy and for sex. In Twentieth-Century America, the automobile and then the motel would become that refuge. This is the search for what a contemporary novelist calls "public privacies."[25]

Still, in Colonial America, the opportunity for serenity in the woods was in many ways no more than an illusion (as it may be in Twentieth-Century America). The wilderness –with good reason – was perceived as a place of unexpected dangers and hostility. William Bradford, governor of the Massachusetts Colony, took a look at his environment and pronounced it "a hideous and desolate wilderness, full of wild beasts and wild men."

"The seeds of the attitude that many British nature lovers still sense in ordinary American life can be seen planted in [Bradford's] story of the Pilgrims Fathers' grim early years in Massachusetts. I can best describe it as a resentful hostility towards the overwhelming power of the wild land; for Bradford, natural America seems a far worse enemy than the Indians or the machinations and failings of his neighboring colonists. Of course it would be ridiculous to speak of hostility to natural America in the modern United States, but there lingers a kind of generalized suspicion about it, or else a cold indifference, as if it may have been officially forgiven the sweat and tears it exacted from the settlers and pioneers, but can't expect to be trusted, let alone loved, for a long time yet."

**British novelist John Fowles,
in Wormholes, 1998.**

If there was limited opportunity for solitude outdoors, there was certainly no opportunity at all within the four walls of the typical colonial residence. The New Englanders regressed, in part, to the ways of a culture two or three generations earlier in England – a time when, in the words of French scholar Georges Duby, "in feudal residences there was no room for individual solitude, except perhaps in the moment of death."[26] It was improper for a man of quality to be alone, except for prayer. "Until the end of the Seventeenth Century, nobody was ever alone," wrote Philippe Aries in *Centuries of Childhood: A Social History of Family Life.* "The density of social life made isolation virtually impossible."

Homes in early America were cramped indeed. Up and down the East Coast a whole family might live in an underground cellar covered with green sod for three or four years or more until the family could afford a frame house above the foundation. Even many wealthy people lived this way.[27]

With all the wealth in Boston, there were not 20 homes with more than ten rooms, according to a census at the time.[28] This, in a community that was the largest in North America at the time, with 6000 inhabitants. There were no ceilings over the rooms, so that sounds could easily be heard from room to room and anybody willing to climb to the roof beams could peer into another room. Many homes, of course, had no room partitions at all. Sometimes a curtain or other flimsy barrier separated man and wife in bed from the children, or from adult family members, or even visitors.

This was the home environment into which Benjamin Franklin was born in 1706. The youngest of 17 children, he lived in a narrow row house. (Families the size of young Ben's were not totally unknown; the average number of children in colonial families in Seventeenth– and early Eighteenth-Century Massachusetts was an astounding seven or eight.)[29]

"People did not like to sleep alone in early America," reported Flaherty. Even strangers who were offered lodging for the night would share a bed with the host, whether of the same sex or not. This was done out of necessity. Early homes did not have enough rooms or even beds to offer the kind of hospitality Twenty-first-Century Americans would expect. It was also done for warmth.

Consider a clergyman in that period casually referring to another clergyman whom he had visited overnight as "my Bedfellow." Or the Rev. John Cotton of Plymouth writing to his cousin, Cotton Mather, "to thanke you for your late courteous entertainment in your bed." Or the English gentleman who noted in his diary, while in Virginia, "I called up my man, who lay in my room with me." Masters and servants often shared the same room.[30]

In the court files of Suffolk County, Massachusetts, was this account: "I Ann James of Boston Testify and declare that living with my brother Phinehas James. . . I frequently used to lodge in the Same Roome where the said Mrs McCarthy lay and two nights William Stone of Boston lay with Mrs McCarthy in one Bead and I lay with her two Sisters Abigail and Elizabeth Floyd in another bed in the Same Roome."[31]

It is easy to appreciate how common bed-sharing was in those times from the complaint of a visitor to North America, who found the custom hard to accept. Francisco de Miranda complained in the 1780s about his landlord "because notwithstanding a formal stipulation he had put another guest in my room; thank God he was not put in my bed, according to the custom of the country." Another traveler from England, Sarah Kimball Knight, traveling on horseback in 1704, stopped for the night at an inn between New York and Boston. She was shocked to awake and find two men unknown to her sharing the bed next to her.[32] These were visiting foreigners, of course; the new Americans themselves would have hardly noticed.

The visitors should not have been totally shocked. These arrangements were known also in parts of Europe, especially in peasant homes.[33] David Hackett Fischer, author of *Albion's Seed*, the analysis of British folkways in America, argues persuasively that to understand the customs of the early Americans you have to look precisely to the regions of Britain and of other countries in Europe where they formerly lived; there was no one European custom nor even one British custom. In *the regions* from which the New Englanders originated, Fischer shows in his 1989 book, these swarming living conditions within residences were common at the time, although they were not common throughout all of Britain.

Flaherty uncovered the testimony of a young woman saying that an unmarried couple apparently did not have sexual intercourse, as accused, on a certain occasion. She knew, because she shared the bed, which was "very Narrow on which the three were and thinks it almost if not wholly impossible that they should be guilty of that Crime without her knowledge and She observed no such thing."

Only with the coming of taverns and coffeehouses and inns did this custom of bed-sharing fade, but not entirely. There is plenty of evidence that families shared rooms and beds for sleeping – as did strangers – well into the last decades of the Nineteenth Century.

Although it was not uncommon for visitors to enter another's home without knocking, the average colonist regarded the home as a special preserve, deserving special protection, even if only conceptually. (The idea of the sanctity of the home can actually be traced to Biblical times.) The maxim that "a man's house is his castle" was brought over from England; the English took it from Roman law. The great Roman orator Cicero said, "What is more inviolable, what better defended by religion than the house of a citizen. . . . This place of refuge is so sacred to all men, that to be dragged from thence is unlawful."[34] Boston lawyer James Otis called this a "right of House," in his famous argument to a British court in Boston in 1761 against the Crown's writs of assistance, which permitted unfettered searches of premises. Otis' eloquent but unsuccessful defense of the sanctity of each modest dwelling place was so vital to John Adams that he later wrote, "Then and there the child Independence was born."

It's important to remember that this solemn protection did not extend to the dwellings of persons of color.

Eavesdropping – listening to others under the eaves of a house – was occasionally punished, and Peeping Toms faced ostracism. The great commentator on American and English law, Sir William Blackstone, in his commentaries of 1783, defined such offenders as: "Eaves droppers, or such as listen under walls or windows, or the eaves of a house, to hearken after discourse, and thereupon to frame slanderous and mischievous tales. . . ." He called them "a common nuisance," and for many years they were deterred by the legal principle of nuisance, not by grand constitutional principles.

Early on, the Colonial community of New Haven enacted a statute permitting the authorities "to search or cause to be searched any man's house, study, closet, or any other place for bookes, letters, wrightings, or any thing else" but only "upon probable grounds" that a crime had been committed, and only in the case of major crimes.[35] The reason for this balancing of privacy and crime control was "that wee may live a quiet and peaceable life, in all [godliness] and honesty."

Prior to entering someone's house for purposes of regulating consumption of alcohol, the tythingmen, constables, and others customarily secured a warrant from a court even though they were not required to under the laws then in effect.

By the 1730s, Benjamin Franklin was concerned about the free hand given to constables. Much later in his life, he wrote in his *Autobiography*,

> "The city watch was one of the first things that I conceiv'd to want regulation. It was managed by the constables of the respective wards in turn; the constable warned a number of housekeepers to attend him for the night. Those who chose never to attend paid him six shillings a year to be excus'd, which was suppos'd to be for hiring substitutes, but was, in reality, much more than was necessary for that purpose, and made the constableship a place of profit; and the constable, for a little drink, often got such ragamuffins about him as a watch, that respectable housekeepers did not choose to mix with. Walking the rounds, too, was often neglected, and most of the nights spent in tippling. . . .

> "On the whole, I proposed as a more effectual watch, the hiring of proper men to serve constantly in that business; and as a more equitable way of supporting the charge, the levying a tax that should be proportional to the property."

The six shillings paid by the neighbors to escape constable duty, incidentally, is equivalent to $800 in the 1990s. Within a few years, people had adjusted to the more formalized establishment of law enforcement and instituted Franklin's ideas.

The importance of protecting the home against law enforcement intrusions is clear from an editorial comment in Philadelphia 50 years later. The writer was arguing, in the debates over the new Constitution, the need for juries of public members to hear criminal cases, not a government-run court that might go easy on a wayward constable. In his argument, the editor was trying to suggest his idea of one of the most outrageous offenses imaginable. "Suppose," he asked "that a constable, having a warrant to search for stolen goods, pulled down the clothes of a bed in which there was a woman, and searched under her shift – suppose, I say, that they commit similar, or greater indignities, in such cases a trial by jury would be our safest resource."[36]

Abuses occurred enough to inspire citizen complaints. As the framers of the constitution sat down to meet in Philadelphia in the 1780s, a pamphlet circulating in Boston proclaimed:

> "Thus our Houses, and even our Bed-Chambers, are exposed to be ransacked, our Boxes, Trunks and chests broke

open, ravaged and plundered, by Wretches, whom no prudent Man would venture to employ even as menial Servants; whenever they are pleased to say they *suspect* there are in the House, Wares, etc., for which the Duties have not been paid. Flagrant instances of the wanton exercise of this Power have frequently happened in this and other seaport Towns. By this we are cut off from that domestic security which renders the Lives of the most unhappy in some measure agreeable. These Officers may under color of Law and the cloak of a general warrant, break through the sacred rights of the domicil, ransack Men's houses, destroy their Securities, carry off their Property, and with little Danger to themselves commit the most horrid Murders."[37]

While there were recorded cases of snooping into residences, there were only a few prosecutions for intercepting or reading private correspondence. This is remarkable, in view of the haphazard non-system for transporting letters among the colonies. Scattered attempts to develop organized mail systems in New England seemed to flounder each time one got underway. And so the settlers entrusted acquaintances, ship captains, or strangers to deliver messages and packages. Usually this was reliable, at least in getting the letters delivered. It did not guarantee confidentiality. Often mail would be left at a tavern or meeting house for the next person traveling in a particular direction to gather up and take to the destination. At least the service was free. But it was not unusual for the person delivering the correspondence to read the letter – even a sealed letter – and even to add his own postscript.[38]

Receiving mail was crucial for the settlers, living in remote rural communities and anxious to know about possible new restrictions coming from England. Life in America was pretty uniform, noted William Byrd of Virginia in his diary in 1736, until the ships come in. "Then we tear open the letters they bring us from our friends, as eagerly as a greedy heir tears open a rich father's will." Early records show evidence that, in at least one court, all proceedings ceased while the participants had a chance to read the newly arrived letters.

In the early years hand-delivered letters were generally not vehicles of personal correspondence. It was mostly the merchants of early America who exchanged letters, and so their correspondence concerned business affairs, not so much personal tidbits. This is true of their diaries as well. Their writings were in many ways more like modern newsletters than personal letters, in that incoming letters were usually circulated around town by the recipients so that more traders could have access to the information.

The non-system for delivering letters is similar to the early years of electronic correspondence 300 years later, in the 1990s. In the Internet age, there is only a slight assurance that your message will be delivered, in confidence, only to its intended recipient and remain forever secret. Yet historians in the future will probably write that complaints were few and Americans – and persons in all cultures – seemed to adapt to the hit-or-miss aspects of the Internet. (Historians may also write that correspondents in the late Twentieth Century used the Internet for sending and receiving business-related matters and frivolous notes, but not intimate revelations.)

For letter writers in the Colonial period, the consequences were serious if their writings were disclosed, especially if the messages appeared to defy the Crown or to be otherwise suspicious. Consequently, persons in official positions, even though they were not reluctant to intrude into homes and into innocent evening activities, were uneasy about ordering mail opened.

To be safe, letter writers developed means for preserving the confidentiality of their correspondence. They used sealing wax and wrapping paper. They used pseudonyms or "pen names." They developed codes for disguising their words. For instance, someone in Ireland described his precautions to John Winthrop, Jr., in Massachusetts in 1635. His comment implies that the two had previously worked out an elementary code for preserving confidentiality:

> "Herewith I send you a casement through which I thinke you may much more securely impart your minde. . . I had written in the way wee agreed on, butt I fownd itt, in my judgment, more tedious, and less secrett."

A man seeking medical advice from Winthrop asked him to be mindful of the sensitivity of his wife's condition when Winthrop wrote back.[39] The man added, "Modo hoc obsecro, ut si aliquid secreti scribus latine scriberes." Translation: "I beseech you to write in Latin anything of a private nature."

For the colonists, using codes to encrypt their messages was a crucial element of exercising free speech. In fact, language itself was a form of encryption. Simply using the written word, whether in English or any other language, prevented most of the rest of the populace from understanding the content. A large number of male residents and probably nearly all women could not read or write

English at the time, and so they could not understand the contents of letters even if they intercepted them. (Illiteracy meant, of course, that most early Americans had to sacrifice their own privacy by having a scribe write their letters and a reader read incoming correspondence aloud).

The importance of encryption as a means of communicating sensitive thoughts was invoked in the late Twentieth-Century debate over whether the government could regulate the use of encryption and regulate its availability to users of electronic mail. Modern-day government prosecutors argued that encryption software is merely a product to be regulated, and they set out to do so. Privacy and free-speech activists countered that since colonial days the ability to encode one's personal correspondence is *a form of language*, a form of expression, to be fully protected by the First Amendment.[40]

In his book, Flaherty wrote, "In 1622 an English correspondent of Governor William Bradford of Plymouth Colony sent his missive sewn into the sole of a new pair of shoes 'for fear of intercepting.' The fear was well founded, for one of Bradford's enemies discovered the letter while on board ship."

Just two years later, Bradford apparently turned the tables. Suspecting that two settlers were plotting to overthrow him, Governor Bradford is said to have intercepted two incriminating letters that they had intended for friends back in England. At a public assembly the two denied plotting an overthrow. As evidence, Bradford produced their personal letters and caused them to confess publicly. The defendants then expressed outrage that their letters had been intercepted. "You think this is evil?" responded the governor. The men "would not say a word," according to Bradford's own account.[41]

Authorities were motivated to develop a formal postal system in the next century. It is clear from the wording of a statute in 1699 that one reason for this was concern about the lack of security.

Obviously, it was crucial for Colonial settlers to keep in touch with family and associates back in England and, later, with those up and down the East Coast. It was a matter of life and death to know what was going on, here and abroad. Here's one account of how information traveled in the early years, jotted down by a day laborer named Abner Sanger who lived in New Hampshire:

"A man might come home from Northfield, Massachusetts, with news of the depredations of the Hessian troops, another might come from Connecticut with reports of French aid to Congress, while a third local traveler might return from Boston with a still wider range of reports.

"One day [a citizen] might go up the main street in Keene, New Hampshire, and hear only of local doings, or he might, as on November 26, 1779, learn of the Comte d'Estaing's defeat at Savannah. At work the talk would be about a neighbor's livestock or, as in November 1777, when [the man] was working for the tanner, news would be passed of Washington's and Howe's armies at Philadelphia.

"News came at random. Thus, near the end of August 1782, he happened to meet a man on the bridge over Keene River 'that tells me there is talk of peace.' Later that day, while he was 'dragging old flood-wood out of the saw mill creek,' he inquired of a passerby, a 'Londonderry man,' who told him 'there [is] much talk of peace with Britain.'

"Similarly in October, while he was digging potatoes, '[a neighbor] come along and tells me that their talk was that Governor Hancock of Boston was dead.'

"In the first two cases the information was accurate, and in the third it was mistaken."[42]

Haphazard as it was, the primitive mail "system" was probably much more reliable for conducting business and for staying abreast of revolutionary fervor than was word of mouth. Still, word of mouth was the primary means of information dissemination for decades to come.

The fact that correspondence could remain fairly private in informal delivery arrangements may have been a testament to the fact that it was not very fascinating. Most of the letters concerned dry commercial and trade data, not personal secrets.

The respect for confidentiality also indicates the deference that the early settlers showed towards the private realm of their neighbors, irrespective of the religious teachings their leaders brought from the Old World.

Already one of the ambiguities of American life was beginning to be established: an intuitive yet informal recognition of others' rights to privacy amidst a governmental and religious structure –

and later a commercial sector – that sought to intrude into that private realm.

| LINKS |

To see how these Colonial values shaped our Constitutional principles, continue to the next chapter, on <u>Serenity</u>.

To see how the new nation developed a confidential mail system, go to the chapter on <u>Mistrust</u>.

To see how Colonial values of sexuality shaped Twenty-First-Century values, go to the chapter on <u>Sex</u>.

Serenity

*The founders' partiality for protecting their private lives,
the inferences of privacy in the Constitution,
and early objections to census taking*

One of the products of the New England Puritan environment expressed his passion for solitude, in his multitude of writings on the status of the emerging nation and his own life. John Adams wrote in his diary in 1761:

> "I must converse and deal with Mankind, and move and stir from one scene of Action and Debate and Business, and Pleasure, and Conversation, to another and grow weary of all before I shall feel the strong Desire of retiring to contemplation on Men and Business and Pleasure and Books. After hard Labour at Husbandry, Reading and Reflection in Retirement will be a Relief and a high refined Pleasure."

And at another time:

> "After attending a Town Meeting . . . a Retreat to reflect, compare, distinguish will be highly delightful. So after a Training Day . . . I shall be pleased with my solitude."

Adams wrote these words years before he was fully engaged in his stressful and dangerous public life. He was to be at the center of controversy during his time, one of the first to propose American independence, a drafter of the contentious Declaration of Independence, a defender of British soldiers accused of murder in the Boston Massacre, the nation's first vice president, and at the end of the century its second President, sandwiched between two of the new nation's most esteemed leaders.

Throughout his life he sought a safe haven from the public arena. In fact, from 1770 to 1773, Adams actually withdrew from public life.

At one point during this period he said that he wanted to "throw off a great part of the load of business *both public and private.*"

> **"I've also found it serviceable to retreat on occasion and spend as much time as possible wholly alone, for without distraction one's thoughts turn automatically to the next day's work or to the unresolved problems of the morning just past."**
>
> **Ambassador and economist John Kenneth Galbraith,**
> ***Ambassador's Journal*, 1969.**

John Adams also claimed the right not to respond to inquiries about his personal life. No, *more than that*. He claimed the right to conceal personal matters by *dissimulation*. Adams wrote in his diary:

> "The first Maxim of worldly wisdom, constant Dissimulation, may be good or evil as it is interpreted. If it means only a constant Concealment from others of such of our Sentiments, Actions, Desires, and Resolutions, as others have not a right to know, it is not only lawful but commendable – because when these are once divulged, our Enemies may avail themselves of the Knowledge of them, to our Damage, Danger and Confusion. So that some Things which ought to be communicated to some of our Friends, that they may improve them to our Profit or Honour or Pleasure, should be concealed from our Enemies, and from indiscreet friends, lest they should be turned to our Loss, Disgrace, or Mortification. I am under no moral or other Obligation to publish to the World, how much my Expences or my Incomes amount to yearly. There are Times when and Persons to whom, I am not obliged to tell what are my Principles and Opinions in Politicks or Religion.

> "This Kind of Dissimulation, which is no more than Concealment, Secrecy, and Reserve, or in other Words, Prudence and Discretion, is a necessary Branch of Wisdom, and so far from being immoral and unlawfull . . . is a Duty and a Virtue."[1]

The comments of our second President would have provided great comfort to our forty-second President nearly 200 years later, when Bill Clinton was beleaguered by public investigations of his sexual activities. "Dissimulation," which Adams claimed to be virtuous, is defined now as "concealing under a false appearance." At least as a young man, Adams regarded concealment of personal matters not only as morally defensible, but also *a branch of wisdom*. This shows the thinking that Adams and his contemporaries contributed to the drafting of our Constitution. Adams' view of the necessity of both a physical haven removed from scrutiny *and* protection from questioning about personal affairs was shared by his contemporaries who were forging the principles for a democracy. Although the word privacy is not mentioned directly in the Constitution – nor even explicitly the concept of privacy – it was an essential part of the framers' understanding of liberty and the pursuit of happiness.

> **"The makers of our Constitution undertook to secure conditions favorable to the pursuit of happiness. They recognized the significance of man's spiritual nature, of his feelings and of his intellect. They knew that only a part of the pain, pleasure and satisfactions of life are to be found in material things."**
>
> **Supreme Court Justice Louis D. Brandeis, dissenting in *Olmstead v. U.S.*, 1928.**

Reading Adams' diary makes it is easy to see the acceptance by the founders of the notion brought from England that a person has a right to remain silent, even in a criminal investigation. The idea was to be embodied in the Fifth Amendment in the Bill of Rights enacted in 1789.

One of the prime movers in the "Miracle at Philadelphia" at which the Constitution was shaped, Benjamin Franklin also found a need for private space away from the stress of public activities. In his *Autobiography* in 1784 Franklin related that in mid-life he attempted to achieve moral perfection in his life. He established a list of virtues that he would try to achieve, and then he arranged them in priority.

First on the list was "Temperance." Second was "Silence – Speak not but what may benefit others or yourself; avoid trifling conversation." Next came "Order – Let all your things have their places, let each part of your business have its time." These came before "Frugality," "Industry," "Sincerity," "Justice," and "Moderation" because, Franklin said, he felt that he could not achieve those virtues until he had achieved the first few on his list. Listed eleventh in his inventory of 13 virtues was a form of privacy: "Tranquillity – Be not disturbed at trifles, or at accidents common or unavoidable."[2] Taken together, these constitute a recognition that personal privacy is a crucial element of what Franklin considered a virtuous life.

George Washington so longed for the sanctuary of his home at Mount Vernon that as he battled British troops in the winter cold he dispatched weekly notes back to construction workers with his specifications. He ordered them to build a private two-story suite within the mansion so that he could do as he pleased beyond the view of houseguests and visitors. As a hero throughout the continent after the Revolutionary War had been won, George Washington reveled in his relative solitude: "I am become a private citizen on the banks of the Potomac," he wrote to his comrade-in-arms, General Marquis de Lafayette, "and under the shadow of my own vine and my own fig tree. Free from the bustle of a camp and the busy scenes of public life, I am solacing myself with those tranquil enjoyments of which the soldier [and] the statesman can have very little conception. I am not only retired from all public employments, but I am retiring within myself, and shall be able to view the solitary walk and tread the paths of private life with heart-felt satisfaction."[3]

Six years later, he was President of the United States.

It is hard for Twentieth-First-Century Americans to imagine that President George Washington simply packed his bags and toured the Southern states and remained completely out of touch with his government for two months. But he did. On his low-key trip, he would show up at roadside taverns without any advanced notice and without much retinue at all, much to the surprise of a series of innkeepers along his 1900-mile route. In a letter to his sister on a previous non-public presidential trip to New England, he said that his objective was "relaxation from business and re-establishment of my health."[4]

"A life spent entirely in public, in the presence of others, becomes, as we would say, shallow."

Political scientist Hannah Arendt, in *The Human Condition*, 1958.

The public men of the 1700s felt a need to articulate this sense that we all deserve respite from our daily grind – whatever it may be – and a right to remain silent against inquisitive inquiries. They seemed to express these views more than did public men and women of the Twentieth Century, more than do public persons in other cultures.

John Adams, according to David Flaherty in *Privacy in Colonial New England,* contrasted "such silent scenes, as riding or walking thro the Woods or sitting alone in my Chamber, or lying awake in my Bed" with the opposite – "the distracting Bustle of the Town and ceremonious Converse with Mankind." Adams shared with Thomas Jefferson a passion for solitary reading. The two of them – John Adams, the urban sophisticate, and Thomas Jefferson, the rural gadgeteer – amassed two of the greatest private libraries in the world.

According to the definitive book *A History of Private Life:*

> "In America's Puritan culture we find the most radical privatization of reading. The book became the center of family life. People read for themselves and for others. They memorized passages, which by dint of frequent repetition became part of their everyday language. . . . The book thus became the companion of choice in a new kind of intimacy. And the library, for those who could afford one, became the ideal place for retreat, study, and meditation . . . a retreat from the world, freedom enjoyed out of the public eye.
>
> "Reading influenced privatization in many ways. It contributed to the emergence of a sense of self, as the reader scrutinized his own thoughts and emotions in solitude and secrecy."[5]

"I can't live without books," Jefferson said at one point. "Books are my disease," said a prominent Quaker, James Logan, who owned about 3000 volumes. It was said that his fellow Quakers in the Pennsylvania Colony valued solitude more than other groups. One of their number, Anne Cooper Whitall, offered this advice in her diary around 1760:

> "Converse as much as may be with God, with his holy Angels, with thy own conscience and complain not for want of company . . . . Decline you may crowds and company, for frequent discourse, even of news or indifferent things, which happens upon such occasions, is sometimes destructive to virtue."[6]

Can there be any doubt that enjoying a safe haven away from interruptions and turmoil is part of the "pursuit of happiness" the founders included in their Declaration of Independence? Surely it was in the minds of John Adams and Benjamin Franklin and Thomas Jefferson.

But reading requires more than solitude. It demands the opposite of privacy – curiosity. Voracious readers, as the public men of the 1700s were, have a voracious curiosity as well – about public events and about the lives of other people.

Ben Franklin is the emblematic character here, a man who felt he could not achieve his goals of industriousness and high performance without a sense of privacy in his life and at the same time a man of immense curiosity. He had to be curious to achieve his goals. He was a remarkable scientist, inventor, publisher, diplomat, essayist, and innovator – all vocations that require an intense inquisitiveness. "Franklin's studies of electricity and many other phenomena were prompted not by practical aims, but by his playful curiosity – which often became obsessive, even antic," said Dudley R. Herschbach, a Harvard chemistry professor and Franklin admirer.

Among Franklin's innovations was the nation's first public library. James Madison, fourth President and author of the Bill of Rights, shared Franklin's passion for libraries.

Franklin personified the conflicting yearnings of the new America – an apparent passion for a safe haven away from the turbulence of daily life and at the same time an undying curiosity about the new world around him, including its inhabitants.

"Three may keep a secret, if two of them are dead."

Benjamin Franklin, in 1728.

Like most people in public life, Franklin preferred to conduct the public's business in private. He campaigned hard to appoint his son as a postmaster in Philadelphia, but so discreetly that one member of the influential Penn family of Philadelphia complained, "The whole of this business has been transacted in so private a manner, that not a tittle of it escaped until it was seen in the public papers; so that there was no opportunity of counteracting, or, indeed, doing one single thing that might put a stop to this shameful affair."

Franklin exemplified the duality in the American character in another way. In every way, he was America's very first celebrity – a popular figure whose image and accomplishments were widely known along the East Coast. Any one who could tame lightning was bound to be a hero; until Franklin's experiments, it had been regarded as a supernatural force with great religious overtones.

"In 1723 Benjamin Franklin landed at Philadelphia, and with his loaf of bread under his arm walked along Market Street toward an immortality such as no American had then conceived," exclaimed Henry Adams in 1889. If there had been printed T-shirts or action figures in the 1700s, they would have depicted Ben Franklin. He was the subject of much curiosity and it irritated him.

Franklin had traveled abroad and could see elements in the American character not readily apparent to those living here. In another setting, in England, Ben Franklin sighed, "It seems I am too much of an American."

Like nearly all of the visitors from Europe and the other Americans who spent time in Europe, Franklin was amazed at his fellow Americans' intense curiosity in the presence of strangers. In the late 1750s stories circulated that he had tired so much of answering endless questions about himself before he could be served at an inn that he would gather the inhabitants for a set speech about himself. Then he would insist on no more questions. "This is all I know of myself, and all I can possibly inform you of," he would say. "I beg therefore that you will have pity upon me and my horse, and give us both some refreshment."

Alexander Hamilton similarly tired of answering personal questions. He complained about a man who apparently stayed with him all the way to Portsmouth, New Hampshire, badgering him with questions. At one point, John Adams dismissed this American trait as "harmless impertinence," but he too recognized it as part of the new American character.[7]

Of course, Secretary of the Treasury Hamilton, as well as Thomas Jefferson, had good reasons to avoid personal questions from the public. Hamilton was preoccupied during his tenure fighting outrage over accurate reports that he had paid cash to a husband to keep silent about Hamilton's sexual affair with the man's wife. The wrongdoing apparently became public when Jefferson leaked information to a friendly journalist in Richmond. The reporter later turned against Jefferson and revealed, apparently accurately, that Jefferson had fathered at least one child by his slave Sally Hemings. No wonder each man sought safe havens – and avoided personal questions.

Jefferson especially had his reasons for shunning the press and the public. In 1800, he had experienced what few other persons ever do. Newspapers up and down the East Coast reported that he had died at Monticello. Later, the erroneous report was attributed to the fact that a slave at Monticello, also named Thomas Jefferson, had died.[8] Ninety years after Jefferson's term as President, Henry Adams provided this insight into the man:

> "As a leader of democracy he appeared singularly out of place. As reserved as President Washington in the face of popular familiarities, he never showed himself in crowds. During the last 30 years of his life he was not seen in a Northern city, even during his Presidency; nor indeed was he seen at all except on horseback, or by his friends and visitors in his own house. With manners apparently popular and informal, he led a life of his own, and allowed few persons to share it. His tastes for that day were refreshingly refined. . . . He built for himself at Monticello a chateau above contact with man. The rawness of political life was an incessant torture to him. . . . To read, write, speculate in new lines of thought, to keep abreast of the intellect of Europe, and to feed upon Homer and Horace were pleasures more to his mind than any to be found in a public assembly."[9]

America's public men in its early history kept wondering why people were so interested in them. Thomas Paine, the Revolutionary activist who was born in England, asked just after his arrival here in 1774 why Americans are always "gazing at each other, with suspicious or doubtful curiosity?"

A long succession of European visitors asked the same question over and over. One of the first, a British writer named Isaac Weld, Jr., complained,

> "On arriving amongst the Americans. . . a stranger must tell where he came from, where he is going, what his name is, what his business is; and until he gratifies their curiosity on these points, and many others of equal importance, he is never suffered to remain quiet for a moment. In a tavern he must satisfy every fresh set that comes in, in the same manner, or involve himself in a quarrel, especially if it is found out that he is not a native, which it does not require much sagacity to discover."[10]

Weld wrote at another point that, without any introductory small talk, he was immediately asked where he was born and "if I was acquainted with any news, and finally my name."

Then again, 100 years later Henry Adams, an astute native-born observer of American ways, said of the ability of Europeans to analyze American traits, "Frenchmen like Liancourt, Englishmen like Weld, or Germans like Bilow were almost totally worthless authorities on a subject which none understood."

"No people could be expected, least of all when in infancy, to understand the intricacies of its own character, and rarely has a foreigner been gifted with insight to explain what natives did not comprehend," Adams said.

Still, in his 1889 book about the United States in 1800, Adams quoted Francois de la Rochefoucauld, the Duc de Liancourt, a French traveler to the new nation, approvingly:

> "One of the traits to which Liancourt alluded marked distinctly the stage of social development. By day and night, privacy was out of the question. Not only must men travel in the same coach, dine at the same table, at the same time, on the same fare, but even their beds were in common, without distinction of persons. Innkeepers would not understand that a different arrangement was possible. When the English traveler Weld reached Elkton, on the main road from Philadelphia to Baltimore, he asked the landlord what accommodation he had. 'Don't trouble yourself about that,' was the reply; 'I have no less than 11 beds in one room alone.' This primitive habit extended over the whole country from Massachusetts to Georgia, and no American seemed to revolt against the tyranny of innkeepers."[11]

Adams quoted an unhappy Philadelphian who said in 1796, "At New York I was lodged with two others, in a back room on the ground floor. What can be the reason for that vulgar, hoggish custom, common in America, of squeezing three, six, or eight beds into one room?" At home, Americans of the time lived in a "shell of boards," according to an English traveler.

"Almost every writer spoke with annoyance of the inquisitorial habits of New England and the impertinence of American curiosity," reported Adams. "Complaints so common could hardly have lacked foundation, yet Americans as a people were never loquacious, but inclined to be somewhat reserved, and they could not recognize the accuracy of the description." Timothy Dwight, President of Yale University and an American whom Adams considered the most reliable of Eighteenth-Century social commentators, "repeatedly expressed astonishment at the charge" of excessive curiosity. By contrast, the British novelist Charles Dickens, said Adams, found Americans taciturn.

And another thing, Adams added: Americans don't simply sit around taverns gossiping and getting drunk, as was commonly reported by European travelers. After all, "no immigrant came to America for ease or idleness."

"Foreigners were constantly struck by the inquisitiveness of the new Americans," wrote Adams. "Idle curiosity was commonly represented as universal, especially in the Southern settler who knew no other form of conversation."

It seems that America's founders institutionalized curiosity in the Constitution they forged. "To promote the Progress of Science and useful Arts" they decreed in Article I, Section 8, Congress would have the power "securing for limited Times to authors and Inventors the exclusive Right to their respective Writings and Discoveries." With this protection, of course, writers and researchers would have increased motivation to probe and to publish, to ask questions and to disseminate their findings. This is in addition to the unprecedented freedom of expression and freedom to publish established by the founders and incorporated into the Constitution in 1791. Can there be any doubt that Franklin, the writer, inventor, and commercial publisher, would endorse such copyright protection and that he would have done so to enhance the quantity and quality of information available to Americans?

Further, on the very first page of the Constitution, the framers required that each person report his or her identity to the government for purposes of enumeration. Censuses were known since Biblical times and the Roman Empire, but this surely was the first nation to enshrine a head count in its Constitution. It was the first to disclose the results of the tally. The purpose of the count originally was to determine with accuracy the highly charged question of apportionment of delegate votes and taxes among the separate colonies. (Benjamin Franklin had offered an alternative plan back in 1754, at the Albany Congress, suggesting apportionment based not on population but on revenues from the various colonies.)

James Madison made clear in 1788 that the census would both determine representation in the federal legislature and determine each state's proportionate share of taxes to be paid to the federal government. This, he thought, would motivate states to neither inflate nor deflate the count.

There was another purpose, stated in Article I itself: to provide only partial representation, through enumeration, to enslaved persons of color. They would count as three-fifths of a person. Madison planned that the first census would categorize persons as (1) free white males, (2) free white females, (3) free blacks, and (4) slaves. Free whites were to be segmented by age – those younger than 16 and those 16 and older.

While there were no adamant objections to a census as an intrusion into the privacy rights of citizens, some of the states were not interested in an enumeration at all. They had abandoned their earlier extensive registration requirements after the Declaration of Independence. Massachusetts, the leader in demographic data collection, kept its requirements, but New Jersey and many others made registration voluntary. North Carolina eliminated its data collection all together. The Virginia Senate in 1785 refused to approve James Madison's proposal for a statewide birth and death registration.[12]

This fear of a census, like the idea of a census itself, came from England. Religious fundamentalists had a particularly acute fear about being counted. The Bible, after all, relates that King David was punished by God for requiring that the people of Israel be counted. In addition, Revelation 13:16-17 and 14:9-10 warn that enumeration will result in "the mark of the beast" on whoever is counted and that those with the mark "shall be tormented with fire and brimstone." The Biblical passage was cited in debates over a census at the Constitutional Convention. Governor William Burnet of the New Jersey Colony in 1726 complained that enumeration makes people "uneasy" – especially New England Puritans influenced by these Biblical admonitions.[13] This Biblical fear of a head count and of assigning identifying numbers to everyone continued into the Nineteenth and Twentieth Centuries.

Back in 1715, the governor of the New York Colony had reported, "The superstition of the people is so insurmountable that I believe I shall never be able to obtain a complete list of the number of inhabitants of this province."[14] When Governor Robert Hunter attempted a headcount of his colony, he was forced to report:

> "I have issued out orders to the several Counties and cities for an account, of the numbers of their inhabitants and slaves, but have never been able to obtain it compleat, the

people being deterr'd by a simple superstition and observation, that the sickness follw'd upon the last numbering of the people [the "torment" mentioned in Revelations]."

After more than 100 years of enumeration in New England, after all, there *had been* an epidemic of diphtheria that killed thousands of children in the mid-1730s. Representatives Samuel Livermore of New Hampshire and John Page of Virginia warned in 1790 that the people would be alarmed by an intrusive census. Page said that the federal government was simply "gratifying idle curiosity." He added, "This particular method of describing the people would occasion an alarm among them."[15]

James Madison told them to relax, that "it was more likely that the people would suppose the information was required for its true object, namely, to know what proportion to distribute the benefits resulting from an efficient General Government." Instead of retreating on the idea of a census, he proposed that the states collect *more* information – for agricultural, commercial, and manufacturing interests, including how each person was employed. This is the kind of information that legislators would need each ten years to govern effectively, Madison argued. But his proposal was defeated before the 1790 head count.

Still, we can credit Madison for making the national census an instrument of precise data gathering about the citizens of America. Madison, as curious as Franklin and his other colleagues, campaigned for an expanded census from the beginning. He wanted cumulative information that would help the state and federal legislatures enact laws relevant to community needs. He envisioned a census as a means of collecting socioeconomic data about the nation's people, not merely as a nose count to separate Indians and persons of color from white Americans.

Madison was not successful at first, but just as Chief Justice John Marshall expanded the role of the federal courts beyond the outlines spelled out in the Constitution, James Madison, as a delegate to the Constitutional Convention and as President, expanded the hollow authority for a population count in Article I, Section 2, into a vehicle for gathering demographic information to guide public policy.

He could never overcome the fears that early Americans had about registering with the government. It was chilling indeed for citizens to be confronted by federal marshals requiring name and address (and race and free status), with the knowledge that the information would be submitted to federal courts and later publicly posted.[16] When Secretary of State Thomas Jefferson announced the results in 1791 showing a population of 3.9 million (95 percent of them living in communities with fewer than 5000 persons), he admitted that there were many omissions. He estimated that four percent of the citizenry was not counted. (By 1960, the undercount wasn't much better – 2.7 percent. Among African-Americans it was 4.5 percent. In 1990 the estimated undercount was about two percent overall, but in minority communities it was twice as much. An estimated 5.4 percent of African-American men and 5.8 percent of Hispanic men were not counted in 1990. The estimated number of minority residents not counted in 1960 and in 1990 exceeded the total number of Americans counted in 1790.)[17]

Madison was disappointed that the 1790 Census did not produce more details about the population. President Washington probably agreed. He is known to have asked for personal copies of the returns. The emissaries whom he sent abroad didn't even know exactly how big was the new nation they represented. Likewise Alexander Hamilton used Census data in his work. Secretary of State Thomas Jefferson reveled in statistics. After he had received a couple of complaints from Madison by mail about the paucity of the 1790 enumeration, he called for "a more detailed view of the inhabitants" in the 1800 count. Among other things he wanted to compare the life spans of Americans with those of non-Americans. (He did not get his wish, and the 1800 Census was as nonproductive to demographers as the first.)[18]

Propelled by the curiosity of these leaders of the new nation, the trend was established: The Census would become an ever-expanding vehicle for gathering demographic data on Americans and their households – for the use of government policy makers, social scientists, and, later, commercial interests. There was actually a small insurrection over counting noses in 1799 when federal agents were dispatched to register the number and size of windows, in order to administer a tax based on house size. Women in northeastern Pennsylvania were indignant when the authorities came to measure their windows, and the resulting disturbance required President John Adams, the man who longed for quiet retirement, to dispatch military force.[19] The essence of the protest was undoubtedly resistance to taxes, although the rhetoric of protest focused on freedom from intrusions into home life.

There is another point to remember about the framers of the nation: "The Constitution of 1787, of course, had itself been written behind closed doors; no reports were published, and all participants were sworn to secrecy 'to preserve the fullest freedom of discussion,'" according to Alan F. Westin in *Privacy and Freedom*, the landmark volume that launched a reconsideration of the value of privacy in the 1970s. News reporters – what news reporters there were in the 1780s – and other outsiders were excluded from "The Miracle in Philadelphia."

The stakes were high, and anonymity was often essential for those who dared to break with England. After all, English laws against seditious libel at the time punished anyone in England or the colonies for writing or speaking words that would incite the citizenry to overthrow the established governmental authority. Back in England, as a way of deterring speech threatening to the state, it had been a requirement that books and pamphlets bear the actual name of the author and printer. The leaders of the colonies in North America knew that anonymous writings were essential to bring about social change. Therefore, they found it a necessity to mask their political writings in anonymity, to prevent recriminations. Alan Westin pointed out, "Contrary to the principle of Seventeenth-Century English licensing laws, which had required books and pamphlets to bear the name of the author and printer, the First Amendment's right of free press protected both anonymous and pseudonymous expressions."[20]

"One historian has estimated that between 1789 and 1809 six Presidents, 15 Cabinet members, 20 Senators, and 34 Congressmen published unsigned political writings or writings under pen names," according to Westin.[21] To realize that men like Richard Henry Lee and Dr. Benjamin Rush, both leaders of the resistance against British rule, protected their anonymity when exposing abuses of the Crown helps us appreciate the courage they showed when they affixed their actual names to the Declaration of Independence.

The Federalist and Anti-Federalist documents in the debate on framing a Constitution are filled with references to "Cato" (thought at one time to be Governor George Clinton of New York but now thought to be a prominent state senator in New York), "Caesar" (a respondent to Cato, once thought to be Alexander Hamilton, but no longer), "An American," "Z," "Dr. Panegyric," and "An Old Whig."[22]

Samuel Adams, the pre-revolutionary patriot in Boston (and for a while preeminent brewery master) who had sponsored the subversive Committees of Correspondence, regularly used a pseudonym in his articles to the *Gazette* in Boston. As perhaps the most anti-British delegate, Sam Adams of Boston brought his own "paper shredder" to the Continental Congress in Philadelphia in 1774 and 1775. In the summer, when there were no fires in the fireplaces, he used his own scissors to cut up sensitive correspondence into tiny pieces.[23]

It was not unusual for letters to the editors of local news sheets of the day to be published anonymously. For instance, in 1789, the *Providence Gazette* in Rhode Island published impassioned letters on whether slavery – or the slave trade – should be abolished in the state. The debate involved two brothers, the merchant John Brown, who was getting rich off the slave trade from Guinea, and Moses Brown, who had released all his slaves, denounced the family mercantilism, and become a Quaker. John Brown's first letter was signed "A Citizen." The first rebuttal was signed "A Foe to Oppression." Then came another detailed response signed "A Friend Through a Monitor to the Citizen." "A Friend" was Moses Brown himself, he admitted in a private letter to his brother two days later in which he said that he was aware that John Brown was "A Citizen." Moses attempted to cool the fight, but "A Citizen" wrote at least two subsequent, increasingly angry responses. Then someone signing a letter "A Citizen and True Federalist" wrote to the *Gazette* defending "A Citizen." The tone of the letter made it sound as if John Brown had written it himself.

Before long, Moses Brown was signing his published letters "M.B.," and his brother even signed his real name to later submissions (including one in which he approvingly cited the views of "A Citizen").

Providence was not a large city, and so local readers pretty much knew who was writing the letters. But this limited anonymity allowed contributors to have what politicians of the 1970s began calling "deniability." It may have been possible to *assume* who was the source of controversial utterings, but it was difficult to prove. This also permitted the letter writer to follow up a published letter with more letters of support signed with other pen names. This was a favorite tactic of John Brown, but his brother Moses knew exactly who the author of the panegyrics was, according to the findings of the Rhode Island Historical Society.[24]

George Washington, Alexander Hamilton, co-drafter of the Constitution Gouverneur Morris, and others regularly used ciphers in their correspondence or signed off with pseudonyms. So did a prominent Virginian, William Byrd. He was perhaps protecting himself against Tory retaliation, but more likely he was protecting himself against personal embarrassment. His diaries included specific references to his sexual activities.[25] Even after the Revolutionary War had long ended and he had served in George Washington's government, Hamilton still wrote under the name of "Camillus." Benjamin Franklin was known to have used at least 42 pen names over a lifetime of writing. He used the name "Richard Saunders" for 25 years as author of the famed *Poor Richard's Almanack*.

In 1785 Thomas Jefferson wrote a letter to James Madison that looked roughly like this:

> "Your reappointment for three years will be notified from the Office of F. Affrs. It was XXXOXOOOXXOO being YZYYZ. XXXOO ZZZ YZO XX OO ZZZ that XXY ZZE YZX on YYY Z. Every ZZZ YYOOO OOOO XX to have YYZZO YYYY."

Another missive in 1787 looked like this:

> "These views are said to gain upon the nation. The 1647 678.914 for 411.454 is 979.996.607.935. of all 789. The 404 is 474.872. ' And an 223 435.918 of some sort is not impossible. The 539 is alarmed, & the surest reliance at this moment for the 809.133.1370 is on their 1091.1312.593.1150. I cannot write these things in a public dispatch because they would 598 into a 1030.7.207 and 884.366.1525."

The decrypted version:

> "These views are said to gain upon the nation. The king's passion for drink is divesting him of all respect. The queen is detested and an explosion of some sort is not impossible. The ministry is alarmed, and the surest reliance at this moment for the public peace is on their 200,000 men. I cannot write these things in a public dispatch because they would get into a newspaper and come back here."[26]

The British political theorist John Locke, who was the framers' source for the concepts of natural rights later incorporated in the Constitution, also wrote anonymously. In fact, his *Letter on Toleration*, which influenced American thinking greatly, was first published anonymously while Locke was living in voluntary exile in the Netherlands around 1689. In it, Locke wrote, "What I call civil goods are life, liberty, bodily health and freedom from pain, and the possession of outward things such as lands, money, furniture, and the like."[27] This is strikingly similar to concepts of privacy and "personhood" developed in the late Nineteenth and Twentieth Centuries.

Locke was influenced, in turn, by American thinkers like Roger Williams of the Rhode Island colony. He even drafted a constitution for the Carolina colony (but it was not enacted). Locke's most prominent contribution to thinking in America was the notion of religious tolerance. This is a form of respect for privacy – for the autonomy of the individual, for the sanctity of private beliefs, for the "right of conscience," and for freedom to choose the way in which a person manifests his or her personal religious faith. This was one of Thomas Jefferson's most strongly held views, that the government has no business inquiring into a person's spiritual beliefs. "It does me no injury for my neighbor to say there are 20 gods, or no god. It neither picks my pocket nor breaks my leg," wrote Jefferson from Monticello in Virginia. (In the 1990s the American Civil Liberties Union published a nationwide survey showing that most Americans respect that Jeffersonian assertion. A clear majority said that they tolerate personal behavior in others that may be in conflict with their own moral or religious beliefs.[28])

During debates leading up to acceptance of the concept of religious freedom that found its way into the First Amendment, James Madison echoed Locke, "This right is in its nature an unalienable right. It is unalienable because the opinions of men, depending only on the evidence contemplated by their own minds, cannot follow the dictates of other men." In fact, Madison's first draft of what became the religion clause of the First Amendment – when he served in the House of Representatives in 1789 – is as much a protection of privacy as a protection of religious tolerance:

> "The civil rights of none shall be abridged on account of religious belief or worship, nor shall any national religion be established, nor shall *the full and equal rights of conscience* be in any manner, or on any pretext, infringed."

But, originally in their non-public deliberations in Philadelphia in the 1770s, the framers – thanks to the persistence of James Madison – were preoccupied with creating a structure of government, rather than itemizing individual rights. (Although in the debates before the Constitution was finally drafted there were plenty of references to the right against unreasonable searches, the right of free speech, and due process, there was strong sentiment in state conventions that to enumerate certain individual rights would be to concede that natural rights were somehow within the purview of government or even subject to majority rule.[29] If certain rights were mentioned in the Constitution, it was argued, those rights could later be abridged by the authorities. The Bill of Rights, which recognizes the essential individual rights of all Americans, came later, in 1791.)

Looking back from his position as an Associate Justice of the U.S. Supreme Court from 1956 to 1990, William J. Brennan, Jr., observed:

> "The Constitution on its face is, in large measure, a structuring text, a blue print for government. And when the text is not prescribing the form of government it is limiting the powers of that government. The original document, before addition of any of the amendments, does not speak primarily of the rights of man, but of the abilities and disabilities of government."

But, Brennan goes on:

> "When one reflects upon the text's preoccupation with the scope of government as well as its shape, however, one comes to understand that what this text is about is the relationship of the individual and the state. The text marks the metes and bounds of official authority and individual autonomy. When one studies the boundary that the text marks out, one gets a sense of the vision *of the individual* embodied in the Constitution."[30]

James Madison would have agreed with this. He pushed for amending the Constitution just two years after its passage, to guarantee individual rights specifically. This "Bill of Rights" was augmented by passage of the Fourteenth Amendment after the Civil War, guaranteeing due process of law and equal protection of the laws and, in effect, extending the Bill of Rights to protect individuals from actions of the states as well as the federal government. After that, there could be no doubt that the Constitution had become, in Brennan's words, "a sparkling vision of the supremacy of the human dignity of every individual."

"This vision," Brennan observed in a speech in Washington in 1985, "is reflected in the very choice of democratic self-governance; the supreme value of a democracy is the presumed worth of each individual."

Or, as a delegate to the Constitutional Convention remarked in arguing that it was not wise nor possible to include in a document all of the possible rights of human beings, "We might just as well put into the Constitution that a man has a right to wear a hat, or not wear a hat."[31]

When the limits of the Constitution were tested again in 1998 during the impeachment of President Bill Clinton, a cartoonist for the *Arkansas Democrat-Gazette* depicted the framers in Independence Hall deliberating over drafts of Constitutional language. One of them remarks, "Maybe it's just me, but I don't think we'll ever need a section in here about phone sex."[32]

Alan F. Westin, who has spent a lifetime researching all of the nuances of personal privacy, asserts that the protection of privacy runs through our Constitution and its Bill of Rights in spite of the fact that you will not find the word anywhere in the document. He wrote in *Privacy and Freedom* in 1967:

> "When the Federal Constitution was drafted and the United States was launched as an independent government in the 1790s, American political thought rested on a series of assumptions – drawn heavily from the philosophy of John Locke – that defined the context for privacy in a republican political system. First was the concept of individualism, with its component ideas of the worth of each person, private religious judgment, private economic motives, and direct legal rights for individuals. Second was the principle of limited government, with its corollaries of legal restraints on executive authority, the rule of law, and the moral primacy of the private over the public sphere of society. Third was the central importance of private property and its linkage with the individual's exercise of liberty; to protect these twin values, property owners required broad immunities from intrusion onto their premises and from interference with their use of personal possessions. Each of these guiding ideas had a common purpose; to free citizens from the unlimited surveillance and control that had been exercised over 'subjects' by the kings, lords, churches, guilds, and municipalities of European society."[33]

Westin goes on to point out, as Associate Justice William O. Douglas had done in 1964, that the words in the Constitution are intended to secure the components of personal privacy: First, the freedom to communicate (or not to communicate), as well as the right to hold your own religious beliefs, implicit in the First Amendment rights of freedom of expression, freedom of association, and freedom of religion. Second, the Third Amendment's prohibition of compelling anyone to house soldiers in his or her own dwelling in peacetime. Third, "the right of the people to be secure in their persons, houses, papers, and effects, against unreasonable searches and seizures" in the Fourth Amendment. Next, the right to remain silent, even in a criminal investigation, guaranteed in the Fifth Amendment.

To this, Justice Douglas added, fifth, the statement in the Ninth Amendment, "The enumeration in the Constitution, of certain rights, shall not be construed to deny or disparage others retained by the people," and, sixth, the overlooked, often ignored, and easily dismissed language in the Tenth Amendment, "The powers not delegated to the United States by the Constitution, nor prohibited by it to the States, are reserved to the States respectively, or to the people."

Others would add "the right of the people to keep and bear arms" in the Second Amendment; the right not to have "private property taken for public use, without just compensation" in the Fifth Amendment; and the right to keep confidences with a lawyer of one's choice implied in the Sixth Amendment's guarantee of the right to legal counsel in a criminal prosecution.

"It is impossible not to conclude that Eighteenth-Century concepts of privacy were the driving forces behind the Bill of Rights."

Privacy law expert John H.F. Shattuck, in 1987.[34]

To read Westin's appraisal of the principles incorporated into the Constitution, as the Third Millennium begins, is chilling. The second principle, that of limited government, has disappeared in America, except in the lip service of some political rhetoric. The third, the inviolability of private property, has been severely diminished if not virtually eliminated, in a contemporary society of zoning laws, environmental protections, and over-population. What remains is the concept of individualism. But in the last half of the Twentieth Century that principle was nearly forgotten, because of commercial forces as much as government action.

⟍ Links

To see how the U.S. Supreme Court interpreted the tacit protection of privacy in the Constitution, go to the chapter on <u>The Constitution</u>.

To realize the mistrust that greeted James Madison's census through the years, continue on to the chapter on <u>Mistrust</u>.

To develop the theme of curiosity in the American character, go to the chapter on <u>Curiosity</u>.

Mistrust

*Development of a postal system, a national census, and a telegraph
system and the fears that they created about confidentiality*

As the Eighteenth Century ended, the young nation was sending
diplomats abroad and engaging in overseas commerce. Its population had nearly doubled to 5.3 million in the 24 years since the nation was established. Literacy and schooling increased. Word-of-
mouth and face-to-face communications and serendipitous delivery
of correspondence were clearly inadequate.

First, the new nation needed a working postal system.

Americans had to have ways to communicate with each other and
to stay current on what was happening in the New World and in
Europe. Americans at all social levels sought out written materials,
no longer for religious study alone, but also for practical information, for business advantages, and eventually for entertainment and
enrichment.

In the early decades of the new nation, Americans did not rely on
newspapers for information. The few that existed were of marginal
importance, with tiny circulations. Not coincidentally, they were
published by postmasters – who believed that they were at the con-
fluence of the flows of information in the community.

The British government had assigned Benjamin Franklin to run the
colonial mails back in the 1730s and he continued in this position
until the Revolutionary War. In wartime, opening of mail by
authorities was neither unusual nor unexpected. Franklin suspected
that his letters were being opened by "some prying persons" at a
tavern or coffeehouse or by authorities in London. This was ironic,
because in a 1753 regulation he had required his employees to
swear "not to open or suffer to be opened any Mail or Bag of Letters."[1] After peace had been assured, the Continental Congress established a National Post Office and named Franklin to run it. It
began formally as a system of 75 post offices along the East Coast.
But the arrangements could hardly be called a system. Delivery
was still haphazard.

It did not help in making postal delivery more methodical that post offices were filled with political appointees. If they felt like reading the correspondence of political opponents, they apparently did so. Franklin felt no qualms about appointing brother John postmaster in Boston and brother Peter postmaster in Philadelphia. Franklin's son, William, was comptroller of the Post Office, and his son-in-law, Richard Bache, succeeded him as Postmaster General.

Even after the formal establishment of a postal service, Thomas Jefferson did not trust the confidentiality of the mails. Jefferson suspected even when he was President that curious postal workers were opening mail that he had sent. "The infidelities of the post office and the circumstances of the times are against my writing fully and freely," Jefferson said in 1798 when he was Vice President. "I know not which mortifies me most, that I should fear to write what I think, or my country bear such a state of things."[2] His archrival, Alexander Hamilton, felt the same way.

George Washington expressed the same opinion. "By passing through the post office," Washington wrote in a letter to French General Marquis de Lafayette the year before he was elected President, "[my words] should become known to all the world."[3] Perhaps General Lafayette needed such outrages explained to him. The favored classes in France, of which Lafayette was one, would "insist on the inviolability of secrets confided to the post so that private letters may never be brought in accusation against individuals," according to Alexis de Tocqueville in *The Old Regime and the French Revolution* in 1856.[4]

As part of a resolution in 1782, the Congress in essence enshrined Benjamin Franklin's earlier requirement of confidentiality. Its legislation included a requirement that clerks could not "open, detain, delay, secrete, embezzle, or destroy" any letter without the consent of the addressee or an approved warrant. This was not an American innovation. British law had similar protections, since at least the Post Office Act in 1710 (although there are those who believe that British authorities set up a postal system in England for the precise purpose of facilitating government access to private correspondence.[5])

Some Americans suspected that postal clerks delivered letters to whoever would pay for them. Thus the innovation, towards the end of the 1800s, of prepayment by the sender, in the form of adhesive stamps, was not only a revenue enhancement for the system but also a privacy enhancement for the sender and receiver. So was the introduction of locks on mailbags at about the same time; small-town postmasters along the way did not have keys. Just the growing volume of mail made informal snooping difficult. By 1800 the system was carrying nearly three million letters a year, an average of nearly one for every free, adult inhabitant.

In 1811, a Louisiana court recognized the sanctity of confidentiality in the mails by ruling that the holder of a letter had no right to publish it without the consent of the sender. A newspaper editor in Louisiana had claimed the right to publish a letter given to him by the recipient. The court based its reasoning not on a copyright or proprietary right in the contents of a letter but on the privacy interest held by the sender.[6]

The operative federal law on the confidentiality of mailed correspondence was enacted in 1825. It applied to all persons, not simply mail handlers. It said then, and says today:

> "Whoever takes any letter, postal card, or package out of any post office or any authorized depository for mail matter, or from any letter or mail carrier, . . . before it has been delivered to the person to whom it was directed, with design to obstruct the correspondence, or to pry into the business or secrets of another, or opens, secretes, embezzles, or destroys the same, shall be fined . . . or imprisoned."[7]

In 1841, a Jeffersonian from Boston on the U.S. Supreme Court, Joseph Story, in a lower court ruling reached a conclusion similar to the Louisiana court's. At about the same time, Story wrote in his noted legal treatise that intruding into the privacy of personal correspondence is "odious":

> "It strikes at the root of all that free and mutual interchange of advice, opinions, and sentiments, between relatives and friends, and correspondents, which is so essential to the well-being of society, and to the spirit of a liberal courtesy and refinement."

Intercepting mail, of course, would cause distress to those who write letters, Story argued, and, more important, "compel every one in self defense to write, even to his dearest friends, with the cold and formal severity with which he would write to his wariest opponents or his most implacable enemies."[8] This is precisely the rationale for protecting communications between a patient and doctor, a penitent and clergy member, a client and a lawyer, and others in trusted relationships. Without an expectation of confidentiality, participants will not be candid, will not be fully forthcoming. Total candor is required in order to make those relationships function. By the same token, without an assurance of confidentiality, people would not be candid in written correspondence. And, as Story said, if that occurred, they would simply not use the medium but seek out another means for conveying sensitive matters, to the detriment of "the well-being of society." Such a result would also create a serious drag on commercial transactions, thus slowing economic growth.

"Gentlemen do not read each other's mail."

Secretary of State Henry Stimson, in 1946.

A special agent for the postal service, James Holbrook, was able to summarize, in a memoir he wrote in 1855:

> "The laws of the land are intended not only to preserve the person and material property of every citizen sacred from intrusion, but to secure the privacy of his thoughts, so far as he sees fit to withhold them from others. . . . Now the post office undertakes to maintain this principle with regard to written communications as they are conveyed from one person to another through the mails. However, unimportant the contents of a letter may be, the violation of its secrecy while it is in charge of the Post Office Department, or even after having left its custody, becomes an offense of serious magnitude in the eye of the law."[9]

In spite of the stiff regulatory language, *The New York Times* complained in an editorial at mid-Nineteenth Century that "the sacredness of the mail-bag has departed," but this referred not to busybodies reading letters but to thieves taking things of value, according to David J. Seipp, an historian at Boston University who has chronicled privacy in the Nineteenth Century.

The growing respect for postal privacy was severely tested during the Civil War, when it was almost too much to expect that postal employees, North and South, could resist examining contents for military intelligence, treasonous statements, or simply news from the front. However, "so sacred was this rule [of confidentiality] even in time of war that, when repeated applications were made by local postmasters of the importance of ascertaining hostile proceedings through letters deposited in the war districts of the country, an order issued from the [federal postal authorities] prohibiting the slightest detention, delay, or tampering in any manner with such letters," Representative John A. Kasson of Iowa said in a retrospective speech in Congress in 1876.[10]

These remarks came in a Congressional investigation prompted by an accusation by a Democratic campaign operative that someone in the New York City Post Office had steamed open his political mailings in the Presidential campaign of 1876. This was the campaign that resulted in the closest election in the nation's history and was regarded as America's first political campaign with mass mailings. The investigators concluded that because of the sheer volume of mail, Americans should be assured that tampering with the mails was rare. Surely the complaints about intrusions were relatively modest during this period.[11] Alan Westin could find no indication that the contents of intercepted mailed was used as evidence in any trials or Congressional investigations.[12]

Nonetheless, there were repeated attempts by those in official positions to pierce through the protective cover of the mail – either to investigate crime, protect the national security, curb indecency, or discover subversives. For example, in 1871, federal investigators sought access to three letters opened by the Dead Letter Office that they believed would help convict a counterfeiter. The Postmaster General announced that the law did not permit him to provide the letters "for that or any other purpose."[13]

In 1877, the Supreme Court ruled that mailed letters and packages are entitled to the protections against unreasonable searches and seizures in the Fourth Amendment to the Constitution. This means that government agents may examine the contents of mail only pursuant to a court warrant or in recognized exceptions to the warrant requirement (as when there is a probability that the evidence will be destroyed or when there is an examination of incoming international mail).

Ironically this landmark decision came as the result of the activities of a man whom many accused of snooping into the mails – or wishing he could. He was Anthony Comstock of the New York Society for the Suppression of Vice, who stirred up a national hysteria in the 1870s over obscenity. At the height of his campaign, Comstock was obligated to assure his public that "there is no one obligation more sacredly imposed . . . than to preserve unsullied the sanctity of the seal."[14] Comstock had been accused of opening mail sent to decoy addresses set up by his organization.

He successfully lobbied for federal legislation banning obscene publications from the mails. What became known as the Comstock Act of 1873 was amended 15 years later to ban obscene references from private letters as well.

Comstock and his followers sought to ban mailed materials concerning gambling, abortion, and birth control, as well as sex, and many states passed their own "Comstock laws." A New York City man named Orlando Jackson challenged the Comstock restrictions in the U.S. Supreme Court. He had been fined for mailing advertisements about a lottery in violation of New York State's Comstock law. The Court held, in *Ex parte Jackson* in 1877, that the government has the power to forbid the delivery of certain materials to prevent fraud or deception or the dissemination of materials for immoral purposes, so long as there were alternatives for distribution. But Associate Justice Stephen Field, for the Court, made clear that the government had no business intruding into first-class mail:

> "A distinction is to be made between different kinds of mail matter – between what is intended to be kept free from inspection, such as letters and sealed packages subject to letter postage, and what is open to inspection, such as newspapers, magazines, pamphlets, and other printed matter, purposely left in condition to be examined. Letters and sealed packages of this kind in the mail are as fully guarded from examination and inspection, except as to their outward form and weight, as if they were retained by the parties forwarding them in their own domiciles. The constitutional guaranty of the right of the people to be secure in their papers against unreasonable searches and seizures extends to their papers, thus closed against inspection, wherever they may be."

Perhaps the judge felt that he was becoming an expert in the use of the mails to persuade voters and consumers. In the same year that he was ruling on *Ex parte Jackson*, Justice Field served on the Electoral Commission that decided America's closest election in favor of Rutherford B. Hayes. It was the first Presidential election in which use of the mails was crucial, both in the campaign and in the outcome.

During the Nineteenth Century, it was the task of the Post Office to wipe out a tradition dating back to pre-Revolutionary times that intercepting mail and reading it was not especially uncommon –

and to replace it with a new respect for confidential treatment of letters in transit. At mid-century, the task was not yet complete. Special Agent Holbrook, in his 1855 recollection, *Ten Years Among the Mail Bags*, admitted:

> "There are many who would recoil from the thought of robbing a letter of its pecuniary contents, but feel no compunction at violating its secrecy for the sake of indulging an idle or malicious inquisitiveness, if the commission of the deed can be concealed. This may not be called a common evil, and yet it exists; and it is one against which Acts of Congress have been leveled almost in vain, for there is perhaps hardly any portion of the laws of that body relative to the protection of correspondence, through the mails, about which there is felt so great a degree of security."[15]

The trend, still, was definitely towards greater protection.

Postal regulations have never been intended to protect the information on the outside of a first-class letter, which investigators may have access to without a court warrant. In fact, regulations in 1887 expressly authorized this, so long as it did not retard delivery of the mail.[16] In these so-called "mail covers," postal inspectors copy the address of sender and recipient from envelopes addressed to a targeted person or location and then send the correspondence on its way. There are about 10,000 of these a year nowadays.[17]

Even though these mail covers do not involve opening and reading mail, they do violate the expectations of users of the mail. In one of many books in the second half of the Nineteenth Century profiling the Post Office Department, Marshall Henry Cushing explained the reason for an existing regulation prohibiting disclosure outside the Post Office Department of "information concerning mail matter received or delivered":

> "The name of the person addressed is written on the outside of the letter for the single purpose of enabling the postmaster to deliver it to the proper person. For any other purpose the postmaster is presumed to have no knowledge of the address. . . . The privacy of the service will be at an end if the postmaster could be required to disclose the name or address of his patrons, except after the legal proceedings should have been taken."[18]

This is the first evidence of a principle of privacy that was to become crucial in the years from 1970 to 1990 – that personal information gathered for one purpose ought not be used for any incompatible purpose, without the consent of the individual. For instance, in the context of postal delivery, an individual places the name and address of the intended recipient on an envelope for the sole purpose of having it delivered correctly. Any other secondary use by the postal service, under this principle, would require the consent of the sender. But any additional use of the information *for the same purpose* – for a private contractor to deliver the mail, say – would not require additional consent, it would not violate this principle of "secondary use." Cushing articulated the principle long before it had a name and long before it became a benchmark among privacy theorists. Fragments of the principle were articulated in the Nineteenth Century within the Census Office as well.

In that period, the greatest protection for postal secrecy came not from a law or regulation, but from a physical innovation. In the mid-1800s adhesive envelopes were introduced, providing for the first time an easy means for sealing one's personal writings before entrusting them to the postal service. This inspired an approving editorial in *The New York Times*, which in 1873 looked back and commented:

> "The ordinary letter, sealed with its red wafer, and into which the prying eyes of the village postmistress so often peeped, was soon superseded by the envelope, which secured the inviolability of the contents from all eyes but those for which they were intended."[19]

The introduction of the adhesive envelope is a good example of how an invention or a physical innovation, as much as a law, can alter behavior and enlarge privacy expectations. There are other examples: the single-party telephone line, automatic telephone-switching (which removes the need for an operator to handle calls), private automobiles and recreational vehicles, fibre-optic telephone lines, telephone booths, motels, sound-proofing, encryption software. Some would say that the automatic display of the telephone number from which an incoming call is coming is such an innovation; others would say that the capability to block the display of one's phone number by such "Caller ID" devices is a privacy-enhancing technology.

After the Civil War, the writer Ralph Waldo Emerson could marvel,

> "To think that a bit of paper, containing our most secret thoughts, and protected only by a seal, should travel safely

from one end of the world to the other, without anyone whose hands it had passed through having meddled with it."[20]

What a contrast to the distrust shown by Franklin, Washington, and Jefferson.

Emerson's ideal was certainly the aspiration of the post office throughout the Nineteenth Century and at least into the first half of the Twentieth Century, and it has been the expectation of Americans who use the mails for their sensitive correspondence. The evolution from mistrust – even among the leaders of the nation and the leaders of the postal service itself – to trust shows how a serious tradition of confidentiality can be inculcated into an institution. It takes persistence and repetition and development of an institutional memory of how the system failed to function when there was no recognition of confidentiality. Once the tradition has been established over the years, employees and customers come to expect confidentiality. And it helps, when developing a tradition of respecting confidentiality, to enforce clearly defined penalties. In the Nineteenth Century, there was a $500 fine and one-year imprisonment for opening mail. In the Twenty-first Century, the penalty is still one year in prison and a fine of an unspecified amount. Through the Twentieth Century only two federal agencies, the Postal Service and the Bureau of the Census, have been able to sustain this tradition of respecting confidentiality. They have done it through persistent training and through enforcement of penalties for breaches of confidentiality.

In the early years of census-taking there was no need to develop such a respect for confidentiality. The government gathered only identifying information, not the indicators of lifestyle and family life that became common in the Nineteenth and Twentieth Centuries. The purpose of the census, as stated in the Constitution, was simply to count the population for purposes of apportioning the federal legislature. Very soon after the undertaking of the first head-count, it expanded into a government effort to collect demographic and economic data about the nation and its citizens – thanks mainly to the curiosity of James Madison. Immediately, this fueled concerns about government intrusiveness.

The anxieties about confidentiality that arose in the third Census, when John Quincy Adams, son of John Adams, was President, came from business owners worried that details of their manufacturing operations would become known. There were 14 inquiries about manufacturing in the 1820 Census, along with inquiries about whether each respondent was employed in agriculture, commerce, or manufacturing. There must have been resistance, because Adams was compelled to announce:

> "As the act lays no positive injunction upon any individual to furnish information upon the situation of his property, or his private concerns, the answers to all inquiries of that character must be altogether voluntary. . . . It is to be expected that some individuals will feel reluctant to give all the information desired in relation to manufacture. . . ."[21]

The collection of this business data was not successful and the queries were omitted from the 1830 survey. But two personal questions were added for the first time: Are you deaf? Are you blind? For the first time, the cumulative data was centralized in Washington. Prior to that time, the states maintained the data. And also for the first time, a uniform printed form was used for collecting data, although the federal government had not yet figured out a method for rapid counting of the results.

(The very name of our sixth President is instructive in showing how increasing populations and the needs of modern states to classify and tax those populations led to the assigning of, first, surnames and, later, identity numbers. Governments, not families, assigned surnames by and large. Just one generation earlier than John Quincy Adams', a single "given name" was adequate for most of the people in the world. When Adams was growing up in New England, for instance, governments in Austria and Prussia were just beginning to mandate last names. "Many of the immigrants to the United States, Jews and non-Jews alike, had no permanent surnames when they set sail," points out James C. Scott in his fascinating study *Seeing like a State*.[22] Yet by the late 1700s it was necessary to identify John Adams' son by *three names* to distinguish him from his father and from the scores of other Adams men in the Boston area. One hundred years after John Quincy Adams left the Presidency, the U.S. found it necessary to identity citizens by numbers as well as first and last names. That began with assignment of Social Security numbers to most adult Americans in 1936.[23])

The curiosity of people in high places about the emerging nation led to a significant increase in the number of Census questions in 1840. Once again, there is evidence that citizens were complaining about possible breaches of confidentiality; the instructions given to enumerators that year told them how to handle complaints:

> "Objections, it has been suggested, may possibly arise on the part of some persons to give the statistical information required by the act, upon the ground of disinclination to expose their private affairs. Such, however, is not the intent nor can be the effect, of answering ingenuously the interrogatories. On statistical tables no name is inserted – the figures stand opposite no man's name; and therefore the objection can not apply. It is, moreover, inculcated upon the assistant that he consider all communications made to him in the performance of this duty, relative to the business of the people, as strictly confidential."[24]

Several counties in the South did not provide answers to Washington (although the objections were to questions about businesses more than about individuals). Retired President Andrew Jackson complained to his protégé, President Martin van Buren, who was unsuccessful in running for reelection, that the Democrats lost Tennessee in 1840 because of "the foolish questions" in the Census that year.

By this time, lobbyists in Washington had begun actively pushing for more and more data to be collected in the decennial censuses. The American Statistical Association, for example, was founded in 1839 largely for this purpose, and to assure accuracy in the counts.

A Census statistician told Congress in 1849 that each time the government added questions to the survey "the people sometimes look with a jealous eye upon the whole subject, without understanding the purpose of it, and refuse to give correct information, or give wrong information."[25] And until this point census takers were still asking for only bare-bones information like name, address, and type of employment.

By 1850 the list of questions had become intrusive: name, sex, age, color, birth place and date, marital status, literacy, property ownership, and whether the person was deaf, dumb, blind, insane, idiotic, a pauper, or a convict. Even in its information collection, America was split into two societies, one black and one white. The Census questions for slaves were different than those for freed persons. Fewer questions were asked about slaves than about whites and freed black persons. This racial bifurcation remained throughout American history. In the 1960s and 1970s and later, there was widespread distrust of the Census in African-American communities and there were estimates that the undercounts in black neighborhoods were three or four times those in white areas. Census officials themselves estimated after the 1960 count that up to 30 percent of non-white men between the ages of 18 and 19 were not counted at all.[26] By the 1980 count there was widespread suspicion among Hispanic-Americans, who feared that Census responses would be provided by the Census Bureau to immigration authorities.

In 1850, Census collectors had to be reminded not to use the information they collected for other purposes. The head of the newly formed Census Board wrote in his instructions:

> "Information has been received at this office that in some cases unnecessary exposure has been made by the assistant marshals with reference to the business and pursuits, and other facts relating to individuals, merely to gratify curiosity, or the facts applied to the private use or pecuniary advantage of the assistant, to the injury of others. Such a use of the returns was neither contemplated by the act itself nor justified by the intentions and designs of those who enacted the law. No individual employed under sanction of the Government to obtain these facts has a right to promulgate or expose them without authority."[27]

Once again, this is an early articulation of the principle on "secondary use," namely that personal information collected for one purpose ought not be used in an individually identifiable form for a second purpose different from the one for which the data was originally gathered, without the consent of the individual. This differs from a rule of absolute confidentiality, which would eliminate *any* disclosure of personal information once it has been collected. Obviously a rule of absolute confidentiality would severely limit the usefulness of information gathered. So long as the additional uses of the information are compatible with the purpose for which the individual provided it originally, it seems fair to use it. It is not fair to use it for other purposes, even within the same organization. That is what the 1850 Census rule is getting at, and what Marshall Henry Cushing, in his discussion on postal secrecy in 1893, was getting at.

Acting on this principle, Census officials denied requests from researchers to see *individually identifiable* data from the 1850 results, reasoning that a lack of trust in the confidentiality of responses lowers the number of candid responses a survey taker can expect.

In 1850, it seems, the concern was that census takers were profiting from the government information with which they were entrusted by selling it, and not so much that they were directly compromising citizens' expectation of privacy. After all, raw Census data was still posted publicly (until 1870) and the public seems to have had access to the information, at least locally, so that they could make corrections. At first this practice was harmless because only the names of heads of households and the numbers of persons in each household were publicly posted. But in the 1830 and 1840 and 1850 counts, more and more family information was publicly posted. The public posting certainly undercut arguments in Washington that individual Census data had to be protected.

There were complaints about the questionnaire in 1850, but the Census Board reported that in only three cases did people violate the law making it a crime to refuse to answer questions. (The criminal penalty is still on the books, but invoked sparingly.) In all three cases the objectors gave in and complied.[28]

Those who mistrusted the Census agency had their worst fears realized during the Civil War. Union General William Tecumseh Sherman planned a scorched-earth raid through Georgia to the sea, not only to defeat the Confederate Army but also to rout Dixie's economy and civilian population. The Census superintendent had been providing to the Union Army the population data and maps that showed concentrations of industry in the South, but no one seemed to take interest in the materials. But Sherman took interest. He used the data in 1864 to rout the very people in the South who had earlier provided the data to the government in the 1860 head count. Census information led his troops to military sites, mills, cotton supplies, population centers, and a lot more in Georgia and neighboring states. The general seemed ecstatic in a thank-you note to the Census superintendent after the war, "The closing scene of our recent war demonstrated the value of these statistical tables and facts, for there is a reasonable probability that, without them, I would not have undertaken what was done and what seemed a puzzle to the wisest and most experienced soldiers of the world."[29]

Although the data released to the general did not identify persons by name, it was used for a secondary purpose and Sherman's use of the data was as threatening – and as traumatic to the victims – as the demand by the military War Command in World War II for

Census information to help locate Japanese-Americans in Western states. The military authorities wanted the data in order to remove Japanese-Americans from their homes for detention in war camps. The Census agency refused to provide names of individuals, but it did provide cumulative data showing concentrations of Japanese residents. This made the roundup easier for military authorities.[30]

During the post-Civil War period there was a continual move towards a "scientific census" that would objectively measure the demographics of the nation and permit intelligent framing of public policy. To do so required confidentiality, as Ohio Congressman James Garfield recognized as chair of the Committee on the Census in the 1860s. "The operations of the Census Office under the present law are not sufficiently confidential. The citizen is not adequately protected from the danger, or rather the apprehension, that his private affairs, the secrets of his family and his business, will be disclosed to his neighbors," said a report by the Garfield Committee in 1870.[31] None of his proposed reforms seem to have been adopted, but Garfield was later to become a leader in the House of Representatives and, in 1880, was elected President.

Widespread distrust of the Census continued for most of the last half of the Nineteenth Century. Both blacks and whites in the post-Civil War South were hostile towards the decennial count. Because of this, there were serious undercounts in the 1870 survey. *The New York Times* in 1870 said that the Census had "inquisitorial aspects." By 1875, the *Times*, in an editorial, said,

> "The universal suspicion of the census is as old as it is unaccountable. . . . There is a popular impression that [the census taker] is an enemy of domestic peace, a busybody in other men's matters, an impertinent spy, upon whom indignation has been poured for generations. . . . The true-born freeman resents nothing more bitterly than any suspected invasion of his domestic privacy."

In the Tenth Census in the nation's history, each Census taker was required for the first time to take an oath of confidentiality and there was a new $500 criminal penalty for violations of secrecy. That was in 1880. Still the emphasis was on protecting commercial information, not personal information.

By 1880 writers in all of the major newspapers logged in their complaints about the increasing intrusiveness of this head counting every ten years. Many commentators and citizens advocated boycotts. The inquiries had grown far beyond what James Madison and Thomas Jefferson had sought from the Census. But as devourers of statistics and facts about the U.S., each man probably would have loved to delve into the results.

"Be kind to the Census man," an 1890s humor magazine called *Life* said sarcastically. "If you must kick him, kick him softly." The Boston *Globe* in 1890 complained that "Uncle Sam's census takers will swarm forth and pump us all dry."[32]

Newspapers in 1890 published stories about attempts to thwart the decennial census – and editorials questioning the authority of the federal government to ask so many questions. Warrants for the arrest of 60 persons who refused to answer the dreaded census taker – most of them women – were issued in New York City. A German man in Manhattan asked, "What for you vant to know all dot beesness?" according to the New York *Tribune* of June 3, 1890. Doctors refused to respond to a Census demand for them to report diseases of their patients. The disdain for the whole process is clear in this verse published in the New York *Sun* in 1890:

> I am a census inquisitor.
> I travel about from door to door,
> From house to house, from store to store,
> With pencil and paper and power galore.
>
> I do as I like and ask what I please.
> Down before me you must get on your knees;
> So open your books, hand over your keys,
> And tell me about your chronic disease.
>
> Are you sure you don't like it? Well, I'm not to blame:
> I do as I'm ordered. Wouldn't you do the same?
> I'm a creature of law, and work in its name
> To further the new statistical game.

A decade later, the Superintendent of the Census admitted, "All over the country could be heard murmurings of discontent and declarations that the people of the United States would never submit to such an inquisitorial inquiry into their private affairs."[33]

The supervisor of the 1870 and 1880 censuses and the framer of the 1890 count, a prominent statistician named Francis A. Walker, pressed on with more and more inquiries and seemed to ignore pleas for confidentiality protections. Perhaps, as a Census veteran, he knew the nature of the American people better than those concerned about privacy did. Americans recognize the need for an accurate census and aren't worried about uses made of the information, Walker wrote in 1888. "What an American doesn't know about his own farm, or, for that matter, his neighbor's, too, is not worth knowing; and all he knows he is perfectly willing to tell."[34]

Sure enough, under Walker, the Census Office was finding Americans willing to tell what they knew about themselves. But the office had no systematic way to count it. The data was nearly obsolete by the time it could all be counted.

To process all of its questionnaires, the Census fostered development of the world's first counting machine. This was the first, but not the last, instance in which federal taxpayers subsidized the development of the modern computer. It happened again in 1946 when the U.S. Army sponsored development of the ENIAC, the first truly electronic processor without moving parts, and again in the 1950s when the Bureau of the Census developed the UNIVAC, the first commercial digital computer. Herman Hollerith, a Census employee, was later to be regarded as one of the fathers of the modern automated data processing machine.

Hollerith joined the Census in 1880, one of a group of bright young professionals hired by the statistics agency. The young Hollerith helped his boss in the vital statistics division, Civil War Col. John Shaw Billings, to tabulate vital statistics "as an amusement." The young man was dating the colonel's daughter. She invited him to dinner one night – a date that "ought to rank among the great serendipitous events of all time." At one point, as they chatted about statistics, the colonel looked at Hollerith and said, "There ought to be a machine." Billings suggested punch cards.[35] Weaving machines, after all, were using punch cards to automate the textile industry. The technique had been perfected in France back in 1804. In the 1820s an English mathematician named Charles Babbage had invented a "Difference Engine," which was used to solve mathematical problems.

Although Hollerith's relationship with the colonel's daughter did not last, he stayed with the Census agency. Within seven years, Herman Hollerith had developed a "census machine" with a keyboard card puncher and an electric tabulator. It was the first device to automate the processing of data and the first counting machine to use electricity.

Hollerith's counting machine was ready for the 1890 Census, allowing the government to cut in half the time needed to count its returns – even though the returns that year exceeded the number received in the previous count by 25 percent.

The implications of Hollerith's machine for confidentiality were two-fold – and paradoxical. The paradox has been true for all of the other technological advances in data processing since then: Automation adds certain anonymity to the process. Data collectors do not have time to absorb the masses of data passing by; in fact, most automated data processing removes personal facts from any inspection by human eyes. Actually, the Census Office in 1890 tried to assuage Americans' fears about privacy by announcing, "Your answers will be tabulated with about 60 million others."[36] On the other hand, the ease of tabulation and later the ease of storage remove any incentive to reduce demands for personal data. In an age of automated data processing, the rule seems to be "When in doubt, collect the information." Automation removes incentives to limit the amount of information demanded.

In addition, by their abilities to categorize individuals instantly – in fact, their *need* to categorize bits of data – the machines affect privacy in another way beyond the loss of confidentiality; they diminish personal autonomy. Hollerith's machine, for example, permitted the Census Office for the first time to break down its tabulations into small units, called Census tracts or Census blocks. His machine literally sorted people – or cards representing people – into separate boxes.

In Hollerith's device, an operator placed a blank paper card next to a larger metal prototype of the card, indicating holes to be punched for age, sex, color, address, and other variables. By pressing a handle, the operator punched holes in the card appropriately.

The punched cards were then fed into an electric counting machine. It had a set of spring-loaded pins pushed against the card. Where there was a hole, a pin passed through and touched a piece of metal on the other side, completing an electrical circuit. This caused a pointer on a dial counter to advance one unit. The counter looked like a clock.

This was essentially the same technology used well into the Twentieth Century. In the 1940s punched paper tape was substituted for the cards. Cards were used into the 1960s, but if they were spilled in the computer room they had to be sorted all over again. On the other hand, paper tape tended to break, and so magnetic tape was introduced. Another drawback of cards was that they would not function if they were altered. On them was printed the everlasting and ubiquitous legend, "Do Not Fold, Spindle or Mutilate." This gave rise to the battle cry in the campus unrest of the 1960s, which in part was aimed at depersonalization in large institutions: "I am a student. Do not fold, spindle, or mutilate." Integrated circuits replaced all of that in the 1970s.

And what became of Herman Hollerith? He started a business called Tabulating Machine Company, which in 1911 he merged with three others into an entity later to be known as International Business Machines – IBM.

Hollerith's invention was probably the least-noticed new technology in the Nineteenth Century that was to have a lasting effect on the dissemination of personal information into the next century. More noticeable to the average person were the relay stations necessary to transmit millions of invisible "dots and dashes" – codes for thousands of business and personal messages. They dotted the wide-open spaces west of the Allegheny Mountains and between the port cities of the East – about every 30 miles. Back in 1836, Samuel F. B. Morse had invented this new method of transmitting telegraphic messages by way of electronic pulses that could be translated into language. Thomas A. Edison enhanced Morse's invention in 1874 by devising a way for telegraph lines to transmit more than one message at a time in both directions. It was an expensive means of communicating at first, and became known as "the rich man's mail."

By 1844, Morse, formerly an artist and sculptor, completed a connection between Baltimore and what was then known as Washington City – thanks to a Congressional appropriation of $30,000. By the time of the Civil War, the East and the South were pretty much wired.

Prior to this, letters were dispatched by relays of men riding horses, the Pony Express. There was hardly time for letter writers to worry about the confidentiality of their correspondence in this privately run mode of delivery because it went bankrupt after just 18 months of operation. Although the Pony Express was later celebrated in American lore, it did not last long. Left behind at 25-mile intervals across the plains and mountains from the Mississippi River all the way to California were hundreds of transfer points where the horses had been rested and the riders relieved. The success of the telegraph, especially the installation of the Pacific Telegraph Company's connection to San Francisco, finished off the Pony Express in 1861.

The new telegraph technology required an enormous leap of faith on the part of the sender. It represented for the first time ever a means of delivery where there was no physical evidence at all that the message was traveling. This required the sender not only to trust that the human decoders of dots and dashes would not intercept and read the messages but also to trust that the technology could actually deliver the message to the intended recipient. Whatever personal information or sentiments were included in the message truly left the control of the originator. Further, unlike the situation with the U.S. Mail, an employee handling telegraph traffic could easily read messages without risking leaving the traces of an unopened envelope. There was no physical evidence of an interception. And, unlike the postal service, the telegraph system permitted the retention of every message. And it was controlled by a profit-making business. Because of the nature of the medium and enormity of the business that operated it, there was only a faceless institution, not a known individual, to hold accountable for the embarrassment or indignity of an invasion of privacy.[37]

On the other hand, this impersonal aspect of the process brought some anonymity to it. Because of the immensity of the operation, if a telegraph employee did peer into the content of a message, there was little chance that he would know the sender or recipient or that he could do much with the information. Computer keypunch personnel in the 1970s and Internet technicians in the 1990s were in the same position. In some ways, the more automated the process and the larger the volume of correspondence, the greater the possibilities there are for confidentiality.

When it was first introduced, many people anticipated that telegraph transmission would be far more secure than the Postal Office had been and that it would provide "impenetrable secrecy," because the messages were coded, or could be coded. But coding was not used for most business and personal correspondence. (The main reason was that a sender could recover damages caused by errors in transmission by the telegraph company but when it transmitted encoded messages its liability was significantly lower.). Because they were being charged by the word, many correspondents quickly learned how to communicate in a "telegraphic style" that omitted articles and extraneous language, to save money. Sometimes this included a mutually agreed basic form of encryption – as in, "Instead of writing out each member of my family, I'll identify each one by a digit in telegrams."

In the first three decades of telegraph service, accusations of abuses were rare. Western Union Co. reported in 1873 that its employees would burn a message rather than be compelled to disclose it. "Telegraph operators all through the land have been faithful," said a company publication.[38] Seven years earlier, without citing evidence, *The New York Times* claimed, "The popular idea that the secrecy of private communications sent by telegraph is always preserved is, we suspect, a good deal of fallacy." Violations of state confidentiality laws, which had been enacted in a bare majority of states, are hard to detect, and Western Union employees are subject to "strong temptations," the *Times* said.[39] The protection that existed was comparable to the hit-or-miss protection for individual account information in a financial institution in the Twenty-first Century: There's a strong tradition and a competitive incentive to protect information – and the possible deterrent of a subsequent invasion-of-privacy lawsuit; but in the end there is no black-and-white protection written in the statute books.

There were not many reported instances of subpoenas compelling the production of telegram transcripts in court. When there were, most courts followed an 1851 precedent in Pennsylvania that the state confidentiality statutes were intended to protect against private gain or the dissemination of damaging gossip, not to prevent use of telegrams in the judicial process.[40]

Congressional investigating committees were interested in using telegraph evidence, especially in the impeachment trials of President Andrew Johnson in 1868 and of Secretary of War William Belknap in 1876. One Congressional committee was said to sift through three-quarters of a ton of discarded messages of the Atlantic and Pacific Telegraph Company.

To investigate America's closest Presidential election in its history, one that had to be decided by the House of Representatives, Congressional committees sought access to telegram messages as evidence. This is the same campaign that produced complaints of mail openings in New York City.[41] Congressional investigators questioned the manager of the telegraph office in New Orleans about messages to and from state Republican candidates. Western Union President William Orton ordered the employee not to respond. He accused Congress of requiring his employees "to become spies and detectives upon and informers against the customers who have reposed in us the gravest confidence concerning both their official and their private affairs." Orton had promulgated a rule against disclosure in 1873. With Democrats supporting disclosure and Republicans supporting confidentiality, the Western Union manager was found in contempt of Congress and ordered to be held in custody until he complied. Orton himself was arrested by a deputy sergeant of arms on Capitol Hill and detained, despite an illness. (Orton must have been frail; he died less than a year after this occurred.)

On page one of the New York *Tribune* of January 20, 1877, the headline read, WESTERN UNION SURRENDERS. In response to a Congressional subpoena, the company delivered 30,000 political telegrams in a trunk to the House Committee on Privileges and Elections in the winter of 1877. "An Electoral Commission having by then been established, the senators never made official use of the messages, and the Democrats on the House committee never saw them, but someone did extract from the lot and publish coded dispatches that imputed serious bribery charges to [unsuccessful Democratic Presidential] candidate Samuel Tilden, the long-remembered 'cipher telegram,'" David Seipp reported in his history of privacy.[42]

Ohio Congressman James Garfield, who at the same time was arguing in favor of confidentiality in the Census, urged his colleagues in Congress to respect the public's expectation of confidentiality in sending telegrams as well. Otherwise, he warned, anyone could require a telegraph operator "to bring in his bundle of dispatches and this inquisitorial body can fish out from among them whatever evidence may happen to suit its passion or its caprice."[43] Other members of Congress said that the "security of society" and "getting at the truth" were more important. A colleague from Kentucky said that Garfield merely had a "newfangled sentimentality" about protecting telegraph confidentiality. As an assertive pro-privacy advocate in the 1860s, Garfield seemed not to prevail among his colleagues. But he did become sufficiently influential in Congress on other matters to get himself elected President in 1880.

In the next years, Congress debated whether Western Union telegraphs should be compared to Post Office material and therefore kept confidential or should be available by subpoena. The public recognized that this was a double-edged sword; a requirement of non-disclosure or of instant destruction of messages would protect privacy but also allow the company to escape liability for errors; the evidence would not be available. In response to comments in the press and in Congress, Western Union reduced the retention time for sent messages. As a practical matter, Congressional committees seemed to resolve the matter by narrowing their demands to see telegrams. Still, the debate continued in legal and academic circles – and on the front pages and editorial pages of the nation's newspapers.

At the same time as the election dispute, the courts of Missouri were considering the identical issue, involving the refusal of the telegraph company to comply with a grand jury demand for telegrams in a gambling investigation aimed at the governor and a police commissioner. In 1880 the Missouri Supreme Court, in a ruling in accord with the practical compromise arrived at in Congress, determined that telegrams had to be disclosed upon lawful demand but that the demands had to be narrowly fashioned.[44]

Also in 1880, a House committee reported out favorably a bill drafted for the committee by Western Union's lobbyists to protect telegrams to the very same extent as sealed letters in the Post Office. But the full House did not act on the proposal.

The public might have been prepared to accept this uneasy truce on privacy, but in 1881 perhaps the most hated capitalist of America's Gilded Age wrested control of Western Union Co. He was Jay Gould, who amassed a fortune in taking over control of major railroads. It was widely believed that his scheming to horde the existing gold supply caused the price of gold to plummet, resulting in one of the worst financial panics in American history, on "Black Friday" in 1869. Gould and his associates gained about $11 million by the maneuver. It was unthinkable that this man could control the main means of long-distance communications in the U.S.

"This individual possesses the power to inform himself of the nature of any intelligence transmitted over the wires, whether it refers to business, to family matters, or to politics," cried a business publication in Philadelphia. Besides, this "one man" was regarded as "a gigantic speculator," "an unscrupulous wrongdoer," "a menace to our free institutions." And, remember, this "one man" through his ownership of Western Union controlled the flow of out-of-town news from the wire services to the newspapers, as well as the flow of thousands of business and personal messages.

A Twentieth-Century account said of Jay Gould, "The financier stood barely five feet four, weighed 110 pounds, and looked more like a bright-eyed boy than a capitalist baron."[45] All of this sounds like what was said at the end of the Twentieth Century of Bill Gates, the bright-eyed boy who founded Microsoft, Inc. He is another unimposing man, incredibly wealthy, who as chief executive officer of Microsoft has the opportunity to have access to billions of bits and pieces of personal writings and to control a crucial means of communications for millions of persons.

After Gould's acquisition of Western Union, long-standing proposals for the government to take over the telegraph system gained momentum. (Congress had turned down Samuel Morse's offer to sell the system in its infancy at whatever price the government named.) Most of the concern focused on possible mischief because Western Union as a monopoly could engage in price gouging and because it was entrusted with masses of valuable business and investment information. But there was concern about privacy as well. A few advocates argued that government control would enhance protection of privacy. The rhetoric expressing fears about privacy in the Western Union system was similar to that about the Internet computer network in the 1990s, except that a possible advantage of the Internet – which its users recognized – was that no one really owned it, certainly no single titan of industry owned it.

In the end, concerns about privacy were subsumed in arguments over whether the government should take over the system or at least regulate it closely. Congress never did so. Jay Gould had his friends in Congress. President Benjamin Harrison reportedly passed the word about Western Union to his postmaster general: "To attack them is political insanity." Harrison was swamped in 1892 when he ran for reelection, but for other reasons. In that same year, Jay Gould died at age 56. And in 1892 as well, the breathless, gossipy reporting of the New York *World*, which Gould had owned before it became successful, was extending the paper's daily circulation towards the one million mark.

A writer for the Springfield *Republican* in Massachusetts at the end of the century was exasperated by the cacophony: "The telegraph and the innumerable newspapers have made the world one enormous ear of Dionysius – a perpetual whispering gallery."[46] Another journalist, this one writing in 1883, was perceptive enough to see how the converging trends related to each other – and affected the rights of individuals over the long term. The development of the frontier, the power of the telegraph, and the pervasiveness of aggressive press coverage. What did they have in common? Charles T. Congdon, a newspaper publisher in upstate New York, wrote, "The simultaneous control of the telegraph, of long lines of railway, and of leading newspapers, by a few men acting in a corporate capacity, or by one man employing the advantages of a corporation, puts the whole public, so far as intelligence is concerned, at the mercy of unlimited power."[47]

⟍ Links

To read about the development of big-business newspapers during the same era, continue on to the next chapter, on Space.

To discover the legal response to the new technology at the end of the Nineteenth Century, go to the chapter on Brandeis.

To read about the spread of electronic surveillance in the Twentieth Century, which grew out of techniques learned in the early telegraph era, go to the chapter on Wiretaps.

To compare the Nineteenth-Century response to new technology with that in the Twentieth Century, go to the chapters on Databanks and Cyberspace.

Space

Frontier attitudes about privacy, living conditions in early suburbs and on plantations, and a New England essayist's retreat to his own space

In many ways, the people of early Nineteenth-Century America had more privacy than any other culture before or since. There were vast, unlimited opportunities for physical separation and a growing affluence to make use of it. The new technological developments that were to permit permanent photo imaging, record keeping, and intrusiveness were still to come. The federal government was growing, to be sure; but it had nowhere near the capacity for information collection and surveillance that was to come in the second half of the Twentieth Century. Even at the end of the Nineteenth Century, the central government collected little if any information about its citizens. The perceived threats to privacy came only from two sources in the private sector: the telegraph monopoly and the pervasive boisterousness of large-circulation newspapers.

Once again, as in the previous century, it was a visitor from Europe who identified the advantages and disadvantages of life in America. Baron von Hubner toured the world after a career as an Austrian diplomat in major capitals. After visiting the United States, he wrote in the 1870s, "What abounds in America is what we lack most – space."

Everything is new and incomplete in the new nation, he said. In Europe people rebuild or restore. In the U.S. people demolish. "To become American would be to presuppose the entire destruction of Europe."

"Life is easy here," von Hubner concluded about America, *"for everybody has space."*

> "To prevent a disagreeable meeting, one has only to cross to the other side of the street; it is wide enough for all. But the day will come, although it is now far-off, when this illimitable space will be narrowed, and when it will be diffi-

cult by flight to escape those who do not share your religious convictions. Even in your country the question of liberty of conscience has not yet been definitely settled.

"To sum up, you have the great advantage of space, which is wanting in Europe; and you are at the growing age. North America offers an unlimited field of liberty to the individual. It does not simply give him the opportunity; it forces him to employ all the faculties with which nature has endowed him. The arena is open. As soon as he enters it he must fight, and fight to the death. In Europe it is just the contrary. Everyone finds himself hemmed in by the narrow sphere in which he is born."[1]

Von Hubner felt that in Europe a person seeks to attain a life of ease; in America a person works to be rich. Not everyone attains it, but everyone tries. He was sure that this is what accounts for our cumulative success.

The physical space available to Americans – already abundant – expanded dramatically in the early part of the century with the Louisiana Purchase in 1803, which annexed most of the land west of the Mississippi and east of the Rocky Mountains. There was even more expansion when Texas became a state in 1845 and California and New Mexico were annexed three years later.

"Nineteenth-Century America was a rich, empty country which lay outside the mainstream of world events, and in which the twin nightmares that beset nearly every modern man, the nightmare of unemployment and the nightmare of State interference, had hardly come into being. There were social distinctions, more marked than those of today, and there was poverty . . . but there was not, as there is today, an all-revealing sense of helplessness. There was room for everybody, and if you worked hard you could be certain of a living – could even be certain of growing rich; this was generally believed, and for the greater part of the population it was even broadly true. In other words, the civilization of Nineteenth-Century America was capitalist civilization at its best."

British journalist and novelist George Orwell, in 1946.[2]

Because of the great expanses available in North America, Americans came to take physical privacy for granted. They also came to assume that they could pack up and move whenever they took a notion to. When Thomas Jefferson was America's envoy to France, he identified this characteristic, in a note to a French scholar in 1786:

> "The present population of the inhabited parts of the United States is of about ten to the square mile; and experience has shown us that wherever we reach that, the inhabitants become uneasy, as too much compressed, and so go off in great numbers to search for vacant country."[3]

A Frenchman who toured the new nation observed the same trait but regarded it less complimentarily:

> "The frontiersman offers complete proof of the American indifference in love and friendship and of failure to form attachments to anything. In the course of a lifetime he may begin as many as four clearings. He abandons, without reluctance, the place where he first drew breath, the church in which he first perceived the idea of a supreme being, the tombs of his ancestors, the friends of his infancy, the companions of his youth, and all the pleasures of his society. He emigrates, especially if he be a northerner, to go South or West, to the backwoods of the United States on the Ohio, disposing of his property, selling the house, the wagon, the horse, the dog, anything that will fetch a price."[4]

Even many "plantations" of the slave-holding South were no more than a collection of modest outbuildings on the edge of the frontier that the owner might abandon after one year of intensive planting had ravished the land. Americans maintained that mobility throughout the Twentieth Century – more than 35 percent of us now do not live in the place where we were raised and about one in five of us changes residences each year. In other words, the French writer Mederic Louis Elie Moreau de Saint-Mery had it right for the Twentieth Century as well as the Eighteenth – four "clearings" in a lifetime for each of us. (Among other things, this means that we are not known to merchants and insurance companies in the localities where we live. Our family reputations are not known there either. This means that businesses must rely on national credit bureaus and consumer reporting agencies to vouch for our credit-worthiness and general reputation.)

Walt Whitman, the great poet of the Nineteenth Century, identified his nation's "pull-down-and-build-over-again spirit." As editor of the *Eagle* in the teeming city of Brooklyn, New York, Whitman wrote in an editorial:

> "Let us level to the earth all the houses that were not built within the past ten years; let us raise the devil and break things!"

And in a poem:

> "Unscrew the locks from the doors! Unscrew the doors themselves from their jambs."[5]

In a continent where all the land had not even been explored or mapped and where anyone could move on a whim and find new neighbors or solitude, Americans developed an assumption of unlimited elbowroom. This presumed entitlement of a space of our own has stayed with us into the more crowded Twenty-first Century.

"When this country was new, a nonconformist or someone who just wasn't making it could always go west. There was always space. Now there is no more space, and the courts have been called on to protect the rights of these individuals. The courts are trying to provide that space."

Associate Justice of the Supreme Court Potter Stewart, in 1982.[6]

In fact, some people believe that the nation's unlimited physical space is the reason that it did not develop a legal regime to protect privacy in the first decades. According to this theory, there was no need for laws recognizing a right to privacy because there were vast opportunities for solitude or for a fresh start far away. Even in the cities, people lived in close proximity without protocols for protecting personal space. Boston hardly had any police force at all in the early 1800s, according to Henry Adams' account. "In most cases an invasion of a man's private life would result in a duel, a horsewhipping, or the shooting of a newspaper editor who was considered to have overstepped the boundaries of good taste or discretion," wrote Thomas H. O'Connor, in a 1968 essay called "The Right to Privacy in Historical Perspective."[7]

For five decades during this period, audiences were entertained by a fictional stage character named Paul Pry, a persistent snooper. But the retaliation against him was a kick in the rear, not a lawsuit.[8] (In the latter half of the Nineteenth Century, "Paul Pry" was a common synonym for busybody.)

On the Tennessee frontier in 1808, an accused eavesdropper argued in his defense that the English law on protection of privacy didn't apply in the new land; it was not "consistent with our mode of living," his lawyer argued, because America was egalitarian and on her frontier a man had other opportunities for enforcing his rights. The judge disagreed, saying that a prohibition against eavesdropping is consistent with "the situation of any society whatsoever."[9]

The defendant was arguing that the West, because it was sparsely settled, required little formal regulation. In its early years, the Internet of the 1990s was similarly an unregulated frontier; in many ways that was its strength. But in some ways it was more dangerous: In contrast to life in the American West, children and others could innocently wander into the dark alleys of the Internet frontier town – the "global village" – without leaving home and without the knowledge of their guardians.

"America was largely settled, and its frontiers expanded, by people seeking to get away from something unpleasant in their pasts, either oppression, painful episodes, poverty, or misdemeanors."

Social critic Vance Packard, 1950s.

Precisely because America did not have the sophisticated system of customs and social niceties and class distinctions that England had developed over centuries, it eventually had to develop a legal protocol to protect a sense of privacy. Still, the legal safeguards have never been fully developed in this country. Privacy even today is protected far more by non-legal means than by enforceable rights. It is stronger as a social concept than as a legal concept. By adjusting our behavior or the behavior of others, by adapting physical space, by using new technologies, by subtly establishing taboos, by scores of little-noticed accommodations each day, we manage to establish the lines of privacy in our own lives.

In addition to these social protections, privacy is preserved by legal protections *indirectly*, not by a law that addresses privacy explicitly. Examples include rules of evidence that exclude as admissible whatever is produced by an unreasonable search, the recognition of privileges between spouses or between medical professionals and patients, and civil or criminal sanctions against trespasses and nuisances.

There were those who believed that it was fair to impute Americans' great curiosity, as well as its interest in privacy, to the nation's abundance of land. Another French visitor – this time it was the French naturalist Francois Andre Michaux – after the obligatory tour of the States, wrote in 1802 that intense curiosity "is natural to people who live isolated in the woods and seldom see a stranger."[10] Or, as Washington Irving's fictitious Ichabod Crane said, distant neighbors who came calling were welcome if they were "carrying the whole budget of local gossip from house to house." For many pioneers, the sound of an ax chopping against wood was a welcome one. It meant that there were people nearby to relieve their loneliness – or satisfy their curiosity. Compare that to the dread that contemporary exurbanites or rural residents experience today when they hear a chain saw or a bulldozer. There was no mistaking the loneliness of the frontier.

> "There are days when the booming of the wind in the pines is like the audible rushing of time – when the sad knowledge of the grave stirs in the subconsciousness and bends the spirit to melancholy; days when the questions that have no answers must insinuate themselves into the minds of the least analytical of men. And there are other days – in July and August – when the nerves wilt under the terrific impact of sun and humidity, and even the soundest grow a bit neurotic; days saturnine and bilious and full of heavy foreboding.
>
> "The loneliness of the country, the ennui of long, burning, empty days, a hundred half-perceived miseries, ate into him and filled him with nebulous discontent and obscure longing."[11]

The brooding chronicler of *The Mind of the South*, W. J. Cash, used this language to describe a Southerner in early America. Discounting somewhat for "half-perceived miseries" – it could apply as well to any rural American in the Nineteenth Century.

Frances Trollope, in her unfavorable observations about America in the 1830s, compared rural farmers to the solitary Robinson Crusoe, and added:

"It seemed to me that there was something awful and almost unnatural in their loneliness. No village bell ever summoned them to prayer, where they might meet the friendly greeting of their fellow men. When they die, no spot sacred by ancient reverence will receive their bones. . .

The wind that whispers through the boughs will be their only requiem. But then they pay neither taxes nor tythes, are never expected to pull off a hat or to make a curtsy, and will live and die without hearing or uttering the dreadful words, 'God save the king.'"[12]

Thus, seeking a respite from the rest of humanity – like that sought by John Adams and his Constitutional colleagues – was not a priority. For safety, efficiency, and companionship, pioneer families in many enclaves stuck together. Many of their communities were a reversion to the compact Colonial New England villages where space between you and your neighbors was not a virtue. It was a risk. Many of their settlements resembled the Mormon communities established in the mid-1800s, which were described as follows: "In every conceivable relation, position, interest, and idea; in every sentiment of hope and fear, of joy and sorrow – there is mutual assistance and sympathy. It enters into all affairs, whether for time or eternity, and to the fullest extent short of communism, mutual assistance in agriculture, commerce, and manufacture."[13]

At the same time, the leader of the Mormon migration to Utah, Brigham Young, preached a kind of personal autonomy quite different from that of New England Puritanism. Speaking of God, Brigham Young, a transplanted New Englander, preached:

"He cannot force his children to do this, that or the other against their will – the eternal laws by which He and all others exist in the eternities of the Gods, decree that the consent of the creature must be obtained before the Creator can rule perfectly."

In another way, though, the Church of Jesus Christ of Latter-day Saints was replicating the church-state coziness in Colonial New England villages. Each town and city in Utah in close cooperation with the church began to keep detailed family histories just as Puritan villages did. "They know in Orderville [in southwestern Utah] exactly who was hungry in 1912 and who committed adultery in 1956, but they also know where somebody's ancestor from the fifteenth century has been given a valid passport to eternal life," wrote Timothy Egan of *The New York Times* in his 1998 book

Lasso the Wind. "No state has more keepers of history, or better archives, honeycombed in climate-controlled vaults, than Utah."

Each local bishop – a male member of the church – prepares a cumulative record on each church member, and a copy is stored in the church headquarters in Salt Lake City. These sheets record the member's progress in the church, identities of parents, spouse, and children, volunteer tasks and missions undertaken, and finally the date, place, and cause of death. A separate record keeps track of regular financial contributions through the years. In addition, because the church believes that all living and deceased persons who were not members of the church will have an opportunity for resurrection, it maintains the largest genealogical database in the world – millions and millions of computerized and manual files on non-church members in the Church of Latter-day Saints Genealogical Society next to its temple in Salt Lake City. When the church made its data on 400 million persons and their family histories available on the World Wide Web in May of 1999, interest was so great that the site at first could not handle the traffic.

While the Western expansion was taking place, new Americans were simultaneously filing the nation's Eastern cities. From 1840 to 1890, the share of the population living in communities with more than 2500 persons jumped from 11 percent to 35 percent. In roughly the same period, 12 million persons immigrated into the U.S., a nation that increased in population from 17 million to 62 million during the same time. In the East, where newcomers crowded New York and other cities, it was harder to see the possibilities for self-reliance. Americans in the cities were becoming more dependent on their neighbors, for shelter, for food, for employment.

In a notable address in 1893, historian Frederick Jackson Turner declared the age of the frontier officially over. And he pointed out that the westward migration had had a profound impact on the mores of American society equal to that of the legacies of British culture in the East. These values were in conflict between East and West, though perhaps in a healthy manner:

> "Legislation is taking the place of the freelands as the means of preserving the ideal of democracy. But at the same time it is endangering the other pioneer ideal of creative and competitive individualism. Both were essential and constituted what was best in America's contribution to history and progress. . . . All that was buoyant and creative

in American life would be lost if we gave up the respect for distinct personality, and variety in genius, and came to the dead level of common standards. To be 'socialized into an average' and placed 'under the tutelage of the mass of us' ... would be an irreparable loss."[14]

Each of us Americans living in the new millennium must ask ourselves, as we rush from shopping mall to shopping mall or from one World Wide Web to the other or bow to demands for our personal credentials or accept camera surveillance at each street corner, "What would Frederick Jackson Turner have said 100 years later?" Is each of us "buoyant and creative," thereby adding to America's "contribution to history"? Or has each of us come to a "dead level of common standards" – giving up our personal privacy and dignity in the process?

It must have been difficult to maintain one's sense of privacy and dignity in the tight Nineteenth-Century living quarters that most Americans lived in. Physical surroundings within the home had not changed much since Ben Franklin's youth in Boston. "These people live in open log cabins with hardly a blanket to cover them," exclaimed a visitor to the Appalachian region of North Carolina in 1767. "They sleep altogether in common in one room, and shift and dress openly without ceremony. . . . Nakedness is counted as nothing."[15]

Log cabins favored by Scotch Irish settlers in rural America, but not by the English, were inconspicuous structures, built to withstand external threats but not to maximize living space – "a style of building well suited to a people who had a strong sense of family and a weak sense of individual privacy," according to David Hackett Fischer in his book *Albion's Seed* in 1989.

"Very often an entire family of a dozen, male and female, adult and child, slept, cooked, ate, lived, loved, and died – had its whole indoor being – in a single room," according to W.J. Cash's account of life in the South. Cash was writing about the poor "yeomen farmers" in the Southern states in the Eighteenth Century, but conditions had not changed much in the first half of the Nineteenth Century.

Most Mormon families in the West had large numbers of children and still lived in a single-room or two-room dwelling, like Benjamin Franklin's family and many others in Colonial New England. A typical set-up was the two-room log cabin in Beaver, Utah, that accommodated 32-year-old Lorenzo Robinson, his wife, and six children. Six more children soon joined the rest of the family, in the same quarters.[16]

Consequently, throughout rural America, more than one child regularly shared a bed. Adult visitors would sleep with children of the same gender, as well, or share a bed with the parent of the same sex. Beds were narrow; physical contact, especially with three or more in a bed, was inevitable, sometimes even between strangers.

Leaders of the Church of Jesus Christ of Latter-day Saints regularly encouraged same-sex bed sharing, as part of some bonding ritual in the church. Its founder, Joseph Smith, urged church members of the same sex to sleep in "the same bed at night locked in each other's embrace talking of their love," according to D. Michael Quinn's eye-opening account, *Same-Sex Dynamics among Nineteenth-Century Americans: A Mormon Example*.

It made sense to embrace each other overnight, regardless of sex, because Nineteenth-Century dwellings were usually cold in the winter. In Colonial New England, even strangers engaged in this coziness mainly to keep warm. But even after heating improved, Mormon authorities encouraged the practice. Church leaders always stayed with church families in their travels and until at least the 1940s, according to Quinn, "continued the practice of sleeping with local leaders and having religious discussions in bed." Some leaders of the Church of Latter-day Saints found this ritual distasteful. Apostle David O. McKay wrote that he would rather sleep on the floor than with another man. Upon sharing a bed with one Mormon leader, local LDS leader Francis M. Lyman wrote in 1876, "He was so dirty that it made me crawl whenever he touched me." But Brother Lyman apparently overcame his distaste – or was more selective – for in 1891, an LDS colleague, L. John Nuttall, noted, "I found Bro. F.M. Lyman in my bed at the Gardo [a church site in Salt Lake City, Utah] & we slept together." In the next several months, Nuttall wrote, the two shared a bed together, although both their wives were elsewhere in the city. And, there was no cold weather to contend with in the spring.

Nuttall, official secretary of the First Presidency, made a special point of noting in the 1890s that when another Mormon couple came to visit, "He slept with me." It's curious that Nuttall felt it noteworthy to mention this; the leaders apparently wanted their followers in the church to be sure to know that these arrangements were encouraged. Nuttall's comment and others like it show that Mormon members, at least the elite in the church, paired off by gender, and not by couples, when it came time to turn in for the night.

By the 1860s a physician warned in his popular medical-advice book that siblings should sleep alone. After puberty, he warned, it's possible for siblings to have erotic encounters if they are bedfellows.

Only with the coming of roadhouses and inns did the custom of bed-sharing by visitors fade, but not entirely. The Duc de Liancourt, one of the more credible foreign observers in the Nineteenth Century, wrote, "The people of the country are . . . astonished that one should object to sleeping two or three in the same bed and in dirty sheets, or to drink from the same dirty glass after half a score of others."[17]

"If I am to write, I must have a room to myself, which shall be *my* room."

Harriet Beecher Stowe, author of *Uncle Tom's Cabin*, 1852.

For two-and-a-half million Americans of color in the Southern states there were not only ramshackle living conditions, but also the total deprivation of privacy that characterized slavery. One Louisiana slaveholder admitted that the cabins for slaves on his plantation afforded "scarcely a shelter."[18] After a tour of the South in 1852, the most prestigious landscape architect of his time, Frederick Law Olmsted, described the typical building housing slaves on the South's 46,000 plantations:

> "A good many old plantations are to be seen, generally standing in a grove of white oaks, upon some hill-top. Most of them are constructed of wood, of two stories, painted white, and have, perhaps, a dozen rude-looking little log cabins scattered around them, for the slaves.

> "The negro cabins here [in South Carolina] were the smallest I had seen – I thought not more than 12 feet square, inside. They stood in two rows, with a wide street between them. They were built of logs, with no windows – no opening at all, except the doorway, with a chimney of sticks and mud; with no trees about them, no porches, or shades, of any kind. Except for the chimney, . . . I should have conjectured that it had been built for a powder house, or perhaps an ice house – never for an animal to sleep in.

"The houses, with respect to their dimensions may be compared to the tiny cells of monks. The height is such that when you stand up your head touches the roof."[19]

According to Olmsted's measurements, each slave *family* had about 441 square feet of living space, roughly the size of a small bedroom in the 1990s. He noted a stark comparison with the modest houses of poor white Southerners. The physical space and frailty were about the same; but, as contrasted to slave houses, white residences displayed an aura of permanence, of freedom and independence, of personal preferences, and of a capacity to use the entire dwelling and its surroundings without fear of theft or retaliation.

"O, nobody knows a who I am,
a who I am, till the judgment morning!"

Southern Negro spiritual "Nobody Knows Who I Am."

Of course, maintaining a semblance of family life, which is one of the basic purposes for seeking privacy, was impossible in the oppressive "peculiar institution" of slavery. Slaveholders disregarded the emotional and physical bonds of family members. Sons and daughters, brothers and sisters, husbands and wives, fathers and mothers were separated and scattered when bought and sold in the marketplace, or forced to flee. Harriet A. Jacobs' classic personal memoir of life as a slave, *Incidents in the Life of a Slave Girl*, related this heartbreak. For instance, when her father died, "I thought I should be allowed to go to my father's house the next morning; but I was ordered to go for flowers, that my mistress's house might be decorated for an evening party. I spent the day gathering flowers and weaving them into festoons, while the dead body of my father was lying within a mile of me. What cared my owners for that? He was merely a piece of property. Moreover, they thought he had spoiled his children, by teaching them to feel that they were human beings. This was blasphemous doctrine for a slave to teach."[20]

Jacobs described the horror when the master of the plantation demanded that the teen-aged slave girl share his bedroom, sleeping next to his bed. It was common in the two previous centuries in America for masters and servants to share living quarters, often the same room. Frances Trollope, the British observer of American folkways, found it amazing that master and servant spent most of the day – and the night – in close proximity and that white people did not seem to resent this restriction on their freedom of movement and privacy. In the context of Nineteenth-Century slavery, room sharing was not for warmth, not for ritual bonding, not at all for lack of space – as it was in Colonial New England and on the frontier. It was for illicit, involuntary sex. The young African-American girl found sleep impossible.

Mary Boykin Chesnut, a campaigner for the abolition of slavery who kept a diary during the Civil War, observed the lack of privacy – and hypocrisy – in the institution of plantation slavery:

> "Like the patriarchs of old, our men live in one house with their wives and their concubines, and the mulattos one sees in every family exactly resemble the white children – and every lady tells you who is the father of all the mulatto children in everybody's household, but those in her own she seems to think drop from the clouds . . . . You see, Mrs. Stowe did not hit on the sorest spot. She makes Legree a bachelor."[21]

She was referring to Simon Legree, the mean-spirited overseer in *Uncle Tom's Cabin* by Harriet Beecher Stowe. One of the reasons planters promptly sold off children in slave families, thus dismantling ties within the African-American household, was to remove reminders and evidence of illicit sexual relations with slave women.

"There are those who argue that the right to privacy is of a higher order than the right to life. That was the premise in slavery. You could not protest the existence or treatment of slaves on the plantation, because that was private and therefore outside of your right to be concerned. That's how they dehumanized us."

Civil rights activist Jesse Jackson, quoted in 1993.

Harriet Jacobs was apologetic for submitting to a white man's sexual advances rather than be victimized by force. But she was not very apologetic:

> "O, ye happy [white] women whose purity has been sheltered from childhood, who have been *free to chose the objects of your affection*, whose *homes are protected by law*,

do not judge the poor desolate slave girl too severely! If slavery had been abolished I, also, could have married the man of my choice; I could have had a home shielded by the laws; . . . but all my prospects had been blighted by slavery. I wanted to keep myself pure; and, under the most adverse circumstances, I tried hard to preserve my self respect; but I was struggling alone in the powerful grasp of the demon Slavery; and the monster proved too strong for me. I felt as if I was forsaken by god and man."

"The dream of my life is not yet realized. I do not sit with my children *in a home of my own*. I still long for a hearthstone of my own, however humble. I wish for my children's sake far more than for my own."

Jacob's human yearnings for freedom to choose, for a home of her own, *for a home protected by law* constitute the very essence of personal privacy. Most of us can take for granted these basics of privacy.

Plantation slaves established their own covert informal customs for establishing a sense of personal territory. In the process they created their own tacitly recognized domains. It might be the stable or the craft shop or a barn. A white man who visited several plantations to tutor white children recalled being assessed fines by slaves for venturing into their space. A slave cook, for instance, might make the kitchen in the "big house" off-limits to anyone not authorized by her.

Slaves established a system of pathways through the woods for visiting each other and for convening celebrations and clandestine rituals. The great abolitionist Frederick Douglass recognized these private trails as the locus of rebellion.

On plantations where slaves were permitted to build their own quarters, they usually built near the woods, as far from the main house as possible. Landowners were quite happy to have the ugly shacks out of sight. The white overseer or the master of the house himself was entitled to make unannounced visits and often did, much like the tythingmen in Colonial New England. But white people also had an attitude that slave quarters were so dirty and chaotic as to be beneath notice. Some slave cabins displayed a horseshoe above the opening to ban evil spirits and distrusted persons, and some white folks on the plantation did not wish to challenge that. Or a "conjuring gourd" might be within reach, for the same purpose.

Especially on large plantations, owners relied on overseers to keep tabs. These were an itinerant, despised bunch; slaves who lived on the premises devised ways to outwit these migratory employees. This provided some cover for slave residents to have modest opportunities for activities free from monitoring. One former slave recalled that her African-born mother took great pride that she "worked without no watchin'," and members of the household knew this.

The degrading physical conditions of slave houses were the least of deprivations of privacy; in fact, the shacks mostly were used only for sleeping anyway, much the way Native Americans used teepees. John Michael Vlach, author of *Back of the Big House, The Architecture of Plantation Slavery*, points out, "Planters were determined to keep their slaves under control by treating them as a collective population rather than as individuals." This made the slave house not a residence at all, but a lock-up for the night or a corral. Along with the inability even to be known by the name you or your parents might choose for you, this loss of individualism was the ultimate deprivation of privacy and autonomy, of course. Access to education and even the right to marry – both components of the constitutional right to privacy recognized in our time – were denied by law. "The characteristic feature of slaves is that they lack self-ownership," in the words of Anita L. Allen, who has written on the relationship of race and privacy. She pointed out:

> "All black mothers were de facto surrogates. Children born to slaves were owned by Master X or Mistress Y and could be sold at any time to another owner. Slave women gave birth to children with the understanding that those children would be owned by others."[22]

And yet this oppression could not erase human dignity and spirit. Within the slave quarters inevitably there was a semblance of vitality and home life, just as is established in other oppressive settings.[23] Bondage did not totally destroy a people. In the words of Ralph Ellison, Twentieth-Century novelist of the African-American experience:

> "Any people who could undergo such dismemberment and resuscitate itself, and endure until it could take the initiative in achieving its own freedom is obviously more than the sum of its brutalization."[24]

As a Czech-born philosophy professor at Boston University, Erazim Kohak, once said, "As long as a person retains the privacy of his soul, he can resist; absolute rulers cannot tolerate that." Think of the *private* in an army, Kohak said, or a prisoner. "There is precious little objective privacy here, and yet how deeply, intensely private can be the thoughts and experiences of each of those men! If you ever were a sergeant shouting orders to a private who was a poet in his civilian life, you know how impenetrably *private* his experience remains to you – and yours to him."[25]

And so when Emancipation came in 1863, many slaves insisted on remaining in the places they had created. They did so not because of a fondness for the institution of slavery or for their former owners. Instead they insisted that they had an ownership interest in the property. They had worked the land, built the structures, and personalized the place. One South Carolina freedman returned from Civil War service with rifle in hand and insisted to his former owner, "Yes, I'm going to work right here. I'd like to see any man put me out of this house."

Decades after slavery had been invalidated, an elderly former slave man known only as Morris objected to an effort to evict him from his home by saying:

> "I was born on this place before freedom. My Mammy and Daddy worked the rice fields. They are buried here. The first thing I remember are those rice banks. I grew up in them from that high. . . . The strength of these arms and these legs and of this old back is in your rice banks. It won't be long before the good Lord takes the rest of poor old Morris away too. And the rest of his body wants to be with the strength of the arms and the legs and the back that is already buried in your rice banks. No, you ain't going to run old Morris off this place!"[26]

Five years after Emancipation, the nation enacted the Fourteenth Amendment to the Constitution, as a way of remedying the ills of slavery in a self-proclaimed democracy. (President Andrew Johnson successfully urged all the Southern states except Tennessee not to ratify it.) The Fourteenth Amendment says, in part:

> "No State shall make or enforce any law which shall abridge the privileges or immunities of citizens of the United States; nor shall any State deprive any person of life, liberty, or property, without due process of law; nor deny to any person within its jurisdiction the equal protection of the laws."

It was intended to provide substantive and due-process rights for millions of freed black Americans and it did so. Among other things, it also eliminated the method of enumerating a slave as three-fifths of a person, a bifurcation that in many ways had caused the founders to be obsessed with collecting an accurate census of the population. Beyond that, the Fourteenth Amendment also provided in the Twentieth Century one of the bases for recognizing a right to privacy for all Americans under the Constitution of the United States.

At about this time, Americans near the teeming cities were emulating, in a way, their sisters and brothers who had gone west in search of autonomy and elbowroom. Everybody seemed to yearn for physical space between themselves and their neighbors. No longer were there the impediments that forced early New Englanders to make their villages compact.

For the rest of the century, there was a drumbeat urging Americans – in both the East and West – to insulate themselves from their neighbors with physical space. One writer at mid-century warned, "The consciousness of contiguity is always an annoyance."[27] Another said flatly that apartment life was not home life.

Just as America was breaking away from its English roots and exploiting new technology to revolutionize its commercial development and to move from a rural to an urban society, it was fashionable in some circles to yearn for the England of old. The same Frederick Law Olmsted who had toured the South seven years earlier toured England just before the outbreak of hostilities between North and South and in a 1859 book reported back on the verdant landscapes that he found. Olmsted saw the need for preserving the natural surroundings for serenity in Manhattan and in other American cities. Based on his observations in England, he designed Central Park and others like it in Washington and Chicago.

Were Americans hustling too much to make money? "Author after author lambasted the houses inhabited by the new urban residents, houses reflecting newly acquired wealth, houses inhabited by idle women vexed by idle servants, houses cramped, airless, and fronting ever more noisy city streets," reported John R. Stilgoe in his 1989 study of American restlessness, *Borderland: Origins of the American Suburb, 1820-1939*. "As early as 1838 [Ralph Waldo] Emerson argued that a proper home offered its occupants – and particularly the businessman – a haven from the trials of public life, a place of 'recreation.' For the debilities caused by 'studies, handiworks, arts, trade, politics,' Emerson proposed the 'balsam' of 'the garden, the house, and the old and new familiar faces therein contained.'"[28]

According to *Borderland*, "The tinkling of a badly tuned piano, the drifting scent of burning liver, the squalling of miserable infants made apartment life, except for the rich, increasingly wearing on already strained men and women."

"Paper-thin walls of apartment houses bring every sound of your neighbors into your bedroom. Nervous breakdowns must have been around since the Renaissance. The more we change, the more we stay the same."

Playwright Neil Simon, in 1999.

But the American farmhouse would not do as a family sanctuary, nor as a place to appreciate plant life. Farmers and pioneers were competing with each other to strip the land of its natural growth as quickly as possible. "Grubbing" it was called. In the Twentieth Century, Americans' greediness would be mocked by the line, "Whoever dies with the most assets wins." Some Nineteenth-Century commentators taunted, "Whoever has grubbed the most land by the time he dies wins."

Americans therefore turned to the English cottage as the model for the perfect family nest. An influential post-Civil War book called *Home Life: What It Is, and What It Needs* argued that the perfect home must provide for seclusion and privacy, as well as a garden and a yard. "A walk through some parts of any large town or city is enough to make the heart ache," wrote the author, John F. W. Ware.

A writer named Alexander Slidell Mackenzie reversed the earlier pattern of Europeans constantly reporting our shortcomings to European readers. Mackenzie, as an American visiting England, reported back to Americans. In 1835, he wrote, "I could not but regret the unfavorable character of the comparison between those charming cottages, and the tasteless masses of brick and mortar in which people of the same class and of greater means are contented to live in my own country."

Back in 1804, in a book published in both London and Philadelphia, Ely Bates had insisted that children must be raised with "a taste for solitude" and that city living fostered only anxiety and conventional thinking. The title of his book said it all: *Rural Philosophy: Or Reflections on Knowledge, Virtue, and Happiness Chiefly in Reference to a Life of Retirement in the Country.* Echoing John Adams, William Penn, and their contemporaries two generations earlier, Bates advised America's frenetic businessmen to take long breaks in the country or risk physical illness, or what we today call "burnout."

All of this thinking led to the creation of America's first suburban subdivison. It was in the 1850s in Orange, New Jersey, one hour by train from downtown New York City (12 miles). Here middle-class Americans could have it both ways – access to the earning potential of the teeming city and the pseudo-adventure of the expansive frontier. The new community was built by Llewellyn S. Haskell, a successful businessman who had always favored living on the fringes of the city. He borrowed an idea from England and created an association of homeowners who purchased one-acre to 20-acre sites. He borrowed another idea from abroad and installed a gate house through which visitors to his Llewellyn Park had to pass after first registering. The gate was closed on Sundays. (Still, Haskell was willing to sell to anyone with enough money, without any social restrictions.) Inside, with its carefully planted shrubbery, rambling carriage pathways, and spectacular views of New York City and the ocean beyond, visitors found the enclave to be what one called "an enchanted ground or fairy ground."

The residents, necessarily, were an affluent, well-connected bunch. But non-residents came to regard them as slightly eccentric, interested in such things as spiritualism, atheism, and communing with nature. Perhaps most subversive about them was that they valued their privacy. What activities could they possibly be hiding, especially in a century in which same-sex relationships, casual sex, and other unorthodoxies were tolerated much more than in our own time?

Llewellyn Park was clearly the prototype for the exclusive gated communities of the 1980s and 1990s, but in the Civil War years the suburban ideal did not immediately catch on. By the 1890s, however, major cities had their share of outlying bedroom Edens. Their names are still on the maps of metropolitan areas, all of them incorporating elements of the great outdoors – Lake Forest, Forest Hills, Forest Grove, Woodland, Chestnut Hill, Woodlawn, Brookdale, Evergreen Park, Cherry Hill. Did the names give residents some sense of serenity in an increasingly stressful industrial economy? "The great curse of American civilization today is that we are living too much on our nerves," warned an article in a contemporary magazine. "Not a day passes but we hear of some man prominent in the professional or business world driven into premature retirement because of a nervous breakdown." The writer entitled his warning, "Nervousness – a National Menace."[29] This was a theme reflected in popular fiction of the time, as well as nonfiction. The clergyman who wrote these words also operated a clinic for those complaining of nervousness. He claimed that, aside from counseling, a walk in the woods might lessen the stress. Or, better still, the Rev. Samuel McComb advised, a vacation in a rural retreat. If a vacation away from the city could revitalize hardworking Americans – perhaps even save their lives – imagine what could be the effect of living in the woods permanently – and still being able to entrain to the city to continue earning money.

Kenilworth, Illinois, was trumpeted as a place that "gives a new lease on life and helps prepare the mind and body for the world's business battles." The Chicago suburb required that houses be set back from the street at least 40 feet, creating what some planners would later call the greatest wasted space on earth: the American front yard. Contrast this to the insistence in early New England villages that homes be located close together and close to the roadway.

The new suburbanites, in their selections of houses, sought privacy as assurance against stress. Physicians even advised suburbanites that they would feel better if they surrounded their plot of land with fences or trellises. The dwellings were placed so that low-hanging trees and shrubs shielded them from view. The residents bought collapsible shields to hide their drying laundry. (It was fashionable at the time for city residents, usually toting a picnic lunch, to catch a trolley or train on a weekend and simply stroll through these blissful residential parks. Many of them found installation of these barriers "un-American" and a few critics agreed. These weekend invasions only motivated erection of more barriers.) In *Borderland*, John Stilgoe noted that the elaborate shrubbery and fences and exaggerated eaves often hid very modest dwellings.

There are those who came to believe that Americans of the time had a great appreciation of trees. The protective tree became a symbol of privacy. But those who saw the frontier being tamed, as Isaac Weld did in his travels a century earlier, knew, as he observed, that Americans seemed to have an "unconquerable aversion to trees."

Suburbanites favored natural shingles and "earth colors" for their houses, to blend with the surroundings and to deter attention; all the right people in these enclaves used wood stains. City dwellers often chose bright paints, to distinguish their row houses from everybody else's.

The fear of nervous breakdowns regardless of where they lived was as great for late Nineteenth-Century urban and suburban professionals as were cholera and other plagues in the first years of the century, according to Stilgoe. He observed:

> "Trees and hedges. . . created a defense against mass society, a *nook*, . . . within which flourished . . . spontaneity, diversity, simplicity, tradition, invention, and a host of other values many women and men came to honor. Love of nature endured in the borderlands, but the love enfolded and masked the ever more powerful love of outdoor privacy, of visual separation from [weekend] pointers and other strangers, of stepping back from views of factories and cities, of spontaneous enjoyment of outdoor space."

It is hard to imagine a scholar celebrating the suburbs of the Twentieth Century as breeding grounds for "spontaneity, diversity, simplicity, tradition, invention, and a host of other values many women and men came to honor"!

Many of the warnings about Nineteenth-Century burnout were aimed at the women who were married to the go-getters generating all the wealth – and the stress.

"The woman, the cat, and the chimney should never leave the house."

Proverb in the second half of the Nineteenth Century.[30]

Especially at the end of the century, with the diminishing availability of servants and the introduction of household devices that wives were expected to operate themselves, women were constantly told of their needs for privacy. A school of landscape architects advised establishing pockets within the typical suburban yard for the wife of the house to call her own. Sligoe points to popular advertising for porch shades: "She Can Look Out, But You Can't Look In." *House Beautiful* magazine reviewed the product, saying, "Passers-by cannot see through them, though you can look out. This affords privacy, and you can serve luncheons or lounge in negligee on your porch without fear of observation." This magazine and others stressed that a woman at home ought to expect privacy outdoors and well as inside, to doze, to read, to mend the family's clothes, perhaps to practice a new craft.

The commuting men of the time were pleased to ease their stress by providing this "niche" for the woman of the house. Or does it go deeper? Was Barbara Welter, then of Hunter College, on to something with this panoramic view in a scholarly article in 1966?

> "The Nineteenth-Century American man was a busy builder of bridges and railroads, at work long hours in a materialistic society. The religious values of his forebears were neglected in practice if not in intent, and he occasionally felt some guilt that he had turned this new land, this temple of the chosen people, into one vast countinghouse. But he could salve his conscience by reflecting that he had left behind a hostage, not only to fortune, but to all the values which he held so dear and treated so lightly. Woman, in the cult of True Womanhood presented by the women's magazines, gift annuals and religious literature of the Nineteenth Century, was the hostage in the home. In a society where values changed frequently, where fortunes rose and fell with frightening rapidity, where social and economic mobility provided instability as well as hope, one thing, at least remained the same – a true woman was a true woman, wherever she was found."[31]

In "The Cult of True Womanhood," Welter went on to describe the portrait that a woman of that period would see in the pages of publications she came across: married, certainly; married for love not for money, of course; a mother, naturally; religious; patriotic; conversant in the great books, but not brainy; and, most of all, contented to be within the privacy of her own home.

A well-regarded feminist of her time, Charlotte Perkins Gilman was not impressed with any notion that the household provided privacy for a wife, affluent or not. In a book called *Women and Economics*, which attracted attention in 1898, she wrote,

> "The home is one place on earth where no one of the component individuals can have any privacy. A family is a crude aggregate of persons of different ages, sizes, sexes, and temperaments, held together by sex ties and economic necessity."

More tellingly, Gilman assailed households with servants as "absurd paradoxes," because the masters and mistresses of the houses chatter about how much they value privacy but do not hesitate to undress or to discuss intimate secrets in front of the hired help. They entrust care of the children and the laundering of their intimate apparel to them as well. Of course, if you view the person in the room with you as a *non-person*, as slave masters did and as many persons with servants did, you presumably feel no loss of privacy, any more than you would if you disrobed in the presence of a household pet.

Gilman agreed with Harriet Beecher Stowe and Virginia Woolf that modern conditions required each person to have a room of one's own. She also knew that this was impractical for most families (even though the average size of families had reduced to four at the time she wrote). Beyond that, she knew that any woman – or child – who sought solitude within the family would be resented.

Now that many of them had gained the skills in literacy that their mothers and grandmothers did not have, women of the period discovered the diary as an outlet for personal expression. And they took pains to protect it from prying eyes. For Puritans in the early years, a diary was a confidential form of confession, similar to the secret verbal confessions of Roman Catholics. The women of Nineteenth-Century America, but not the men, seemed to stick to that custom. This was the European way; a person wrote a diary in order to know himself or herself better, with the assumption that no one would read it, except perhaps descendants after the writer had died. People wrote *for themselves*.

In 1817 a 26-year-old woman named Anne Listed began a diary of her intimate relations with other women, including a daily account of their shared orgasms. Later in the century, an Eastern intellectual named Mabel Loomis Todd recorded in her diary every sexual activity and orgasm she experienced with her husband from their marriage in 1879.[32] For them, confidentiality was crucial. They were not the only women of the time to provide intimate journals that provided later historians an unfiltered view of sexual practices in America at the time.

By contrast, the personal journals of most Nineteenth-Century men – like Walt Whitman, Henry David Thoreau, and others – seemed intended for publication eventually. Especially after he became famous, Whitman wrote in the third person in his diary, in a tone that sounded more like an autobiography than an intimate journal.[33] Thoreau's famous journal of his two years at Walden Pond in Massachusetts was intended for a wide audience.

In his personal diary, one prominent man in South Carolina admitted his own sexual philandering and said that he deserved "condemnation," but he seemed also to be preaching to a wider audience. "In all ages and countries down to our day and nation the very greatest men that have lived have been addicted to indulgences with women," James H. Hammond noted in an entry in 1846. "It is the besetting sin of the strong, and of the weak also, of our race. Among us now Webster and Clay are notorious for it." He was referring to two of probably the most notable U.S. senators in American history.[34] Regardless of the validity of Hammond's rationalization, it could have provided great solace for President Bill Clinton's during the public debate in 1998 over his sexual leanings.

True privacy was hardly attainable for women, whether they spent their time at home or at work. In the 1830s, living in Concord, Massachusetts, Thoreau knew that the solitude he sought was not possible for everyone. "Consider the girls in a factory," he wrote, "never alone, hardly in their dreams."[35]

Just 12 miles away, in Lowell, Massachusetts, the thriving textile mills provided another kind of home life for American women. And privacy was not a part of it. Owners of the mills provided their own boardinghouses for employees as a way of controlling their lives – and assuring that it would be very difficult for them to quit. One mill in Lowell had the following regulations:

> "All persons in the employ of the Appeleton Company are required to observe the regulations of the overseer of the room where they are employed. They are not to be absent from their work, without his consent, except in case of sickness, and then they are to send him word of the cause of their absence.
>
> "They are to board in one of the boarding houses belonging to the Company, and conform to the regulations of the house where they board.
>
> "A regular attendance on public worship on the Sabbath is necessary for the preservation of good order. The Company will not employ any person who is habitually absent.

Another mill had these regulations:

> "The tenants of the Boarding House are not to board, or permit any part of their houses to be occupied by any person except those in the employ of the Company.

> "They will be considered answerable for any improper conduct in their houses, and are not to permit their boarders to have company at unseasonable hours.

> "The doors must be closed at ten o'clock in the evening, and no one admitted after that time without some reasonable excuse.

> "The keepers of the boarding house must give an account of the number, names, and employment of their boarders, when required; and report the names of such as are guilty of any improper conduct, or are not in the regular habit of attending public worship.[36]

Hundreds of young women left their families in the countryside to live in the boardinghouses, six to a room and – in the Nineteenth-Century way – two to a bed. The women were required to live in, unless they had special permission from the mill agent. Most men had no alternative, and so they lived in, too, in separate quarters. Alcoholic beverages were prohibited, and so was "intemperance," whether on the job or off. One mill said that it expected the employee quarters to be "tranquil scenes of moral deportment."

And so they were. There were few complaints, especially from young women away from home for the first time. Having a paying job was paramount, even if it meant sacrificing human dignity around the clock. One doleful song of the period went:

> "Oh, isn't it such a pity, such a pretty girl as I – Should be sent to the factory to pine away and die?"

Early in the century Americans experienced the shock of, for the first time, earning wages in a place beyond the home, at a place that was often impersonal and sometimes ruthless. But at least they knew the boss. That changed after the Civil War with the gradual expansion of manufacturing plants. For instance, McCormick Tractor Co., in Chicago, went from a work force of 123 before the war to 1400 in 1884. By the 1880s, the railroads and textile mills employed a thousand or more workers each. Supervision was delegated to a foreman, in an arrangement similar in structure to the overseer system in the South.

There was simply no such thing at work as a respite from constant monitoring. A carriage shop in New York City in 1878, for instance, had the same rules about compulsory church attendance and a 10 p.m. curfew as the New England textile mills. The boss also collected ten percent of all wages for the employees' "declining years." At least in New York, employees were granted "one evening a week for courting purposes." In the same decade, an editorial in *The New York Times* called for increased surveillance of government workers and gave the following reasons:

> "In his private business, every careful citizen investigates a man's character before he trusts him. He often investigates a great many things likely to throw light on character which it is unpleasant for the employee to have looked into. He does not hesitate to inquire as to a clerk's associates, or a cashier's habits of expenditure, or the places in which a bookkeeper passes his leisure time."[37]

At the turn of the century, in the words of a scholar on the working conditions of the time:

> "There came into existence a number of hitherto unfamiliar agents acting on behalf of the private, commercial, and industrial order. These were the industrial police, the coal and iron police, the railway police, and a host of private operatives. A man could retreat to the privacy of his home, but during working hours he was to discover that he had to surrender more and more of his own individuality."[38]

No wonder the intellectuals gathering regularly in the Boston area came to believe that America had lost sight of its lofty constitutional aspirations, blinded by "selfish competition." Led by Ralph Waldo Emerson, the transcendentalists celebrated the capacity of the individual – at a time when captains of industry were not looking for individualism in the workers they sought to build railroads or to manufacture clothing.

"One of the points of a liberal democracy is to create and enlarge the private space where friendships breathe and grow."

Author Andrew Sullivan, in 1999.[39]

The transcendentalists especially treasured the letters they exchanged with one another, recounting intimate revelations about themselves. This would have not been possible without a sense of mutual trust and confidentiality – not for oneself but *within the group*. Emerson grieved when his intimate friend Margaret Fuller perished in a shipwreck in 1850. In the process he panicked when he learned that a trunk containing her correspondence had been recovered and opened.

One of Emerson's crowd, Bronson Alcott, drew a line in the dust:

> "Individuals are sacred. The world, the state, the church, the school, all are felons whensoever they violate the sanctity of the private heart."[40]

Alcott had his daughter tutored by Emerson and Henry David Thoreau, a young intellectual who was influenced by the circle when – in the Nineteenth-Century way – he lived at Emerson's home for a year or two. The daughter, Louisa May Alcott, became a popular author of books for young readers. Thoreau, at age 28, decided to test whether an individual could live on his own self-reliance, in harmony with nature. Taking up residence in a shack on Emerson's property at Walden Pond west of Boston between 1845 and 1847, Thoreau sought a private space away from the clamoring curiosity of his times. He included these observations in his essay *Walden or Life in the Woods*:

> "For what reason have I this vast range and circuit, some square miles of unfrequented forest, for my privacy, abandoned to me by men? My nearest neighbor is a mile distant, and no house is visible from any place but the hilltops within half a mile of my own. I have my horizon bounded by woods all to myself; a distant view of the railroad where it touches the pond on the one hand, and of the fence which skirts the woodland road on the other. But for the most part it is as solitary where I live as on the prairies. It is as much Asia or Africa as New England. I have, as it were, my own sun and moon and stars, and a little world all to myself. At night there was never a traveler passed my house, or knocked at my door, more than if I were the first or last man; unless it were in the spring, when at long intervals some came from the village to fish. . . .

> "There can be no very black melancholy to him who lives in the midst of nature and has his senses still.

"I have never felt lonesome, or in the least oppressed by a sense of solitude, but once, and that was a few weeks after I came to the woods, when, for an hour, I doubted if the near neighborhood of man was not essential to a serene and healthy life. To be alone was something unpleasant. But I was at the same time conscious of a slight insanity in my mood, and seemed to foresee my recovery.

Henry David Thoreau

"Every little pine needle expanded and swelled with sympathy and befriended me. We are the subjects of an experiment which is not a little interesting to me. Can we not do without the society of our gossips a little while under these circumstances, have our own thoughts to cheer us?

"By a conscious effort of the mind we can stand aloof from actions and their consequences; and all things, good and bad, go by us like a torrent.

"I find it wholesome to be alone the greater part of the time. To be in company, even with the best, is soon wearisome and dissipating. I love to be alone. I never found the companion that was so companionable as solitude. We are for the most part more lonely when we go abroad among men than when we stay in our chambers. A man thinking or working is always alone, let him be where he will. Solitude is not measured by the miles of space that intervene between a man and his fellows. The really diligent student in one of the crowded hives of Cambridge College is as solitary as a dervis in the desert. The farmer can work alone in the field or the woods all day, hoeing or chopping, and not feel lonesome, because he is employed; but when he comes home at night he cannot sit down in a room alone, at the mercy of his thoughts, but must be where he can 'see the folks,' and recreate, and, as he thinks, remunerate himself for his day's solitude; and hence he wonders how the student can sit alone in the house all night and most of the day without ennui and 'the blues'. . . .

"Society is commonly too cheap. We meet at very short intervals, not having had time to acquire any new value for each other. I have a great deal of company in my house; especially in the morning, when nobody calls. "If a man does not keep pace with his companions, perhaps it is because he hears a different drummer. Let him step to the music he hears, however measured or far away.

"I went to the woods because I wished to live deliberately, to front only the essential facts of life, and to see if I could not learn what it had to teach, and not, when I came to die, discover that I have not lived. I did not wish to live what was not life, living is so dear; nor did I wish to practice resignation, unless it was quite necessary. I wanted to live deep and suck out all the marrow of life, to live life so sturdily and Spartan-like as to put to rout all that was not life, to cut a broad swath and shave close, to drive life into a corner, and reduce it to its lowest terms, and, if it proved to be mean, why then to get the whole and genuine meanness of it, and publish its meanness to the world; or if it were sublime, to know it by experience, and be able to give a true account of it in my next excursion. For most men, it appears to me, are in a strange uncertainty about it, whether it is of the devil or of God, and have somewhat hastily concluded that it is the chief end of man here to 'glorify God and enjoy him forever.'"[41]

Which of us who longs for a private haven of solitude and privacy in the Twenty-first Century cannot identify with Thoreau's remark that a man like him was "born in the nick of time"? When his own century had begun, America provided seemingly endless possibilities for a new frontier, a new start in life, an opportunity to know nature up-close, a respite from commercialism and urban sprawl. When his life began, Thoreau was in synchrony with his times. By the time he published *Walden* in 1854, he, before all others, realized how out of touch he was with his own times. At Walden Pond, he was truly *a voice in the wilderness*.

\Links

To realize the cacophony that Thoreau was escaping, read the next chapter, on Curiosity.

Curiosity

Foreign visitors' observations about Americans' obsessive curiosity and how British-trained journalists exploited that curiosity by developing profitable mass-circulation newspapers.

"In England, every one appears to find full employment in his own concerns; here, it would seem that the people are restless until they know every person's business," wrote Charles William Janson, a British writer who toured the United States in the beginning of the Nineteenth Century. In his 1807 study he identified what was to become a theme for the century to come:

> "If the Americans have any national trait, which has been denied by some writers, it is this intrusive curiosity. Nor is it to acquire useful information that these people pester strangers; it is habit, for they act in the same manner towards each other; and on meeting, they propose, as it were, in one breath, a long string of questions to each other."[1]

Janson was apparently warned before he embarked for North America that "unbounded curiosity was a prominent trait in the character of the Americans."

If the previous century was an era when individual rights were asserted and a governmental structure was created to assure those rights, the Nineteenth Century found Americans catching up with European society in knowledge and culture. Throughout the century, the acquisition of knowledge – in this unruly, diverse democracy – was accompanied by a uniquely American preoccupation with tidbits of information about other people. The century ended with a frenetic battle among cheap newspapers to exploit the public's fascination with details about the lives of other people. Gossip became institutionalized.

By the end of the century many of America's leading thinkers had come to realize this national trait and to plead guilty to the charge lodged by Charles William Janson at the beginning of the century. They had to, because Janson was only one of many observers of American society who identified the same trait.

Henry Adams, America's own homegrown chronicler, was forced to admit,

> "Foreigners were struck by what they considered popular traits, which natives rarely noticed. Idle curiosity was commonly represented as universal, especially in the Southern settler who knew no other form of conversation. . . . Almost every writer spoke with annoyance of the inquisitorial habits of New England and the impertinence of American curiosity. Complaints so common could hardly have lacked foundation, yet the Americans as a people were never loquacious, but inclined to be somewhat reserved, and they could not recognize the accuracy of the description."[2]

The French naturalist Francois Andre Michaux wrote this in his journal after a trip to Kentucky:

> "The public houses are always crowded, especially so during the sittings of the courts of justice. Horses and lawsuits comprise the usual topics of conversation. If a traveler happens to pass by, his horse is appraised. If he stops, he is presented with a glass of whiskey, and then asked a thousand questions, such as: Where do you come from? Where are you going? What is your name? Where do you live? What is your profession? Were there any fevers in the different parts of the country through which you came? These questions, which are frequently repeated in the course of a journey, become tedious, but it is easy to check these inquiries by a little tact, their only object being the gratification of that curiosity so natural to people who live isolated in the woods and seldom see a stranger."[3]

Frances Trollope, an accomplished woman married to a lawyer who simply could not make a living in Bristol, England, moved her family to Cincinnati in 1827. There Thomas Trollope tried to build a retail business. Once again, he failed, and Mrs. Trollope took the family back to England. A year later she wrote *Domestic Manners of the Americans* based on her three years in the States. She too apparently was on the receiving end of ceaseless inquiries from the Yankees around her, mainly while traveling. "The Americans love talking," she wrote; she entitled one chapter, "Yankee Curiosity." At another point in her book she referred to a friendly neighbor in Ohio as practicing "violent intimacy."

It shouldn't surprise modern Americans that visitors noticed this trait of curiosity mainly when the visitors were sharing public transportation with Americans. Who has not sat next to a total stranger on a plane, bus, or train and heard far more than he or she needed to know about the stranger's gall bladder surgery, unruly in-laws, bad debts, or interest in pornographic videos? And who has not, in turn, found himself or herself revealing intimate details, upon minimal prodding from the stranger? But that is the point. We find this kind of exchange perfectly normal. Europeans find it perfectly American.

"The ordinary American himself is extraordinary," wrote the French humorist Paul Blouet under the pen name of Max O'Rell late in the century.

> "Meeting you in a railway carriage, he will ask you point blank where you are going, what you are doing, and where you are from. By degrees, he grows bolder, and if the fancy takes him, he will touch the cloth of your coat and ask, 'What you gave for that.' He has not the least intention of being disagreeable. He, in his part, will give you all the information you care to have about himself. He takes it for granted that you are as inquisitive as he is, and he is ready to satisfy your curiosity. He is obliging."[4]

Twenty-First-Century pollsters, direct marketers, government information collectors, school teachers, employers, and, eventually, television talk show hosts would come to rely on this readiness of Americans to share information about themselves. There is no doubt of our willingness to answer any question, and to answer often with more detail than requested. There is not an application form we are unwilling to fill out, and to fill out fully. Indeed, at the same time that the French humorist was making his observation (in the late 1880s), the director of the Census was marveling at the willingness of Americans to tell government agents anything about themselves, even though they complained about it.

Paul Blouet, like most male observers, felt that women more than men engaged in gossip. "Everyone is interested in what the others do. . . . You need only live a couple of months in one of the larger American cities, no matter which, in order to know everyone, and all their doings." Modern Americans might dispute this accusation – made light-heartedly, of course – and deny that it's remotely possible in a large American city today to know what everyone else is doing. They should contemplate for a moment the typical big-city newscast and the preoccupation in our print and electronic news media with the doings of celebrities and public officials.

And what about Europeans? Do they not have this trait? Janson, the British "stranger in America," thought not. Another commentator in 1889, Frances Power Cobbe, thought, "The average Englishman, from the highest to the lowest, entertains a profound conviction that privacy is an invaluable privilege." Europeans are reticent and reserved, according to the lore reported in the research of David J. Seipp of Boston University.

To protect themselves, the English rely on a sense of reserve – or so it is said. To avoid being intrusive, they rely on unwritten and unspoken cues from others. They are able to preserve confidentiality in a group setting by their manner of speaking and by an expectation that others nearby will respect privacy.[5] Germans use physical barriers (like curtains, closed doors, and high fences), as well as the notion of *lebensraum*, a necessary buffer – or elbow room – between persons and between nations. The French, like other Mediterranean peoples, are willing to co-exist in closer physical proximity to one another without a feeling of intrusiveness, according to popular perceptions.

Persons from other cultures have a curiosity about the world around them, of course. But, they seem quite willing to sit quietly on an airplane or train without feeling the need to pry into the work life and home life of a stranger nearby. By contrast, our curiosity seems to be insatiable – and leads to a willingness to provide far more personal information to strangers than is appropriate for our own good. Americans regard silence as a vacuum that must be filled. Only when another person removes himself or herself physically will an American recognize that person's desire to be let alone.

Most Americans, after all, lived in remote areas until the last century. The results of the 1790 Census showed that 95 percent of Americans lived in small communities, with fewer than 5,000 residents. In the years just before 1900, about 66 percent of Americans lived in rural areas. Why wouldn't they look forward to grilling visitors about the latest news and why wouldn't they be willing to share personal information about themselves, especially to a visitor from overseas whom they expected never to see again?

But it was not just rural Americans who showed this trait. Those who lived in large port cities seemed to show the same characteristics. Janson wrote in his memoir, "The first salute we received was from at least a dozen voices, inquiring the news from England."

William Byrd, a socially prominent planter in Virginia, noted in his diary, "Our lives are uniform without any great variety, til the seasons bring in the ships. Then we tear open the letters they bring us from our friends, as eagerly as a greedy heir tears open a rich father's will."[6]

**"As long as gossip was oral, it spread,
as regarded any one individual, over a very small area,
and was confined to the immediate circle of his acquaintances.
His peace and comfort were, therefore,
but slightly affected by it."**

Journalist E.L. Godkin, in 1890.[7]

A lot of Europeans' surprise at Americans' supposed inquisitiveness has to be attributed to the visitors' amazement that average people would dare speak to them at all. The visitors, after all, came from the elite classes of Europe and expected to be insulated from mere mortals.

In her portrayal of *The Miracle at Philadelphia*, historian Catherine Drinker Bowen captured this aspect of the phenomenon:

> "A traveler sees what he wishes to see, and the American curiosity concerning strangers was insatiable, especially in rural districts – which meant nearly everywhere. No European peasant, no British yeoman would have dared such questions. Isaac Weld traveled out into Lexington, Kentucky. 'Of all the uncouth human beings I met within America,' he writes, 'these people from the western country were the most so; their curiosity was boundless. Frequently have I been stopped abruptly by one of them in a solitary part of the road, and in such a manner that had it been another country I should have imagined it was a highwayman that was going to demand my purse.'"[8]

The most reliable of United States-watchers, Alexis de Tocqueville, had it right:

> "In America, where the privileges of birth never existed and where riches confer no peculiar rights on their possessors, men unacquainted with one another are very ready to frequent the same places and find neither peril nor advan-

tage in the free interchange of their thoughts. If they meet by accident, they neither seek nor avoid intercourse."[9]

Thus, the visiting European was shocked that American egalitarianism permitted casual conversation "between classes." Once overcoming that, any visitor should not have been surprised that thirst for information should increase as one moved west into America's frontier.

Imagine the loneliness of rural life in the Nineteenth Century. It should be no wonder that if an Isaac Weld or a Charles William Janson should happen along a dusty road, the solitary farmer would cry out, "What's new?" Discovering that the stranger had a European accent and that he was actually interested in discovering a piece of Americana would only motivate the man more to ask about the visitor and to share with him details of his own life. Sharing personal details with a European passing through involved little risk – comparable to chatting with an airline companion who will soon be racing off to a connecting flight.

In the early Nineteenth Century, newspapers did not quench this thirst for information. Most of them reprinted documents from the London papers and did so long after the originals had appeared. Diaries from the time reflect that few men and women relied on newspapers for their information. Almanacs, not newspapers, provided the information that a farmer needed.[10] In New York City, a metropolis with 250,000 persons in 1820, the largest selling newspaper reached only 1,200 customers.

One of the earliest publishers who struggled to reach a viable circulation was Benjamin Franklin's grandson, Benjamin Franklin Bache, publisher of the *Aurora* in Philadelphia during George Washington's presidency. "Lightning-Rod Junior," they called him. Bache scrupulously reprinted government documents and was viciously critical of both President Washington and President John Adams, but his newspaper never covered the private matters of private citizens. After his death, his widow and her new husband edited the *Aurora*.

In fact, private letters had more credibility than newspapers, reported University of Connecticut historian Richard D. Brown in his 1989 book *Knowledge is Power*. Thus, merchants, who were the most frequent letter writers after the nation had been established, were the source of a lot of the information in a town, more than the clergy, more than politicians, and more than judges and lawyers. If salacious material about other persons and their personal lives appeared in these missives, it was rare. If it ever did, the circulation of the material was severely limited by the medium.

Following the Revolutionary War, the merchants who relied so much on correspondence among themselves began to publish regular newspapers. Their customers were the new immigrants – clerks, laborers, retailers. These Americans had language skills that Americans working the fields did not have. They had some discretionary income. They needed more information than the political documents used by the elite classes, the statistics of market conditions used by businesspersons, and the horticultural hints in almanacs. They also expected to be entertained. They were America's new middle class.

From England during the 1830s came the innovation of the "penny press," cheap news organs that satisfied the curiosity of readers about the failings of people in high places. Some of these British scandal sheets reached American audiences. More importantly, they reached a few entrepreneurs who saw the possibilities for this country.

In 1833, a 23-year-old printer named Benjamin Day launched his own four-page newspaper in New York patterned after the successful "penny press." His *Sun* would, for the first time in American journalism, be affiliated with no political party and would provide concise news for the people – all for a penny. Day, the direct descendant of a signer of the Mayflower Compact and the founders of Connecticut, imported British journalists to replicate the successful cheap papers of London. In the first issue of the *Sun* were accounts like these:

> "Bridget McMunn got drunk and threw a pitcher at Mr. Ellis, of 53 Ludlow st. Bridget said she was the mother of 3 little orphans – God bless their dear souls – and if she went to prison they would choke to death for the want of something to eat. Committed. Bill Doty got drunk because he had the horrors so bad he couldn't keep sober. Committed."[11]

The editor who wrote those items had trained as a police reporter for the *Morning Herald* in London.

Within four months, Day's innovative paper reached a circulation of 4,000, almost equaling the reach of the existing dailies in New York City. Within six months, the New York *Sun* surpassed 8,000 in circulation. It did so – in a time of economic depression – with stories about drunkenness, reckless carriage driving, wife beatings, brawls, petty crimes, unusual animals, and often unusual human beings. The *Sun* also showed for the first time that readers would be interested in news about the social events of affluent persons.

In the mid-1830s, Day hired Richard Adams Locke, another London-trained editor who immediately had a major impact on American journalism with stories like these:

> "Margaret Norris, a wretched drunken, dissipated being, disgracing the very name of female, was brought up yesterday afternoon by a couple of citizens who had the misfortune to know her, and then requested that she might be provided for, as she was a habitual drunkard, and in the frequent practice of insulting every person who chances to pass when she is under the effects of liquor.

> "She felt very eloquent, and holding onto the rail, begged permission of this 'Honrable Honor," and the 'Jontlemon of the Jury,' to 'plade' her own cause. Her request was granted, and it would have puzzled the most skilled stenographer to have kept pace with her tongue. She talked about justice, honesty, sobriety, mercy, but her forte was 'Vartu.' Committed."

There were not enough cases in the New York courts to supply the insatiable *Sun*. Locke was said to reprint stories from London newspapers with slight changes to make them appear to be local. (In the late 1990s many ratings-hungry local news broadcasts would do much the same thing, using videotapes from out of town because there weren't enough juicy local crime stories to fill their airtime.) Within a short time, Locke had beefed up the number of reporters covering police and court activity to a dozen, of whom at least nine were British, not American.[12]

It was then accepted practice in London to fabricate stories to make a readable product. Most readers realized this and regarded the lurid newspapers as no more than good entertainment, but not reliable sources of information and news. For news, readers would rely on "the qualities." Day and Locke fabricated stories for the New York *Sun* as well, but in the United States, readers were accustomed to giving credibility to the written word, even in the penny press.

In 1835, Locke wrote a series of articles that presented evidence of living beings on the moon. Other newspapers picked up on the "scoop." The "Moon Hoax" boosted circulation for the *Sun* to 19,000 copies a day, then the largest in the world.[13] Day boasted that the *Sun* had a circulation "double that of all the six-penny respectables combined."

The success of the *Sun* brought competition within two years – the New York *Herald*, founded by Scots-born and London-trained James Gordon Bennett. Then came the New York *Transcipt*, which with the help of its London-trained police reporter, offered the most sensational coverage of all.

Penny press newspapers were launched in Boston, Philadelphia, Baltimore, and elsewhere. The new breed of press entrepreneurs was relying on innovative techniques that for the first time allowed production on a daily basis. These included a new process for reproducing half-tone illustrations, faster photolithography printing, the new Napier cylinder printing press, and, of course, the typewriter, in 1878. The coming of the bicycle and of the trolley car provided possibilities for rapid delivery.

The papers rode the wave of a great population explosion. In the half century before the Civil War, the nation was growing at a rate six times the global average, with most of the increase in the large cities. New York went from 124,000 in 1820 to a million inhabitants by 1880.

This intensification of journalism occurred when there were virtually no protections against libel and slander and absolutely no protections against invasions of privacy by news reporters. Courts simply did not recognize lawsuits against a news organization for truthful but intrusive and emotionally distressing publication of purely personal matters. "Juries still considered a libel suit a somewhat cowardly alternative to the time-honored manner of settling newspaper attacks by dueling," according to privacy historian David Seipp.

There were constant objections about the intrusiveness of the "new journalism," of course, and just as many responses from the press lords that they were merely giving the people what they want. "Every where their influence is felt," wrote the poet Walt Whitman. "No man can measure it, for it is immeasurable." Walt himself was to join the payroll of the *Herald* in 1888, contributing several poems. At mid-century, the popular poet himself had become one of America's first true mass-media celebrities and the object of attention from these "keyhole journalists." (There was even a

"Walt Whitman Cigar" on sale, with the poet's face as the logo on the wrapper.)[14]

More than one editor pointed out that items published about the parties and balls of the upper classes came from the participants themselves, usually in their own handwriting. In the same way, in the late Twentieth Century, editors and television producers pointed out defensively that the celebrities who complain about intrusive press coverage are the same ones who, with their press agents and social secretaries, use the press to publicize themselves.

The editor of the New York *Graphic* after the Civil War, David G. Croly, defended the new journalism:

> "Human beings are very curious about one another. Nothing is more interesting to them in a newspaper than what their fellow-beings are doing. A newspaper that satisfies this desire will have a very great measure of success."[15]

In 1836, the *Herald* found the story it needed to challenge the *Sun*. On April 10 of that year, Helen Jewett was found bludgeoned to death in a burning bed in a house of prostitution. Richard Robinson, the unfortunate soul who was her customer, was charged with the murder. All in, there had been at least 20 homicides in the same part of Manhattan in the preceding months and none of them would have attracted much attention were it not for the insatiable appetites of the cheap popular newspapers[16]

But the *Herald* had a way of elevating stories to a daily obsession for thousands of readers, the first time this had occurred in American journalism. The *Herald*'s publisher himself, Bennett, visited the crime scene and interviewed the suspect, then persuaded his readers that Robinson was guilty. The *Herald* generated so much interest in an otherwise low-interest case that 6,000 persons tried to jam into the City Hall in New York City for the five-day trial. (The judge was the grandson of the inspiring Colonial preacher Jonathan Edwards.) The intense public interest gave birth to a new business, commercial publishers who could rush the transcript of the proceedings to print and to an awaiting public.

During the trial, Bennett reconsidered, and, in print, begged for justice and an acquittal. The *Herald*'s circulation tripled to 15,000. The traditional newspapers of the day shunned coverage of the Robinson-Jewett trial but the penny press loved the story. The *Herald*'s competitor, the *Transcript*, saturated its pages with the story, selling all 15,000 copies of an extra edition with the trial transcript. An all-male jury eventually acquitted Robinson, after deliberating less than 15 minutes. The acquittal fueled speculation about who actually killed Helen Jewett. For months after, the penny papers filled their pages with columns of speculation about the murderer.[17]

In 1851 a new newspaper joined the competition: *The New York Times.* It too sold for one cent. It capitalized on the innovative distribution methods of the rest of the penny press and adopted most of its journalism from English traits. But *The Times*, as it proclaimed in an early editorial, used as its model *The Times* of London, then probably the world's most respected newspaper. Once again American journalism was being fashioned on standards developed in the British culture, not the American culture. Now it was importing both its highest standards and its lowest.

Across town Horace Greeley's *Tribune* was much more discreet. He had an unwritten rule, for instance, that his Washington correspondents were not to expose the private sins of public officials. He fired one of his columnists, the first woman to be admitted to the Congressional press gallery, Jane Swisshelm, for violating the policy. (She also lost her seat in the press gallery.) In 1850, Swisshelm published a column in a Pittsburgh newspaper attacking Massachusetts Senator Daniel Webster, whom history portrays as an accomplished litigator and orator. He was also widely regarded as a compulsive philanderer. When he was conciliatory to the South because he passionately wanted to preserve the Union, campaigners for the abolition of slavery attacked him with no conciliation at all. Swisshelm, an abolitionist who enjoyed attacking public figures, wrote that she had discovered a strong "moral stench" in the nation's capital. "Nearly everyone knows that [Webster] sometimes drinks to excess and his friends here say he requires to be excited by wine to make him approachable – civil. His mistresses are generally, if not always, colored women – some of them big black wenches as ugly and vulgar as himself." Twenty years earlier "a colored boy" apparently went to the Senate chamber and said that Senator Webster was his father.

Even after losing her column at the *Tribune*, Swissholm continued her "expose," writing that "the God-like statesman. . . was a great nasty beast, . . . dangerous and loathsome, . . . his whole panoply of moral power was a shell – that his life was full of rottenness." She said that two members of Congress "assured me of the truth of what had been told me, but advised me to keep quiet."

Although there was general agreement that Senator Webster was homely, the journalist never provided proof for her accusations of sexual misconduct, and she was later discredited. But her comments were reprinted in newspapers throughout the nation (showing perhaps that these kind of contemporary reports do little to mar a public official's ultimate reputation in history). The Lowell *American* newspaper in Webster's home state, wrote, "We have never before heard that Mr. Webster's 'mistresses' were 'colored women,' but the fact that he has 'mistresses' of some color is, we suppose, as notorious as any other fact concerning him."

Earlier, in 1842, an article in the Louisville *Daily Journal* in Kentucky had accused Webster, then Secretary of State, of having attempted to rape a clerk in the Department of State, saying to her as he pounced on her, "This, my dear, is one of the prerogatives of my office." The accusation is not much different from the original accusation that led to the impeachment of President Bill Clinton – that when he was in a position of political power he made an unwanted suggestion to a female subordinate presumably as a prelude to sex; during the investigations in 1998 of his conduct he was also accused of committing a rape before he became President, but the charges were never substantiated. When Webster denied the accusation and affirmed the denial under oath before a magistrate, the Louisville editor who wrote the article retracted it.

Still, Webster was widely detested. No wonder the senator enjoyed a trip to England, where he experienced "a queer feeling" of not being recognized when simply "poking around *incog.*" "A stranger in London is in the most perfect solitude in the world. He can touch every body, but can speak to nobody. I like much these strolls by myself."[18]

The sensationalizing newspapers eventually knocked each other out of the market and discovered that they had lost sight of their original mission: to provide a realistic view of the world to average people. By the end of the 1850s, readers were more interested in the increasing tensions between North and South than in the freaks, murderers, and misfits profiled in the penny press.

But after the Civil War, the popular press got its second wind. One of the many immigrants flocking to the United States was Joseph Pulitzer, a 17-year-old from Hungary who immediately joined the cavalry to fight for the Union Army against the Rebels. In peacetime, he became an American citizen, then reported and edited the news in St. Louis. Later, he formed the *Post-Dispatch*, which delighted in publishing stories about the private foibles of the "best families in St. Louis," under headlines like ST. LOUIS SWELLS, AN ADULTEROUS PAIR, and LOVED THE COOK. The saturation coverage that Pulitzer insisted on included details of a heiress's quarrel with her family over her plans to marry an "unsuitable" man and an expose of the drinking habits of Protestant clergy in Roman Catholic St. Louis (DOES REV. MR. TUDOR TIPPLE?). The *Post-Dispatch* sensationalized the death of a businessman in a downtown hotel – with the front-page headline A WELL-KNOWN CITIZEN STRICKEN DOWN IN THE ARMS OF HIS MISTRESS.

This may have been too much for St. Louis, and so Pulitzer – without relinquishing ownership of the *Post-Dispatch* – headed for New York, where he regarded the papers as atrophied and moribund. First he went to England, as he had done often before. There he studied British ways of practicing journalism, especially those of his associate, the renowned British tabloid publisher, Lord Northcliffe. Later Pulitzer regularly recruited his staff in London. The important staff on his papers were all trained in London. For a brief time, Pulitzer reported the news for the brawling New York *Sun*; in fact, for the *Sun*, he covered the commission that decided the nation's closest Presidential election, in 1876. By age 36 he was the owner of the New York *World*, which became known for its self-generated stunts and personal crusades, for publishing flashy color and comics and eye-catching maps and diagrams, and for exploiting stories of crime, lurid sex, violence, and corruption in high places. Marc Osgoode Smith reported in his research:

> "The *World*'s first issue chronicled a murder, a lynching, a suicide, several robberies and muggings, and for good measure, a grave robbery. The second issue showed that Pulitzer intended to maintain his newspaper's adherence to sensationalism. The front-page headline blared: SCREAMING FOR MERCY. The story detailed the last moments before the hanging of an unrepentant murderer. Witnesses apparently never heard the man 'scream.' The bottom half of the page offered a detailed account of a society divorce case and a barroom brawl. Page Two offered the story of tornadoes in the Midwest with a headline DEATH RIDES THE BLAST."[19]

Pulitzer had purchased the moribund *World* from the same Jay Gould who was terrifying everyone with his unscrupulous takeover of the Western Union Co. just two years earlier. Within a year of purchasing the *World*, Pulitzer had quadrupled its circulation to 60,000. By 1898, the *World* reached the million mark.[20] It was by far the most successful paper in the U.S.

Pulitzer's main rival in New York towards the end of the century was a young Harvard dropout named William Randolph Hearst, who owned the New York *Morning Journal* and the *Evening Journal*. With both papers, Hearst reached 1.5 million readers, a previously unheard of circulation figure. He did it using techniques from the earlier penny press and from Joseph Pulitzer. The *Morning Journal*, in fact, was a newspaper that Pulitzer's brother had founded. Of the young Hearst it was said, "He began where Pulitzer had the virtue to stop."[21] These two created the first truly mass medium in the U.S. They did not wait for news to happen; they created news. The acerbic columnist Ambrose Bierce, a long-time Hearst employee, said the competition produced news reporting with "all the reality of masturbation." Their rivalry was so intense that their news coverage aroused Americans into waging the Spanish-American War in Cuba at the end of the century. Their aggressive, sensationalized form of reporting became known as yellow journalism, after a popular color comic strip called "The Yellow Kid," which both Hearst and Pulitzer claimed the rights to publish.

This aggressiveness allowed Pulitzer to proclaim at the turn of the century, "There is not a dodge, there is not a trick, there is not a swindle, there is not a vice which does not live by secrecy." He could have added, but did not, "There is not a newspaper, there is not a magazine, there is not a news organization that does not live by secrecy."

A much less intrusive *World* thrived until 1931 long after Joseph Pulitzer's death in 1911. Hearst's *Journal* lasted into the Twentieth Century, when it was absorbed by other New York dailies.[22]

During all of the time of the Pulitzer-Hearst rivalry, free public education and compulsory attendance at school were making it possible for millions of Americans to learn to read. Was this new literacy merely addicting Americans to gossip mongering? It was easy to believe that. Certainly Charles Dudley Warner did. The editor of *The Hartford Courant* in Connecticut and pal of Mark Twain, looked back in 1890 with a dark perspective: "Perhaps it is this very ability to read conferred upon multitudes whose taste is low that accounts for the greater circulation of journals suited to the low taste," he wrote.[23] The end result when a person reads

American newspapers at the end of the century, Warner said, was that "the mind loses the power of discrimination, the taste is lowered, and the appetite becomes diseased." And he was a journalist himself.

As they became addicted to daily newspapers, average Americans were developing resentments of large corporations and the wealthy people who profited from them. Many of the rich, consequently, became wary of publicity about their social events and their extravagance. For many, it was prudent to disguise their luxurious lifestyles and the affluence that made it possible.[24]

Two widely circulated books at the end of the century highlighted this class conflict. One was *Society as I Have Found It* by Ward McAllister, which chronicled the extravagance of the rich and famous. McAllister was the proprietor of the list of "Four Hundred," which determined eligibility to join the elite class, at least in New York. The other was *How the Other Half Lives*, by Jacob Riis, which portrayed, with photographs, the misery of tenement life in New York. It was one of the first ventures into photojournalism, the process of telling a story through photographic images. And who was Jacob Riis? Born in Denmark, he served as police reporter of the New York *Sun* for many years.

The exuberance of the press also has to be attributed to the new experience of total freedom it came to enjoy in the Nineteenth Century. Just 30 years before the founding of the New York *Sun*, several journalists, including Benjamin Franklin's son-in-law, faced jail time for what they had written. In the years before 1826, just five years prior to the founding of the *Sun*, a newspaper could not defend itself from a libel suit by showing that what it had published was true. After that courts came to accept truth as a defense in a libel lawsuit. In other words, until then, the press was vulnerable if it published damaging utterances about individuals, even if it could prove the truth of them.

In the new climate, the press faced no censorship from the government and virtually no threat of private lawsuits. Reporters and editors in the U.S. did not even face the restrictions they had faced when they trained in England – prohibitions against reporting on the Royal Family or against negative comments about governmental actions.

Presidents and First Ladies of the period decried the aggressiveness of the press, with perhaps even more reason than their successors at the end of the Twentieth Century. Mary Todd Lincoln tried unsuccessfully to escape the press while vacationing on the New Jersey shore in 1861. Reporters from James Gordon Bennett's New York *Herald* stalked the exhausted First Lady there and ridiculed her constantly for avoiding the press. Former President Ulysses S. Grant, as he lay dying of throat cancer in Saratoga, New York, at age 63, was subjected to news reports revealing, in the words of a writer at the time, "all his private, personal habits, as to the neatness or the lack of it, capping the whole business with a minute description of the state of his teeth, the accumulation of tartar upon them, and his neglect of the toothbrush."[25]

Reporters dogged 49-year-old President Grover Cleveland and his new wife on their honeymoon in the mountains of Maryland in the second year of his presidency, in 1886. They crowded a nearby platform to spy on his honeymoon cottage with binoculars; they counted the letters delivered to him; and they even lifted the covers of the dishes sent to the couple at mealtime. Ever since 1884, when newspapers reported in the midst of his campaign for the Presidency that he had fathered an illegitimate child, Cleveland hated the press. He thought that reporters were "animals." After his honeymoon experience he wrote to the *Evening Post* in New York that nosy reporters "were doing their utmost to make American journalism contemptible in the estimation of people of good breeding everywhere." The *Post* had earlier condemned the "keyhole journalism" on display in Maryland. Six months after his honeymoon, in a speech at Harvard University, the President, who apparently was shy and had a strong sense of dignity, said that such tactics "violate every instinct of American manliness and in ghoulish glee desecrate every sacred relation of private life."[26]

"The newspaper, in its eager search for the sensational, [does not hesitate] to invade the sacred privacy of the family and squat in repulsive familiarity on the hearthstone."

Press critic Conde Benoist Pallen, in 1886.[27]

The excesses of the period forced the leading law reformer of the time, a respected scholar who had studied England's legal system, to lose patience. In an article in a law journal in 1876, David Dudley Field could actually argue that press freedom was a legal doctrine that had lost its significance. The painful lessons about press censorship of a generation earlier, he wrote, had happened "long ago." A constitutional amendment was needed not to protect the press but to restrain it. "The right of reputation should be declared one of the fundamental rights of men."[28]

Another legal scholar, Herbert Spencer Hadley, expressed similar heresies in 1895. He had to admit that in an age of profiteering, concerns about protecting the safe haven of one's home or protecting one's reputation get lost. But why, he wondered, was the individual's recourse no greater than his or her right to collect an unpaid debt in small claims court?[29]

"The whole character of the nation is there: spirit of enterprise, liveliness, childishness, inquisitiveness, deep interest in everything that is human, fun and humor, indiscretion, love of gossip, brightness."

French humorist Paul Blouet (Max O'Rell), writing about American journalism, in 1891.[30]

Amid all the news about drunkenness, corruption, petty crimes, adultery, and high society in the Nineteenth Century, the published items with the most lasting impact on the right to privacy appeared in the *Saturday Evening Gazette* of Boston in 1890 about a "Mrs. S. D. Warren, Jr." The newspaper reported in one sentence in March that Mrs. Warren had given a dinner party for 12 friends and in June that she and her husband had transformed their home at 155 Commonwealth Avenue into a "veritable floral bower" for a wedding breakfast for his cousin.[31]

The *Gazette*, the namesake of the newspaper published by Ben Franklin's brother in pre-Revolutionary Boston, was one of six daily newspapers in the city in 1890, each of them with society pages. It enjoyed a high regard in Boston for its coverage of current events, but fully one-third of its text "consisted primarily of social gossip and other items of social interest," according to a Twentieth-Century analysis of the *Gazette*'s content during the 1880s.[32]

The *Gazette* itself, in a defensive editorial in August of 1884, gave a hint of the strong disapprovals it was hearing from the people of Boston – and at the same time it engaged in bashing its spiritual patron, Benjamin Franklin, by innuendo:

> "In an age when interviewing has developed a taste for more personal details and scandal to which unscrupulous journalism does not hesitate to pardon, protesters forget the

universal and instinctive interest which attaches to the personality of eminent men. Tell the truth, treat it with sympathy, intelligence and proportion. Dr. Franklin, for instance, would not forfeit his great and just fame if some passages of his life were told, instead of just being whispered."[33]

Was the *Gazette* positioning itself as the thinking-person's gossip sheet? All during the 1870s and the 1880s, after all, it was publishing every single day across five columns its "Out and About" column, a combination of harmless handouts about social events and more enticing, whispered second-hand stories about the rich and famous. A sample, in 1888:

> "It was Miss Grant, though, who among others, popped corn and ate baked apples with the second Comptroller and Congressman Ned Burnett the other afternoon in their bachelor quarters."[34]

Or, in 1890:

> "In some of the finest houses in Newport, there is a great deal of misery."

The items about Mrs. Warren, in retrospect, seem harmless enough. What hurt the finer people of Boston more, perhaps, were items like the one published in the *Gazette* in January of 1890, which could easily be read as a threat of extortion:

> "The state of society never seemed so depraved as at present. If the gossip at the clubs can be believed, the stories that are openly told are so shocking that, if even hinted at in print, they would hardly be accepted. There are few of the leaders of society whose names have not been dragged down by the scandalous backbiters, and the worst of it is that there is often a germ of truth in such reports. . . . The stories that have recently found their way to the offices of the *Saturday Evening Gazette* are much worse than anything printed by the London or New York Society papers. Respect for the position of the people implicated has buried these tales in oblivion."[35]

"Social Boston," said the writer of this item, "is standing on a volcano."

\Links

To read about the immediate response to press coverage in Boston, continue on to the next chapter, on <u>Brandeis</u>.

To read how the sensational press coverage of the Nineteenth Century altered sexual mores, go to the chapter on <u>Sex</u>.

To discover the current impact of British-trained journalists on the tabloid press of the 1990s, go to the chapter on <u>Torts</u>.

Brandeis

How the din of sensational news coverage and of new technology at the end of the Nineteenth Century led two Boston lawyers to come up with a remedy.

At his home in Boston, Samuel D. Warren, Jr., was experiencing an eruption of his own. An outstanding graduate of Harvard Law School who was forced to give up the practice of law to take over his family's paper business, Warren was apparently outraged by Boston press coverage of social activities.

It may not have been the discreet items about Mrs. Warren's entertaining, for the references were infrequent and harmless enough. But it surely was the cumulative impact of intrusive reporting by the press over the years. Warren's mother, father, and sister – their vacations and their parties – were frequently mentioned in the society pages of Boston's newspapers. His wife's father, Senator Thomas Francis Bayard of Delaware, was the subject of frequent negative news coverage. Of course, Bayard was a public figure, a controversial candidate for President in 1884 and then Secretary of State under the eventual winner in 1884, Grover Cleveland.

The *Gazette* in Boston had noted Bayard's departure from office with an editorial saying, "Happily he has but a few days more in which to strut about like a pompous turkey-cock with wings drooping in defiance. . . . Secretary Bayard will go into private life unwept, unhonored, and unsung, and it is to be sincerely hoped that he may be kept there for good and all."[1] This is not an invasion of privacy but is surely the kind of language that would motivate an upstanding son-in-law to take on the press, especially in view of the fact that the *Gazette* was the newspaper read by all the finer people in Boston.

Warren turned to his close friend, Louis D. Brandeis, to devise a "right to be let alone" that would permit an aggrieved person to collect damages for press reports of sensitive matters that, because they were true, could not be reached by the law of libel. There could not have been a more potent pair. Brandeis, before he had even turned 21, had been first in his class at Harvard Law. Warren had been second.

When Brandeis had developed eye trouble at Harvard, his friend Sam Warren read the required material to him for a time. They had formed a thriving law practice together in Boston for a brief time after law school. Brandeis, of course, would later become a distinguished member of the U.S. Supreme Court.

Together they drafted an article that the *Harvard Law Review* published in December 1890. Warren seemed to provide the passion and the evidence of a need for protection, and Brandeis provided the legal wisdom.

They wrote:

> "The press is overstepping in every direction the obvious bounds of propriety and of decency. Gossip is no longer the resource of the idle and of the vicious, but has become a trade, which is pursued with industry as well as effrontery. To satisfy a prurient taste the details of sexual relations are spread broadcast in the columns of the daily papers. . . .

> "The intensity and complexity of life, attendant upon advancing civilization, have rendered necessary some retreat from the world, and man, under the refining influence of culture, has become more sensitive to publicity, so that solitude and privacy have become more essential to the individual; but modern enterprise and invention have, through invasions upon his privacy, subjected him to mental pain and distress, far greater than could be inflicted by mere bodily injury."[2]

More than an attack on the press, the Harvard article was largely a response to new technology: "Recent inventions and business methods call attention to the next step which must be taken for the protection of the person and for securing to the individual . . . the right 'to be let alone,'" it said.

"Instantaneous photographs and newspaper enterprise have invaded the sacred precincts of private and domestic life; and numerous mechanical devices threaten to make good the prediction that 'what is whispered in the closet shall be proclaimed from the house-tops.' For years there had been a feeling that the law must afford some remedy."

What "numerous mechanical devices" were they talking about?

Some were obvious:

1873 Manufacture of the first effective typewriter by E. Remington and Sons.

1876 Invention of the telephone (and the microphone), by Alexander Graham Bell.

1876 Invention of the first sound recording device (a dictating machine) by Thomas A. Edison.

1886 Linotype machine introduced at the New York *Tribune*, permitting high-speed typesetting by line, not by letters.

1887 First gramophone or phonograph for playing back sounds of performances.

Other mechanical devices that made gossip and intrusiveness possible were not as obvious:

1884 The free-flowing fountain pen, marketed by Louis Waterman.

1884 First patent for roll film, by George Eastman.

1887 Development of the forerunner to the modern computer, by Herman Hollerith at the U.S. Census Office, a landmark invention not generally known to the public at the time.

1888 Development of revolutionary "Kodak" camera allowing impromptu, and often clandestine, "snap" photographs.

1891 First automated switching equipment for routing phone calls without human operators, in Kansas City.

Other developments that were no longer surprises to the people of 1890 but nonetheless critical in their impact on personal privacy:

1839 First photographic process perfected, in France.

1844 Sending of the first public telegram, on a device invented by Samuel Morse.

1849 Formation of first wire service, Associated Press, to accelerate transmission of the news.

1877 First moving pictures developed.

1883 First large-circulation magazines.

All of this change within just 20 years. Two observations: Prior to the Civil War, news reporting was what one editor called the stuff of "small beer and scandal"; now it was a wholesale enterprise, whether or not the subject matter was especially newsworthy. Just as importantly, prior to Alexander Graham Bell's telephone, a person had to be located in close physical proximity to a conversation in order to intercept it. When Brandeis and Warren published their article, that was no longer the case – conversations could be overheard from afar.

The development of photography had a special impact. Imagine for the first time seeing a facsimile of your own image – and a permanent image. Prior to this, only a very few rich and powerful persons could have seen painted portraits of themselves.

Realize, too, that in the years before the development of photography in the mid-1800s, even mirrors were not universal in British and American home life. Imagine the realization that for the first time the very essence of your being – your visage – could be captured by someone else – used and controlled by someone else.

At mid-century, photography was so cumbersome and the sittings so prolonged that at least no one's image was captured without their fully knowing it – there was informed consent. (To process his famous pictures of the Civil War, Matthew Brady was forced to take a horse-drawn processing studio with him into battles.)

But all of that changed in 1888 with Eastman's "snap camera." This hand-held camera, for the first time, permitted amateurs to take photographic images – and to take them clandestinely. Imagine the shock, for the first time, of having a stranger take a photograph of you without any warning and without your knowledge or permission. ("You Press the Button; We do the Rest," proclaimed advertisements for Eastman Kodak's new camera.)[3]

In fact, in the years after this, there were several complaints about photographers selling negatives or prints without permission for use in advertising and about others blackmailing victims through the use of candid photographs.[4] Some legal scholars argued that there ought to be a remedy.

Then imagine the possibilities of instantaneous reproduction of those images in newspapers circulated throughout the country – never before remotely possible.

All of this future shock occurred within a span of fewer than 45 years – between 1839 and 1884, less than a lifetime. A generation

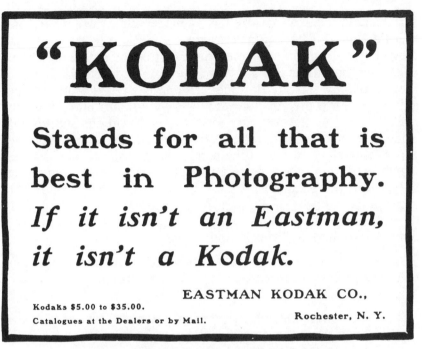

Advertisement in *Harper's Monthly*, 1901

not accustomed to being photographed at all could now readily identify with the tenet in Native American cultures that "whoever takes my picture takes a part of my soul."

Consider how these new technological possibilities shocked Marion Manola, who discovered that she had been photographed from one of the boxes while she performed in tights at the Broadway Theatre in New York City on June 14, 1890. The tempestuous star was reported to have "thrown her mantle over her face and run off the stage" in reaction to the flash of the camera. She had not agreed to be photographed beforehand. In fact, she had made clear that her modesty prevented her from allowing photographs while she was in tights. Miss Manola was said to fear having her school-aged daughter stumble upon an immodest picture of her mother in shops along Broadway.

The famous opera prima donna returned to the stage to finish her performance. What else could she do? At the time, a person had no legal right to prevent commercial use of a photograph of himself or herself. In spite of that, Marion Manola succeeded seven days later in getting a court to bar, at least temporarily, use of the photograph for publicity purposes.[5]

The Manola incident occurred as Brandeis and Warren were putting the final touches on their article, "The Right to Privacy" (and they mentioned it in a footnote). Seeking to combat this new brand of exploitation, Brandeis and Warren did what lawyers often do – they argued by analogy: If American courts already protect values akin to personal privacy, why should they not also protect privacy itself? Courts permit recovery for libelous distortions and untruth. They protect corporate trade secrets, privileged communications, and relationships of trust (like a fiduciary). They compensate for mental suffering. They protect an individual against being compelled to testify against himself or herself, under the Fifth Amendment to the Constitution. And they permit ownership of intangible ideas and thoughts, under the copyright and patent protections written into the Constitution.

Then the two did what lawyers do almost as often – they argued that their proposed rule of law was no more than an affirmation of existing principles:

> "The principle which protects personal writings and any other productions of the intellect or of the emotions is the right to privacy, and the law has no new principle to formulate when it extends this protection to personal appearance, sayings, acts, and to personal relation, domestic or otherwise. If the invasion of privacy constitutes a legal *injuria*, the elements for demanding redress exist, since already the value of mental suffering, caused by an act wrongful in itself, is recognized as a basis for compensation."

The recognized protection afforded to one's writings, thoughts, and sentiments, they concluded, is no more than an instance of "the more general right of the individual to be let alone."

Warren and Brandeis were willing to build on what had come before, to accept the notion of their time that the protection of private property was the paramount human freedom. This notion goes back to the English Magna Carta of 1215, and even before that to Roman legal concepts in the Middle Ages: the sovereign had nearly unlimited powers *except to interfere with ownership of one's private property*. Rather than challenge that, they simply sought to nudge that concept to a higher plane. "The basis of this right to prevent the publication of manuscripts or works of art . . . is stated to be the enforcement of a right of property; and no difficulty arises in accepting this view," they wrote. Then, in the next breath: "But where the value of the production is found not in the right to take the profits arising from publication, but in . . . peace of mind, . . it is difficult to regard the right as one of property, in the common acceptance of that term." The right at stake is the right to privacy.

Good lawyers know that judges and other lawyers do not like to stray from prior precedents; they prefer to build on them.

The two were careful to point out that their right to privacy would not prohibit publication of newsworthy material, nor prohibit dissemination of "privileged communications" like those uttered in a court or other official proceeding, nor provide damages in most instances of verbal dissemination, nor bar dissemination once an individual had consented or published the information himself or herself. They conceded that the right to privacy must necessarily be limited and that it would be difficult to enforce. (Their notion that an invasion of privacy must be *unwarranted*, in order to be actionable, has become a part of our contemporary law. The federal Freedom of Information Act of 1966 permits government agencies to withhold documents from disclosure if they include personal information, but only if the invasion of privacy will be *unwarranted*.)

Then Brandeis and Warren went on to provide their ideas of appropriate remedies once an individual proved an invasion of privacy by another person or entity. In just 26 pages, the law review article succeeded in virtually creating a new right of action for aggrieved individuals where none had existed before. It did so because the authors made a strong case for the existence of a problem and were extremely conservative in shaping a remedy. The parameters they set for an invasion-of-privacy claim remain essentially the same today.

At first blush, the ills Brandeis and Warren complained of seem to have no similarities, except that they are grouped under the rubric of "invasions of privacy." But Brandeis and Warren identified the connecting link. The combination of gossip journalism, commercial use of personal information, intrusive snooping into private lives, and reckless use of cameras and recording devices "*both belittles and perverts. It belittles by inverting the relative importance of things, thus dwarfing the thoughts and aspirations of a people.*" In other words, it not only victimizes the subject of the gossip; it also cheapens the culture of a nation.

The brilliant young lawyers from Boston did not invent the term "right to be let alone." They acknowledged borrowing it from Thomas McIntyre Cooley, the noted judge and legal scholar who two years earlier had published a treatise on *The Law of Torts*, which included this language:

> "Personal Immunity. The right to one's person may be said to be a right of complete immunity: to be let alone."

Judge Cooley was actually explaining the legal maxim that an attempted physical touching of a person is an injury for which the victim may recover damages just as surely as if the attack lands a blow ("There is very likely a shock to the nerves, and the peace and quiet of the individual is disturbed.") He was not recognizing a right to privacy, as Brandeis and Warren were doing, but merely using the words that since his time have labeled the right to privacy – "the right to be let alone." But in the course of their argument, Brandeis and Warren borrowed the idea from Cooley that the law will provide compensation for threats that cause consternation or severe distress, even if no physical injury results. This is a form of privacy protection, they argued.[6]

Cooley's treatise in 1888 discussed torts – the possible lawsuits that an individual might have against another person or private entity for a personal injury or insult. In 1868 he wrote a book discussing another branch of the law – constitutional law. That is the body of law concerning the rights of a citizen vis-a-vis governmental power. The legal principles of torts govern disputes between two private individuals or entities, in contrast to constitutional law, which involves the rights of the individual against the state. Thus, an invasion of privacy could constitute a tort or it could be a violation of the constitution; it depends on who's doing the invading. A conservative legal theorist who believed that the less government the better, Cooley wrote in his book on constitutional law, "It is better oftentimes that crime should go unpunished than that the citizen should be liable to have his premises invaded, his trunks broken open, his private books, papers, and letters exposed to prying curiosity."[7]

The more immediate inspiration for Brandeis and Warren might have been a landmark article not by a lawyer but by, of all people, a journalist (or, as the two lawyers acknowledged in their legal article, "an able writer"). As editor of the influential weekly magazine *The Nation* and a liberal reformer, E. L. Godkin had become concerned about the excesses of the press. He was a thinking person's journalist. Of the British-born Godkin, the philosopher William James said, "His influence has assuredly been more pervasive than that of any other writer of the generation." On the other hand, as editor of the New York *Evening Post*, Godkin was on the receiving end of a five-year civil libel lawsuit and of criminal libel charges for his reporting on the powerful Democratic political machine in New York City, the Tammany Society, or more familiarly Tammany Hall. Thus, although he championed the right of all citizens to be free of outside intrusions, he did not advocate legal recognition of the right to privacy. Instead, in an influential article in *Scribner's* magazine in July of 1890, Godkin proposed educating the public to ostracize news organizations that invade privacy.

In the article, entitled "The Rights of the Citizen – To His Own Reputation," Godkin wrote in *Scribner's*, on the one hand:

> "The right to decide how much knowledge of his personal thought and feeling, and how much knowledge, therefore, of his tastes, and habits, of his own private doings and affairs, and those of his family living under his roof, the public at large shall have, is as much one of his natural rights as his right to decide how he shall eat and drink, what he shall wear, and in what manner he shall pass his leisure hours."

He went on to say, on the other hand:

> "In truth, there is only one remedy for the violations of the right to privacy within the reach of the American public, and that is but an imperfect one. It is to be found in attaching social discredit to invasions of it on the part of conductors of the press."[8]

Godkin, like Brandeis and Warren, was reacting to the increased urbanization of American life, the unsettling impact of new technology, the competitiveness of the press, the loss of opportunities for serenity. "Privacy," he wrote, "is a distinctly modern product, one of the luxuries of civilization, which is not only unsought for but unknown in primitive or barbarous societies."

Godkin did not have to look far for evidence of intrusive technology. Just a few months before his article was published, *Scribner's* published an advertisement for private detectives showing a bowler hat with a built-in hidden camera.[9]

As an eminent journalist, he correctly identified the trend of the times; a certain kind of newspaper, he wrote, had "converted curiosity into what economists call an effectual demand, and gossip into a marketable commodity." The Godkin essay appeared just six months before the article by Warren and Brandeis.

Brandeis and Warren noted in their article that France, since 1868, had a law protecting privacy and that the case law in England protected intellectual property. They could also have noted, but did not, that an English philosopher 17 years before them had written:

> "To define the province of privacy distinctly is impossible, but it can be described in general terms. All the more intimate and delicate relations of life are of such a nature that to submit them to unsympathetic observation, or to observation which is sympathetic in the wrong way, inflicts great pain and may inflict lasting moral injury. Privacy may be violated not only by the intrusion of a stranger, but by compelling or persuading a person to direct too much attention to his own feelings and to attach too much importance to their analysis. The common usage of language affords a practical test which is almost perfect on this subject. Conduct which can be described as indecent is always in one way or another a violation of privacy."[10]

Sir James Fitzjames Stephens was right. The right to privacy covers only "the more intimate and delicate relations of life," not every incidental fact about a person or his or her identity. To this day, that is the rule in the U.S.

Sir James was right in a more subtle respect. Each of us knows that exposing the unclothed body to a nurse or doctor in a medical setting may be uncomfortable but it is generally not threatening. This is *observation*, but not *unsympathetic observation*. Exposing the naked body involuntarily to a news photographer is threatening because it is *unsympathetic observation*. By the same token, no one objects to sharing embarrassing details with trusted friends – that is not a sacrifice of personal privacy. Such candor among a select circle actually enhances a sense of privacy. Most of us would object, however, to having those same details pried from us by a news reporter or commercial investigator – or worse, having them pried from some third party. That is, in Stephens' words, "observation which is sympathetic in the wrong way."

In fact, one American court (probably unwittingly) had accepted Stephens' notion of "unsympathetic observation" nine years before the Brandeis-Warren opus. The Supreme Court of Michigan ruled that the mother of a newborn infant was entitled to damages against her doctor, who invited an untrained ("unmarried, young") medical assistant to observe the home delivery. The parents believed the assistant to be trained. The court could not very well say that this was a trespass, a traditional right of action in the courts; but it was an invasion of privacy, an *unsympathetic observation*. The state supreme court ruled, "The plaintiff had a legal right to privacy of her apartment at such a time, and the law secures her this right by requiring others to observe it."[11]

"It is likely that the Warren and Brandeis article has had as much impact on the development of law as any single publication in legal periodicals."

George Trubow, privacy expert at John Marshall Law School, Chicago, in 1992.

Thus, the notion of a right to privacy was not totally unknown in American courts before the Brandeis-Warren article. And just a few months after the article appeared, although most likely with no prompting by it, the U.S. Supreme Court recognized the right to privacy. It ruled on the appeal of a woman who objected to being compelled to disrobe and submit to a surgical examination without her consent, as a condition of continuing her lawsuit against a railroad to collect damages for a physical injury. It was not uncommon at the time, especially in the West and South, for a court to order such a physical exam. A federal court in Indiana had said that it had no power to compel the examination. Witnesses testified as to the woman's injuries, and the court awarded Clara Botsford $10,000 anyway. The railroad appealed. The U.S. Supreme Court agreed with the trial court. Before citing Thomas Cooley, it proclaimed,

> "No right is held more sacred, or is more carefully guarded, by the common law, than the right of every individual to the possession and control of his own person, free from all restraint or interference of others, unless by clear and unquestionable authority of law. . . . The inviolability of the person is as much invaded by a compulsory stripping and exposure as by a blow. To compel any one, and especially a woman, to lay bare the body, or to submit it to the touch of a stranger, without lawful authority, is an indignity, and assault, and a trespass."[12]

This definitive language must have surprised lots of lawyers and judges in 1891 who had until then searched in vain for such protection in the courts. Of course, the Supreme Court was talking about the sanctity of bodily privacy, not the right to preserve one's reputation. These are separate branches of the concept of personal privacy. The court's ruling in the *Union Pacific* case has long been an aberration in American case law, separated by decades from other court decisions on privacy and strangely omitted in nearly all discussions of the subject. For some reason, it is usually not included in the line of cases supporting a right to privacy, even though it is the first and perhaps the most unequivocal Supreme Court case to do so.

Fifteen years after the landmark Harvard article appeared, a lawyer named Elbridge Adams published his own law review article, suggesting that E.L. Godkins' article probably motivated Brandeis and Warren. It was a favorable review of their work. Thus, Brandeis, still practicing law in Boston, borrowed the article from the Boston Social Law Library (which still has an estimable collection on the right to privacy) and mailed it to his co-author. In an accompanying note, Brandeis said, "My own recollection is that it was not Godkin's article but a specific suggestion of yours, as well as your deep-seated abhorrence of the invasions of social privacy, which led to our taking up the inquiry."[13]

Warren wrote back, "You are right of course about the genesis of the article."

"The article is a model of how effectively presented legal scholarship can lead to a change in the law."

Arthur R. Miller, author of *The Assault on Privacy* and professor of law, Harvard University, in 1990.

Brandeis had a certain ambivalence about the piece, according to his biographer, Lewis Paper. He admitted in a letter to his fiancee that he was not sure that the piece was "as good as I thought it was" when he saw the page proofs for the first time. A few years later, he did not respond to Warren's urging that he draft a criminal law punishing abuses by the press and present the proposal to the Massachusetts state legislature.

Like Warren, Brandeis hoped, in his words, "to make people see that invasions of privacy are not necessarily borne – and then make them ashamed of the pleasure they take in subjecting themselves to such invasions." In other words, he wanted to tell the victims of abusive press coverage or commercial misappropriations, "You don't have to take it." But he realized, "All law is a dead letter without public opinion behind it" and "The most perhaps that we can accomplish is to start a backfire." He knew that there were at the time no legal protections at all and that the only hope was outraged public opinion – "a backfire."[14]

Brandeis, in fact, felt that he should be addressing the opposite side of the coin – the need for exposing secret actions in government. He was, after all, a crusading public-interest lawyer until President Woodrow Wilson named him to the high court in 1916. "Lots of things which are worth doing have occurred to me," he wrote to his fiancee shortly after the Harvard article appeared. "And among others to write an article on 'The Duty of Publicity' – a sort of companion piece to the last one that would really interest me more. . . . If the broad light of day could be let in upon men's actions, it would purify them as the sun disinfects."[15] Brandeis never did write an article on access to governmental records.

As for the article on privacy, Lewis Paper went on to say in his biography, "The reaction to the article was nothing short of incredible. Lawyers read it, magazines reviewed it, and courts relied on it – all to the seeming end of creating a new right to privacy."

There was even a feminist critique. In 1898, Charlotte Perkins Gilman, a women's advocate of the period, argued in her book *Women and Economics* that as patricians Warren and Brandeis adopted the myth that within the confines of the home there was privacy. In fact, women at home enjoyed no privacy or autonomy, even if they were safe from outside intrusions.[16]

"If two lawyers wrote such an article today, there would be absolute outrage. There was no recognition at all of the First Amendment."

James C. Goodale, lawyer for *The New York Times*, in 1990.

Although the early reaction was favorable, there have been unfavorable appraisals in later years, especially from advocates for an unfettered press and for purity in the development of case law. Press advocates severely criticized the article for presumably ignoring the First Amendment right to publish, even if what was published included personal information about an individual. In fact, the article did recognize that newsworthiness would be a limitation on a claim of a right to privacy.

Much of the negative reaction stems from early mythology that Warren was overreacting to press coverage of society events involving himself and his family. A biography of Brandeis in 1946 perpetuated this account. The mythology deepened after an inaccurate – but widely disseminated – assertion by a respected expert on privacy, William L. Prosser of the University of California. Prosser wrote in 1960 that Samuel Warren had been outraged by the press coverage of his daughter's wedding. Searching for a spin, Prosser compared Warren's daughter to "the face that launched a thousand lawsuits."[17] Subsequently, in the 1970s, Boston lawyer James H. Barron took the time to discover that Warren's daughter was no more than seven years old in 1890.[18] Prosser – or an eager student researcher – must have erred after reading press coverage of the doings of Mrs. S.D. Warren Sr., and her daughter, Samuel Warren, Jr.'s *sister*. Further, Barron's search through old Boston newspapers found no outrageous press coverage of Samuel D. Warren, Jr., or Louis D. Brandeis themselves. Having deflated the myths surrounding the article, Twentieth-Century legal scholars seemed then to ask, "What's all the fuss about privacy? The press never crucified Warren – or Brandeis either!"

And what was the immediate reaction of E.L. Godkin, the enlightened journalist? Ten days after publication of the Brandeis-Warren article, Godkin wrote again about privacy in *The Nation* weekly, saying that it was unlikely that any court or legislature would recognize privacy as a legal right. The reason? In order to seek a remedy for a legally enforceable right to privacy, an aggrieved individual would "have to expose himself to a great deal more publicity." People simply wouldn't do that, Godkin believed. Indeed, this "Catch 22" that you have to file suit through public court documents and expose more details of your private life in order to get redress is the ultimate outrage. And this ironic reality has deterred many lawsuits for invasion of privacy in the years since 1890.

Godkin presented another reason that a legal right to privacy would never catch on: "There is nothing democratic societies dislike so much to-day as anything which looks like what is called 'exclusiveness,' and all regard for or precautions about privacy are apt to be considered signs of exclusiveness."[19]

Indeed, in the years leading up to 1890 and after, the public seemed to believe that privacy was essentially something for the elite classes to worry about. This feeling was reinforced when one of the first lawsuits filed after the Harvard article, and surely the most prominent, was by a nephew and other relatives of the late Mrs. Mary Hamilton Schuyler, a wealthy blue blood who had lived at a country manor near Saratoga Springs, New York. "Her figure is majestic, features handsome," said a contemporary description. The nephew sought to prevent her from being celebrated with a statue as the "Typical Philanthropist" in a display at the 1893 World's Fair in Chicago. She was to be posed next to a likeness of the great feminist Susan B. Anthony. He did not succeed in the end, largely because the New York Court of Appeals ruled that a right to privacy, if it exists, expires with death.[20] That same view has been held by courts throughout the Twentieth Century (although a half-dozen states have reversed that with statutes).

Tossing poor Godkin, the working person's newsman, in among the "swells," privacy scholar Alan F. Westin added his voice to this "elitism" interpretation about the origins of privacy. Westin has written:

> "The movement begun by the Godkin and Warren-Brandeis essays was essentially a protest by spokesmen for patrician values against the rise of the political and culture values of 'mass society.' For the patricians, the gossip press, commercial advertising, and exposure of the doings of the socially prominent were aggressive and unjustified intrusions by publishers pandering to 'mass' curiosity and tastes. Conservative traditionalists among the patricians, such as Samuel Warren and Brook Adams, fused concern over the immunities of high society with anger at press muckraking of political and social scandals, though this was one instrument which brought the widespread business and governmental corruption of the era under minimum public controls. Liberals among the patricians, such as Godkin and Brandeis, joined a concern over the privacy of the socially prominent with a fear that the artistically sensitive or intellectually unpopular would be harmed by press intrusions – long a minority position in dominant American cultures."[21]

Brandeis and Warren were guilty as charged. They were patricians. (Although you have to wonder how much Brandeis as a Jew and a social reformer was accepted among the upper crust of Boston in the 1890s. You have to ask who else, especially in that century, made intellectual breakthroughs, except for the intellectual elite.)

Both were associated with the group of breakaway members of the Republican Party who refused to support their nominee in 1884 and instead backed the Democratic candidate, Grover Cleveland (who ironically had beaten Warren's father-in-law, Senator Bayard, to secure the nomination). It was said that they longed for America's values before it had become urbanized, industrialized, and crowded with new immigrants and emancipated black Americans. Part of their ethos, clearly, was a passion for individual autonomy. These gentrified Republican dissidents were labeled Mugwumps. That derisive name came from a writer for the *Sun*, the newspaper that had invented journalistic excesses half a century earlier in New York.

Surely, Brandeis and Warren's advocacy coincided with the desires of the elite classes who were offended by newspaper coverage – or any public awareness at all – of their spending and their socializing. For this reason, a knee-jerk reaction to concern about privacy ever since has been that it is "an upper-class issue." This may have been true of the origins of the legal concept in the United States. But in the Twentieth and Twenty-first Centuries, public-opinion surveys and strong anecdotal evidence continually show that fears about privacy span all income groups. It is in *the priority* that people give to different types of privacy invasions that class differences appear. For instance, affluent men and women when they think of privacy cite unwanted mail advertising and disclosure of tax information and financial information; indigent persons mention police searches and government paperwork requirements and intrusions at work.

A Denver, Colorado, lawyer writing in 1989 argued persuasively that the privacy of upper-crust Easterners, if they had lived amid the European values of the Old World, would have been protected by customs and entitlements. It is precisely because America was a raucous, egalitarian place that Brandeis and Warren and their well-born and privileged cohorts had to turn to the rule of law for a new *legal* right.[22]

The best response to charges of elitism came just two months after the *Harvard Law Review* article, when an editor of *Scribner's* magazine responded to Godkin's equation of privacy with "exclusiveness." (It was in *Scribner's* six months earlier where Godkin had fired up the debate.) The editor wrote in *Scribner's*:

"In the great future battle of the world between the two systems of Socialism and Individualism, one of the vital points of difference is to be *privacy*; and it is important to note that it *is* between individualism and socialism that the point of difference lies, and that privacy is not by any means an attribute of aristocracy as opposed to democracy. That Western citizen who raised the curtain of the new-comer's shanty and desired to know 'what was going on so darned private in here,' was the typical socialist, not the typical democrat."[23]

Indeed, in 1835, Alexis de Tocqueville in his appraisal of the young country had equated individualism with the sense of privacy, the sense of reserve, and the sense of retirement from a bustling community that John Adams and his contemporaries cherished:

"Individualism is a novel expression, to which a novel idea has given birth. . . . Individualism is a mature and calm feeling, which disposes each member of the community to sever himself from the mass of his fellows and to draw apart with his family and friends, so that after he has thus formed a little circle of his own, he willingly leaves society at large to itself."[24]

(The reference in *Scribner's* to "what was going on so darned private in here" is to a story told by E.L. Godkin in his 1890 piece in the same periodical: "There is the story of the traveller in the hotel in the Western mining town who pinned a shirt across his open window to screen himself from the loafers on the piazza while performing his toilet; after a few minutes he saw it drawn aside roughly by a hand from without, and on asking what it meant, a voice answered, 'We want to know what is so darned private going on in there!'")

Courts had a few opportunities in the decade of the Gay Nineties to embrace the emerging doctrine of a legally protected right to privacy, and they accepted the reasoning of Brandeis and Warren. This included at least two lower-court decisions in New York State.[25] A new legal right, almost instantaneously, had been created.

An intermediate court in New York State in 1901 quoted Thomas Cooley approvingly and recognized a claim for invasion of privacy. The loser in the case, a flour manufacturing company in Rochester, appealed to the highest court in the state, called the

Court of Appeals. Thus, at the turn of the century, the highest court in New York was presented with a case that posed the issue perfectly.

A shy, attractive teenaged girl in Rochester named Abigail Roberson had discovered that a lithograph of her was displayed on 25,000 flyers advertising Franklin Mills Flour, with the caption "Flour of the Family." She had not given her consent. Her innocence had been stolen before she had reached adulthood. Her young face, the image of purity, had been displayed on barrels in warehouses and in saloons across the country. The involuntary poster girl complained that many of her acquaintances had recognized her, some had scoffed and jeered her. Her lawyer said that the humiliation resulted in illness and severe nervous shock, for which she sought medical help. She asked for $15,000 in damages and an injunction to stop use of the photograph. There was no allegation that Miss Roberson had been libeled; in fact, the likeness was flattering. But it was exactly the kind of abuse that others had complained about, as photography became more widespread during the second half of the Nineteenth Century and instant photographs were used for commercial exploitation or blackmail without any legal restrictions.

Chief Judge Alton B. Parker, for the New York Court of Appeals, admitted that the Brandeis-Warren article was "presented with attractiveness, and no inconsiderable ability," and was even "clever." He seemed ready to use the word "cute," if it had been available to him at the time. But, no thanks, said the chief judge. He did not buy the idea of a legal right to privacy.

> "If such a principle be incorporated into the body of law through the instrumentality of a court of equity, the attempts to logically apply the principle will necessarily result not only in a vast amount of litigation, but in litigation bordering upon the absurd, for the right of privacy, once established as a legal doctrine, cannot be confined to the restraint of the publication of a likeness, but must necessarily embrace as well the publication of a word-picture, a comment upon one's looks, conduct, domestic relations or habits. And, were the right of privacy once legally asserted it would necessarily be held to include the same things if spoken instead of printed, for one, as well as the other, invades the right to be absolutely let alone. An insult would certainly be in violation of such a right."[26]

Loosen up, said a dissenting opinion by John Clinton Gray and two other justices that deserves more recognition than it gets in the historical record. Photography is a new medium; the courts must adapt to new conditions; and the law must guard against commercial exploitation without consent, Gray wrote. Otherwise, the resulting invasion of privacy may be "more formidable and more painful in its consequences than an actual bodily assault." As important to the dissenters, there were no prior court decisions in New York State rejecting a right to privacy.

The result of Chief Judge Parker's ruling was that persons like Abigail Roberson in New York, as in all other states, were still left without recourse against commercial exploitation of their own images. Advertisers, publishers, and marketers were free to use anybody's photograph or persona for their own profits. The editors of the *Yale Law Journal* pointed out that the decision preserved for an arrogant press the prerogative "to pry into and grossly display before the public matters of the most private and personal concern."[27]

Someone wrote in a letter to *The New York Times* that because the high court in New York clearly protected *property* rights but not personal privacy, Miss Roberson might well have won her case had her dog, not herself, been portrayed on the flour posters. The public disapproval of the decision was great enough to prompt one of the four members in the majority, Judge Denis O'Brien, to write an article in the *Columbia Law Review* defending it, an extraordinary step for a judge. And he did so within a few months of the decision.[28]

Let the legislature create a right to privacy, if it wishes, wrote Judge Parker, but the courts will not. In 1903 at its very next session, just one year later, before the ink was dry on the *Yale Law Journal*'s dire prediction, the New York legislature did just that. New York became the first of several states to recognize by statute a right to sue for invasions of privacy. The 1903 New York law is still on the books, and the courts in that state accepted its concept more than 100 times throughout the last century.

"The right to privacy is very much a child of the Twentieth Century, and, as such manifests all of the impetuousness, zeal, and occasional inconsistency of youth."

Literary attorneys Harriet F. Pilpel and Jerry Simon Chasen, in 1990.[29]

Section 51 of the New York Civil Rights Act enacted in 1903 and still on the books reads:

> "Any person whose name, portrait, or picture is used within this state for advertising purposes or for purposes of trade without the written consent first obtained as above provided may maintain an equitable action in the supreme court of this state against the person, firm or corporation using his name, portrait or picture, to prevent and restrain use thereof; and may also sue and recover damages for any injuries sustained by reason of such use, and if the defendant shall have knowingly used such person's name, portrait, or picture in such manner as is forbidden or declared to be unlawful by this act, the jury, in its discretion, may award exemplary damages."

At the end of the Twentieth Century, 12 other states had laws like this. In 45 other states, courts had recognized such a right in the common law, irrespective of whether a statute exists. No state has expressly rejected it.

Some cynics have said that the most immediate effect of the New York law and others like it was to give models for artists and photographers the opportunity to increase their fees for posing. Prior to this legal trend, they didn't have much leverage; they had no rights to their own images.

Alton B. Parker denied recovery for Abigail Roberson's ills and claimed that his decision saved the courts in New York State from being buried under an avalanche of "absurd" litigation. Then, while still on the Court of Appeals, he ran for President against Theodore Roosevelt in 1904. (He won the Democratic nomination over William Randolph Hearst, the 41-year-old practitioner of sensational journalism.)

As a candidate, Parker tried to declare a moratorium on "promiscuous" photography of himself and his family. He refused to pose for news photographers. After his wife was obligated to flee her home to avoid photographers, Judge Parker warned, "I reserve the right to put my hands in my pockets and assume comfortable attitudes without being everlastingly afraid that I shall be snapped by some fellow with a camera."[30] Abigail Roberson, now barely 21 years old, wrote an irate letter to *The New York Times* about this indignity. It appeared on the front page July 27, 1904. She sympathized with Parker's wife but said Parker had no right to restrict photographs of himself, citing Parker's own decision in her case as her "very high authority." Ms. Roberson said that she could find

> "no reason why you or your family have any rights of the nature suggested which do not equally belong to me. Indeed, as between us, I submit that I was much more entitled to protection than you. I was a poor girl making my living by my daily efforts, and never had courted publicity in any manner. You, on the other hand, are a candidate for the highest office in the gift of the people of the United States, and that fact makes you the legitimate center of public interest. It may fairly be said that you invited the curiosity which we have both found to be somewhat annoying."

Ms. Roberson said that it all just proved to her the truth of the maxim that "it makes a difference whose ox is being gored." Score one for Abigail Roberson – or the lawyer who undoubtedly drafted her letter.

"The privacy tort was the brainchild of Nineteenth-Century men of privilege, and it shows. . . . The privacy tort bears the unmistakable mark of an era of male hegemony. . . . The Warren and Brandeis article was a lofty defense of values of affluence and gentility."

Law professor Anita L. Allen and lawyer Erin Mack, in 1990.[31]

Perhaps those commentators who insist that "privacy is an elitist issue" should look closer and discover, in fact, that privacy is important to people at all economic levels; regrettably, it is afforded most often to the elite. Alton Parker was the first of a significant number of Twentieth-Century American politicians who disparaged the right to privacy at every chance they got but invoked it later in their careers when they needed to. Those who changed their views on privacy depending on their personal circumstances included Richard Nixon, Judge Robert Bork, Associate Justice Clarence Thomas, Bill Clinton, and former Chief Justice Warren Burger. (Despite his public prominence and his coolness towards granting a constitutional right to privacy for others, Burger hated to be photographed and often would not attend an event if news photographers were permitted to attend.)

Teddy Roosevelt didn't appreciate the mob of photographers who dogged him any more than did his opponent Judge Parker. (The press coverage of both public men was modest by the standards of the 1990s). Of course, at the turn of the century, it was still an intimidating experience for anybody to be photographed, even a public official. It would have been doubly worrisome to a man who became President when his predecessor, William McKinley, was shot down amid a friendly crowd. Still, TR exposed himself and his family to mass-media style news coverage and publicity. The *New York Times* had reported in 1902, less than a year after Roosevelt became President:

> "The present President of the United States has been so much annoyed by photographers who have attended his down-sittings and his uprisings and spied out all his ways, . . . that it is reported that only his respect for the dignity of his office has upon one or two occasions prevented him from subjecting the impertinent offender to the appropriate remedy. . . of personal chastisement."[32]

Roosevelt surely was reflecting the frustration of his constituents, especially the well-heeled people from which he came. During his presidency, a writer in *Harper's Weekly* said that the "petty gossip, mean curiosity, and idle scandals" of the daily newspapers were driving people into hiding. Middle-class businessmen came to complain about the constant interruptions in their workday – and it wasn't any better at home. "We have all become so accessible, by telephone, by telegraph, or by post," said another writer in 1914, Robert J. Shores, "that we are at the mercy of almost anyone who chooses to make a demand upon our time."[33]

And as for gossip and the newspapers, they, according to Shores, had one effect on the poor reader: "He has impressed upon him, through the press and by word of mouth, his responsibility for all the poverty, vice, ignorance, and crime that exist in the world today." This simply caused the average person to withdraw into a private circle of family and friends. Shores was certainly not the last one in the Twentieth Century to weigh in with that complaint.

In 1975, Lawrence Baskir, then counsel to the Senate Judiciary Subcommittee on Constitutional Rights chaired by North Carolina Senator Sam Ervin, was teaching a seminar on privacy law at Georgetown University Law Center in Washington. Robert Ellis Smith was a student in the class, his first full exposure to a subject that was to become his career interest for the next 26 years. Baskir began the first class by announcing that the reading list would begin with the Brandeis-Warren article and then the *Roberson* opinion. A young woman at the end of the table, no older than Abigail Roberson when she filed her lawsuit, spoke up in a delicate voice and said, "Oh, my great-grandfather wrote that decision."

Her great-grandfather did not have the last word, for in 1905, after Parker's defeat in the presidential race, the Georgia State Supreme Court issued a ruling that relied on Brandeis and Warren and on Justice Gray's dissenting opinion in New York, not on Parker's majority opinion.

Not only is a person whose image is misappropriated deprived of profits and subjected to stress, the Georgia court said, but he would also be justified in feeling that "*his liberty* has been taken away from him" and that he is "for the time being, *under the control of another*, that he is no longer free, that in reality he is a slave without hope of freedom, held to service by a merciless master."[34] This idea that privacy results in *a loss of control* – over one's personality, one's freedom to move and to act, one's physical features, and one's personal information – recurred in statutes and court opinions about privacy throughout the new century.

The Georgia case was blatant. Paolo Pavesich had been reading the *Atlanta Constitution* one day when he came across two photographs that looked like a "before" and "after" comparison. One man was portrayed as sickly. He had not purchased insurance from New England Life Insurance Co. The other man pictured was Pavesich himself! Luckily, Pavesich was portrayed as a healthy, satisfied customer. But he was still peeved, because he had not consented to the use of his image. Pavesich had never even done business with New England Life. But the publication of his picture implied that he was endorsing the product, an element not obviously present in the *Roberson* case.

The unanimous Georgia Supreme Court issued a closely reasoned opinion that paved the way for courts elsewhere around the country. The court made clear that its ruling did not threaten First Amendment rights of news reporters. Its ruling involved commercial exploitation of personal images, not restrictions on opinion and free speech. At first, other courts were preoccupied with the question of whether the right to privacy exists at all in American law, but after the decision in *Pavesich* judges began instead to articulate the nature of that right. It is not the mere use of a name or an image that is prohibited; anyone may use or publish any name he or she likes, even if it happens to belong to a celebrity. Nor is the use of a picture of a person's body, or a part of it, prohibited if the person himself or herself is unrecognizable. It is only forbidden when another person makes use of the name or image to pirate the individual's identity for some advantage, especially some monetary advantage.

Sam Warren died at the age of 58 in 1910. One biographer of Brandeis said that Warren was mortified by a bitterly contested trial to determine the distribution of his father's estate.[35] The embarrassing family feud was reported in the newspapers of Boston. It was the ultimate horror for a sensitive man who believed passionately in the sanctity of a private life.

In February 1916, at a U.S. Senate hearing to consider the nomination of Louis D. Brandeis to be a Supreme Justice, the proud dean of the Harvard Law School, Roscoe Pound, testified that the Brandeis-Warren article "did nothing less than add a chapter to our law."[36]

Once on the Supreme Court, Justice Brandeis became increasingly disenchanted with the extent of surveillance he discovered within the government. The right to privacy no longer meant protecting the social activities of the patrician classes, if it ever did, to Brandeis.

Brandeis fumed in several letters to Harvard Law Professor Felix Frankfurter about government law-breaking and spying. "Couldn't you get started through your men a series of the HLR covering the danger of arbitrariness etc. in the several federal Depts. & Bureaus?" he wrote, referring to the *Harvard Law Review*. "I omitted to ask you what progress is being made in the effort to reduce the appropriations for spies in the public service. . . . Wouldn't it be possible to interest [Harvard Law School professors and students to write] articles bearing on the redress for the invasion of civil and political rights through arbitrary, etc. governmental action, by means of civil suits? I think the failure to attempt such redress as against government officials for the multitude of invasions during the war and post-war period . . . is disgraceful. . . . Americans should be reminded of the duty to litigate. . . . Wouldn't it be possible to have some one in Congress move for a Claims Commission to make reparations to American citizens for the outrages incident to the Jan. 20 Palmer raids? An article on the Sedition law reparations would prepare the way."[37]

Government "espionage" is "un-American. It is nasty. It is nauseating," Brandeis said.

It is quaint that he had such faith in the power of law review articles to change social policy. But why not? He had seen it work in the case of privacy, within less than two decades' time.

The Palmer Raids he referred to in his correspondence with Felix Frankfurter were staged by Attorney General A. Mitchell Palmer under President Woodrow Wilson, with the participation of a young aide named J. Edgar Hoover. After mysterious bombings in various cities in 1919, federal agents conducted brutal raids in 12 cities and arrested hundreds of suspected Communists, anarchists, and "alien filth." They had the helpless detainees summarily deported by ship, despite the fact that far fewer than ten percent of them turned out to be deportable immigrants. And, this was simply a dress rehearsal. In the following January, the Immigration Bureau and local police groups called "red squads," along with agents from the forerunner to the Federal Bureau of Investigation, rounded up from 5,000 to 10,000 suspected radicals, conducted searches without warrants, installed unauthorized wiretaps, made arrests without warrants, detained people incommunicado, and subjected them to brutality.[38]

"Brandeis was willing to use all available resources in the service of eliminating illegal and unethical intrusions by government into the lives of the people," wrote Philippa Strum in her biography of Brandeis. "Ironically, neither Brandeis nor Frankfurter knew that throughout the period of their correspondence about government spying, the Massachusetts state police, concerned about the Sacco-Vanzetti murder case in which Frankfurter was playing a major role, maintained a wiretap on Felix Frankfurter's telephone."[39]

Brandeis was constantly badgering his friend, who was to succeed him on the Supreme Court in 1939, to talk with Senator Burton K. Wheeler, the influential Roosevelt Democrat from Montana, and other members of Congress to terminate the U.S. government's active surveillance program during the 1920s, by denying Congressional appropriations for this purpose.

Within six months, Brandeis had a small victory. The Senate rejected a $500,000 appropriation request for undercover activity aimed at liquor bootleggers during Prohibition. Yet he was realistic about the pace of lasting change:

> "It may take a generation to rid our country of this pest, but I think it probably can be done, if the effort is persistent and we are prepared for action when, in the course of time, 'the day' comes. The temper of the public at some time in

conjunction with some conspicuous occurrence will afford an opportunity & we should be prepared to take advantage of it."[40]

Brandeis' correspondence with Frankfurter offers an early articulation of what privacy activists between 1980 and 2000 came to call the "oil spill" theory of social reform. They knew, as environmental activists knew, that it takes a major disaster like an oil spill to motivate the public, and ultimately their elected representatives. As Brandeis had written in his letter to Samuel Warren about campaigning for recognition of a privacy right, "All law is a dead letter without public opinion behind it."

Several of those "oil spills" occurred in the privacy field in the last three decades of the Twentieth Century – the proposal for a Federal Data Center described in the chapter on Databanks, the government abuses in the 1970s known as Watergate, "browsing" through tax returns by employees of the Internal Revenue Service, abuse of personal information by prisoners employed to process it, the sex-related investigation of President Bill Clinton, the constant leaks of personal data from World Wide Web sites, and a few more – but none apparently had the requisite drama to prompt lasting outrage in the American public.

Eleven years after his appointment to the Court, Justice Brandeis showed his continuing interest in privacy, in a concurring opinion in the case of *Whitney v. California*:

> "Those who won our independence believed that the final end of the State was to make men free to develop their faculties; and that in its government the deliberative forces should prevail over the arbitrary. They valued liberty both as an end and as a means. They believed liberty to be the secret of happiness and courage to be the secret of liberty. They believed that freedom to think as you will and to speak as you think are means indispensable to the discovery and spread of political truth."[41]

Brandeis' activism from his position as a member of the Supreme Court, intended to influence the Executive Branch, was rare for a justice. But lobbying within the Court among the Justices is not rare at all. Within a few months he had an opportunity to lobby inside the Court for a ruling to declare wiretapping without a court order a violation of the Fourth Amendment "right of the people to be secure in their persons, houses, papers, and effects, against unreasonable searches and seizures."

The Supreme Court was presented with the appeal of Roy "Big Boy" Olmstead and more than 50 of his cohorts whose liquor-smuggling operation across the Canadian border in Washington State was broken up through covert wiretaps installed on their office and home telephones by federal agents. ("Big Boy" was a lieutenant in the Seattle Police Department!) For five months, the agents listened to all sorts of conversations, some of them personal and many of them dealing with illegal sales; some of them involving police officers and the mayor. In all, they collected 775 pages of notes (modest in today's electronic-surveillance procedures, in which the *average* federal tap lasts 28 days and tape-records 200 persons in 2000 separate conversations).

No court had given its approval to the surveillance, which would be a requirement today. The state of Washington even had a law prohibiting electronic surveillance, but a federal trial court ruled that was not relevant and permitted the use of the evidence collected through the telephone surveillance to be used in criminal trials of the conspirators. The agents had not trespassed into private property to install their listening devices; instead, they monitored the conversations from afar. The issue for the U.S. Supreme Court was whether the Fourth Amendment prohibited such extensive snooping and whether the suspects were denied "due process of law" under the Fifth Amendment to the Constitution.

Brandeis was not necessarily ready to tackle the constitutional dimensions of the case, perhaps sensing there were not the votes among his colleagues for a decision by the Court finding the surveillance unconstitutional. The fact that federal agents had violated state law was disturbing enough. By condemning that, he reasoned, the court need not reach the constitutional issue in this case. That could be saved for "the day" when the public – and the Supreme Court – were outraged enough.

On February 8, 1928, he expressed his view in a handwritten memo to his colleagues:

> "Crime is contagious. In a government of laws, the Government must observe the law scrupulously. It teaches the whole people by its example. If it becomes itself a lawbreaker, it destroys respect for the law. It invites every man to become a law unto himself. It invites anarchy."[42]

His law clerk, Henry Friendly, persuaded Brandeis to address the constitutional issue and reach for a uniform national standard limiting this kind of invasion of privacy. The justice went to work revising his memorandum, using language from the article on privacy he and his late friend had written 38 years earlier:

"The makers of the Constitution appreciated that to civilized man, the most valuable of rights is the right to be let alone. They did not limit its guarantees of personal security and liberty against danger to the enjoyment of things material. Happily, the law recognizes that only a part of the pain, pleasure and profit of life lies there. The law gives protection to beliefs, thoughts, emotions and sensations. . . . Experience has taught that the danger of invasion by the Government of these rights of the individual is greatest where its purposes are benevolent. Men born to freedom are alert to resent the arbitrary invasion of their liberty by evil-minded rulers. It is in the insidious encroachments by the well-meaning – by those of zeal without understanding – that the greatest danger lurks."

The Court had to interpret the constitutional protections in light of new technology, Brandeis argued to the other justices. He echoed the theme of his *Harvard Law Review* article:

"Discovery and invention have made it possible for the Government to obtain by means far more effective than stretching upon the rack disclosure of 'what is whispered in the closet.' Through television, radium and photography, ways may soon be developed by which the Government can, without removing papers from secret drawers, reproduce them in court and by which it can lay before the jury the most intimate occurrences of the home."

The mention of television in a memorandum written in 1928 is remarkably prescient. Brandeis knew what he was talking about. Researchers much later discovered in his files that the justice had clipped and saved an Associated Press news story of January 13, 1928, announcing the Radio Corporation of America's first successful laboratory transmission of television pictures. However, Brandeis' clerk, who was to become a highly respected chief judge of the U.S. Court of Appeals in the Second Circuit, tried to persuade the justice that television wasn't relevant here. "Television doesn't work in a way so that you can take it and beam it across a street into an apartment building and see what somebody is doing," the 24-year-old Henry Friendly said.

"That's exactly how it works," replied the justice. Still, the reference to television was deleted from what Brandeis authorized to be published later.

Elected representatives and judges have not been as sophisticated about television as Brandeis was in 1928. To this day, no law regulates the use of covert video surveillance, without sound. This is curious because the invasion of privacy is as intense as, perhaps more intense than, when audio alone is used. The reason for the omission is that the current federal law on electronic surveillance was written and rewritten at times when no one apparently anticipated that video cameras would be readily available to individuals and amateurs and could be used without the full knowledge of everybody involved – in the same way that George Eastman's hand-held "snap camera" could be used without consent.

After oral arguments on "Big Boy" Olmstead's appeal, the justices voted in late February of 1928 to uphold his conviction and to rule that the seizure of electronic conversations was constitutional. Brandeis' internal memo was evolving into a dissenting opinion. He hoped to persuade his elder colleague on the bench, Oliver Wendell Holmes, Jr., to join in the dissent. But the man known on the court as "The Great Dissenter" voted with the majority this time.

Holmes, 87, had great respect for Brandeis' views; the distinguished Civil War veteran was also from Boston and from Harvard Law School. (He represented an early Twentieth-Century reversal of the mores of his Puritan forebears, who virtually required everyone to get married; by contrast, the judge required that his law clerks *not* be married – an employment policy that is now illegal because it invades the privacy of employees.)

Holmes could not be swayed. "I fear that your early stated zeal for privacy carries you too far," Holmes told his younger colleague. Brandeis, now 71, still saw the possibility of persuading a majority on the court to rule simply that the criminal conviction of Olmstead should be reversed because government agents violated the law. This irritated Chief Justice William Howard Taft, who wanted the justices to hold to their earlier determination that the case would be decided on constitutional grounds. There was bad blood between the two. Taft had opposed the nomination of Brandeis to the Supreme Court and then had been heard making anti-Semitic remarks in his direction once the two were on the Court together. As a crusading lawyer, Brandeis had opposed some actions of

Taft's tenure as President from 1909 to 1913. Taft thought the young liberal justice had too much influence over the elderly Oliver Wendell Holmes, Jr. "Brandeis gets two votes not one," the chief justice complained.

Taft was irate when Brandeis succeeded in getting Holmes to change his mind and vote against upholding the conviction. Holmes drafted a separate dissenting opinion based on the fact that law enforcement agents had violated state law. In it was Holmes' famous declaration, "I think it a less evil that some criminals should escape than that the Government should play an ignoble part." (Compare Holmes' comment with what Thomas Cooley had to say back in 1888: "It is better oftentimes that crime should go unpunished than that the citizen should be liable to have his premises invaded, his trunks broken open, his private books, papers, and letters exposed to prying curiosity.") Wiretapping, Holmes wrote, "was dirty business" and the courts should not accept it.

Taft wrote the opinion for the Court, saying that "only" listening to conversations is neither a search nor a seizure. After all, nothing tangible had been seized.

In a letter to his brother a few days later, the Chief Justice said that he was deeply hurt by Holmes' desertion – calling it "the nastiest opinion." Then he went on to justify his own decision:

> "The telephone might just as well have been used to carry on a conspiracy to rob, to murder, to commit treason. The truth is we have to face the problems presented by new inventions. Many of them are most useful to criminals in their war against society and are at once availed of, and these idealist gentlemen urge a conclusion which facilitates crime by their use and furnishes immunity from conviction."[43]

Brandeis managed to get only two other justices to go along with him and Holmes. Each of the four members of the minority wrote separate dissenting opinions. And so the conviction, in spite of the government's law-breaking role, was upheld, in a 5-4 vote. "Big Boy" Olmstead surrendered to authorities at the federal penitentiary in Washington State and served the balance of his four-year term. Later he became a model citizen and earned a Presidential pardon.

In his *Olmstead* dissent, Brandeis polished the language in his internal memorandum and issued one of his most notable opinions, in a losing cause. It is a dissenting opinion that has been quoted far more often than Taft's majority opinion:

> "Clauses guaranteeing to the individual protection against specific abuses of power must have a . . . capacity of adaptation to a changing world. . . . Time works changes, brings into existence new conditions and purposes. Therefore a principle to be vital must be capable of wider application than the mischief which gave it birth. This is peculiarly true of constitutions. . . .

> "The progress of science in furnishing the government with means of espionage is not likely to stop with wiretapping. Ways may some day be developed by which the government, without removing papers from secret drawers, can reproduce them in court, and by which it will be enabled to expose to a jury the most intimate occurrences of the home. Advances in the psychic and related sciences may bring means of exploring unexpressed beliefs, thoughts and emotions. . . .

> "Whenever a telephone line is tapped, the privacy of the persons at both ends of the line is invaded and all conversations between them upon any subject, and although proper, confidential, and privileged, may be overheard. Moreover, the tapping of one man's telephone line involves the tapping of the telephone of every other person whom he may call, or who may call him. As a means of espionage, writs of assistance and general warrants are but puny instruments of tyranny and oppression when compared with wiretapping. . . .

> "The makers of our Constitution undertook to secure conditions favorable to the pursuit of happiness. They recognized the significance of man's spiritual nature, of his feelings and of his intellect. They knew that only a part of the pain, pleasure and satisfactions of life are to be found in material things. They sought to protect Americans in their beliefs, their thoughts, their emotions and their sensations. *They conferred, as against the government, the right to be let alone – the most comprehensive of rights and the right most valued by civilized [persons].* To protect that right, every unjustifiable intrusion by the government upon the privacy of the individual, whatever the means employed, must be deemed a violation of the Fourth Amendment."[44]

The consummate lawyer was showing here an ability to anticipate the direction of new technology and to convey to the American people the interrelationship of technology and the welfare of a free people. In saying, "Ways may some day be developed by which the government, without removing papers from secret drawers, can reproduce them in court," wasn't Louis Brandeis anticipating the Internet of the 1990s? Prior to Brandeis, the American political figure who could best relate the impact of technological change on a democratic society was Benjamin Franklin.

Back in 1926, Brandeis had predicted to Felix Frankfurter, "It may take us a generation to rid our country of this pest. . . . I think it can be done, if the effort is persistent and we are prepared for action when, in the course of time, 'the day' comes."

He was right on target. Twenty-one years after the death of Louis D. Brandeis – and five years after Felix Frankfurter ended his own 23–year tenure on the court – the Supreme Court succeeded in finally setting limits on federal wiretappers. One year later, in 1968, Congress did the same.

Links

To follow the development of electronic surveillance technology and its constitutionality, follow on to the chapter on Wiretaps.

To learn what may have been the real motivation for the Warren-Brandeis article, see the story of the Beecher-Tilden scandal in the chapter on Sex.

To follow the legal development of Brandeis and Warren's conception of a legal theory to its culmination, go to the chapter on Torts.

To follow the development of the right to privacy as a constitutional right after Brandeis left the Court, go to the chapter on The Constitution.

Wiretaps

How the Supreme Court and Congress resolved six decades of confusion about the limits of electronic surveillance.

What Justice Brandeis called an "unjustifiable intrusion" and Justice Holmes less delicately called "dirty business" increased continually in the years after the Supreme Court's decision in the *Olmstead* case, as Brandeis had anticipated.

Indeed, wiretaps were discovered on the telephones of Supreme Court justices themselves in 1935 and 1936 and at the White House as well. Wire devices were attached to the phone of the Mayor of New York City in 1929 and of the Mayor of Philadelphia in 1938. The governor of Rhode Island had a tap installed on the telephone of the state attorney general in 1940.[1]

For both federal and state authorities, there were plenty of rationales. Masses of Americans were participating in protests over working conditions in the nation's new industrial plants. Waves and waves of new immigrants – unfamiliar faces speaking unfamiliar languages – were entering the country. There had been urban riots protesting wartime military conscription and campaigns against involvement in World War I. Many entrepreneurs were smuggling or selling alcoholic beverages illegally in the years 1920 through 1934 when liquor sales were prohibited by the Eighteenth Amendment to the Constitution. During these years, law enforcement officials seemed to believe especially that new immigrants were agitators, criminal bosses, common thugs, or instigators of violence. In later years in the Twentieth Century it was Communists, then organized-crime syndicates, then hippies, then student anti-war protesters, then suspected terrorists from Arabic cultures, then suspected dealers of illegal drugs – each group in successive periods providing the rationales for government surveillance.

Local police departments were limited in their effectiveness against any of these perceived threats. They did not have sophisticated equipment, and they regarded direct confrontation with the participants in these threatening activities as reactive, not pro-active. Direct confrontation with suspected criminals was also risky. How much easier and safer it was for law enforcement to monitor phone calls among confederates and then choose their moment to round up the targeted malefactors.

"Do we have to wait until the bomb goes off and people are killed or injured?

Or can we act while the fuse is still sputtering?"

An official of the FBI justifying wiretapping, in 1976.

With the advent of the Twentieth Century came a new technology that law enforcement needed for non-confrontational collection of intelligence about possible criminal behavior, in advance: hidden microphones for the monitoring of telephone calls and of in-person conversations. Consequently, law enforcement agencies resorted to electronic surveillance and infiltration to keep tabs on the threat of the moment.

Electronic surveillance had the additional advantage to law enforcement of creating an impression – perhaps only to police personnel themselves and to no one else – that law enforcement was all-knowing, all-seeing, all-powerful.

At the same time, listening in on telephone calls and in-person conversations was labor-intensive and often inefficient. It usually required sitting in a musty basement somewhere monitoring hours and hours of conversations filled with profanities and static and trivialities. It surely was "dirty business," in Justice Holmes' words.

It was also threatening to the civil liberties of many innocent persons. Just one installation would intrude upon thousands of conversations. A wiretap, of course, would pick up the words of anyone who happened to call the telephone of a targeted person. In the process, the snoopers picked up lots of information that was unrelated to crime and lots of information that provided no more than opportunities for prurient dabbling or tangential indulgence.

It had been this way since the beginning, for interceptions were reported almost as soon as the first wire communications system was established – the telegraph introduced by Samuel Morse in 1844. During the Civil War, forces on both sides tapped each others' lines. Confederate General J.E.B. Stuart was said to have had his own "wire man" accompany him in the field. Newspapers regularly reported incidents of telegraph tapping to steal information about stock tradings, horse races, or political messages. In the frenetic years of the penny press and "yellow journalism," insatiably curious newspapers were known to intercept each other's wire transmissions to gain a competitive advantage.[2] As soon as the telephone, the microphone, and the dictograph recorder were invented in the 1870s and 1880s, these devices were used for surreptitious listening and recording of conversations.

Consequently, in the early years of telephone service there was no realistic expectation of privacy; part of the shock of the new technology of amplified sound was precisely that person-to-person conversations could no longer be contained between the two persons involved. This was especially true in the early decades of telephone service. One "party line" would serve four or more customers. Simply by picking up the telephone, one of the customers could hear the conversation of another if the line were in use. In fact, this was common because a party-line customer would have no other way of knowing whether the line was free to place a call except to pick up the phone and listen. There was no dial tone in those days; live telephone operators would direct the call manually at a switchboard. In small towns, you could simply ask the operator for the name of the person you wanted to reach; you didn't need a number. If the operator had previously tried to place a call to the same person and gotten no answer, she might tell the caller that the person wasn't home and wouldn't need to place the call. Certainly, in the course of their work, operators knew who was talking with whom, if not the content of the conversation.

"If someone would invent a contraption to shut out the other nine when a person wanted to use the tenth [on a "party line"], he would be richer and more famous than Edison. But he'd be forever unpopular with us farmers for we'd never know each other's business."

Harry S. Truman, when a 26-year-old farmer, in a letter to his wife in 1910.

This feature of early telephone service led to an invention that changed the nature of the service forever. In 1889 an undertaker in Kansas City, Missouri, named Almon P. Strowger suspected that he was losing business because telephone operators were intercepting his calls from potential customers and diverting them to his competitors. Strowger invented a "girl-less, cuss-less" system that could automatically route the calls. He figured that this would allow calls in Kansas City to be routed without female intervention and without the profanities brought on by frustration. Automated switching did not eliminate party lines, but it lessened the number of operator-assisted calls.[3] Thus, automated switching created an expectation of privacy in telephone calls. After it was introduced, Americans became comfortable using the telephone for personal and sensitive matters. And when that occurred, there came good reasons for others to want to intercept the calls surreptitiously.

The Dictograph Co. in 1907 built a cumbersome device that seems to be the first put together expressly for the purpose of monitoring conversations. It consisted of a heavy microphone, a pair of uncomfortable headphones, a dry-cell battery, a metal switching device, and several spools of wire all fitted into a bulky black briefcase.[4] Instructions accompanying the device suggested hiding the microphone in plants or light fixtures and behind furniture, paintings, or radiators. A Los Angeles private detective named Nick Harris apparently used the cumbersome bugging device to gather evidence against "Nimble Anne, Queen of the Safecrackers," mass murderer James Watson, and other master criminals

Scientific American magazine reported in 1912 how the Burns Detective Agency had successfully broken a case of dynamiting as well as a celebrated bribery case through the use of an early version of a Dictograph. The detectives would place a small transmitter "in an inconspicuous place" in a hotel room and connect it to a speaker in the adjoining room. There a stenographer transcribed the content of a conversation between an *in cognito* detective and a suspect who did not believe that his words were being memorialized.[5] This is an example of a bug, used to monitor an in-person conversation – as opposed to a wiretap, used to intercept a wire conversation.

One of the first uses of a bug was reported in the annual *Report of the Postmaster General* in 1895. It said that by hiding a recording device in his top hat a postal inspector successfully recorded the words of a lawyer suspected of illegal use of the mail. The lawyer taunted the inspector by admitting in front of him that he had sent an incriminating letter. He knew that he could easily deny this in a trial and that he would do so. But, he was surprised to be confronted with the evidence of his admission. To his shock, it had been secretly preserved on tape.

The police commissioner of New York City, after his department was caught intercepting telephone calls in two celebrated cases in 1916, declared that no one should be surprised that the police or anyone else could monitor telephone calls:

> "Telephone conversations from their very nature cannot be private in the way that letters can be, since the employees of the telephone company cannot help hearing parts of conversations and may, if they are inclined, easily hear all."[6]

Telephone subscribers felt otherwise, especially with the introduction of single-party lines, automated switching, and dialing capability, all of which removed the involvement of human operators on most local calls. And telephone companies felt that conversations were entitled to protection – or so their executives said.

To devise legal protections, lawyers and judges – as lawyers and judges do – had to determine whether the new medium was more analogous to telegraph service, postal service, or something else.

Several states protected the confidentiality of telephone calls by amending their laws that had been enacted to protect telegraph messages.[7] California, for instance, in 1905 extended its 1862 law against the interception of telegraph messages to telephone service. But into the first third of the Twentieth Century there was no federal law on interception of telephone calls.

The practice was frowned on, to be sure. Even the U.S. Department of Justice said that it regarded the practice as unethical, and the Director of the Bureau of Investigation within the department, J. Edgar Hoover, said that he agreed. "No sir," he told a Congressional committee in 1931. "We have a very definite rule in the bureau that any employee engaging in wiretapping will be dismissed from the service of the bureau. . . . While it may not be illegal, I think it is unethical, and it is not permitted under the regulations by the Attorney General."[8]

The discoveries of interceptions were dramatic but not overwhelmingly numerous. The *Olmstead* case reached the U.S. Supreme Court in 1928 precisely because police in Washington State had violated one of several state laws prohibiting interception of telephone conversations.[9]

Six years after the Supreme Court decision in the *Olmstead* case – but not in response to it – Congress enacted the Federal Communications Act of 1934, which became the definitive scheme for regulating broadcasting and telecommunications. Section 605 of the act provided that:

> ". . . no person not being authorized by the sender shall intercept any communication and divulge or publish the existence, contents, substance, purport, effect, or meaning of such intercepted communications to any person."

The telephone companies were pleased. After all, they had argued to the Supreme Court in *Olmstead v. U.S.* for Justice Louis D. Brandeis' restrictive position. They told the Court that the function of the nation's telephone system was to allow any two persons at a distance to converse privately as if both were present in person in the home or office of one of them. The purpose of the system was not to catch crooks, although it might provide a means for doing so. "A third person who taps the lines violates the property rights of both persons then using the telephone, and of the telephone company as well," said the telephone companies' legal argument in the *Olmstead* case.[10]

The 1934 language restated the anti-interception provisions of the Radio Act of 1912 and the Radio Act of 1927; those laws, in turn, borrowed restrictive language similar to what was in the telegraph confidentiality laws enacted by about two-thirds of the states by the turn of the century.

But the 1934 law was never effective in limiting wiretapping by either law enforcement or private entities. Section 605 was primarily about *divulging*. For many years, law enforcement argued that the full statute was merely intended to regulate broadcasting, that it was no more than a restatement of existing prohibitions. They were right about that. Then they argued that it prohibited interception by law enforcement only if the contents of the conversation were divulged outside of the government. And they argued for many years that the words "no person" really didn't include government operatives. Those arguments required a stretch. But law enforcement got some judges to agree with them on all three points.

Because it dealt with broadcasting and wire communications, the 1934 law clearly did not prohibit listening devices not connected to a telephone wire. In other words, it did not apply to "bugging," the non-consensual interception or recording of conversations not over a telephone or a wire. The law affected only "wiretapping," the interception of wire communications. Both wiretapping and bugging are subsumed within the category of "electronic surveillance," a term synonymous now with "eavesdropping."

A covert listening device, whether a wiretap or a bug, is essentially a miniature radio broadcasting station, powered by a tiny amount of electricity. A tap connected to a telephone line (either inside a targeted premises or outside) or a bug must pick up the sound, then *amplify it* into an electrical signal, and transmit the signal to a receiver. Transistor technology (developed by Bell Laboratories in the 1940s) replaced the cumbersome vacuum tubes that had once been necessary in receivers. After that breakthrough, the challenge of electronic surveillance was to improve the quality of the sound and to extend the distance across which it could be transmitted – and to make the devices smaller and smaller, to prevent detection. Eventually even smaller integrated circuits replaced the tiny transistors, making it almost impossible to detect the presence of a wiretap. A victim now could not discover a tap or a bug through finding tangible evidence of it. Nor could a victim necessarily detect a discernible drain of electric current through the phone line. About the only way to discover the presence of a tap was through someone else's confession or by finding out that information that could have become known only through telephone monitoring had been divulged. Still later, tape-recording machines attached to wiretaps became voice-activated. Because they turn on and record only when there are conversations, voice-activated recorders remove the need for a human being to monitor long hours of silence and irrelevant conversations. Thus, voice-activated recorders overcame a primary deterrent to law enforcement agencies installing electronic surveillance as an investigatory tool, the labor intensity of the task.

"Show me a person who doesn't eavesdrop, and I'll show you a person with a serious hearing problem."

Surveillance-law expert Herman Schwartz, American University, in 1965.

To defeat a wiretap, persons who use the telephone regularly for sensitive matters can use a scrambler. The caller speaks into a microphone in the scrambling device and the conversation is made unrecognizable before being transmitted along telephone wires to the recipient. The recipient then unscrambles the conversation, with a descrambler using the same code used by the caller's telephone. Today this scrambling and unscrambling is done by software, called encryption.

Because the language in the 1934 federal law emphasized the *disclosure* of intercepted conversations, the Supreme Court ruled in 1937 that evidence obtained by wiretapping without consent in violation of Section 605 could not be used as evidence in court. This time Justice Brandeis was in the majority. The defendant in the case, Frank Carmine Nardone, was then retried and convicted a second time of smuggling alcohol into the U.S.; he appealed to the Supreme Court again. In the second *Nardone* case, the Court went a step further, ruling that not only could illegal wiretap conversations not be used as evidence to convict a person, they could not be used for leads that resulted in an indictment or conviction.[11] This second *Nardone* decision was based on an existing principle that law enforcement could not use the "fruit of the poisonous tree" as a basis for criminal convictions. In the same year the Court ruled, as expected, that the Federal Communications Act applies to virtually all calls, whether interstate or within a state, a ruling that is valid today.[12] The *Nardone* cases, for the first time, created limits to the broad authority granted under the *Olmstead* decision for law enforcement to install electronic surveillance freely and use the evidence in court – even if a state law made it illegal.

After the 1939 cases, law enforcement knew this much: they could not use as evidence in a trial either the contents of the conversations they overheard in violation of federal law or the information they developed as the result of the listening. But the high court had not said explicitly that they could not install the devices and continue listening.

And so they kept listening.

In 1940 a Senate committee held a hearing and concluded that federal agents were using wiretapping to investigate the political activities and beliefs of government employees and private citizens. The hearing produced a report generally critical of wiretapping as an investigative technique, and Attorney General Robert H. Jackson re-issued an official ban. But with the nation engaged in war the Senate did not enact reforms. Nor, even then, did federal agents cease using electronic surveillance.[13]

With the coming of World War II, law enforcement's rationale for wiretapping shifted from liquor and gambling violations to "subversion" from abroad or within the United States. With this shift in emphasis, what was now known as the *Federal* Bureau of Investigation could tell itself that its electronic surveillance didn't need to comply with the case law, all of which involved *domestic* cases.

The FBI's director succeeded in getting President Franklin D. Roosevelt to issue a directive on September 6, 1939, ordering the bureau to coordinate espionage and sabotage investigations and asking local authorities to cooperate. This came right on the heels of Attorney General Jackson's official ban. FBI Director Hoover used that authority from Roosevelt – and a verbal go-ahead he claimed to have received from the President in 1936 and an FDR memo in 1940 – to justify the bureau's covert activities. After a thorough analysis of surveillance since then, Athan Theoharis of Marquette University concluded in his 1978 book *Spying on Americans*, "These directives did not formally authorize FBI investigations of 'subversive activities and related matters.' By misinforming Presidents Truman and Eisenhower and then Attorneys General . . . about Roosevelt's 1939 directive, FBI Director Hoover obtained tacit approval for ongoing FBI investigations of dissident activities."[14]

> **"A tyrant should also endeavor to know**
> **what each of his subjects says or does,**
> **and should employ spies, like the . . . eavesdroppers;**
> **for the fear of informers prevents people**
> **from speaking their minds, and if they do,**
> **they are more easily found out."**
>
> **Aristotle, *Politics*, 384-322 B.C.**

The first *bugging* case reached the Supreme Court in 1942, three years after Justice Brandeis' retirement. The federal communications law was not applicable here, because there was no interception of a *wire* conversation. In its decision, the Court reached back to the *Olmstead* case, ruling that so long as no physical intrusion into the premises had taken place in installing a device, there was no violation of the Fourth Amendment protection against unreasonable searches. In this case, *Goldman v. U.S.*, federal investigators used a "detectaphone" in an adjoining office that was sensitive enough to pick up and amplify sounds in the suspects' office. A stenographer transcribed the conversations as she heard them. This is precisely the primitive technology that the Burns Detective Agency used back in 1912. What she heard were lawyers and others conspiring to violate the bankruptcy law. The interception was legal and the transcribed conversations were admissible as evidence, the Court said.[15] It was able to look past the fact that investigators had in fact trespassed the night before into the suspects' office to install another listening device in *an opening* in the office wall connected by a wire to earphones. But that device had failed to function.

The minority view on the Court that this kind of electronic "searching" was unconstitutional was becoming stronger. Through nine years of appointments, President Roosevelt by now had created a seven-member majority on the Court attuned to his more liberal politics. His appointments included former Attorney General Robert H. Jackson, who had issued the 1940 official ban on taps, and Felix Frankfurter, who seemed to share Brandeis' disdain for the practice. Justice Frank Murphy, a 1940 Roosevelt appointee, wrote in dissent in the *Goldman* case:

> "Science has brought forth far more effective devices for the invasion of a person's privacy than the direct and obvious methods of oppression which were detested by our forebears and which inspired the Fourth Amendment. Surely the spirit motivating the framers of that Amendment would abhor these new devices no less."

What about a foot-long microphone – a "spike mike" – inserted through a wall to pick up sounds through a heating duct? That was *a physical penetration*, the Court later ruled, and could not be installed without court approval. But the decision came 20 years later, in 1961, when technology and the Court's attitude towards electronic surveillance had decidedly changed. Justice Potter Stewart, in writing the Court's opinion, called it "frightening paraphernalia." Still, how long could the Court rely on the idea that the extent of physical penetration in a warrantless bug was the difference between constitutional and unconstitutional? In the 1961 case, although the device was a foot long, the penetration was a mere five-sixteenths of an inch. Then three years later the Court found that penetration by the length of a thumbtack was unconstitutional. Under this doctrine, the confidentiality of a conversation depended upon law enforcement's choice of equipment, not on a right to privacy.[16]

The director of the FBI must have regarded the *Goldman* ruling in 1942 as a green light. In the same year, Hoover authorized a program of illegal break-ins to install listening devices as well as to steal or copy documents.[17] Hoover created a separate filing system – a "Do Not File" file – to collect the secret documentation relating to the trespasses. Two years later, he persuaded an assistant attorney general, Alexander Holtzoff, to provide a Department of Justice cover for the bureau's procedures. Holtzoff's memorandum to Hoover declared, "Microphone surveillance is not equivalent to illegal search and seizure" and "Evidence so obtained should be admissible" even when "an actual trespass is committed." This does not reflect an accurate reading of the *Goldman* decision.

In 1949 Hoover directed that information about questionable electronic surveillance "which would cause embarrassment to the bureau, if distributed" should be mentioned only in a separate cover page in an investigatory file, never in the report of the investigation itself. In that way, if a court ordered the FBI to provide a defendant with an "investigative report" (a Supreme Court requirement), the defendant would never discover that he or she had been the victim of questionable electronic surveillance.[18] Bureau agents usually cited "a reliable source" whenever describing the origin of information that in fact had come from a wiretap.

In 1951, Hoover informed President Harry Truman's Attorney General, J. Howard McGrath, that the FBI was installing hidden microphones in some investigations, even if this required a trespass. Hoover said that when a trespass was involved the FBI realized the evidence was inadmissible. Still, it collected information in this way "for intelligence." McGrath responded, "Please be advised that I cannot authorize the installation of a microphone involving a trespass under existing law."

J. Edgar Hoover, typically, was undeterred. This ended his formal authorization of the practice, but not the practice itself. It continued on an informal basis, between 50 to 60 times a year, according to documents released much later.

He continued to badger Department of Justice officials to give him the latitude he said that he needed. He was successful in the early months of Dwight D. Eisenhower's administration. Later, in 1954, Eisenhower's Attorney General, Herbert Brownell, issued a secret authorization to install microphones, even with a trespass, even if the purpose were not to gather evidence for prosecution. There had been a Supreme Court decision shortly prior to that in 1954 apparently prohibiting precisely this,[19] but Brownell was able to say in his memo that the latest Court opinion didn't apply to snooping on "espionage agents, possible saboteurs, and subversive persons."[20] The Eisenhower Administration effectively rescinded the Truman Administration's ban on this kind of surveillance.

In its 1954 decision, the Supreme Court expressed disapproval of what it said was an excessive invasion of privacy in installing an illegal microphone in a bedroom. The Attorney General and the Director of the Federal Bureau of Investigation were able to rationalize to themselves that the FBI was not doing that sort of thing, and besides the bureau was pursuing political subversives and saboteurs. It created a distinction between what it was doing and what the Supreme Court had just prohibited.

By the late Fifties hysteria over national security threats within the country had subsided. But when in 1957 federal investigators uncovered and photographed a gathering of organized crime kingpins in Apalachin, New York, they effectively elevated the existence of organized crime to a nationwide concern. Federal officials then could point to the threat from organized crime syndicates as a new rationale for wiretapping. Tapping had produced crucial information about the nefarious Apalachin get-together.[21] In 1963, when an underworld informant named Joseph Valachi described in great detail in nationally televised Congressional hearings how a crime syndicate works, the public became fully aware of the threat.

And then came the olive in the martini.

A private detective in San Francisco named Hal Lipset took advantage of miniature transistor technology to develop the ultimate gimmick for showing just how covert a bugging device could be. As he prepared to testify before a Senate subcommittee in 1959, Hal Lipset had what he thought was a great idea; "First I thought I'd dazzle them with an array of miniature devices they had never seen before; then I would surprise them by playing back my own testimony from a recorder I had hidden before the hearing."[22] Not surprisingly, the senators were highly offended by Lipset's stunt and regarded it as dramatic evidence that private electronic snooping had gotten out of hand, both because of striking "improvements" in the technology and the lack of any prosecutions for violations of the weak prohibition in the current law.

Lipset learned his lesson. The next time he was asked to testify, before a hearing called by Senator Edward V. Long of Missouri in 1965, he alerted Senate staff members in advance to his plans for a dramatic gesture. In fact, the staff encouraged him to come up with something to create headlines, as Congressional staffers often do. First, Lipset thought that he would place a bug in turds produced by his pet dog. But then he realized that people might wonder why there was excrement on the witness table. Then he and his associates came up with idea of implanting a tiny microphone inside a fake olive inside a cocktail glass. "No gin was used – that would cause a short," he recalled.

Long, chair of the Senate Judiciary Subcommittee on Administrative Practice, was alerted in advance and played along, first innocently asking about flowers left at his desk. Why, said Lipset, if you look under the large petal on the left you'll see a hidden bug. The witness played back Long's opening statement (which he had tape-recorded surreptitiously). And then he demonstrated the bug in the olive, as newspaper and television cameras captured the moment.

Lipset then moved on through his testimony, but the Senators were transfixed by the martini glass. They kept referring to it. Would it work with vodka as well as gin? How about an onion, not an olive? No one seemed to care that the antenna disguised as a toothpick in the olive had a very limited range and that the microphone would not work at all if there were actually liquid in the glass. Even if it was impractical, the gimmick succeeded in showing how small and inconspicuous bugging devices could be. Senator Long told his colleagues that miniaturization could actually permit hiding a listening device in an aspirin tablet.

The public was transfixed as well. Wherever people gathered to decry the loss of privacy, the "bug in the martini" was a common reference point. "The Bug in the Martini Olive" became a catch phrase in the 1970s for the unfettered ability to intercept conversations by anyone who cared to. Divorcing spouses, unhappy suitors, labor-management negotiators, industrial spies, storefront detectives – anyone could now get a miniature covert listening device installed. And it would be extremely difficult to detect it visually.

When Hal Lipset died in 1997, *The New York Times* reported in its obituary, "Working closely with an electronics expert, Ralph Bersche, Mr. Lipset let his imagination run wild, once winning over a skeptical prospective client by playing a recording of a conversation they had had while sitting naked in a steam room. (The suspicious client had neglected to inspect his bar of soap.)"[23]

**"I felt that eavesdropping was not quite an honorable practice,
...but when a person has once taken to it,
...it is somehow very difficult to give up."**

**James Payn, English author
of *The Eavesdropper: An Unparalleled Experience*, in 1888.**

On its cover dated May 20, 1966, *Life* magazine, the most widely circulated magazine of its time, published a full-color picture of a beautiful woman pulling back her dress and revealing a tiny transmitter taped to her bare back. Inside, *Life* reported that law enforcement officials could argue that electronic surveillance helps in their work, but:

> "That justification does not exist for the growing legions of private citizens – businessmen, union officials, employers, suspicious spouses – who find it ridiculously easy to indulge in electronic spying. They can choose from a vast array of inexpensive, easy-to-install snooping devices which can be bought over the counter with no questions asked."

Accompanying the text, *Life* published an 11-inch high colored photograph of a cross-section of a tiny transmitter inside a fake plastic olive inside a cocktail glass with a clear liquid in it. "Plopped in a martini, it can transmit cocktail party conversation 100 feet," said the caption. Price: $500.

On the opposite page was a full-page photograph with the caption, "MASTER EAVESDROPPER. Bernard B. Spindel, regarded as the U.S.' No. 1 eavesdropper, uses a dentist's drill to bore holes in a tiny amplifier. It can transmit a signal from a mike 10 miles over a telephone line."

Life was correct in its prediction:

> "So rapidly is the field developing that today's devices may soon be outmoded by systems utilizing microcircuits so tiny that a transmitter made of them would be thinner and smaller than a postage stamp and could be slipped, undetected, virtually anywhere."

Life reported as well:

> "In Florida, where eavesdropping is frequently employed in divorce suits, private eyes like Jack Harwood of Palm Beach, shown above with some of his gear, do a thriving business. Harwood, who boasts, 'I'm a fantastic wire man,' was hired by tire heir Russell Firestone to keep tabs on his estranged wife, Mary Alice. She in turn got one of Harwood's assistants to sell out and work for her and, says Harwood, 'He plays just as rough with the bugs as I do.' A court recently ordered Russell and Mary Alice to stop spying on each other."

Life **magazine, 1966**   **The bug in the martini**

Elsewhere at the time, an attorney named Bruce Tara related this war story:

> "I cannot help but recall a very prominent man who was given a fine desk lamp as a gift for his office. He not only accepted it with great thanks but gave it a very prominent place in his office. The person giving him the lamp had concealed a transmitting device in the base of the lamp and was thereby able to monitor any and all conversations carried on within earshot of the lamp. (Beware of the gift horse – it may not be Trojan – it may be electronic.)"[24]

In the 1960s, federal and state investigators still could not really be sure that the evidence they had gathered by wiretapping or bugging would be admissible in a trial. Generally courts were permitting the evidence only if it was gathered without any trespassing.

In 1963, in *U.S. v. Lopez*, the Supreme Court ruled that wearing a concealed listening device on oneself was legal and the evidence was admissible.[25] In other words, an investigator or a police informer could equip himself or herself with "a wire" and tape-record a conversation with a suspect. The evidence could be used in a criminal prosecution. In *Lopez*, the court said that this was not a trespass – and that at least one party had consented to the surveillance, the person who had wired himself. We all run the risk that any of our conversations will be memorialized by a person's later note-taking or by his or her recall. A bug planted on someone to whom we speak, even if we don't know about it, does no more than assure an accurate reconstruction of the conversation, the Court ruled.

In other words, the postal inspector who wore a top hat fitted with a hidden bug to an interview with a suspect in 1895 would not be violating the law, then or currently.

The move finally to find reasonable ground rules for governmental wiretapping – and some stricter proscriptions against installations by private citizens – began, as is not uncommon in legal history, with a dissent in the U.S. Supreme Court. This time it was Justice William J. Brennan, Jr., who began a process that was to refashion the nation's approach to electronic surveillance. In his notable dissent in 1928, Justice Brandeis had *anticipated* how future technology (including what would become known as the Internet) would alter traditional Fourth Amendment assumptions. In his dissent in the *Lopez* case in 1963, Brennan also anticipated the impact of future technology on the Fourth Amendment. Brennan wanted to correct the notion of the Court's six-member majority that tape recordings were accurate renderings of a conversation. It was then generally assumed that audiotape and videotape could not be cut and spliced and altered and counterfeited, making it often unreliable as evidence. But, at least to William Brennan, it could be *anticipated* that new technology would change that. In dissent (in which he quoted the Warren-Brandeis article of 1890), he wrote:

> "A mechanical recording is not evidence that is merely repetitive or corroborative of human testimony. To be sure, it must be authenticated before it can be introduced. But once it is authenticated, its credibility does not depend upon the credibility of the human witness. Therein does a mechanical recording of a conversation differ fundamentally from, for example, notes that one of the parties to the conversation may have taken. A trier of fact [a judge or jury] credits the notes only insofar as he credits the note taker. But he credits the . . . recording not because he believes [the informer] accurately testified as to [the defendant's] statements but because he believes the [tape recorder] accurately transcribed those statements."

Certainly a person runs the risk that someone will repeat what is said in a conversation or even that someone will secretly tape record it to corroborate his or her memory. But should a person also have to run the risk that a (possibly altered) mechanical device could testify about a conversation without being corroborated by a living person who was present, Brennan asked. He wrote:

> "There is only one way to guard against such a risk, and that is to keep one's mouth shut on all occasions. . . . Surely high government officials are not the only persons who find it essential to be able to say things 'off the record.' . . . In a free society people ought not to have to watch their every word so carefully."

Four years later, in 1967, the Court invalidated New York State's permissive statute on law enforcement bugs. Justice Brennan joined the majority. The ruling sent shock waves through police ranks, even though the court did not topple the 39-year-old holding in the *Olmstead* case. The issue in *Olmstead* was whether wiretapping without any physical entry was permissible. This was not at issue in the 1967 case of *Berger v. New York*. In fact, the 60-day wiretap that collected evidence against a man named Ralph Berger of New York City was installed pursuant to a court order. On the basis of that evidence, Berger was convicted of attempting to secure a liquor license through a bribe.One reason that law enforcement people had to be upset was that the opinion by Associate Justice Tom C. Clark, who had been President Harry S. Truman's Attorney General, stated flatly that there were no statistics to prove law enforcement's claim that wiretapping is an essential technique in investigations. And Clark had been on the receiving end of J. Edgar Hoover's entreaties about investigative techniques for six years in the Department of Justice.[26]

The Court ruled that New York's scheme for securing a warrant for police to eavesdrop, "is too broad in its sweep resulting in a trespassory intrusion into a constitutionally protected area." Among other things, a warrant under the Fourth Amendment must be precise in "particularly describing the place to be searched, and the persons or things to be seized" including the nature of any conversations to be "seized." The New York law didn't do that.

There were lots of objections to the decision, especially from three dissenting members of the Court. But G. Robert Blakey, a law professor at the University of Notre Dame advising the Senate Subcommittee on Criminal Laws and Procedures, saw it as "laying down a constitutional blueprint for electronic surveillance, . . . an invitation by the Court to Congress to get down to the difficult business of drafting a fair, effective, and comprehensive electronic surveillance statute." Blakey, then 31 years old, set out to do just that. But exactly what were the perimeters available to the drafters in Congress?

Six months later, the Supreme Court provided the answers:

"The Fourth Amendment protects people, not places."[27]

The *Olmstead* ruling was dead.

The "pest" that had tormented Louis Brandeis had been tamed.

What was called "Four Decades of Indecision"[28] had ended.

What Harvard Law School privacy expert Arthur Miller called "the bizarre distinctions" were coming to an end.[29]

Once again, the principal in a Supreme Court wiretapping case was a seedy character convicted of violations related to illicit liquor or drug sales or gambling. This time it was Charles Katz of Los Angeles. Tipped that Katz was transmitting betting information by long-distance phone from a booth they had seen him use, FBI agents attached a listening device to the outside of the glass partition on the booth. Sure enough, through a tape-recorder at the other end of their wire, the agents captured incriminating conversations. On the basis of the evidence Katz was convicted in federal court. As happens in these cases, the defendant appealed to the federal Court of Appeals, which affirmed his conviction, and then to the U.S. Supreme Court. He claimed that the evidence used against him at trial was gathered illegally, and therefore should have been ruled inadmissible by the trial judge.

Seven of the nine members on the Court were ready to rein in the wiremen. They agreed that the wiretapped conversations could not be used at trial and therefore that Katz' conviction had to be reversed. Charles Katz never did serve time; federal prosecutors used him after that as a witness against other defendants.

Justice Potter Stewart wrote the opinion. There had been no trespass here, no intrusion into private property, and not even a penetration into an outside wall. (And that's one reason why Associate Justice Hugo L. Black, in a lengthy dissent, saw no violation of the Fourth Amendment. He went further to say, as the *Olmstead* decision had said, that there had not even been a seizure of tangible "things" and so the Fourth Amendment didn't even apply.) But none of that mattered, said the majority opinion. Katz had "justifiably relied" on the privacy within the phone booth.

Among many people, the *Katz* decision came to stand for the idea that the Fourth Amendment protects "reasonable expectations of privacy." But the term does not appear in the Court's opinion. (The Court itself spoke of "the privacy upon which he justifiably relied.") The idea comes from language in Associate Justice Harlan's *concurring opinion*, in which he was trying to characterize the majority opinion:

> "My understanding of the rule that has emerged from prior decisions is that there is a twofold requirement, first, that a person have exhibited an actual (subjective) expectation of privacy and, second, that the expectation be one that society is prepared to recognize as 'reasonable.'"

What the majority opinion actually said was that notions of private property and of trespass were not really relevant in protecting the constitutional right to privacy. What is relevant is what a person "seeks to preserve as private, even in an area accessible to the public." Stewart wrote:

> "The Fourth Amendment protects people, not places. What a person knowingly exposes to the public, even in his own home or office, is not a subject of Fourth Amendment protection. But what he seeks to preserve as private, even in an area accessible to the public, may be constitutionally protected."

It's a common view among lawyers and non-lawyers alike that the right to privacy – not just the Fourth Amendment, but privacy in general – provides protection where there is *a reasonable expectation of privacy* and only where there is such an expectation. But there is no basis for this in case law over the years.

Justice Stewart's language highlights an overlooked reality about the right to privacy: Many activities that take place within public view may be entitled to privacy protection, as found in the Constitution. The legal cases say as much. One has a constitutional right to expect that the government will not intrude into – nor keep a record of – the friendships and associations a person has (even if exposed to public view), the expression of political views (even in a public park), a person's comings and goings for medical treatment or to worship, or one's physical appearance or choice of dress (which is inevitably within view of others).

Henceforth, after the *Katz* decision, electronic surveillance could be installed only under the strictures of a "reasonable search and seizure" with a court warrant. The warrant must be issued in advance (except in emergencies and "exigent" circumstances), based on a sworn statement of particulars, with a time limit and a precise description of the premises, and evidence of probable cause that a crime had been committed.

While the Court had been considering its two pivotal cases, both the Executive Branch and Congress had been moving to fashion workable guidelines for wiretapping. The *Berger* and *Katz* decisions now made the efforts urgent. Except for the weak protections in the 1934 federal law – enacted long before transistors and before inexpensive and portable over-the-counter tape recorders and before fake olives – there were no prohibitions against amateur phone tappers, as opposed to law enforcement officers. Against persons who installed room bugs, there were no protections, not even the 1934 law. Nicholas de B. Katzenbach, Attorney General under President Lyndon B. Johnson, said, "It would be difficult to devise a law more totally unsatisfactory." (A 1966 regulation by the Federal Communications Commission technically requires telephone companies to prohibit private persons from tape-recording a telephone conversation without the consent of all parties. But it provides no criminal penalty; the sole penalty for violations is loss of telephone service. In 1978, the FCC removed a requirement that a "beep" on the line warn that a telephone call is being recorded.)

Amid all the obsessions with governmental use of electronic eavesdropping, policy makers and prosecutors had devoted very little attention at all to eavesdropping by private citizens. Between 1954 and 1961 in the entire nation there had been only 12 prosecutions and 10 convictions for violations of Section 605 by private parties. Prosecutions in states that prohibited wiretapping by law were virtually non-existent. (In the 1990s, the situation had not changed much; there was an average of only seven persons each year convicted of the crime in the mid-Nineties, and a total of 15 in the year 1997. This amounted to one person per 100 million population being punished for illegal wiretapping.)[30] Prosecutors simply find it hard to convict suspects of this crime or they give it a low priority in their agendas.

Beginning in 1961, the Kennedy and Johnson Administrations had been submitting proposals to Congress to clarify the limits of legal wiretaps. At the same time, the Federal Bureau of Investigation and other federal agencies were still using electronic surveillance – without any court supervision. The Department of Justice continued its tortured theory that the 1934 act permitted Justice agents to intercept telephone calls so long as no *disclosure* of the contents outside the department occurred.[31]

In Senator Long's hearings, Senator Wayne Morse of Oregon pointed out:

> "Even though the official policy of the various federal agencies of government has been to restrict the use of electronic monitoring excepting in cases where national security was involved, the Long Subcommittee has revealed that over 60 government agencies have at their disposal extensive electronic monitoring gear. The committee finds that these agencies do not hesitate to use such devices as part of the normal investigative procedure."[32]

Since 1964, the Department of Justice had been making lots of federal money available for localities to purchase the latest snooping gear. This was during the military build-up for the war in Vietnam, and critics began to detect what some called a "paint-it-blue syndrome." That meant that military contractors would develop fancy electronics for the Vietnam War and then "paint it blue" and market the same devices to the cops back in the U.S. There had been a variation on the "paint-it-blue syndrome" in the previous century. The first experts on wiretapping were men trained in the devices during their Civil War military service.

After the *Berger* and *Katz* decisions, Senator John L. McClellan, Democrat of Arkansas, convened hearings of his Judiciary Subcommittee on Criminal Laws. This was the seventeenth set of Congressional hearings on the subject since 1934.[33] Within a few months the subcommittee fashioned a bill that would essentially prohibit anyone from using electronic surveillance unless one party to a conversation had consented to it or unless it was a law-enforcement installation with permission from a court. In other words, a private party could not install a listening device unless at least one person in a telephone conversation had given consent. Influential Republicans in Congress were cooperating in the effort once and for all to establish national standards for eavesdropping.

Coincidentally, back in 1965, President Lyndon B. Johnson appointed a Commission on Law Enforcement and Administration of Justice to come up with recommendations "to get tough on crime." This was in response to public fear about street crime, organized crime, anti-war dissidents on university campuses and elsewhere, urban demonstrations among African-Americans, and a political assassination. (Malcolm X, the black nationalist leader, had been shot down in February.) The commissioners spent a lot of time debating what to do about law-enforcement wiretapping, with Robert Blakey acting as a consultant, just as he was to do for the McClellan Senate subcommittee three years later. In January of 1967, as the commission was finishing up its work, President Johnson made clear where his administration stood. In his State of the Union message that month, he said:

> "We should protect what Justice Brandeis called 'the right most valued by civilized men' – the right to privacy. We should outlaw all wiretapping, public and private . . . except when the security of the nation itself is at stake and only then with the strictest safeguards. We should exercise the full reach of our constitutional powers to outlaw electronic 'bugging' and 'snooping.'"

Less than a month after the President's State of the Union speech, Johnson's crime study commission announced recommendations that were far more permissive on wiretapping than the President or his current Attorney General would have liked.

Some members of the commission recommended no eavesdropping by the government. But a majority recommended "carefully circumscribed authority for electronic surveillance to law enforcement officers" consistent with the *Berger* case then being considered by the Supreme Court. Katzenbach, whom Johnson had moved to the number-two job at the Department of State, generally supported the recommendation of the commission that he chaired. At least on one of the crime commission's findings there could be agreement: "The present status of the law is intolerable."[34]

Johnson's brand-new Attorney General at the time, Ramsey Clark, regarded wiretapping as ineffective in law enforcement, even against organized crime. His Department of Justice disavowed the recommendations of the Katzenbach report. The Executive Branch was no longer insisting that Congress grant it wide-ranging authority to use wiretaps in criminal investigations. In March, he so testified before the House Judiciary Committee. For too long, he told Senator Long's subcommittee later, his colleagues in the Justice Department had interpreted the 1934 law as saying "that interception alone is not an offense." Attorney General Clark sent a proposal to Congress, the Right of Privacy Act, that would have kept the government out of the wiretapping business except in cases when the President ordered it to confront a "serious threat to the security of the United States."[35] (After he left office, Clark told a Congressional committee in 1971 that 26 federal agencies, including the FBI, the Central Intelligence Agency, the Postal Service, the U.S. Army, and the Selective Service, had engaged in wiretapping during the time that the Johnson Administration had been discouraging its use. And, all this time, the Department of Justice was funding purchases of electronic equipment by local and state police forces. There was also evidence that Johnson enjoyed the fruits of illegal eavesdropping, even if he disavowed the practice publicly.)[36]

Clark's father, Tom C. Clark, had expressed the identical view about the ineffectiveness of wiretapping in the majority opinion he wrote in the *Berger* case in 1967. (As Attorney General himself in the 1940s, however, the father had acceded to FBI demands to expand its wiretapping authority in investigations involving national security threats.) Justice Clark announced in 1967 that he would retire from the Supreme Court so that his son could become Attorney General without a conflict of interest. For a few months, there was an actual conflict. Ramsey Clark was appointed attorney general on March 10, 1967, and testified twice against wiretapping at the same time that his father was drafting the *Berger* opinion against wiretapping. Only when the Court announced Justice Clark's *Berger* decision, on June 12, 1967, did Tom Clark leave the Court.

J. Edgar Hoover, at least outside the FBI, made a total about-face on electronic surveillance. In March of 1965 Attorney General Katzenbach had ordered him to get the Attorney General's approval for all electronic surveillance. In September Hoover notified Katzenbach that he was eliminating the use of bugs and curtailing other covert surveillance. Hoover was most likely responding to President Johnson's strong distaste for wiretapping. Incredibly, Hoover now was willing to shrug his shoulders in front of Congress. He told the Long investigating committee in 1967:

> "I don't see what all the excitement is about. I would have no hesitance in discontinuing all techniques – [what Hoover called] technical coverage, microphones, trash covers, mail covers, etc. While it might handicap us, I doubt they are as valuable as some believe and none warrant FBI being used to justify them."

Hoover could recognize the political and legal trends. He saw the split recommendations of the crime commission, Johnson's strong words, the Department of Justice's lack of enthusiasm about granting wiretap authority, and the *Katz* and *Berger* decisions from the Supreme Court.

Members of Congress saw the same trends, but they also heard the strong dissenting opinions in both Supreme Court cases, and Republican Presidential candidate Richard M. Nixon's "get tough" entreaties. There was no enactment of a wiretapping law in 1967.

And 1968 was an election year – and one of the most turbulent years in the Twentieth Century. Nixon was campaigning effectively for President on a theme of "law and order." Congress was not about to ban all domestic wiretapping.

An excerpt from a Supreme Court opinion that same year showed – despite the "clarification" in the Berger and Katz opinions – the utter confusion that was presented to any law enforcement officer: "In view of the *Nardone* and *Benanti* decisions, the doctrine of *Schwartz v. Texas* cannot survive the demise of *Wolf v. Colorado*."[37] It sounded as if the Court expected police officers to have copies of four different legal opinions with them when they installed eavesdropping devices.By June, Congress had an agreement. It enacted the Omnibus Crime Control and Safe Streets Act, Title III of which began:

> "To safeguard the privacy of innocent persons, the interception of wire or oral communications where none of the parties to the communication has consented to the interception should be allowed only when authorized by a court of competent jurisdiction and should remain under the control and supervision of the authorizing court."[38]

Under the law, federal agents planning electronic installations must secure a warrant in advance from a federal court. An application for a warrant must be based on probable cause that a crime has been committed or is about to be committed and state why other investigative techniques are unlikely to succeed. A warrant will be approved only in investigations of certain major federal crimes. There are expedited procedures for emergencies. Evidence gathered in violation of the law will not be admissible in a trial. Agents must *minimize* the recording of irrelevant conversations. The contents of the tapes may be divulged only under carefully guarded circumstances. And within 30 days of the end of the surveillance, the court must provide a full report to the Administrative Office of the United States Courts in Washington, which issues a cumulative report in May of each following year. Further, within 90 days of wiretapping or bugging, the target of the surveillance, and sometimes other persons overheard in conversations, must be notified of the surveillance. The law provides similar procedures for surveillance by state authorities, if the state has its own wiretap-authorizing law. Just about all states have wiretapping statutes, 10 of them virtually identical to the federal law.

"Must everyone live in fear that every word he speaks may be transmitted or recorded and later repeated to the entire world? I can imagine nothing that has a more chilling effect on people speaking their minds."

Supreme Court Justice William O. Douglas, in 1971.[39]

Title III, also known as the federal wiretap law, is silent on procedures for using other new electronic devices that do not record the contents of conversations but capture electronic data. These include a "pen register," which logs the telephone numbers dialed from a targeted phone; a "trap and trace" device, which logs phone numbers of all incoming calls; or a "bumper beeper," which transmits the whereabouts of a vehicle.

Addressing non-law enforcement taps, Title III makes clear that "any person who willfully intercepts, endeavors to intercept, or procures any other person to intercept or endeavor to intercept, any wire or oral communication; or . . . willfully discloses . . . the contents of any wire or oral communication knowing or having reason to know that the information was obtained through the interception of a wire or oral communication in violation [of this law]" is guilty of a crime. Prosecutors have not pressed many charges for violations of this section for several reasons. One is that their resources are consumed by more serious crimes. Eavesdropping in marital disputes or political fights are often winked at, not viewed seriously.

The drafters of the 1968 wiretap law undoubtedly built upon the prohibition in the 1934 communications act, but included an important exception: *It is not a violation of federal law to intercept a conversation if one party to it provides consent,* so long as the interception is not for purposes of committing a crime or tort. Thus, under federal law, it's not a crime to tape-record your own phone conversations because as one of the parties to the conversation you're consenting to it. (Tape-recording your own telephone calls still may violate a telephone company rule that the government requires as a condition of granting the company permission – a "tar-iff" – to operate a phone system.)

The laws in California, Connecticut, Florida, Hawaii, Illinois, Louisiana, Maryland, Massachusetts, Montana, Nevada, New Hampshire, Oregon, Pennsylvania, and Washington are more strict than the federal law; they require the consent of *both parties*, or *all parties*, in the conversation before it may be intercepted by a private party. (A state prosecutor indicted Linda Tripp for secretly tape recording her telephone conversations from her home in Maryland as Monica Lewinsky described her sexual activities with President Bill Clinton. Tripp consented to the recording, of course; but in Maryland she needed the consent of *both* parties to the conversation, and Lewinsky was unaware of it.)

There are two other important exceptions to the general federal prohibition: It does not apply to providers of telephone services, which of course must monitor the quality of their equipment. More importantly, it does not apply to "an operator of a switchboard," who intercepts and discloses conversations as a "necessary incident to the rendition of his service or to the protection of the rights or property of the carrier of such communication." Over the years, this language has been broadly interpreted to permit any entity that has phone service (not necessarily "a switchboard") to monitor the telephone calls of employees. It is the basis for what companies call "service monitoring" of employees' telephone calls, mainly those employees who deal over the phone with the public.

But this broad latitude extends only to monitoring to protect the rights or property of the organization or for assuring the quality of its service. Thus, it does not extend to intercepting purely *personal* conversations that have no impact on the business.

The 1968 law also makes it a federal crime to manufacture, distribute, possess, advertise, sell, or ship any electronic device *primarily useful* for surreptitious monitoring of conversations. The phrase "primarily useful" has been a significant deterrent to vigorous enforcement of this provision. Companies engaged in making or selling listening devices – like "spy shops" and retail electronic stores throughout the U.S. – can argue that voice-activated tape recorders, miniature recorders, and other high-tech devices are primarily useful for benign purposes, not illegal eavesdropping.

"Title III, in the form proposed by the administration was properly described as the Right to Privacy Act," opined Senator Hiram Fong of Hawaii. "As accepted by Congress, Title III is more appropriately described as the End to Privacy Act."[40] This is a common trait in Congress. Proposed laws advertised as great protections of privacy end up – because of loopholes inserted into the text – leaving Americans with less privacy than they had before the bill became law. Look at the Bank Secrecy Act of 1970, which in fact requires banks to provide to federal authorities piles and piles of data about customers' transactions. The Financial Right to Privacy Act of 1978 actually authorizes federal agents to have access to customer records held by banks. The Social Security Independence Act of 1994 requires jurors to provide Social Security numbers. In the same way, in George Orwell's anti-utopian novel, *1984*, slogans and titles took on opposite meaning, as in "Freedom is slavery."

President Johnson didn't like Title III at all. He signed the omnibus crime bill because many of its elements had been suggested by his administration in the wake of the assassinations of Martin Luther King, Jr. and Senator Robert F. Kennedy in 1968. Perhaps influenced by Attorney General Ramsey Clark (and ignoring J. Edgar Hoover), Johnson grumbled when he signed the bill that his administration would continue to confine "wiretapping and eavesdropping to national security cases only – and then only with the approval of the Attorney General." He urged Congress to repeal the "unwise" provisions in Title III.[41]

Clark didn't use the authority granted by Title III to the Department of Justice for the six months remaining in his tenure as Attorney General. He told federal agents not to exercise their powers in the new law. The Attorney General viewed electronic eavesdropping as both immoral and ineffective.[42]

His successors as attorney general utilized the authority, however, beginning with the Nixon Administration's John N. Mitchell. Here are the statistics on wiretap installations approved by federal courts in the years since Title III was enacted:

Nixon	
1969	33
1970	182
1971	285
1972	206
1973	130
Nixon/Ford	
1974	121

Ford

1975	108
1976	137

Carter

1977	77
1978	81
1979	87
1980	81

Reagan

1981	106
1982	130
1983	208
1984	289
1985	243
1986	250
1987	236
1988	293

Bush

1989	310
1990	324
1991	356
1992	340

Clinton

1993	450
1994	554
1995	532
1996	581
1997	569
1998	566
1999	601
2000	479

Bush

2001	486
2002	497

The numbers show, first, the enthusiasm in the Nixon Administration for the new wiretapping authority; then, after Richard Nixon left office discredited, the abrupt public distaste for eavesdropping, because of the Watergate scandal; next, the Reagan Administration's pursuit of drug offenses; and, finally, the record-breaking increases in the Clinton years, also mainly in drug-related investigations.

The numbers seem modest enough, until you include two factors: The number of installations by state investigators rises with the federal totals; they usually total from 100 percent to 200 percent of the yearly federal figure. Also, a single wiretap overhears, on average, a total of about 200 persons and 2,000 conversations. That means that the combination of federal and state taps in 1997, for instance, overheard an estimated 237,000 individuals and 2.5 million conversations.

Part of the obstacle in enacting wiretap legislation before and after World War II had been disagreement between the Executive Branch and Congress over authority to install surveillance in cases involving national security, whatever that meant. One thing it meant was that whenever administrations – Democratic or Republican – felt that a wiretap was needed to protect major threats to the U.S. – it would go ahead with the surveillance, without any approval by a court. The Roosevelt, Truman, Eisenhower, Kennedy, and Johnson administrations had done this a total of about 10,000 times, according to figures released in 1975.[43] The Johnson Administration exerted this authority far less than its predecessors did.

The Executive Branch (including the Johnson Administration) had continually sought unfettered, warrantless authority to resort to wiretapping in such cases; members of Congress were adamantly opposed. The result of the stalemate was that there was no legislation at all. In 1968, Attorney General Katzenbach and Senate Republican leader Everett M. Dirksen reached an agreement that resulted in an unsatisfactory compromise. Title III as passed simply excluded "national security" wiretaps from any restrictions at all:

> "Nothing contained in this chapter or Section 605 of the Communications Act of 1934 shall limit the constitutional power of the President to take such measures as he deems necessary to protect the Nation against actual or potential attack or other hostile acts of a foreign power, to obtain foreign intelligence information deemed essential to the security of the United States, or to protect national security information against foreign intelligence activities. Nor shall anything contained in this chapter be deemed to limit the constitutional power of the President to take such measures as he deems necessary to protect the United States against the overthrow of the Government by force or other unlaw-

ful means, or against any other clear and present danger to the structure or existence of the Government."

Professor Blakey, who had helped Democrats draft the legislation and who had recommended a provision much like the one that eventually passed, looked back in 1976 and declared:

> "The inclusion of the language was probably one of the prices that had to be paid for the passage of the general criminal and civil provisions protecting privacy and the court order system strengthening law enforcement. I was not entirely convinced in 1968 that its inclusion was wise. Events since have convinced me that it was probably unwise."[44]

Richard M. Nixon liked unfettered authority for wiretapping in cases of national security. In fact, he used the mantra of "national security" to avoid disclosing actions by his administration to foil the activities of dissidents opposing the War in Vietnam or racism. He borrowed a technique of J. Edgar Hoover's as well, ordering the FBI to keep no records or indexes on any electronic surveillance installed under the "national security" authority. Later he ordered the Department of Justice to transfer any records that existed to the White House.

Attorney General Mitchell said that the "national security" authority in the 1968 law would permit wiretaps of *domestic* groups, without a warrant. During his time the Department of Justice admitted that it had used this "national security" authority to wiretap persons involved in purely domestic activities. There had been no court warrant and no probable cause of criminal activity. This was legal under the President's inherent powers to protect the nation, the department said. Nixon called the public objections to this "hysteria."[45]

"There was of course no way of knowing whether you were being watched at any given moment. . . . You had to live – did live, from habit that became instinct – in the assumption that every sound you made was overheard, and, except in darkness, every movement scrutinized."

George Orwell in *1984*.

By an 8-0 vote the Supreme Court in 1972 rejected the Nixon Administration's approach. It is true that the 1968 law did not limit the powers of the President in investigations involving the national security, the Court said, but the Fourth Amendment does. The authority to install electronic surveillance without court approval does not extend to threats *within the U.S.* from dissidents, radicals, or anyone else who has "no significant connection with a foreign power, its agents, or agencies." The President's broad "national security" authority is reserved for collecting or protecting *foreign* intelligence or combating *foreign* threats to the U.S.[46] (The Nixon Administration did not give up on this point; in 1975 the U.S. Court of Appeals had to tell it, no, the President has no authority to wiretap without a warrant domestic groups like the Jewish Defense League even if the installation is somehow related to foreign matters.)[47]

The Supreme Court's youngest and newest member did not participate in the 1972 ruling. He was William H. Rehnquist, who as an assistant attorney general had provided the intellectual underpinning and legal justification for Nixon's bold assertion of Presidential authority. Rehnquist defended the policy in testimony before the Senate Subcommittee on Constitutional Rights in March 1971. The 47-year-old lawyer said that federal power to investigate cases where the Executive Branch felt the nation was threatened derived from the President's inherent powers in the Constitution to "take Care that the Laws be faithfully executed." "Implicit in the duty of the President to oversee the faithful execution of the laws is the power to investigate and prevent the violation of federal law," he told North Carolina Senator Sam Ervin and other members of the subcommittee.

Rehnquist expressed no fear that this wide-open power could be abused. To the contrary, in a passage that has been quoted by dissident groups ever since, Rehnquist testified,

> "I think it quite likely that self-discipline on the part of the executive branch will provide an answer to virtually all of the legitimate complaints against excesses of information gathering. . . . Isolated imperfections . . . should not be permitted to obscure the fundamental necessity and importance of federal information gathering, or the genuinely high level of performance in this area by the organizations involved."[48]

Rehnquist had no basis for his assertions. Further, he was concealing abuses within the Executive Branch that he was in a position to know about. In the hemorrhage of disclosures about Watergate-related abuses, it was revealed that not only had Rehnquist provided intellectual cover for Nixon's unfettered snooping on and harassment of U.S. citizens but also that he was very close to the action.[49]

One year after he justified the Nixon Administration policy in testimony before the U.S. Senate, Rehnquist as a member of the U.S. Supreme Court was asked to review the constitutionality of that policy. Reluctantly, he disqualified himself from the case.

Just two days before the Supreme Court decision on the President's claim of "inherent power" to violate the privacy of American citizens for broadly defined "national security purposes," operatives of the Nixon White House were arrested for engineering a break-in at the Watergate office of the Democratic National Committee for purposes of installing listening devices. The extent of Nixon's own direct involvement in this scheme was never made known publicly; he continually invoked "national security" as a rationale for not disclosing information about the litany of privacy abuses that came to be known under the rubric of "Watergate."

Among the Watergate disclosures was evidence that in the early months of his Presidency, in the spring of 1969, Nixon ordered the FBI to install wiretaps on the home or office telephones of 13 current or former government officials and four news reporters. (One of the targets was Nixon speech writer William Safire, who was so offended that years afterwards as a columnist for *The New York Times* he crusaded repeatedly for protection against electronic surveillance and other high-tech intrusions by government agencies.) In late 1970 the Secret Service even installed a wiretap on the telephone of Donald Nixon, the President's brother. There was no legal authority for any of this electronic surveillance.

It is no wonder that alarmed civil libertarians came to agree with Robert Blakey, one of the drafters of the 1968 wiretap law, that the law's silence on "national security" surveillance was a mistake.

The 1968 legislation also established a National Commission for the Review of Federal and State Laws Related to Wiretapping and Electronic Surveillance, which began meeting in 1974. Its chair was Justice William H. Erickson of the Colorado Supreme Court. Members included Professor Blakey, then of Cornell Law School; Alan F. Westin, the Columbia University scholar who had written

Privacy and Freedom in 1967 and an informed law review article earlier in 1952 on the status of electronic surveillance; Democratic Senator John L. McClellan and Republican Senator Roman Hruska; and the grandson of the man who had written the majority opinion in *Olmstead v. U.S.*, Congressman Robert Taft Jr., of Ohio.

Westin could not resist observing that the impressive documents appointing him to the commission in 1973 were signed by the President "destined to go down in history as the chief executive whose administration used wiretapping and electronic eavesdropping more than any other in illegal pursuits, and in ways that fundamentally violated the citizenry's constitutional rights of privacy and due process." That was Richard Nixon. The appointment was also signed by a Secretary of State who was sued by one of his assistants for ordering a wiretap placed on the assistant's home telephone. That was Henry Kissinger.[50]

Westin said that his experience on the study commission had "a strangely dream-like quality," because the group studiously avoided any discussion of electronic-surveillance abuses by the FBI, the CIA, and the White House in the previous months. While the commission was at work, newspapers and television news were providing a steady stream of new disclosures about wiretapping abuses during the Nixon years.

There were three crucial areas that the commission did not scrutinize adequately. One was the lack of legal protections against interception of non-voice, data communications. The law covered only "aural" communications (what could be heard by ear), and by 1973, as the commission members were told, the percentage of long-distance traffic devoted to *data*, not spoken conversations, was approaching 50 per cent. In other words, it was perfectly legal at the time to intercept a massive telephone transmission of payroll information or medical files, for instance, but not a spoken conversation between two persons discussing the same information. It took Congress 14 years to close that huge gap in federal law, despite repeated warnings.

Next, the commission did not tackle the question of the appropriateness of the tacit approval from Congress for the Executive Branch to install wiretaps to collect or to defend foreign intelligence (known as national security taps).

Lastly, Westin, in a dissent to the wiretap commission report, echoed Louis Brandeis' fears about new types of snooping technologies. He identified the third gap in the federal eavesdropping law:

"Title III also did not include the use of *visual* surveillance techniques and technology within its regulatory scheme. It is very hard to see why it did not, given the fact that penetrating places where individuals go in the reasonable expectation that they will have privacy for their actions is as much a part of the constitutional right to privacy as the enjoyment of private speech. Furthermore, the rapid development and proliferation of new photographic surveillance devices during the past decade, and their growing use by law enforcement and private investigators, makes this a topic of prime importance for application of privacy safeguards. At the least, the use of cameras, closed-circuit TV mechanisms, and long-distance scanning devices to observe persons not in plain public view but on private premises and taking reasonable precautions to be in private, could be subjected to warrant procedures, preservation of evidence rules, and similar controls in the spirit of Title III."

The reason that Congress did not include protections for video surveillance without sound is that in 1968 no one anticipated that video equipment would be small enough and inexpensive enough to be in the hands of individuals, much less that it would be small enough to hide while it was in use.

Private eye and wireman extraordinaire Hal Lipset had his own explanation:

"The reason – beyond the fact that insurance companies [which use hidden cameras] have a more powerful lobby than private investigators [who use audio] – is that to the public mind, photographs are safe, recordings are dangerous. A photograph, people think, can't be faked. An expert can always tell. But a recording is inexplicable. People are afraid of it, afraid that what they say in a moment of anger may be the painful truth; afraid their words will be misconstrued or, worse, may be altered by someone else."[51]

By 1986, however, when Congress amended the 1968 wiretap law, the capabilities of hand-held video cameras were well known. Congressional committees even had a legal ruling by a prominent federal appeals court judge in the Midwest begging them to fix this problem. While overturning a trial judge who had disallowed use of 130 hours of court-approved FBI videotaping of alleged bomb-making by a secret Puerto Rican terrorist group, U.S. Circuit Court of Appeals Judge Richard Posner nonetheless wrote in the year of 1984:

> "Television surveillance is identical *in its indiscriminate character* to wiretapping and bugging. . . . We would think it a very good thing if Congress responded to the issues discussed in this opinion by amending Title III to bring television surveillance within its scope."[52]

Robert W. Kastenmeier, Democrat Congressman from Wisconsin, a dissenting member of the 1976 wiretap commission, was listening. He introduced a bill in 1985 to do exactly that. Still, Congress failed to act, to include protections against visual electronic surveillance without sound or even to authorize TV surveillance with or without a warrant. Judge Posner had written in 1984, "Television surveillance (with no soundtrack) just is not within the statute's domain." That is still true.

In Nixon's last year in office, the number of taps or bugs installed to collect or protect foreign intelligence information – without any court approval or supervision – surpassed the number installed in criminal cases with court approval under the 1968 wiretap law. President Gerald Ford's Attorney General, former University of Chicago Law Dean Edward H. Levi, not only reined in the FBI's infiltration tactics, he also chopped the number of national-security taps in half. The administration of Jimmy Carter then brought the frequency back to the level of the Nixon years.[53] Carter's Attorney General, Griffin Bell, told Congress that no American citizens were the targets of this surveillance, but because most of the taps were installed on foreign embassies in Washington, Americans who did business with the embassies were certainly overheard on these interceptions. Based on evidence at trials and information disclosed by the government, experts estimated that half a million persons were overheard on these warrantless taps.

Carter officials said that, under current law, if the administration had sought court warrants in national-security cases, it would have been conceding that the President does not have the authority to order such surveillance without court approval. At the same time, the Carter Administration was supporting legislation to require court approval. (It also reduced the number of installations in criminal investigations.)

Eventually, legislation drafted by the Department of Justice and by Senator Edward M. Kennedy of Massachusetts was approved in 1978, setting up a special seven-member court of judges assigned from other federal courts to meet in secret in Washington to approve applications for foreign-intelligence eavesdropping. The law says that the court must approve an application to install a listening device, but that application need not be based on probable cause of criminal activity, as in the case of Title III. Enactment of the Foreign Intelligence Surveillance Act of 1978[54] meant that virtually all electronic surveillance conducted by federal and state investigators without the consent of at least one party to the conversation must be approved in advance by a court – either a federal or state court reviewing applications in criminal cases or the special court reviewing foreign-intelligence taps. President Carter issued an executive order in 1978 prohibiting the Central Intelligence Agency from using electronic surveillance within the United States.

In 1985, Representative Kastenmeier, in addition to his proposal on national-security taps, introduced a separate bill to make clear that the growing mass of *data* communications on telephone lines was protected to the same extent as oral conversations. Thus, a warrant would be required to intercept them. Senators Patrick Leahy of Vermont and Charles McC. Mathias of Maryland introduced similar legislation in the Senate. Both proposals also would have required court approval for installing pen registers, "trap and trace" devices, and "bumper beepers." Civil libertarians and the telephone companies endorsed the proposals, but President Ronald Reagan's Department of Justice testified that current law was adequate to protect digital transmissions. After the sponsors persuaded the Justice Department to accept the bill, it had clear sailing in the Democratic House. In the fall of 1986, the Senate approved the proposal and President Reagan signed it as the Electronic Communications Privacy Act of 1986.[55] It amended the federal wiretap law to protect *cellular telephones, electronic mail, pagers, and electronic data transmissions.* Semi-public communications like paging devices with no message (only a tone), ham radio, mobile and airline radios, police scanners, and the radio portion of a cordless phone call are not covered. In other words, neither consent nor a warrant is needed to overhear them. In the first year of enactment, the Reagan Administration sought approval for eavesdropping on 55 of the new-generation technologies, and state prosecutors sought approval 13 times.

The new technologies – plus services like call forwarding, voice mail, electronic messaging and conference calls, as well as consumer choices in long-distance service – were providing telephone users with unprecedented flexibility in configuring telephone devices for their personal convenience. But the FBI was edgy, feeling that these new technologies and services were making it difficult to install listening devices and actually expect that they would capture conversations of the targeted persons. The bureau said that it had no capability, for instance, to intercept integrated services digital networks (ISDN), the increasingly common capacity for transmitting high-speed video, voice, and data all over the same phone line. It was easy to tap the traditional analog system of transmitting calls, but the bureau insisted that telephone companies must be required to alter their new digital systems so that the FBI could maintain the same ability to install intercepting devices.

The FBI persuaded the Bush Administration in its last months and then the incoming Clinton Administration of the urgency of its "digital telephony" proposal. Vice President Al Gore embraced the idea wholeheartedly. Civil libertarians were outraged. Members of Congress were skeptical. For nearly two years the bureau could not get a single member to sponsor the proposal. But it got its new director, former federal judge Louis Freeh, to breathe new life into the proposal late in 1993.

The FBI agreed to include in its proposal language that law enforcement agencies, in order to get access to customer information from on-line Internet providers like America On-Line, must procure an administrative subpoena or comparable legal process based on "specific and articulable facts." This standard is higher than police need to procure lists of telephone numbers called by a customer and to get customer records from a financial institution, but it is lower than that required to listen in on the content of telephone calls or electronic mail.

The addition of these protections caused some public interest groups in Washington to accept the "digital telephony" legislation, although other groups continued to oppose it. In fact, disagreement over whether to accept the digital telephony legislation created a schism among privacy advocacy groups that remains today. With the administration pushing the proposal, members of Congress agreed in 1994 to enact legislation approving the FBI proposal in most respects. For the first time in the Twentieth Century, Congress moved to alter the ground rules on telephone interception without considered debate. The central provision of the Communications Assistance for Law Enforcement Act of 1994 states:

> "A telecommunications carrier shall ensure that its equipment, facilities, or services. . . are capable of expeditiously

isolating and enabling the government, pursuant to a court order or other lawful authorization, to intercept, to the exclusion of other communications, all wire and electronic communications carried by the carrier within a service area to or from equipment [and] to access call-identifying information."[56]

In other words, telephone companies would have to redesign their technologies so that law enforcement could continue to have the capability to conduct electronic surveillance. Manufacturers of phone equipment would have to do the same. Further, the law eased police access to "call-identifying information." The FBI said after the act was passed that the law authorizes the bureau to determine the ultimate destination of a call to a targeted individual. The FBI says that it needs to know the digits that a person punches *after* a phone call is completed, apparently to trace a call to a particular extension. But this could also include access to account numbers when a person uses a long-distance calling card, bank-account numbers, a personal identifying number (PIN), or a code for accessing voice-mail messages, because these too are "call-identifying information."

The inclusion of "call-identifying information" in the language of the law is important. In conventional telephone transmissions, access to the routing information that directs a call on its way doesn't do you much good if you are looking for access to the *content* of a call. But in Internet transmissions of phone calls, an increasingly common occurrence, the content and routing information are transmitted in such a way that they may be inseparable. If so, law-enforcement access to "call-identifying information" could end up giving it access to the content of conversations as well, without a warrant specifically stating this.

Telephone companies hated the proposal. And who would pay for all of this? Congress agreed to authorize an astounding $500 million of taxpayers' money to reimburse the telephone companies. That's more than Congress provides to the National Institute on Alcohol Abuse or to support historically black colleges. When Congress tossed in a promise of money, the telephone companies swallowed hard and went along with the idea.

But in Congress, *authorizing* funds is not the same as *appropriating* them. In the years following enactment of the law, the political parties in Congress could not agree how, or whether, actually to fund the scheme. Civil-liberties lobbyists in Washington told Congress that the Federal Bureau of Investigation had not yet complied with the law in laying out its exact needs. In any event, said watchdog groups like the Electronic Privacy Information Center, the FBI was trying to push phone companies into design changes not required by the act. For instance the bureau said that it is entitled to listen in on a conference call once the target of its warrant has hung up, entitled to know the location of a targeted cell-telephone caller, entitled to know whether a target has voice mail, and entitled to record the voice mail. The bureau's wish list went far beyond what Congress had in mind in passing the law, according to James X. Dempsey, who had helped hammer out the original language when he worked for the House of Representatives. His organization, the Center for Democracy and Technology, began arguing that the FBI was going far beyond the compromise authorization that CDT itself had endorsed in 1994.

As law enforcement lobbyists were quick to point out, the "CALEA" legislation did not confer any new authority on law enforcement; court approval, based on probable cause, would still be required for electronic surveillance.

Still, for the first time, the legislation mandated that America's system of telephonic communications would have to be redesigned to facilitate criminal investigations. From its invention until 1994, telephone technology had been designed exclusively to enhance communications. Telephone executives had made this point to the Supreme Court in the *Olmstead* case in 1928. Now, the Communications Assistance to Law Enforcement Act would require altering technological development for another purpose – investigating crimes.

The CALEA law marked the first significant retreat in providing privacy protection for telephone use since the Supreme Court's decision in the *Olmstead* case.

Links

For more on J. Edgar Hoover's inquisitiveness, continue on to the next chapter, on Sex.

For the development of the constitutional right to privacy, go to the chapter on The Constitution.

For more on William H. Rehnquist's impact on constitutional rights, go to the chapter on The Constitution.

For an insight into Richard M. Nixon's contribution to *pro-privacy* legal developments, see the chapter on <u>Torts</u>.

To read about the development of concern about "informational privacy" at the same time that the 1968 wiretapping law was enacted, go to the chapter on <u>Databanks</u>.

Sex

A G-man targets secret sex in motels, the 1990s bring more disclosure but not more comfort with sex, and an 1870s Clintonesque scandal changes formerly casual attitudes.

J. Edgar Hoover had a view on just about everything – and a covert private life that most likely included some of the behavior he publicly condemned. Over his 55-year career, Hoover used his regular newspaper columns, his articles in popular magazines, the books that he wrote, FBI consultation with the producers of radio and television crime shows, and well-attended public lectures to alert the public to threats that Hoover and his G-men found in Twentieth-Century life in America.

Among his targets: intellectuals, the weak-minded ("jellyfish"), parental permissiveness, civil rights activism, the dangers of hiring baby sitters and of playing bridge, self indulgence, neglect of duty, the international Communist conspiracy, "the danger from within" and public lethargy, violence portrayed on television, and "sexual goings on."

In the late 1930s he and his agents discovered the popularity of tourist camps or motor courts – what we today call motels. Hoover devoted his regular ghostwritten article in the popular monthly, *American Magazine*, to warning the American people of the dangers that lurked in these substitutes for downtown hotels. Tourist camps offered far more privacy – no need to traipse through a public lobby, no need to dress properly, no need to engage a bellhop. Especially for local customers, there were two additional advantages: there was no expectation that a guest would register with a real name or with any name at all, and there was no possibility of being spotted on a city street or sidewalk when entering the premises.

In an article entitled, "Camps of Crime," in the February 1941 edition of *American Magazine*, Hoover warned Americans of this new threat. He began by asserting that nothing less than *a majority* of the 35,000 tourist camps in the U.S. were hiding places or bases of operations for "gangs of desperadoes." He used as his criterion whether the camps had received approval in the American Automobile Association's new rating system, which was aimed more at cleanliness and amenities for tourists than at the popularity of the establishments among lawbreakers. In its first ratings system the AAA listed about 4000 motor courts, of which only 1000 received its top recommendation. Here are excerpts from Hoover's article:

> "The files of the FBI are loaded with instances of gangsters who have hidden out in unregulated tourist camps, while officers combed the country for them. . . .

> "The larger hotels are quick to report suspicious characters, . . . but the tourist camps are often situated at the outside fringes of town where police jurisdiction stops and county officers seem unable to exert much authority. There is no regular checking of their registers by detectives – often there are no registers at all, or merely ledgers filled with indiscriminate scrawls, and an endless repetition of 'John Smith and wife.'

> "There are few major cases in the FBI involving an extended pursuit in which the roadside crime-nest is not responsible for some form of easy lawlessness, for providing convenient hide-outs, for concealing criminals through loose registration regulations.

> "Appearances can not always be counted upon. Some camps which cater to the underworld element do everything possible to achieve an appearance of respectability. Such was one camp which sought recognition by the AAA. Investigation showed that while it was one of the most beautiful camps in the community, it was actually little more than a depository for the drunken persons from a nearby town.

> "Many of the places frequented by gangsters are spots of dubious entertainment on municipal outskirts, where boys and girls, often from reputable families, go for a night of thrills. This is particularly true where a 'Dine-and-Dance' or night club is run in conjunction with the tourist cabins. .

> "With laxity so prevalent, with often only a porter on duty, with little curiosity about the clientele, it is often the conditions surrounding a camp which attract crime, rather than

any actual participation of the owner in a plot to outwit the law or harbor a hunted criminal. . . .

" 'Of all the tourist camps which line that particular road,' an officer reported, 'there are only one or two proprietors who can be depended upon to observe confidences. The rest of them would immediately broadcast the news to any wanted person to hide out, because the law was on his trail!'

"In many camps, there is a sound reason for this ignorance about guests; business would fall off sharply were there an attempt at identification. Thus a large number of roadside cottage groups appear to be, not tourist camps, but *assignation camps*. On a survey made by a Southern university near a large city, it was found that over a weekend one group of camps was visited by more than 2000 apparently amorous couples. Here every stratum of life was represented as the patrons drove into the auto-court, quickly shutting off their lights as porters herded them to various cottages.

"Generally, such assignation camps are closed to the traveling public on Saturdays and Sundays, when anyone whom the proprietor even suspects of being a tourist is turned away, with the excuse that 'the place is full.' This is not due to any altruistic attitude of the proprietor; there is more money and a faster turnover in the 'couple trade.'

"However for the rest of the week, when the 'couple trade' slacks off, the assignation camp is ready for tourist business, no matter what type. Thus, men, women, and children of respectability are herded into the same cottage group with those engaging in illicit relations. . . .

"Nor is this the end of the assignation camp's influence.

"It is haunted by that lowest of parasites upon law enforcement, the divorce detective, who seeks evidence of some indiscretion by which he can either bring about a heavy settlement in divorce actions, or, through a partnership with some unscrupulous attorney, cause divorce suits to be instituted by presenting his evidence to the injured husband or wife.

"Marijuana sellers have been found around such places.

"The sooner the Crime Camps, Assignation Camps, Hide-Out Camps are wiped out, the more restricted will be the field of the criminal. Certainly there is a place for the well-conducted, clean, wholesome type of camp which can offer a quiet night's rest to decent people, especially those who cannot afford the higher charges of city hotels. . . .

"Law enforcement, working in conjunction with the owners of honest establishments, has a definite responsibility to outlaw the renegade tourist camp. This can be done by constantly striving for tighter regulations, and for officers who will enforce them. . . .

"Until our laws are actually aimed at true control of camps, we shall continue to have pestilential conditions along our highways."[1]

"Professor Henry Hill" in *The Music Man* could not have provided a more eloquent warning.

Hoover's main concern seemed to be that *a lack of curiosity –* about what was happening in the next cabin – was *un-American.* A review of the increasingly intense curiosity of the American people through the Nineteenth Century and into the Twentieth Century shows that he was probably right – a lack of curiosity *was* un-American.

**"The FBI are dabbling in sex life scandals
and plain blackmail
when they should be catching criminals."**

**U.S. Senator Harry S. Truman,
in the early 1940s.**

Hoover's article appeared on page 14 of *American Magazine.* Articles on the surrounding pages showed America's mixed messages regarding sexuality:

Pages Nine and Ten: "Tonight is Mine." ("She was so young and generous and loving, and he was experienced, darkly dangerous, careless of women. They never should have come together, but they could not stay apart.")

Page 16: "Let Me Alone." ("Two things Avril wanted to avoid: autograph hunters, and people who wanted to see what an actress looked like when she took an ocean voyage with her lover.")

Page 32: "The Boys I Left Behind," by Elizabeth Ann Selby. ("And now comes a maiden to write the truth about her ex-boyfriends.")

Hoover's enthusiasm echoed the hysteria of Increase Mather, the pastor of Boston's North Church in 1673:

> "And there are some that ought to do more than merely pray against [drunkenness]. . . .It concerns those that have any Civil Power in their hands, to bear witness against it in their way. . . . Townsmen, Constables, Grand Jurymen, etc. Behold the Word of the Lord is upon you in particular this day. . . . Especially see that you keep a vigilant eye over these private, dark alehouses."[2]

"Predictably, motel operators were angered by Hoover's broadside, and they became even more unhappy when they heard that some hotels were handing out reprints along with customer bills," according to a history of motels in America by Paul Lancaster.[3] Most motel owners suspected that hotel owners were behind Hoover's entire campaign against motor courts in the first place.[4]

It was no secret that motels were convenient places for covert sex. That had been true almost since their beginnings, between 1900 and 1925. The first ones began as adjuncts to gasoline stations or as primitive shelters built by municipalities. As automobile ownership increased from the mere 600,000 units manufactured in 1912, demand for a convenient, informal place to stay along the highway increased. Travelers were thrilled to get a roof over their heads for $1 a night. Automobile travelers found that traditional hotels were located as conveniences to rail passengers, but not to motorists. And hotels were generally designed to appeal to male business travelers, not to families. Often they required wearing "suitable attire." On the other hand, camping grounds without cabins required loading the car with tents – and waiting in line to use the communal toilet.

Family travelers preferred roadside tourist courts, which originally were also known as "cabin camps," "tourist camps," "auto courts," or "motor courts," because they were conveniently located along highways. In 1925, in San Luis Obispo, California, an owner came up with the term "motel," but it apparently was not in common usage in 1940 when Hoover wrote his article. The detached cabins commonly in use in the 1920s and 1930s afforded even more privacy than the later modern versions with shared walls. "Individual cabins were desirable for many reasons – they were or could be cute, attractive, and cozy, and they connoted a sense of privacy and individual 'ownership,'" according to *Home Away from Home: Motels in America*, by John Margolies.

But the reputation of motels for simplicity and for covert sex meant that on some highways they were known as "shacks with spigots," "hot-pillow joints," "hot-sheet motels," "Mr. and Mrs. Jones hotels," and – in later parlance – "the No-Tell Motel." Owners of respectable motels down the road called the customers of these places the "bounce-on-the-bed trade." One joke of the time: "Kids turn into teenagers, but what do teenagers turn into?" Answer: "Motels." Or another one: "What is motel spelled backwards?" Answer: "Let'om." *Hotel Management* magazine in 1929 reported on the new competition from motels with an article entitled, "Tourists Accommodated – and No Questions Asked."[5]

The study of sexual behavior by young people that Hoover cited in his article was conducted by students in the sociology department at Southern Methodist University in 1935. The graduate students paired off as couples and then rented cabins for the night in the Dallas area "to determine the function and significance of the urban tourist camp." They spent the night seated by the windows of their rooms observing customers come and go. They did a count of the different states listed on the license plates of automobiles parked overnight.

Their findings, as reported in the university's scholarly journal *Studies in Sociology* in 1936: "At least 75 percent of the camps' business consists of Dallas couples who find in the anonymity and privacy afforded them ideal conditions in which to engage in illicit sex relations."[6] The researchers tallied 2000 "quickie" customers at 38 area motels on a typical weekend. The study reported that, at one site where a researcher was able to compare auto registration plates with the establishment's front-desk register, 102 of the 109 Dallas-area customers had given fictitious names and addresses. Many Dallas residents must have been scared when the study reproduced a map plotting where in Dallas the customers lived, based on auto registrations. Most were from middle-class and affluent neighborhoods.

The primary conclusion about one establishment that was part of the SMU study used loaded language: "This tourist camp is no resting place for the weary, but is an abode of love, a bower of bliss in which amorous couples devote themselves to the worship of Venus." In context, the remark implied that this is a bad thing.

Many motel owners acknowledged that in fact they did not accept tourists on weekend nights because they could make more money by holding rooms for local visitors. "Ninety percent of my customers use the cabins for immoral purpose," said one owner. "Tourists are a nuisance," another owner told the researchers. "We can't rent to tourists on weekends or busy nights because it would ruin our couple trade." From this quote in the SMU study, Hoover and his co-author developed the notion that motor courts were primarily for sexual trysts. His assertion that dangerous gangsters lurked in the privacy of darkened tourist camps seemed secondary. It undoubtedly came from the fact that law enforcement agents firing machine guns cornered the notorious killers Bonnie Parker and Clyde Barrow at the Red Crown Cabin Camp in Missouri. The pair escaped. This occurred seven years before Hoover's article appeared.

"The direct access from room to car makes it easy to steal from motels, and patrons have been known to stuff television sets and even beds into the backs of their cars, in addition to routine pilferage of ashtrays and towels," according to Paul Lancaster. For a period during the 1930s, motels turned away local customers, like the one in Roanoke, Virginia, that would not accept couples with license plates indicating a residence within a 50-mile radius; it also turned away couples deemed to be "suspicious." Colonial Cottages in Louisville, in the early 1940s hung a sign out front: "NO LOCALS – Strictly Tourist."[7] Into the 1950s, it was not unusual for "respectable" motels not to accept guests without luggage.

Travelers knew from their own experiences that in the 1920s and 1930s "couples were often hard-pressed to find a place where they could shut the door on the world," as Lancaster put it. The roadside cabin provided what the open field provided in Colonial times and the abandoned shack provided in the Nineteenth Century and the automobile itself provided in the decades after World War II. It was a private place for sex.

Night after night, Humbert Humbert, the demonic professor in Vladimir Nabokov's novel *Lolita*, knew the drill:

> "I soon grew to prefer the Functional Motel – clean, neat, safe nooks, ideal places for sleep, argument, reconciliation, insatiable illicit love. . . . a prison cell of paradise, with yellow window shades pulled down to create a morning illusion of Venice and sunshine when actually it was Pennsylvania and rain."

After the war, motels thrived more than ever, for different reasons. National hotel chains took an interest in building new ones, with higher standards and nationwide uniformity. These national companies took advantage of brand names and graphics instantly recognizable to motorists. The first Holiday Inn opened in 1952. With the construction of the Interstate highway system beginning in 1956 – which many in the tourist industry originally opposed – motor inns proliferated. The chains – especially Holiday Inn, Hilton, Howard Johnson, and Marriott – made special efforts to show that they had Christian values. They made their establishments appropriate for children. They began to offer amenities comparable to city hotels – including public lobbies and observant bellhops. The individuality of each establishment diminished, of course – as did opportunities for clandestine trysts.

"Powerful organizations must confront the fact that the great decisions of the world are made by solitary couples – male and female – and are made in bed, to boot."

U.S. Senator Daniel Patrick Moynihan, in the 1980s.

By 1948, Hoover had another target – a scholar at Indiana University, Alfred C. Kinsey. He was the author of a book called *Sexual Behavior in the Human Male*, quickly known as "The Kinsey Report." It was three pounds and 804 pages of narrative text, charts, and statistics, costing twice as much as the average book in the Forties. Yet it challenged *Gone with the Wind* in setting sales records.

Kinsey's work, based on interviews with 12,000 students and others, was the most comprehensive account of private sexual behavior ever published. It told Americans for the first time that, according to their own accounts, 90 percent of men had masturbated, about 85 percent had had sex before marriage, up to 45 percent had sex outside of their marriages, 70 percent had patronized prostitutes, and 37 percent had experienced at least one homosexual encounter reaching a climax. The book "swept away the last remnants of the taboos that had inhibited Americans from engaging in public discourse about their erotic lives," wrote James H. Jones in *Alfred C. Kinsey: A Public/Private Life* in 1997.[8] "However awkward, prurient, or naughty they might feel, Americans suddenly had permission to talk about sex." If Kinsey's statistics were accurate, far more than half the men in America had violated the sex laws then on the books, against adultery, prostitution, fornication, and sodomy.

The Kinsey Report may have been liberating, but it was also threatening – threatening to Americans who believed these topics should not be discussed or that the findings either were based on an aberrant minority or would license others to engage in unorthodox sexuality.

Once again, FBI Director Hoover took it upon himself to warn the American people. *Reader's Digest,* one of the highest circulation periodicals in the 1940s, quoted him as saying that The Kinsey Report was a threat to "our way of life." After Alfred Kinsey became enormously popular, Hoover ordered the FBI to keep a dossier on Kinsey and Kinsey's Institute for Sex Research at Indiana University.[9] The FBI file even included a review of the Kinsey Report by the special investigator in charge of sex-offender investigations.

Eight years after the report was issued, a House of Representatives subcommittee investigated charges that Kinsey's work undermined the American family. Jones' 1997 biography of Kinsey established that the man indeed had kinky interests in sexual behavior and may have skewered his results in favor of more adventurous sexual activities. He personified, in a way, the idea – more often attributed to Europeans – that a barrier can appropriately be erected between one's private life and one's public reputation.[10] (Of course, covertly, Hoover believed the same thing.)

In a lecture to students in 1940, Kinsey avowed, "I believe in marriage as an institution. . . . It is quite possible to walk through life alone but not as efficiently as when there is someone else to go with you to share your plans and your ambitions, to stand by when few others will support you, to help at every turn." What Kinsey did not say is that he also believed in sexual experimentation with partners besides his wife.

He knew from his own studies that even within marriage people did not reveal the truth about their sexual fantasies or behavior. To get at the truth in his study of human sexuality, he developed his own techniques for establishing rapport and candor. "Early in his research, Kinsey realized that his respondents would be more trusting and cooperative if he could not only guarantee confidentiality but avoid the use of written questionnaires," Jones wrote in his biography. "Accordingly, he produced no written key to his interview, preferring to memorize the questions and the order in which they were asked. If a subject balked, or gave an answer that suddenly suggested a new area for discussion, Kinsey had to be able to leap to another round of questions, while keeping mental count of the items in each round. This enabled him to move smoothly through the hundreds of items covered in each history without losing eye contact, and insured that only he and a handful of researchers he had trained knew the specific questions asked, and the answers elicited. Still, some kind of notation was necessary, so Kinsey devised a form and a code for recording sex histories which made his records unintelligible to outsiders." No one else could decipher the sheet of notes that Kinsey compiled on the entire sex history of an interview subject.

"What we really like to do is watch. Today, we know more about what people do in bed – not to mention trains, planes, and automobiles – than ever before."

Harvard University Professor of Afro-American Studies Henry Louis Gates, in 1997.[11]

In 1953, Kinsey compiled his interviews with women in *Sexual Behavior in the Human Female*, which also liberated thinking in the United States about sexuality. At least it made sex front-page news again. Traditional men did not believe Kinsey's finding that half of all married women were not virgins when they married – and that 70 percent of the respondents expressed no regret about this.

Kinsey's controversial research especially caught the eye of a graduate student at Northwestern University who later would have a greater influence on American sexuality. "Why does tolerance turn to intolerance, rationality to irrationality, when man contemplates the problem of sex?" he asked in a 1950 term paper entitled "Sex Behavior and the U.S. Law." "Let us see if we cannot begin to find our way out of this dark, emotional, taboo-ridden labyrinth, and into the fresh air and light of reason." His name was Hugh Hefner.[12]

Three years later, Hefner sat at the kitchen table of his Chicago apartment making plans to create a new magazine for men on love and sex. But the magazine was to be about more than sex; it was to be about a man's private space. "We like our apartment," he wrote in his prototype. "We enjoy mixing up cocktails and an hors d'oeuvre or two, putting a little mood music on the phonograph and inviting in a female for a quiet discussion on Picasso, Nietzsche, jazz, sex." Consequently, the young man's new monthly magazine, *Playboy*, not only depicted explicit sexuality to men, it told them regularly that they could function as real men by being unmarried or living alone. (At the time *Playboy* was launched, ten percent of Americans thought that an unmarried person could be happy; 80 percent thought that bachelors were sick, neurotic and immoral.)

An early issue of the magazine featured an article by Philip Wylie saying, "The American home, in short, is becoming a boudoir-kitchen-nursery, dreamed up by women, for women, as if males did not exist as males."

Hefner's popular new magazine seemed to exploit the notion that in the conformist years of the 1950s, sex – practiced in private, of course, but with abandon – represented one of the few opportunities to express individuality.

Kinsey, Hefner, and others paved the way for more open discussions of sex; in fact, in the 1950s and the years since, it seemed that all Americans did about sex was to talk about it or see it portrayed. A U.S. Supreme Court decision on obscenity in 1957 and cases that followed it made this possible. Although it permitted the conviction of a book distributor under the Nineteenth-Century Comstock anti-obscenity law and said that obscenity is not protected by the First Amendment, the Court clearly outlined limits to governmental restrictions on depictions of sex, whether in print or in film. "Sex and obscenity are not synonymous," the 6-3 majority of the Court said in *Roth v U.S.*[13] "The test in each case," said Associate Justice William J. Brennan, Jr., "is the effect of the book, picture or publication considered as a whole, not upon any particular class, but upon all those whom it is likely to reach. In other words, you determine its impact upon the average person in the community." Brennan and five colleagues were able to tell the nation that sex is "a great and mysterious motive force in human life." That made it official.

In 1960 the immediate, widespread availability of "the pill," a reliable oral contraceptive, changed sexual relationships in more ways. In the next ten years, two sex researchers from St. Louis named Dr. William Masters and Virginia Johnson documented just how different things were, in their post-Kinsey books, *Human Sexual Response* and *Human Sexual Inadequacy*. A wildly popular illustrated guidebook *The Joy of Sex* in 1972 "took sex out of the bedroom and put it on the coffee table," according to *Playboy*'s historian on sex in the Twentieth Century, James R. Petersen.

Then women took over: Nancy Friday with her book of female fantasies, *My Secret Garden*, Erica Jong's *Fear of Flying*, and Sheri Hite's *The Hite Report on Female Sexuality*, "to let women define their own sexuality – instead of doctors or other (usually male) authorities."

**"Lovers give themselves to each other.
They lay bare their innermost feelings to each other;
they are lewd and foolish with each other,
they stand naked before each other.
Between themselves there is no individual privacy,
nothing is held back. But the premise for giving up
individual privacy in love is the feeling
that what is shared so intimately
will not be broadcast to the world at large."**

**Rutgers University privacy scholar
Edward J. Bloustein, in 1977.**[14]

By now, young people in the streets and legions of psychotherapists could chant, "Let it all hang out." Here was the antithesis of privacy.

The noted market researcher Daniel Yankelovich, a man with his ear always to the current public sentiment, assessed America in the post-Woodstock Seventies. What he found, he wrote in a 1978 essay, was a society high on autonomy and free choice, if not privacy:

> "We see the beginnings of an ethic built around the concept of duty to oneself, in glaring contrast to the traditional ethic of obligation to others. In reaching for 'something more than success,' the new breed also press for the individual – freedom to express impulses and desires that people have been accustomed to suppress. Sexual desires are the most obvious, hence the greater openness of homosexuality, pornography, nakedness, and casual sexual encounters. But other forms of freedom 'to do what I want to do' are almost as prominent: freedom to enjoy life now rather than in some distant future; freedom to elevate one's own desires to the rank of entitlements; freedom to give one's own ego

more room in which to maneuver; freedom to pull up stakes and move on without having to pick up the pieces."[15]

In the early Seventies a pornographic movie made for $25,000 named *Deep Throat* would make more than $100 million, and introduce – to men and women – the talents of a new star named Linda Lovelace. Did the "playfully pornographic," socially acceptable explicit film move sex from the home to the theater? Ironically, the label "Deep Throat" became short-hand code for a confidential source used by *The Washington Post*'s Bob Woodward and Carl Bernstein in their investigation of the Watergate scandals in the Nixon Administration in the 1970s. But the original "Deep Throat" in the movie was anything but a symbol for confidentiality and reticence.

Kinsey, Masters and Johnson, Hefner, and the producers of *Deep Throat* were great advocates of "sexual privacy" – by which they meant the protection of sexual activity from governmental intrusion. Thus, in subsequent years, sexual privacy came to mean the right to engage in extramarital behavior without legal consequences, not necessarily the right to keep one's sex life private. In the great American tradition, these liberators of sexuality were also satisfying the *curiosity* of men and woman about the sexual practices of others. The American notion of sexual privacy would not unduly interfere with American curiosity.

This idea that sexuality was none of the government's business yet was something to talk about freely culminated – if that is the right word – on a bright Saturday morning in October of 1991, when young children all over the nation would expect to see cartoons on television. Instead, on all three national networks and the cable news channel, all they and their parents saw were solemn male policy makers talking openly about pubic hairs in Coke cans and someone named "Long Dong Silver."

When President George Bush nominated Circuit Judge Clarence Thomas to become an Associate Justice of the Supreme Court, the already unpopular choice was jeopardized by the testimony of a former assistant, who said that Thomas had made crude sexually oriented remarks to her and that he was a connoisseur of pornography. There were no limits at all now as to words and phrases about sex that public people or actors playing roles could use on national television. The public seemed not to dissolve in embarrassment. News coverage of the Thomas confirmation hearing accustomed reporters and editors to make increasingly explicit references to sexual activities and intimate body parts, much more so than in the "let it all hang out" Sixties and Seventies. By 1995, with only the slightest reticence, reporters for all the respectable news organizations found themselves speculating about "identifying characteristics" on the penis of the President of the United States.

Perhaps this new candor – or what passed as candor – had its healthy side. In 1994, the American Civil Liberties Union could report that the results of a public opinion survey it had commissioned showed that most Americans, with regard to private sex, were truly willing to "live and let live." This is true irrespective of their own views of proper practices. Six in ten Americans at the time believed that "homosexuality is against God's law," yet 80 percent of those holding that view agree that gay sex among consenting adults is a private matter. "Just over half agree that 'homosexuality threatens the values of the American family.' Yet three-quarters of those same respondents *also* agree that a homosexual relationship is a private matter," the ACLU reported. Self-identified "born-again" or evangelical Christians showed less concern than others about privacy in these matters, but three-quarters of them showed a tolerance for private conduct that is contrary to their views.[16] Four out of five respondents agreed that an abortion is a woman's personal decision, yet 61 percent agreed that an abortion is morally wrong. In fact, nearly half, 45 percent, agreed with *both* statements, that abortion is a private matter and that it is morally wrong.

A popular cigarette advertisement of the time aimed at women said, "You've Come a Long Way, Baby," but it was the civil rights of homosexual men and women that had come a long way. James Petersen, in his extensive retrospective on sex published in 1996 through 1998 in *Playboy*, noted that the 1950s brought a "panic about homosexuality," just as surely as it brought a panic about Communism. In the Fifties, it was hard to separate the two phobias. "Communists, deviants – they're one and the same," said Senator Clyde Hoey of North Carolina.[17] Advocates for the rights of homosexuals were forced to testify before the House Committee on Un-American Activities, just as surely as suspected Communists were. As Wisconsin Senator Joseph McCarthy sought to scour federal agencies for Communists – "the enemy within" – other Senators looked for "perverts" in the federal government. McCarthy identified 205 Communists in the government; Senator Hoey found 4954 deviants, most of them in the military.

J. Edgar Hoover, despite the fact that later he was widely regarded as a latent homosexual himself, joined in. He told Congress that FBI investigators knew about 406 "sex deviates" in government service. Congress provided money for a special Sex Deviates program in the bureau.

Perhaps not coincidentally, McCarthy's undoing was an investigation into charges that he and a staff member, Roy Cohn, pressured the U.S. Army for favorable treatment of a former staff member who had been drafted into the Army. Both the staff member and Cohn were widely believed to be homosexuals.

Not until the 1970s were there two defining moments that encouraged homosexuals to risk "coming out of the closet" and living openly as gay men and women. One, coming four years after the 1969 uprising by gay men routed by police from the Stonewall Bar in Greenwich Village, was the vote by the American Psychiatric Association to remove homosexuality from its list of mental illnesses.

The other stemmed, ironically, from the ultimate invasion of privacy – the public airing of a family's entire private moments. This occurred two decades before the release in the late 1990s of two popular films on this theme, *The Truman Show* and *Edtv*, and the MTV program *The Real World*. The husband, wife, and five children in a "typical" family, the Louds of Santa Barbara, California, permitted a Public Broadcasting System TV crew to capture virtually every moment of their home lives – their interesting times and their routine moments, their ups and their downs, and ultimately their marital discord. A fascinated nation watched weekly for 12 weeks beginning in January 1973. Americans came to know the son, Lance Loud, whose facial make-up, effeminate dress, and theatrical ways led people to come to terms with the reality that the boy next door might be gay. Lance acknowledged his homosexuality during the series and then grew up to become a gay-oriented writer and performer in Hollywood.

This oppression and suppression about matters sexual was not always the norm in America. In his 1995 book *Walt Whitman's America*, David S. Reynolds gives this account:

> "The sexual atmosphere before the Civil War was far more varied than is commonly believed. From a governmental standpoint, this was a hands-off period when, despite sporadic crackdowns by local authorities, moral regulations were few. There was no government-authorized moral po-

lice of the Anthony Comstock type, which after the Civil War crusaded against all kinds of explicit materials, including Whitman's poetry. Before the war there were individual moral-reform groups, but none was long-lasting and several actually came into disrepute because of their sensational tactics. Only four states had obscenity laws, and obscenity cases were rarely heard by American courts. In 1842 a ban was imposed on the importation of obscene pictures, but printed matter was left untouched, so that by 1847 Whitman could lament the 'cataracts of trash' flowing from abroad. The same printing improvements that sped the production of mass-oriented sensational newspapers also permitted the growth of an underground industry of pornography, much of it foreign but a growing amount of it written indigenously and peddled in railway stations and at street bookstalls."[18]

Sexual affection was fluid and flexible until the last decades of the Nineteenth Century, when they became rigidly categorized, according to Reynolds. The label of *homosexual* wasn't even used until the very last decade, *lesbianism* only in the 1920s. You couldn't find those words or the term *heterosexual* in a turn-of-the-century dictionary. In 1985 a historian named Michael Lynch examined more than 75,000 indictments in the New York City district attorney's office between 1796 and 1893 and found only about 30 for sodomy, of which only two, in 1847 and 1849, led to convictions. There was not a single indictment in the whole century for non-violent, consensual sodomy. Nor could Lynch find any suggestions in court papers or news reports that such sexual activity was threatening or dysfunctional.[19] But there were severe criminal penalties in the colonies – sometimes death – for engaging in homosexuality. Thomas Jefferson's Virginia code of 1779 decreed castration for sodomy, rape, bestiality, and polygamy.[20]

In his "cultural biography" of Whitman, Reynolds points out that the great intellectuals of the period celebrated same-sex friendship, intimacy, sensuality – whether or not sexual gratification was a part of it. Walt Whitman and Ralph Waldo Emerson were two of the most prominent. "Men often made strikingly ardent confessions of love to each other, as did women," in their diaries, their correspondence, and their public writings, according to Reynolds. Massachusetts Senator Daniel Webster, a celebrated lawyer and orator before the Civil War, said at age 22, "I don't see how I can live any longer without having a friend near me, I mean a male friend." He pined to a friend about the same age, "James, I must come; we will yoke together again; your little bed is just wide enough." Webster went on to establish a reputation as an awkward but incurable philanderer with women.[21]

At least before the war, displays of affection in public were not rare at all – hugging, kissing, verbal expressions of affection – between men and women, women and women, and men and men. And, well into the Nineteenth Century, Americans at all levels of life continued the Colonial practice of sleeping together in the same bed, whether family members or visiting strangers, whether of the same sex or of the opposite sex.[22]

David Reynolds began his book by saying:

> "In Nineteenth-Century America, same-sex friends of all ages held hands while walking down the streets of cities and towns. Few people regarded it as remarkable when same-sex friends kissed each other 'full on the lips' in public or private. Fewer still saw anything unusual in the common American practice of same-sex friends sleeping in the same bed, sometimes for years at a time. Rather than regarding this sleeping arrangement as a grim necessity of overcrowded houses, American teenagers and married persons of that era indicated that they looked forward to their next opportunity to share a bed with a same-sex friend. Whether in privileged societies or working-class culture, letters between same-sex friends in the Nineteenth Century had emotional intensity and passionate references. These are manifestations of . . . 'homocultural orientation' of Nineteenth-Century America."[23]

In the practices of the Church of Jesus Christ of Latter-day Saints at the time, there was further evidence that casual shows of affection between those of the same sex did not shock Nineteenth-Century Americans at all. Kissing, hugging, and bed-sharing between men was common. Mormons, who promoted some tenets that would have pleased the Puritans – including the solidarity of the conventional family – actually encouraged close bonds between male adults. D. Michael Quinn, who resigned as a professor of history at the church's Brigham Young University and was excommunicated in the 1990s as the result of his controversial historical studies, has researched this phenomenon in the church. According to his book *Same-Sex Dynamics among Nineteenth-Century Americans: A Mormon Example*:

"In 1835, outside church headquarters, some Mormon men routinely kissed whenever they met. An LDS apostle visiting an overly 'enthusiastic' branch of 19 members in New York State found that 'the Elders seemed to [lack] almost every quality except Zeal and that they had abundantly – even to saluting with a Kiss.' However, such pro forma greetings did not take place at church headquarters in Ohio, where Joseph Smith [founder of the Church of Latter-day Saints] had revised the New Testament text to rephrase 'holy kiss' into a verbal greeting of 'holy salutation.' Nevertheless, same-sex kissing was common among Mormon women and men in the Nineteenth Century as a spontaneous expression of their religious devotion and personal affection. At Kirtland headquarters in 1837, Mary Fielding Smith wrote, 'Some of the Sisters while engaged in conversing in tongues, their countenances beaming with joy, clasped each others hands & kissed in the most affectionate manner.' Although they did not usually specify it, this same-sex kissing between adults was probably 'full on the lips,' which one Mormon said was the practice of brothers in his family. Several Nineteenth-Century Mormons who became LDS presidents were accustomed to kissing other men."[24]

In Mormon settlements at mid-century, men danced with other men, even inside the temple. The same was true at mostly-male mining camps. It was not unusual in the American West for tough cowboy types to dance with each other at celebrations. It was either that or no dancing at all. Wild Bill Hickok, the frontier marshal in Kansas in the 1870s celebrated for his bravery, was repeatedly referred to as "effeminate" and "sissy." Mormon leaders went further – sponsoring all-male dances and encouraging genial physical contact between men. This encouragement of same-gender relationship was found throughout the American West in the Nineteenth Century. In the East, these living arrangements between women were called "Boston marriages." Henry James called his novel about one such relationship *The Bostonians*.

A fear of erotic arousal overnight led the author of a popular physician-advice book in the 1860s to recommend that post-puberty siblings not sleep together. "Their sexual functions are more than ordinarily active," said the book.

"I wish I could be with you present in the body as well as the mind & heart – I would turn your *good husband out of bed* – and snuggle into you," wrote one American woman to a female friend in 1832, in a passage that was not atypical.

One popular advice book issued in seven editions between 1836 and 1849 encouraged hand-holding, kissing, and caressing between girls so long as they were reserved for "hours of privacy, and never indulged in before gentlemen." It is curious that this was acceptable in America; in Victorian Europe physical contact was censured. This was one of many signs that Americans were breaking away from the Anglo traditions that created the nation.

After the Civil War public attitudes about sexual conduct changed radically. Reynolds described what happened:

> "Several forms of sexual experimentation that had gone unchecked before the war now met with censorship or outright suppression. Street prostitution, which had been rampant before the war, became the target of several prolonged vice campaigns that closed brothels and made prostitutes wary. Free love, which had occasioned only a police raid or two before the war, now came under the moral ban, as evidenced by the arrest of the free-lover Ezra Heywood in the 1880s for defying the authorities by printing some of Whitman's sex poems. John Humphrey Noyes' Oneida [utopian community in New York State], where communal sex had been part of daily life since 1848, found itself after the war challenged by government and church authorities, contributing to its demise in the 1870s. Pornographic literature and entertainments, against which little organized action had been taken before the war, became the special target of the postwar vice campaigners, most notably Anthony Comstock, who helped pass obscenity laws used to suppress, among many other works, Whitman's *Leaves of Grass*."[25]

What caused the change? Why did men and women cease showing intimate affection for each other without fear of societal condemnation? Did the emergence of an industrialized, profit-based economy after the Civil War make it necessary for men and women in the workplace to adopt clearly defined roles? Did modern warfare require men to project fearlessness and masculinity? Did the movement to promote voting rights and equality for women create sharp lines of sexuality? Did many men feel compelled to define themselves as even more manly, more assertive?

With gender roles now clearly distinct, any deviation from them had to become a private matter. If sexuality and displays of affection were no longer casual and open, authorities began to feel compelled to pry into intimate encounters between individuals. The sudden increase in the density of city living may also have prompted authorities to believe that certain forms of sexuality had deleterious effects on society. Sex on the farm – whether kinky or not – was one thing; sex in the tenement next door was perhaps more threatening. Then again, the nation was moving more to a profit-motivated, industrial society. Is there something about capitalism that requires poking into the business of others, that requires regulating private behavior?

"Throughout the major portion of the Nineteenth Century prevailing legal abortion practices were far freer than they are today."

U.S. Supreme Court, *Roe v. Wade*, 1973.[26]

With the coming of a new century in America, sexuality went underground. Spontaneity and uninhibitedness, which are the essence of sexuality, had now to be hidden from view and denied. Consequently, to Twentieth-Century Americans, *privacy* came largely to mean the effort to hide sexuality, whether it was illicit or within a recognized relationship. Privacy, it seems, no longer stood for the quest to provide breathing room and tolerance for a whole list of human endeavors, as Louis Brandeis, Samuel Warren, E.L. Godkin, and John Adams had envisioned. It was no longer regarded as a value to protect one's standing in the community, one's family life, one's financial affairs, one's religious practices, one's intellectual aspirations, or something as simple as one's daily journal. In the Twentieth Century, privacy came to be regarded as no more than a chance to keep secrets about sex, or what many Americans regarded as the sleazy part of human life. That attitude lasted through the century.

The change in gender roles may have been sparked by Sigmund Freud's turn-of-the-century research into the mind. Did this create an obsession with the mechanics and the psychological aspects of sex that led Americans to establish clear boundaries between the genders – and to talk about sex rather than actually do it? Freud came to believe that Americans had peculiar attitudes towards sex, although he probably never attributed that to his own work. In 1909, when he made his only visit to the United States, he said that modern men were cursed by both prudery *and* lasciviousness. "They do not show their sexuality freely," he said in his lectures at Clark University in Worcester, Massachusetts. Instead, people "wear a thick overcoat – a fabric of lies" to conceal their sexuality "as though it were bad weather in the world of sex." A few months earlier, Clark University had heard the opposite view from the person more responsible than any other for driving sex underground before the turn of the century, the crusader against vice Anthony Comstock. After he went home, Sigmund Freud grumbled, "America is gigantic, but a gigantic mistake." Four decades apart, both Sigmund Freud the psychotherapist and Walt Whitman the poet noted that Americans are both prudish *and* leering in their approaches to sexuality.

"The sexual act is of no more concern to the community than any other private physiological act. It is an impertinence, if not an outrage, to seek to inquire into it."

British sex psychologist Havelock Ellis, in 1928.

H.L. Mencken, the celebrated journalist of the 1920s and 1930s, had his own theory: *Prosperity* created the officious censors of the decades after the Civil War. He wrote in 1917:

> "Wealth, discovering its power, has reached out its long arms to grab the distant and innumerable sinner; it has gone down into its deep pockets to pay for his costly pursuit and flaying; it has created the puritan entrepreneur, the daring and imaginative organizer of puritanism, the baron of moral endeavor."[27]

The American puritan, noted "the sage of Baltimore," "was not content with the rescue of his own soul. He felt an irresistible impulse to hand salvation on, to disperse and multiply it, to ram it down reluctant throats, to make it free, universal and compulsory." Puritans had instituted "a campaign of repression and punishment perhaps unequaled in the history of the world."

Elsewhere, Mencken ridiculed the "intolerable prudishness and dirty-mindedness of puritanism" and its "theory that the enforcement of chastity by a huge force of spies, stool pigeons and police would convert the republic into a nation of moral esthetes. All this, of course, is simply pious fudge. If the notion were actually sound, then all the great artists of the world would come from the ranks of the hermetically repressed, i.e., from the ranks of old maids, male and female. But the truth is, as everyone knows, that the great artists of the world are never puritans and seldom even ordinarily respectable. No moral man – that is moral in the YMCA sense – has ever painted a picture worth looking at, or written a symphony worth hearing, or a book worth reading, and it is highly improbable that the thing has ever been done by a virtuous woman."

That reference to the YMCA was a dig at Anthony Comstock, who worked for the Young Men's Christian Association during his anti-smut crusade.

For those who look to single events that demarcate a change in cultural attitudes, they need look only to the sensational public trial of Henry Beecher in the 1870s. It was the *trial of the century* – if you accept the notion that centuries usually have several more than one "trial of the century." It fundamentally changed notions about sexuality and privacy. After it was over, every American understood the public ridicule – if not the loss in public stature – that followed getting caught. The parallels to the scandal involving President Clinton in the late 1990s are striking.

In fact there were two trials. They involved the Rev. Henry Ward Beecher, the most charismatic preacher of his time. Beecher's evangelical oratory packed the Plymouth Church in Brooklyn, New York, with 3000 persons each Sunday. Before the Brooklyn Bridge was completed, they flocked from Manhattan on ferries known as "Beecher boats." One of those who did was presidential candidate Abraham Lincoln. Beecher's Congregational church, often mobbed in front on Sundays, came to be called "Beecher Theatre." Every year, "the most successful church in America" held a big auction to sell off the best pews. Beecher even endorsed products in newspaper advertisements. His sermons were reprinted in newspapers across the nation.

In the summer of 1870, Elizabeth Richards Tilton, 35-year-old mother of four, confessed to her husband, Theodore, that she had been involved in an adulterous sexual affair with Beecher, her pastor. They agreed not to disclose this to anyone. Theodore Tilton idolized the famous preacher; they were both avid abolitionists – and women's rights advocates as well. Beecher had officiated at the wedding of the Tiltons in Plymouth Church in 1855. Through the efforts of Beecher and church members, Tilton came to edit the leading religious journal in the nation, the *Independent*.

As a few people came to know about their pastor's adultery, Beecher met in December with Elizabeth and dictated to her a written retraction of her confession and had her sign it. Beecher expected that this would keep the matter a secret. Tilton, however, got into a fight with his boss, the man who had hired him to edit the *Independent*, Henry C. Bowen. Bowen was also the most prominent member of Plymouth Church, the man who had brought the famous preacher to Brooklyn. Bowen wanted his editor, Tilton, to write more favorably about Plymouth Church. Enraged, Tilton responded, how could he? Beecher had seduced his wife! This was interesting news to Bowen, who had heard his own wife, the mother of ten children, make a confession about Beecher on her deathbed identical to Elizabeth Tilton's!

Beecher was a proponent of "Free Love," a philosophy that regarded marriage vows as unnecessary for sexual or affectional satisfaction. Elizabeth Tilton once said, before her affair, that "at the mention of his name. . . or better still, a visit from him, my cheek would flush with pleasure." This reaction was typical of "all his parishioners of both sexes," she said.[28] (In this respect, he was not different from Brigham Young, the leader of the Church of Latter-Day Saints 2000 miles away in Utah at the same time, who was able to integrate into his charismatic theology the view that he was entitled to sex with any women he wished. His adherents seemed to accept this.)

At Bowen's urging, Theodore Tilton, Elizabeth's husband, wrote to Rev. Beecher demanding his resignation and departure from Brooklyn "for reasons which you explicitly understand." Beecher was unfazed by the threat. Tilton then had his wife sign a confession, in direct contradiction to the retraction she had signed for her pastor just days before. A mutual friend named Frank Moulton offered to "manage the affair" and keep it under wraps. He sent off to boarding school a young girl who lived in the Tiltons' home and knew of the illicit relationship. He persuaded Beecher to pay her tuition. Moulton had the three male principals – Beecher, Tilton, and Bowen – sign a treaty requiring secrecy (and a payment of $7000 from Henry Bowen to Theodore Tilton for firing him).

The efforts of middleman Moulton succeeded for a while. Then the two most prominent feminists of the period, Susan B. Anthony and Elizabeth Cady Stanton, learned about Beecher's adultery from Theodore Tilton's own indiscreet chatter with them at one of the frequent dinner parties held at his house for journalists and suffragettes. In a move she later came to regret intensely, Stanton told what she knew to a renegade feminist named Victoria Woodhull.

The loose-cannon Woodhull was a fellow adherent of Free Love, but she had a different definition of it than did Beecher. And so she considered the preacher a hypocrite. By exposing him, she said, she hoped actually to propel him into national attention as a totally committed advocate so that he would give public support to the many average Americans who, she was sure, were actually practicing Free Love in private but pretending to conform to conventional morality regarding sex. Just like Henry Beecher. Both Woodhull and Tilton felt that the 57-year-old Beecher only flirted with radical politics.

Woodhull, in tactics perfected by Washington insiders in the 1990s, decided to "send a message" to Beecher and Tilton. In a letter to the editor published in the New York *World* denouncing hypocrisy, she tauntingly wrote, without mentioning names, "I know of one man, a public teacher of eminence, who lives in concubinage with the wife of another public teacher of almost equal eminence."

Beecher got the message. He, Tilton, and Moulton conspired to win Woodhull's silence. Their plan was to have Tilton, editor of the *Independent*, flatter Woodhull by writing an admiring biography of her. The scheme fell apart when Woodhull was angered by public attacks on her by Beecher's sister, the celebrated anti-slavery novelist Harriet Beecher Stowe, and another sister, anti-feminist Catherine Beecher. In the process of interviewing Victoria Woodhull for his flattering book, Tilton became very intimate with her, if not sexually involved. But then they had a falling out. Woodhull felt that Tilton and Beecher did not take seriously her quixotic run for the Presidency that year.

The Beecher-Tilton affair became publicly known a year later not through the sensationalizing newspapers of the time, but in the pages of an alternative news sheet self-published by Victoria and her equally eccentric sister, Tennessee Claflin. After reading the lurid account in *Woodhull and Claflin's Weekly*, Anthony Comstock had his friends at the U.S. marshal's office arrest the sisters and indict them for violating the brand-new Comstock Law against mailing obscene materials.[29] In court, the federal prosecutor said that the sisters, aside from the formal charge, "have been guilty of a most abominable and unjust charge against one of the purest and best citizens of the United States whose character is well worth-while the Government of the United States to vindicate."[30]

Although bail was available, on Election Day 1872 when she was on the ballot as the Presidential nominee of the Equal Rights Party, Victoria Woodhull was in jail. Theodore Tilton returned to Brooklyn from a campaign appearance for *his* candidate, Horace Greeley, and was presented with a copy of *Woodhull and Claflin's Weekly* by his wife. It was, he claimed, the first time that he had realized that the affair had become common knowledge.

New York City's newspapers loved the story. Among other angles, Commodore Cornelius Vanderbilt, one of the hugely rich capital-ists whose private lives fascinated the New York press, was smit-ten with Woodhull's sister, Tennessee, and had set up the weekly newspaper for them to report on stock tips, spiritualism, and women's rights. In an irony that occurs regularly *only in America*, the weekly that the nation's premier capitalist originally funded flirted with Marxist ideas, becoming the first publication in the United States to publish the full English text of the Communist Manifesto.

In the Nineteenth-Century way, the protagonists in this drama had revealed their most intimate thoughts in the letters that they ex-changed with each other. Thus, instead of tape-recorded conversa-tions or electronic-mail correspondence, the public had a vast col-lection of juicy writings to sustain their interest in the scandal. Most of the written correspondence back and forth started to ap-pear in the daily newspapers. All of the Tiltons' love letters of the past four years were reprinted in the Chicago *Tribune*.

A staff member of the New York *Tribune*, also a church member, anticipating that he would end the scandal and help Beecher, pub-lished the text of the Bowen-Beecher-Tilton agreement. But this had the effect of making Bowen and Tilton look like schemers. Then there was the letter from Rev. Beecher shortly after Eliza-beth's confession apologizing to Theodore but denying all. Beecher had even offered to resign when the news broke, but Til-ton said that that would reflect badly on him and his wife.

The first result of the news coverage of the scandal was that public opinion turned against Theodore Tilton for slandering the idol of good Christians. (In fact, it had been reported that he was fre-quently on the road and had had several affairs himself with mar-ried women. He was also nasty to Elizabeth.) Amid the publicity, Tilton was booted out of Plymouth Church. Still, Tilton was not prepared to go public. A rival congregation in Brooklyn, the Church of the Pilgrims, was keeping interest alive, not Tilton. Then a series of pro-Beecher articles in the *Independent* newspaper called Tilton a "knave" and a "dog." That was it; Tilton told his side of the story in a long reply that he sent to the major newspapers. Even then, in his manifesto he could not bring himself to renounce his love of Henry Ward Beecher.

News reporters staked out the homes of the participants and even followed Tilton to the beach at Coney Island. One of them perched in a tree opposite Moulton's Brooklyn residence.

Beecher then tried to quell the storm by appointing a Church Investigating Committee (with six of his closest friends). This simply stoked the public's curiosity about the case. During August of 1874, the committee took testimony and the full transcripts were published in the new mass-audience newspapers. Readers could not wait for each day's revelations. At the hearing there was ample evidence of the affair, including Frank Moulton's affirmation that it had occurred. Still, Mrs. Tilton continued to deny it in her appearance before the tribunal. In fact, she turned on her husband.

The pastor's lawyer did not contest the facts but argued that Beecher's popularity should make the charges not credible. In his summation, the lawyer read a letter from an admirer. "For a man who has done so much good," the woman wrote, "a little aberration of this kind instead of being excused, should be justified." This acceptance – ambivalent as it is – encapsulated the attitude of a majority of Americans in 1998 towards their President during a strikingly similar sex scandal a century later.

Beecher's carefully worded presentation to the committee included a complaint that "Not a great war nor a revolution could have more filled the newspapers than this question of domestic trouble, magnified a thousand-fold. . . . It is time that this abomination be buried."[31]

The committee quickly announced Beecher's "entire innocence and absolute personal integrity." Moulton, once the loyal go-between, tried to protest the finding at a mobbed church meeting but was shouted down. As the jubilant parishioners sang, "Praise God from whom all blessing flow. . . ," Moulton was escorted out of the church by police.

Sex scandals never die if people do not want them to die. Angered at the man whom he had virtually created as a national celebrity and who had committed adultery with his own wife, as well as Tilton's wife, Bowen had Tilton file a lawsuit against Rev. Beecher. The subsequent six-month trial attracted the leading lawyers in the land. Both sides were reluctant to call Victoria Woodhull to the stand because of her unpredictability; instead, she conducted a popular lecture tour on the West Coast. Up to 3000 persons a day were turned away from the trial in the Brooklyn City Court House when they could not find tickets from scalpers. Vendors sold opera glasses to the lucky ones who got in.

After two million words of evidence and 52 ballots, the jury said that it could not reach a verdict. The congregation of Plymouth Church held a big celebration and voted a $100,000 raise to pay Beecher's legal expenses. That's the equivalent of more than $1.6 million in 1990s currency. Bowen, Mrs. Moulton, and others who had testified against him were excommunicated from the church. (Bowen took his influence to the rival Church of the Pilgrims.)

In 1878, Elizabeth Tilton finally reversed herself and admitted the affair publicly. Every newspaper in the nation reprinted her brief statement. For this, she was excommunicated from Plymouth Church as well. Thereafter, she never allowed newspapers in her home. Beecher's huge popularity waned, but only a tiny bit. During all of this, Beecher, Tilton, and Mrs. Beecher managed to write novels that give their perspective on events. Later, Beecher was especially sympathetic to New York Governor Grover Cleveland when in the midst of his campaign for the Presidency in 1884 news stories reported (accurately) that he had fathered an illegitimate child. "If every man in New York State tonight who has broken the Seventh Commandment voted for Cleveland, he would be elected by a 200,000 majority," Beecher thundered to an audience in Brooklyn. Rev. Beecher felt that Cleveland's election victory helped exonerate Henry Beecher.

When Beecher died, the Mayor of New York declared a holiday and thousands of mourners, most of them women, flocked to Plymouth Church. Just months later, the reclusive Elizabeth Tilton was buried in the same cemetery. The spirits of all the participants in the sordid mess seemed to have been broken except one – Victoria Woodhull's. She lived the good life in Europe – enriched by hundreds of thousands of Cornelius Vanderbilt's dollars, which he had promised to share with her if one of her stock tips brought a profit.

One protagonist who stayed in the background was Eunice Beecher. She was a traditional spouse suspicious of her husband's flirtations with new ideas and liberated women. She disapproved of everything he stood for and made his life, in Henry's words, "a hell on earth." Mrs. Beecher came to despise Theodore Tilton and barred him from her home. "I have never had so relentless an enemy," said poor Theodore. Rev. Beecher had found the Tiltons' home – with prominent suffragettes and journalists coming and going – much more fun than his own.

The lesson the great Protestant preacher drew from his years of public agony was simple: cover-up is good for the soul. Henry Ward Beecher believed that the public had no right to know anything about his or his church members' private conduct. In fact, he was trying to free New England Congregationalists from idea in Colonial New England that all areas of a person's life ought to be subjected to public scrutiny. There would be no glaring eye painted on the pulpit at Plymouth Congregational Church in Brooklyn.

"No man, for any considerable period, can wear one face to himself, and another to the multitude, without finally getting bewildered as to which may be true. "

Nathaniel Hawthorne,
in *The Scarlet Letter*, 1850.

A recurrent theme of Beecher's sermons was that an individual's "hidden self" can be a source of purity and that in any event another person or the collective public could never understand or be in a position to judge the inner self. Besides, especially for a person in a prominent position, like the pastor of a major church, public opinion could be arbitrary and capricious, robbing one of a hard-earned reputation. "Public sentiment," said Beecher from the pulpit in 1868, "refuses to be just and earnest."[32] Therefore, it was just and proper to deny to the masses any knowledge of the private actions of those public men operating on a higher plane. Private conduct need not be explained to the public, he felt. This notion explains why Beecher twice sought to calm the storm around him by quiet, *private* diplomacy, orchestrated by himself. For a short time it worked.

Beecher's message is a valid one, but one more effectively delivered *before* a public personage gets into trouble. It's doubtful that most Americans at the end the Nineteenth Century – or at the beginning of the Twenty-First Century – accept this theory that individuals in public positions are entitled not to be questioned about their private moral conduct. But a succession of evangelical preachers and their adoring adherents certainly accepted it. And most Europeans would agree with Beecher's sentiments about public men and privacy.

Two lawyers in Boston, Louis D. Brandeis and Samuel Warren, undoubtedly were reading the unavoidable daily accounts of the Beecher trials. They must have agonized over the outrageous public exposure of a man of their class and breed whom they would have presumed to be upstanding. More than that, Brandeis and Warren probably had friends in the two Brooklyn churches; many of the members were transplanted New England Yankees. Both Beecher's crowd and the associates of Brandeis and Warren in Boston were breakaway Republicans later known as Mugwumps.

Brandeis and Warren complained in their *Harvard Law Review* article, just two years after items about the Beecher-Tilton case continued to appear in daily newspapers, "To satisfy a prurient taste, the details of sexual relations are spread in the columns of the daily papers." Yet legal scholars never mention the sensational press coverage of the Beecher scandal as a motivation for the "creation" of a legal right to privacy only a couple of years after the headlines faded.

Historians have tried to present the principals in the Beecher case as illustrative of various character types in the radically changing

Henry Ward Beecher

Louis D. Brandeis

America of the second half of the Nineteenth Century: Henry Ward Beecher as symbol of the new middle class, as well as an emblem for casual pre-war Nineteenth-Century sexuality; Elizabeth Tilton as representative of the emerging emancipated American woman realizing her sexual powers; Theodore Tilton as the urban want-to-be transforming the Protestant ethic into Gilded Age upward mobility; Henry C. Bowen, the devout New Englander trying to bring evangelical Puritanism to New York. (That explains why the church that Bowen founded in New York City was called Plymouth Church. But when Beecher arrived, he eliminated the Colonial New England-styled scrutiny of candidates for membership in the congregation.)

Americans in the Twenty-first Century can as productively view each of the principals as counterparts to the players in the sex scandal that enveloped the Clinton Presidency. The parallels between the two affairs are striking:

The charismatic, popular (and "exonerated") leader, sexually addicted and unfazed by the shame of public exposure, a man whose command of the language is so brilliant as to allow him to make "admissions" without revealing the truth and who when confronted with evidence of misconduct could feign genuine surprise and who said that he never read a word of the mountains of evidence involving him:

Henry Ward Beecher   Bill Clinton

The "go-between" who attempted to fix everything:

Frank Moulton   Presidential friend
                                                       Vernon Jordan

The renegade, discredited freelancer who exposed the scandal through unorthodox channels:

Victoria Woodhull   Internet muckraker
                                                       Matt Drudge or
                                   Literary agent Lucianne Goldberg

The confidante, angered by attacks upon her character in print, who wanted to make everything all right by her disclosures:

Loose-cannon   Best friend
Victoria Woodhull   Linda Tripp

The "strangely earnest brunette" who would rush to the front row to hear the man she admired speak, who engaged in a 13-month sexual affair with him and received souvenir gifts from him when he returned from travel, who said, "I invited it," and who never betrays him in multiple public retellings of her story:

Elizabeth Tilton   Monica Lewinsky

The devoutly Christian prosecutor who had his own motives for his persistence – and ultimately had a losing cause:

Henry C. Bowen   Kenneth Starr

*The apparent victim who **enables** the dysfunctional behavior by gratuitously defending the perpetrator whom he or she adores:*

Theodore Tilton   Hillary Clinton

The communal enablers:

Congregation   Donors to Clinton's
of the Plymouth Church   Legal Defense Fund

The ultimate appraisal by the American people:

"It's all about money."   "It's all about sex."

Links

To read about the development of privacy as a legal concept immediately following the Beecher trials, turn back to the chapter on Brandeis.

To understand the intensity of Nineteenth-Century press coverage, go back to the chapter on Curiosity.

Torts

The cases of the child prodigy, the wronged left-handed pitcher,
the wacky surfer boy, and the bitter ex-Vice President of the U.S.
– and how they all contributed to the restricted legal development
of privacy.

In the year that the Rev. Henry Beecher died, a brilliant 13-year-old Ukrainian girl arrived at the Castle Garden immigrant entry port at the tip of Manhattan, to begin a new life in America like so many others. While a medical student in Boston five years later, she married an equally brilliant Ukranian psychology student at Harvard who had arrived at Castle Garden a year before the girl, in 1886.

Sarah and Boris Sidis had a baby boy on April Fool's Day 1898 and named him after Boris' mentor at Harvard, the renowned philosopher and psychologist William James. "We decided from the start that we would treat Billy just like a grown up," Sarah wrote in a book she wrote later called *How to Make Your Child a Genius.* "So many parents. . . treat them like babies, and then spank them for not behaving like grandfathers. . . . He had all his meals with us. He couldn't creep, and he couldn't walk and he couldn't talk, but he could observe."

Within three months Billy was speaking and spoon-feeding himself; at six months, he wrote his first word; at three years he was typing and teaching himself Latin. At five, he wrote a treatise on anatomy, and by age six he spoke seven languages fairly well and was coaching Boris through the father's studies of anatomy. Boris, an accomplished expert on abnormal psychology whose notable intellect was compared to Sigmund Freud's, sought admission for Billy at Harvard when he was nine and again when he was ten. Harvard balked, but a year later admitted the amazing prodigy. Was he the only Harvard undergraduate in Harvard history to be taken to school by his Mom and picked up by her after classes? (He probably was not; Franklin Roosevelt's mother had moved to Boston to be near him during his time at Harvard.)

On its front page of October 11, 1909 (five years after reporting on its front page the anger of young Abigail Roberson when the New York Court of Appeals rejected her privacy claim), *The New York Times* ballyhooed "Harvard's Child Prodigy." Billy Sidis was now a national celebrity – or national oddity. The newspaper erroneously reported that the boy was 13 years old and had attended Tufts University for two years, then repeated these errors six days later in its Sunday magazine. The original story "was riddled with inaccuracies," according to Amy Wallace in her riveting biography, *The Prodigy*. She wrote of Billy:

> "Thinking – analyzing, pondering abstractions – was his refuge, his place of privacy and play. The more he hungered for privacy; the more famous he became, and the more reporters hounded him."[1]

A friend of the family, a retired Harvard professor, wrote a letter to the *Harvard Graduate Magazine* pleading with the public to understand that Billy Sidis was not a freak, that he was enrolled at Harvard not as a stunt but only to take two courses as a nonresident special student so that he could realize his intellectual potential. The boy was "full of fun." Billy, in fact, was only one of a half dozen young prodigies at Harvard University at the time.

Newspapers everywhere – including the New York and the Boston papers that irritated Louis Brandeis and Samuel Warren and wallowed in the plight of Henry Ward Beecher – continued to report on William James Sidis. *The Times* – which Sidis himself had read on and off from age two – once reported the news that he had the flu, then "rumors" that he had suffered a "nervous breakdown." Other newspapers reported later that the boy tried dormitory life but was so humiliated when classmates ridiculed him for being unable to make change for a telephone call that he moved to an apartment. "Even after they complete their college careers," wrote *The Times* of the Harvard prodigies, "the eyes of the world will be upon them, and the effect of the several theories involved in their education will be universally studied." The precocious youngsters were coping with anti-Semitism as well as America's fear of child prodigies, but still most of them turned out very successfully. Among them were the World War II diplomat A.A. Berle, the composer Roger Sessions, and Sidis' close friend Norbert Wiener, the mathematician who founded the field of cybernetics. The great engineer and philosopher Buckminster Fuller was a friend to them at Harvard.

When Billy Sidis graduated from Harvard he said, "I want to live the perfect life. The only way to live the perfect life is to live it in seclusion. I have always hated crowds." But, Boris Sidis had not taught his son how to avoid news reporters, only how to manipulate them. Billy agreed to an interview with *The Boston Herald*. When he revealed that he would remain celibate and never marry, other newspapers ridiculed him mercilessly, even saying that what he needed was a good seduction. The boy was merely 16 at the time.

In his twenties after an unhappy time at Rice Institute in Houston, he returned to Boston and became a Socialist and a conscientious objector. That only provided the press with more grist for its mill. The headline in the *Houston Post* was WILL SIDIS AGAIN IN THE LIMELIGHT – FORMER RICE INSTRUCTOR WHO DEFAMED HOUSTON GIRLS IS NOW RED FLAGGER. *The New York Herald Tribune* discovered him at age 26 working – by choice – in a clerical job in New York City and criticized him for not attending the funeral of his father (because Billy was feuding with his mother). William had intentionally not told his employer of his genius, which had produced several scholarly, if obscure works. In an editorial the next day, *The Times* told parents what they apparently wanted to believe, "PRECOCITY DOESN'T WEAR WELL." The press repeated so often that William James Sidis had suffered a breakdown that his close friends came to accept it as fact. In turn, he became obsessed with remaining anonymous, whether in his pedantic writings or job searches. (Years later, when he was in his forties, his use of several pseudonyms in his writings and his socialist leanings brought him briefly to the attention of the FBI.)

After a decade of relative freedom from intrusive and mocking press coverage, William Sidis picked up the *Boston Sunday Advertiser* in August 1937, to read, "Genius in a tawdry South End boarding house. That is the story of William J. Sidis, child prodigy and mathematical wizard, who yesterday was discovered working as a clerk in a Boston business house. William J. Sidis, now 39, was once declared by a group of eminent scientists to be a coming innovator in the field of science, with potentialities as great as Einstein and as brilliant as Marconi. Yet yesterday, a *Sunday Advertiser* writer found him in a small room, well-papered and dark, where for the past five years he had lived unknown, unsung, uncaring."

Sidis was doubly insulted when *The New Yorker* magazine published a profile of him in its "Where Are They Now?" series, with the cruel headline "April Fool!" The author of the article hid behind a pseudonym – something the press would not allow William Sidis to do. The author in fact was James Thurber, the famous humorist.

The article repeated the inaccuracies in *The New York Times* story 28 years earlier, then reported comments about Billy's demeanor, from a former landlady in New York ("He had a kind of chronic bitterness, like a lot of people you see living in furnished rooms"), and observations about his personal effects ("There was a large, untidy bed"). Sidis' friends suspected that a mole had infiltrated a small circle of intellectuals who gathered regularly at Billy's residence. But William himself was confident that no stranger had gotten into his room.

Thereafter, reporters and photographers besieged the place where Sidis lived, and he was afraid to go out, even to his job. This time Sidis fought back. He sued the Boston newspaper and also sued the owner of *The New Yorker* for $150,000, claiming a violation of the New York State civil rights law enacted after Abigail Roberson's unsuccessful privacy lawsuit at the turn of the century.[2] His lawsuit also made claims under similar laws enacted in five other states, where *The New Yorker* was distributed. He helped prepare some of the legal briefs in his own case, arguing that the article had damaged his employment opportunities and distressed him, causing "grievous mental anguish, humiliation, and loss of reputation." His close circle of friends did not doubt that this was true.

The prestigious New York law firm representing the magazine argued in the federal district court in New York that Sidis was an object of public interest and that it could not have harmed his reputation because he was already known as eccentric and difficult. It filed a motion to dismiss the case. In response, Judge Henry W. Goddard found *The New Yorker* coverage fair and not abnormal. The privacy statutes in New York and elsewhere, he said, are reserved for instances of *commercial exploitation* of a person's name or likeness, as experienced by Abigail Roberson. They do not cover instances of intrusive news coverage. He ruled that the First Amendment protects publication of newsworthy articles unless they are libelous (untrue and damaging to one's reputation). Therefore, he dismissed the case.

On appeal two years later, the Second Circuit Court of Appeals found the article "merciless in its dissection of intimate details of its subject's personal life." And it gave a nod to the landmark law review article by Warren and Brandeis. But the end result for William Sidis was no different than it was in the trial court. The federal appeals court said:

> "Despite eminent opinion to the contrary, we are not yet disposed to afford to all of the intimate details of private life an absolute immunity from the prying of the press. . . . We would permit limited scrutiny of the 'private' life of any person who has achieved, or has had thrust upon him, the questionable, and indefinable status of a 'public figure.' . . . Even if Sidis had loathed public attention at that time, we think his uncommon achievements and personality would have made the attention permissible. Since then Sidis has cloaked himself in obscurity, but his subsequent history, containing as it did the answer to the question of whether or not he had fulfilled his early promise, was still a matter of public concern.[3]

Despite Sidis' plea, the U.S. Supreme Court let the decision stand. In 1941, by contrast, he won his suit against the *Boston Sunday Advertiser* and collected $375.

Of course, Sidis and his lawyer had not sought "an absolute immunity from the prying of the press," as the appeals court had claimed. But ever since 1940, the decisions of both the trial court and the appeals court in the *Sidis* case have raised the threshold facing any subject of press coverage who wants to recover damages for truthful, but excessively intrusive news coverage. The threshold is so high that now very few individuals ever prevail in a privacy lawsuit against the news media.

The court of appeals said that William Sidis' correct remedy against *The New Yorker* was to allege untruths and sue for libel. Sidis did exactly that afterward and ended up settling the case out of court for a minimal monetary payment.

The appeals court had hinted that Sidis might have a cause of action later in his life after additional years out of the public eye, but only if the revelations are "so intimate and so unwarranted as to outrage the community's notions of decency."[4]

If either court had wanted to, it could have relied on a 1931 decision by a state appellate court in California involving a movie called *The Red Kimono*. It depicted the unsavory life of a former prostitute named Gabrielle Darley, who had been acquitted of murder back in 1918. Thereafter, in the words of the California court, "she abandoned her life of shame and became entirely rehabilitated," married and settled down, and "thereafter at all times lived an exemplary, virtuous, honorable, and righteous life."[5] Therefore, the California court ruled in her favor in a lawsuit against the producers of the film.

The decision in Gabrielle Darley's case stands today for the proposition that a once newsworthy person may have a claim for invasion of privacy if the same information, having once been published, is revived long after he or she has sought to live a private life. James Thurber interpreted the law differently. Years later, he interpreted the *Sidis* decision as standing for the proposition, "Once a public figure, always a public figure." But that is not the case. In 1979, the U.S. Supreme Court endorsed the theory that with the passage of time a person who had been the subject of news coverage could re-claim his status as a private person. The case involved a libel claim, not a privacy claim, by a man who had been convicted 16 years earlier for failing to respond to a grand jury subpoena and found himself the subject of an article in *Reader's Digest.*[6]

In fact, the *Sidis* case represents the principle that a plaintiff in an invasion-of-privacy lawsuit against the news media must show that in the coverage there is a lack of newsworthiness and that it offends "the community's notions of decency."

Long after the *Sidis* case, did the editors of *The New Yorker*, who knew well the institutional history of the magazine, still have resentments about it and accept James Thurber's erroneous interpretation? In 1985 they published a cartoon by Warren Miller showing an irate plaid-suited bumpkin in the office of a New York City publishing attorney. "This man's name happens to be Ichabod Crane," says the receptionist to her boss, "and he wants to know if it's too late to sue the estate of Washington Irving."

In 1971 the California Supreme Court declined to apply the "passage of time" doctrine in another case involving *Reader's Digest.* A man convicted of hijacking and then rehabilitated in the intervening ten years sued *Reader's Digest* for publishing an account of his earlier life. Even though the man had become respected in his community, he could not recover damages, the court said, because the coverage was not malicious and the original hijacking remained a matter of public interest.[7]

In the decades between the 1880s and the 1930s, as virtually all courts around the country came to accept the notion of a tort cause of action based on invasion of privacy, they seemed to show greater deference to the modesty of innocent, victimized women than to the hurt feelings of men. One exception was the victory of Paolo Pavesich in the Georgia Supreme Court, the first recognition of a right to privacy.[8] (While it is true that Abigail Roberson lost her case in New York, the state legislature quickly made amends.)

"Why did the former prostitute prevail and the child prodigy lose? Viewed in social context, the woman who wished to conceal a past of prostitution may have presented a more compelling claim than the man who wanted to conceal that he had failed to have the brilliant career anticipated, precisely because she was a woman and he was a man."

Law professor Anita L. Allen and lawyer Erin Mack, in 1990.[9]

William J. Sidis and the other principals in these cases discovered, of course, the great irony in protecting your own privacy: If you sue to protect your reputation or to recover a sense of privacy, you must endure even more public scrutiny of your life, for many years to come.

Because the First Amendment limits a court from unduly restricting the freedom of the press, judges are cautious about entertaining invasion-of-privacy lawsuits against portrayals by the news media. They are more receptive to invasion-of-privacy lawsuits against *commercial* exploitation of personal information or pictures. Sometimes publications publish articles that are protected by the First Amendment, even though inaccurate, *and* exploit the articles commercially; this creates a hybrid disclosure-of-private-facts/misappropriation claim by the victim.

Between 1900 and 1990 all but one state came to recognize a right to privacy, either by statute or court decision. That means that the states permitted lawsuits seeking damages because an individual or a private entity had invaded the victim's privacy. The courts in Minnesota, a state characterized by assertive litigation by newspapers and broadcasters, always held out. Actually the courts there did recognize a right to sue for commercial misappropriation of one's personality or image, but they did not dare label it "invasion of privacy."

Finally in July 1998, Kathleen Blatz, Chief Judge of the Minnesota Supreme Court, announced:

> "Today we join the majority of jurisdictions and recognize the tort of invasion of privacy. The right to privacy is an integral part of our humanity."[10]

The case involved a photograph of two university students taken in the nude while the women were vacationing in Mexico. They asked a Wal-Mart store to develop the film but were told that the store would not do so because of the nudity. The women then learned that a copy of the photo was circulating in the community, causing them humiliation, embarrassment, and emotional distress. Their subsequent lawsuit against the store was dismissed twice by judges who said that courts in the state had never awarded damages for invasion of privacy. The state supreme court reversed those dismissals. The unprecedented campaign by Brandeis and Warren to establish legal recognition of the right to privacy was complete, 108 years after it had begun.

But what are the similarities between the cases of Abigail Roberson, Paolo Pavesich, William J. Sidis, the two women in Minnesota, and a "Human Cannonball" named Hugo Zacchini, who objected when a local news program broadcast his entire act – getting shot from a cannon?[11] Some of the cases involve commercial misappropriation of one's image, others involve intrusive press coverage. Yet they are grouped together as "privacy" cases.

It was left to a torts law professor in California to make sense out of the seemingly diverse rights protected by the legal notion of privacy that Brandeis and Warren had created.

After surveying the cases to date and the state laws on privacy, William L. Prosser of the University of California wrote, in a notable law review article in 1960:

> "What has emerged from the decisions is no simple matter. It is not one tort, but a complex of four. The law of privacy comprises four distinct kinds of invasion of four different interests of the plaintiff, which are tied together by the common name, but otherwise have almost nothing in common except that each represents an interference with the right of the plaintiff, in the phrase coined by Judge Cooley, 'to be let alone.'"[12]

Another legal scholar, Edward J. Bloustein, saw privacy as one unified tort, not four. The common link among the different privacy actions, he wrote, is "an interference with individuality, an interference with the right of the individual to do what he will."[13]

Bur Prosser's formulation is generally accepted today. University of San Francisco torts expert J. Thomas McCarthy complains that Prosser's theory has become "gospel" among American courts. (Tell that to William Sidis.) Once again a law review article had influenced the direction of privacy law in the United States.

In the years since the 1930s, the American Law Institute, a learned society of professors, judges, and attorneys, has attempted to summarize what the law is, or ought to be, through its "Restatements of the Law." Restatements do not have the force of law, but judges often refer to them and try to conform to them.

As developed in Prosser's writings, the Restatement of Torts, and prior court decisions, courts agree that there are four aspects of the privacy tort:

One right of action covers the widespread **disclosure of truly intimate facts** about a person, even if true – a disclosure that is offensive and objectionable to a person of ordinary sensibilities. The disclosure must be widespread, not merely incidental. A defense to a "disclosure" lawsuit would be that the information is newsworthy, that it is of legitimate interest to the public. Or the publication could defend itself by arguing that the disclosure is not offensive to most people.

Next, the dissemination of personal information (even if "true") or of a picture of somebody that is published out of context, placing a person in "**a false light**," can create a right to sue for damages. This is the type of invasion-of-privacy claim that William Sidis pursued, although it did not have the label of "false light" in 1938.

The third branch of the privacy tort concerns the commercial use of an individual's name or face without permission. Courts often look to whether a commercial endorsement is implied. This has come to be known as **misappropriation** or "the right of publicity." The *Roberson* and *Pavesich* cases are examples. Many celebrities sue under this theory, saying that personal facts about them or their images have been used for someone else's profit. In this branch of the privacy tort, the complaint often does not involve factors that are commonly equated with privacy at all. Under this theory, for instance, a "human cannonball" in a traveling show successfully sued a television station for showing his entire act on its evening news show, and Bette Midler sued Ford Motor Co. for imitating her unique style in a TV commercial. Will the time come when a court will permit a person to sue under this theory for misappropriation of his name and address, without consent, on a commercial sales mailing list, for someone else's profit?

Lastly, courts will regard a physical **intrusion into a person's solitude** – similar to a trespass – as an invasion of privacy. One court said, for instance, that a person's "sense of seclusion, the wish to be obscure and alone" should not be violated without cause.[14] Billy Sidis' lawsuit had elements of this claim as well.

The general rule is that a claim for invasion of privacy expires when the person dies. It is uniquely a personal right that only the person affected can claim. But states with high concentrations of celebrities – like California and – with their country and Western stars – Kentucky, Oklahoma, Tennessee, and Texas – have passed laws extending the "right of publicity" beyond the death of the celebrity.

The families of Dracula film portrayer Bela Lugosi, John Wayne, Martin Luther King, Jr., and Elvis Presley have been especially vigorous in preventing others from using a deceased celebrity's name on souvenirs or as part of product endorsements after death – in the same way that this right is protected during a person's lifetime. In addition, one's expectation of confidentiality in secrets shared in a privileged relationship, as with one's attorney, survives death.[15]

What's the difference between a lawsuit based on libel and one based on invasion of privacy? Libel applies to publication of *untrue* information that damages a person's reputation, even if the publication extends to only one or two other persons. By contrast, invasion of privacy applies to the *widespread* and *highly offensive* dissemination of *true* information that is highly sensitive and intimate. The harm occurs not because the disclosure necessarily damages one's reputation but because it is humiliating or emotionally distressing.

Edward Bloustein stated the difference succinctly, in 1964: The essence of a libel or slander action is creating a false opinion about a person, whether in the mind of one other person or many others. The essence of a privacy case is degrading a person by disclosing private facts to the public at large.[16] It is always a defense to an invasion-of-privacy claim that the person consented to it.

> **"The recognition of a right of action for invasion of privacy is an outgrowth of the complexities of our modern civilization."**
>
> **Arizona Supreme Court, in 1945.**[17]

Lawsuits for invasions of privacy rarely come before a jury. The main reason is that, as is clear from the language of the Restatement, there is a significant threshold for a victim to cross in proving his or her case. At the same time, any lawyer defending a publication or other entity accused of damaging the psyche of an individual does not want at all to place the case in the hands of a jury that will undoubtedly be sympathetic to the plight of the victim, irrespective of the fine points of the law. Consequently, defense lawyers invariably file a motion to dismiss the lawsuit, just as the lawyer for *The New Yorker* did in the *Sidis* case. The plaintiff's lawyer responds with an argument that what happened fits neatly into one of Prosser's four categories. A judge, not a jury, then decides whether the claim does fit within the Prosser analysis – or the Restatement. After the trial judge either grants the motion to dismiss or rejects it, the loser usually appeals that decision to a higher court. In privacy cases, therefore, both the trial court and the appeals court make decisions based on depositions and lawyers' arguments, not on live, moving testimony from the victim.

If the appeals court rules in favor of the plaintiff going ahead with the lawsuit, he or she has great leverage then to talk the defendant into a settlement, without going to trial. And that is usually what happens. Even in his libel suit, William Sidis never got to tell his story before a jury, and most victims in these cases do not either.

Two of the few persons to prevail in an invasion of privacy lawsuit were two of the most famous persons of their time.

Jacqueline Kennedy Onassis, probably the most photographed person in the world in the 1960s, was offended and threatened by a freelance photographer named Ronald Galella. He personified the European paparazzi who pursue a subject so relentlessly as to provoke the person into a startled or hostile pose that can be captured on film. The more provocative the pose, the more likely it is that news publications are willing to pay freelance photographers for celebrity photos. For using this technique, Marlon Brando once gave Galella a broken jaw.

The Secret Service, assigned to protect the former First Lady, sought to keep Galella at a distance from Mrs. Onassis and her two children. He sued her for interfering with his livelihood on the sidewalks of New York, and she countersued, claiming an invasion of her privacy. The photographer responded that he was immune from such lawsuits because he was exercising his First Amendment right to gather the news. A court in 1973 ordered him to stay at least 25 feet away from Mrs. Onassis and her children, John and Caroline Kennedy, even when they walked the streets of New York. The court ruled that President Kennedy's widow, though a newsworthy personality, retains a "reasonable expectation of privacy and freedom from harassment." The U.S. Court of Appeals for the Second Circuit agreed.[18] Mrs. Onassis' plight involved precisely the elements that nettled Louis Brandeis and Samuel Warren: overzealous journalism, aggressive photography, and disturbance of the lives of the social elite. Caroline Kennedy grew up to become a lawyer and wrote a well-received book in 1995 called *The Right to Privacy*. It profiled several persons who had to sue to vindicate their rights to privacy but makes no mention of Ms. Kennedy's own involvement in one of the most notable court rulings on privacy in the century.

"The right of privacy, in short, establishes an area excluded from the collective life, not governed by the rules of collective living."

Legal scholar Thomas I. Emerson in *The System of Freedom of Expression*, 1970.

The other rare winner in a right-to-privacy torts case was Ralph Nader, who panicked the automobile industry in the 1960s with his pointed criticism of the design and safety of American cars. General Motors Corp. attempted to learn all it could about the self-effacing bachelor of modest needs by trailing him everywhere and peeking into the windows of his residence. GM's agents questioned Nader's friends about his political, social, and religious views and his sexual activities. They shadowed him around Washington, sent women to try to seduce him into illicit relationships, made harassing phone calls to his home at all hours of the day, and installed wiretaps and eavesdropping devices to overhear his private conversations. Nader sued the corporation for interference with his ability to make a living and invasion of privacy, as well as intentional infliction of severe emotional distress (a claim very similar to invasion of privacy). A trial court denied General Motors' motion to dismiss the claims.

Upon review, Nader's case ended up before the same tribunal that in 1902 had dismissed Abigail Roberson's claim for invasion of privacy. In a unanimous ruling in 1970, the seven-member Court of Appeals in New York State said that the trial court was right not to dismiss Nader's lawsuit. In analyzing his claim under the law in the District of Columbia, where the abuses had occurred, the court said:

> "The mere gathering of information about a particular individual does not give rise to a cause of action. . . . Privacy is invaded only if the information sought is of a confidential nature and the defendant's conduct was unreasonably intrusive. . . . The plaintiff must show that the conduct was truly 'intrusive' and that it was designed to elicit information which would not be available through normal inquiry or observation."[19]

Thus, a victim can't collect for mere annoyances. Making repeated harassing calls and sending women to seduce Nader did not involve disclosures of private facts about him and so they were not properly claims for invasion of privacy, New York's highest court said. (Still, they were surely grounds for a separate claim, the intentional infliction of emotional distress, the court ruled).

The appeals court could not ignore the electronic surveillance, which clearly constituted the tort of "intrusion upon solitude." Further, General Motors' gumshoes had looked over the consumer advocate's shoulder to scrutinize withdrawals from his bank account. Nader could continue his lawsuit on these two privacy claims, the court held unanimously. Not surprisingly, General Motors, which at a televised Congressional hearing admitted the stalking and apologized for it, reached a major cash settlement with Ralph Nader. Instead of using the proceeds to buy a fancy house or – of all things – a luxury automobile, the consumer advocate endowed some of his consumer-advocacy projects, to keep them functioning for many years into the future.

Chief Judge Alton Parker, in the Roberson case in 1902, may have been right in predicting that the New York courts would be kept busy with privacy litigation, even if not the "absurd" litigation that he had anticipated. After all, you would expect that many privacy cases would arise in New York, where the nation's major book and periodical publishers are based.

New York publishers felt particularly threatened by a case brought in the 1960s by Warren Spahn, the legendary left-handed baseball pitcher for the Boston Braves and then the Milwaukee Braves. Spahn complained that Julian Messenger, Inc., had published an unauthorized biography of him full of factual errors. The author, Milton Shapiro, apparently had invented dialogue, created imaginary incidents, attributed thoughts and feelings, and manipulated chronology, without doing any significant research or interviewing anyone who had known Warren Spahn. Because the Messenger company was making a profit on sales of *The Warren Spahn Story*, Spahn felt exploited and sued under Section 51 of the New York Civil Rights Act, the law that was enacted after Abigail Roberson lost her appeal. He asked the court to stop distribution of the book.

The same New York Court of Appeals that had considered Abigail Roberson's case at the turn of the century and Ralph Nader's case in the 1970s was asked to overturn a trial court decision favoring the Hall of Fame pitcher, the left-hander with the most wins in baseball history. The court this time ruled that a victim could make a case against not only an advertisement or product that misappropriated his or her name but also a "biography" that was not factual. If the falsity is severe enough, the subject of a biography may successfully sue over a writing that shows "reckless disregard," the high court in New York ruled.[20] This New York case was to have a significant national impact just two months later, as related later in this chapter. Ironically, its effect was to diminish a victim's right to recover damages.

"It is common knowledge that many prominent persons (especially actors and ballplayers), far from having their feelings bruised through public exposure of their likenesses, would feel sorely deprived if they no longer received money for authorizing advertisements, popularizing their countenances, displayed in newspapers, magazines, buses, trains, and subways."

U.S. Court of Appeals, Second Circuit, in 1953.[21]

Most states apply the misappropriation tort only to uses of a person's name or face *that implies a commercial endorsement*. New York's more assertive stance has importance because it would apply to any works published in New York – and lots of them are. The legal standard in New York is not totally clear; perhaps all that is required to prevent a privacy lawsuit is for the producer of a text or a play to make sure to label it fiction, or to say that a piece was "inspired by" the experiences of a real person, but not "based on" that person's life.

Lots of famous people have taken advantage of the misappropriation tort to protect against the use of their names or personas in commercial contexts that they do not consent to. Johnny Carson, for instance, sued to prevent the distributor of portable toilets from naming them "Here's Johnny" ("The World's Foremost Commodians"), thus misappropriating a sobriquet of Johnny Carson's popular TV show from 1962 to the 1990s. (The court said that his right to publicity, if not his right to privacy, had been invaded even if his "name or likeness" had not been used.)

Former New York Jets quarterback Joe Namath objected to a "blow-in" subscription card depicting his picture on the cover of *Sports Illustrated* with no royalties to him. (He lost, because the commercial use was incidental.) Former television and movie actress Shirley Booth sued when *Holiday* magazine illustrated an advertisement for subscriptions to the magazine with its cover photo of her. (She lost.) Famed conductor Serge Koussevitzky objected to an advertisement for a biography about him. Movie star Ann-Margret objected when a still photo from a movie showing her nearly nude was reprinted on the cover of a racy men's magazine. The ex-husband of feminist author Betty Friedan objected to a magazine's publication of his name and a photograph of him taken 25 years earlier. (All three lost because they were objecting to what had been purely editorial content, not commercial products, and because there were no allegations of untruth.) Judge Alton Parker's dire prediction at the turn of the century was on target; all five of the cases mentioned in this paragraph, and many more, were heard in the courts of New York.

Elroy Hirsch, running back for the University of Wisconsin and the Los Angeles Rams in the Forties and Fifties, sued because *his nickname* was used in a commercial product. Everyone knew Hirsch as "Crazylegs." The marketers of a shaving gel decided to name their product the same thing. "Crazylegs" wisely chose to sue in Wisconsin, where he was a special hero, and the state supreme court agreed that he enjoyed rights to a nickname as well as his given name.[22]

What do these cases have to do with protecting intimate personal facts about an individual or protecting him or her from harassing intrusions? Not much. The misappropriation tort now protects interests beyond what Brandeis and Warren had in mind in 1890. In an age of intensive marketing of commemorative T-shirts, coffee mugs, action figures and statuettes, theme parks, compact discs, and assorted other souvenirs, perhaps celebrities have misappropriated the misappropriation tort. Some, like Elvis Presley, have even managed to do this from the grave.

Lawyers for Cher, the singer and actress, seem to be the first to extend the misappropriation tort beyond its traditional context. They argued to the Ninth Circuit Court of Appeals in the early 1980s that the widespread promotion and advertising of an article about a celebrity could constitute a violation of the misappropriation tort if there is falsity involved. They had sued *Forum*, a sexually oriented magazine, which falsely claimed an interview with Cher was an "exclusive." In fact, the writer had originally told Cher that it would appear in another publication. The appeals court permitted the lawsuit against the advertising, but not the content of the article itself.[23]

Lawyers for movie star Clint Eastwood piggybacked on Cher's success in merging the distinction between a periodical publishing editorial content and exploiting its product in advertising. This time, the target was the *Enquirer*, the supermarket tabloid, which widely advertised its April 13, 1982, issue with a cover story, "Clint Eastwood in Love Triangle with Tanya Tucker." The report of his infatuation with Tucker while he was engaged in a relationship with actress Sandra Locke was untrue, the actor said. Lawyers for the tabloid responded that a person could sue for misappropriation only if an endorsement of a product was implied. That's right, said a trial court in Los Angeles. No that's not right, said a state appeals court. For the first time, magazines and newspapers in California now had to deal with new ground rules: California's right-to-publicity statute covers news reporting – at least it covers gossipy reporting if it is untrue and is used to exploit sales of the publication. "The appearance of an 'endorsement' is not the *sine qua non* of a claim for commercial exploitation," said the appeals court. Further, "We do not believe the legislature intended to provide an exemption from liability for a knowing or reckless falsehood under the canopy of 'news.' . . . The first step toward selling a product or service is to attract the consumers' attention. Because of a celebrity's audience appeal, people respond almost automatically to a celebrity's name or picture."[24]

Other courts have not picked up the rationale of the *Eastwood* decision; still it was enough for Clint Eastwood to say to the *Enquirer* "Make my day." Shortly afterwards, it was forced to reach a settlement with him out of court. Tom Selleck, the TV and movie actor, sued the same tabloid on the same matter – it had linked him romantically with actress Victoria Principal. He said the two had never met at the time. A state court in Los Angeles permitted his lawsuit at the same time the court of appeals ruled in Eastwood's favor. In 1985, the *Enquirer* had to pay up to Tom Selleck, out of court, as well.[25]

The current standard for judging whether press coverage constitutes a disclosure of private facts – or an intrusion upon solitude – and therefore whether a victim may collect damages – was articulated by a federal trial court in California. Once again an important privacy case involved a publication of Time, Inc. The company refuses to settle these lawsuits; it insists on fighting them in court as long as it takes.

Mike Virgil was just as insistent about winning. He was a local celebrity, a body surfer at the renowned "Wedge," a public beach near Newport Beach, California. At the peak of his invasion-of-privacy tussle with Time, Inc., a judge wrote that he "can be seen as a juvenile exhibitionist, but on the other hand he also comes across as the tough, aggressive maverick. . . ." Perhaps he was a beach-blond Seventies version of Billy Sidis, without the genius IQ.

Mike Virgil had agreed to an interview with a writer for *Sports Illustrated* magazine. When he discovered later that the article would focus more on his eccentric nature than his athletic skills, he called the reporter and revoked his consent and asked him not to write about him. The magazine published its article about him anyway, describing Virgil as "quiet and withdrawn, . . . considered to be somewhat abnormal." It said he once extinguished a lighted cigarette in his mouth and on another occasion burned a hole in the back of his hand. The article said that Mike Virgil dove headfirst down a flight of stairs – "just because," and "bit off the cheek of a Negro in a six-against-30 gang fight." Virgil's wife was quoted as saying, "Mike also eats spiders and other insects and things."

The aim of the aggressive strategy of Time, Inc., is to prevent privacy cases like this from ever coming before a jury. A jury might like a guy like Mike Virgil. As expected the publisher of *Sports Illustrated* filed a motion for summary judgment. In other words, it wanted a judge to dismiss the case before a trial, because, it argued, Virgil's case did not fit within the permissible scope of an invasion-of-privacy lawsuit. Besides, he had consented to the interview; as we have seen, consent is always a defense to an invasion-of-privacy lawsuit by a victim. Virgil argued that he had revoked any consent he had given and that the article publicized private facts about himself. Time, not Mike Virgil, got wiped out in this wave. The trial court denied Time's motion, and the company appealed.

The appeals court said that agreeing to an interview "can be construed as a consent to publicize. However, if consent is withdrawn prior to the act of publicizing, the consequent publicity is without consent." The court found that Virgil's complaint fit the tort of "Publicity Given to Private Life" as defined in the Restatement of law. Further, Virgil was not barred from suing on a privacy claim because he did not claim that anything written about him was untrue. In a privacy claim, it's precisely the truth that hurts. In language that celebrities liked, the court said,

> "Accepting that it is . . . in the public interest to know about some area of activity, it does not necessarily follow that it is in the public interest to know private facts about the persons who engage in that activity. The fact that they engage in an activity in which the public can be said to have a general interest does not render every aspect of their lives subject to public disclosure."

In other words, there should be no compulsion for a stage performer to open up her family life simply because in her profession she appears before the public or even seeks publicity. Theatrical talent or skill on the athletic field – while of interest to a lot of people – do not compel full disclosure of one's off-hours activities.

The court then relied on a comment accompanying the Restatement saying:

> "In determining what is a matter of legitimate public interest, account must be taken of the customs and conventions of the community; and in the last analysis what is proper becomes a matter of the community mores. The line is to be drawn when the publicity ceases to be the giving of information to which the public is entitled, and becomes a morbid and sensational prying into private lives for its own sake, with which a reasonable member of the public, with decent standards, would say that he has no concern."[26]

Thus, Virgil's "victory" was a hollow one. The obstacle the Ninth Circuit had erected – for a victim at trial to show "a morbid and sensational prying for its own sake" by the press is extremely difficult.

In May 1976, the U.S. Supreme Court let the Ninth Circuit opinion stand. In December, the original trial judge wearily reconsidered Time's motion for summary judgment and concluded that Mike Virgil this time would be the victim of what the judge called a "wipeout." He did not even get a trial.

> "Any reasonable person reading the *Sports Illustrated* article would have to conclude that the personal facts concerning Mike Virgil were included as a legitimate journalistic attempt to explain Virgil's extremely daring and dangerous style of bodysurfing at the Wedge. There is no possibility that a juror could conclude that the personal facts were included for any inherent morbid, sensational, or curiosity appeal they might have."

District Court Judge Gordon Thompson, Jr., however, tossed a bone to celebrities with this footnote: "This opinion should not be read in any way endorsing no-holds-barred rummaging by the media through the private lives of persons engaged in activities of public interest under the pretense of elucidating that activity or the person's participation in it." The point remains that the case of the insect-chewing surfer left us with the legal principle that only persons who can show that they did not consent to publication *and* that the reporting is "morbid and sensational prying for its own sake" can prevail in a suit based on public disclosure of private facts. And that explains why so few individuals have even tried.

"Prying sensationalism robbed American life of much of its privacy to the gain chiefly of morbid curiosity."

Historian Arthur Schlesinger, Sr., describing journalism at the end of the Nineteenth Century, in *The Rise of the City*, 1933.

An invasion of privacy is a *tort*, a wrong committed by one private person or organization against another, as we have seen in all of the cases in this chapter. Privacy is also *a constitutional right*, as when an agency of the government restricts the freedom of a private individual. This is unique in the law. The jargon can be the same, but the principles are quite different. By contrast, libel is a tort but there is no constitutional right against libel. Stifling free speech violates a constitutional right, but there is no tort for telling a person to keep quiet. Invasion of privacy, by contrast, arises both as a tort and as a constitutional violation. The constitutional right to privacy is the subject of the next chapter.

Actually there is a *third* context for privacy in the practice of law, and that is when interpreting a statute that is designed to protect it. Judges have to determine whether a privacy-protection law goes too far, and infringes on someone else's rights or has a chilling effect on the exercise of free speech. In two major cases in 1989, the U.S. Supreme Court grappled with this third aspect of privacy. On both occasions, the Court considered the constitutionality of state laws that, in the name of privacy, punish the publication of the names of victims of sexual assaults or the names of juvenile offenders. Do such laws infringe on the First Amendment rights of news publications? The Supreme Court has not answered that difficult question definitively. Its latest word on the subject seems to be:

> "Where a newspaper publishes truthful information which it has lawfully obtained, punishment may lawfully be imposed, if at all, only when narrowly tailored to a state interest of the highest order."[27]

In its most curious "pro-privacy" decision – and a unanimous one at that – the Court in 1989 ruled that a state may prevent the disclosure of databases with information about past arrests, at least to the extent that the records may be retrieved by a person's name. The decision seems not to apply to the disclosure of arrest information in chronological lists, in contrast to data listed by the names of individuals.[28] It was extraordinary because 13 years earlier the Court had found no privacy interest in a person's pharmacy records and because the same justice, John Paul Stevens, wrote both opinions. (In his last opinion as a federal appeals judge in Chicago, Stevens had written earlier that he could find no privacy interest to invalidate a county hospital's rule barring fathers from a delivery room. Yet he could find a privacy interest in an arrest or even conviction record!)[29] The 1989 decision by the Supreme Court was curious also because all nine members of the Court gave a ringing endorsement of a person's privacy interest in police records after many years of not recognizing a privacy interest in much more sensitive information, like financial records, prescription records, non-marital sexual activity, and one's choice of hairstyle.

In the arrest-records case, the Court relied on a cogent dissenting argument from the federal Court of Appeals in the District of Columbia saying that there could be a privacy interest in arrest data in a cumulative database even if the information had been public at some time, in some place in the past. This led to the Supreme Court's finding that,

> "Plainly, there is a vast difference between the public records that might be found after a diligent search of courthouse files, county archives, and local police stations throughout the country, and a computerized summary located in a single clearinghouse of information."

The author of the persuasive dissent was Kenneth Starr, who served as a federal appeals judge for six years before becoming Independent Counsel in the investigation of President Clinton.[30]

In a footnote to its decision, the Supreme Court noted the difference between the constitutional right to privacy and the tort of invasion of privacy. Non-lawyers and lawyers alike, as well as many judges, are confused by this dichotomy.

One lawyer understood this perfectly, but his brilliant analysis did not persuade a majority of the U.S. Supreme Court in a tort case that shaped the broad leeway the press enjoys when reporting on private citizens. The lawyer came as close as he possibly could to winning but his side did not prevail.

In 1962, a jury in New York decided an invasion-of-privacy case against Time, Inc., in favor of a Connecticut couple who felt they had been portrayed in a false light. Leonard Garment, a New York City lawyer, represented James and Elizabeth Hill at the trial. Time, Inc., appealed, eventually to the Supreme Court in 1965.

As Garment was preparing to argue against the appeals of Time, Inc., a lawyer with very little in-court experience moved to New York City and joined Garment's law firm. He was Richard M. Nixon. A year and a half after leaving the vice presidency, Nixon had lost a bitter election campaign for governor of California and took leave of the state with a notorious morning-after press conference in which he had blasted the news media and implied he was finished with electoral politics. The partners in the law firm were anxious to show off their new acquisition, in a case with public visibility, but one in which his untested skills – or lack of them – might not be costly. Garment thought that the Hills' appeal offered that opportunity. "It also offered an attractive political twist: Richard Nixon who had apparently passed from the political scene, arguing for the right of privacy against one of the nation's largest publishers," Garment recalled in a 1997 memoir. "In arguing their case, Nixon would have the best possible forum in which to express his deeply held feelings about press abuses of privacy. He would be seen as a disciplined advocate respectful of constitutional principles, not as the bitter politician who after losing the California gubernatorial race had lashed out at the press in his famous 'last press conference.'"[31]

The Hills had been victims of a siege upon their home in suburban Philadelphia in 1952 when three escaped convicts held them, their three daughters, and twin sons as hostages for 19 hours. The episode was widely reported in the press throughout the nation. Everybody heard about it. In the early Fifties, it shocked the nation to realize the possibilities for terror in the suburbs. In fact, the escapees had treated the family respectfully, even though the incident ended in a gunfight with police. The Hills promptly moved to Connecticut to free themselves from the memory of their ordeal, and they subsequently sought to shield themselves and their kids in the aftermath. They turned down the endless requests for press interviews, despite the apparent need to correct widespread speculation that members of the family had been harmed or even sexually assaulted.

A writer named Joseph Hayes wrote a popular novel called *The Desperate Hours* motivated by the incident, but he recounted a fictionalized, more terrifying story than what the Hills had experienced. In the fictional account, the criminals were sadistic and brutal, the daughter was sexually threatened, the mother panicked, the father was beaten unconscious. When a play based on the novel played in Philadelphia prior to its Broadway run, *Life*, the popular pictorial magazine, sent a photographer to the Hills' former residence in the suburbs to show cast members portraying scenes from the play. *Life* said that the play "reenacted" the Hills' ordeal. It labeled its account "True Crime." It did not mention that Hayes' novel and the play were fiction, not actually close to the real-life experience at all. *Life*'s account said that "the desperate ordeal of the James Hill family [was] reenacted in Hayes' Broadway play," and this was not true.

At trial, Garment had argued that *Life* had portrayed the Hills in a false light; yet he wove into his argument two other elements of the privacy tort: The article was an intrusion upon the solitude of the Hill family by showing their former home and it commercially exploited the Hills' names and personalities for profit without their consent. This overcomes any claim of newsworthiness, especially in view of the inaccuracies, he had argued. Time, Inc., owner of *Life* magazine, had responded that, irrespective of the inaccuracies, publishing the article was fully protected by the guarantee of freedom of the press in the First Amendment.

A jury awarded Mr. and Mrs. Hill $75,000 for their trauma; then after an appeal and a retrial on the amount of damages, a judge reduced that to $30,000. Time, Inc., which had developed a policy of never settling a privacy lawsuit, appealed again.

The Supreme Court was faced with a classic collision of the right of aggrieved individuals to vindicate assaults upon their personal space and sense of privacy versus the broad right of a news publication to publish free of governmental restraint. Where's the potential *governmental* restraint in a lawsuit brought by a *private* family? As in a libel suit, if a court accepts a standard for prevailing in a privacy lawsuit against a news publication that is too low, the action of the court, which after all is an arm of the government, would be curtailing press freedom in violation of the Constitution. Who decides whether the standard is too low? The U.S. Supreme Court. This is a conflict in values that arises only in privacy lawsuits against an entity that enjoys First Amendment protection. It did not arise in the lawsuit against General Motors, but it did arise in the lawsuits against *The New Yorker* and against the press photographer Ron Galella. Thus, Garment recalled:

> "The legal stakes were substantial, and for Nixon, who was preparing to seek the 1968 Presidential nomination, the political and personal stakes were just as high. He could not afford to stumble before his old political adversaries or be seen as simply continuing his war against the press by new means, in a new forum. The only possible answer to these concerns was, as Nixon saw it, meticulous preparation, and I consequently had the opportunity during 1965 and 1966 to see how Nixon prepared himself for a professional 'crisis' such as periodically marked his public career.
>
> "He began by reading and virtually committing to memory not only the trial record and the state-court decisions in the Hill case but copious quantities of additional material, including federal and state case law, law-review articles, and philosophical writings on libel and privacy. He read his way through the First Amendment analyses of various law

professors and philosophers, including Alexander Meiklejohn, Thomas Emerson, William Prosser, and Edward J. Bloustein.

"His preparation was almost obsessive; he left nothing to chance. His behavior was not only a matter of professional pride but a sign of his determination not to let his recent defeats drive him from the political arena."

On April 27, 1966, the Supreme Court heard the oral arguments, first from the attorney for Time, Inc., the eminent First Amendment attorney and experienced Supreme Court advocate Harold Medina. The falsity in the *Life* article was incidental, he argued, and New York's privacy statute, enacted after the high court in that state turned its back on Abigail Roberson, was overbroad because it would punish constitutionally protected publication of even newsworthy materials if they were sold in a commercial market.[32]

Then it was Richard Nixon's turn to face the nine Justices, some of whom had had strong political differences with the former vice president in the past. There was Chief Justice Earl Warren, former California governor who never had any use for Nixon as a Congressman from California. There were Hugo L. Black, William O. Douglas, Tom C. Clark, and Abe Fortas, all New Deal Roosevelt Democrats who were dismissive of Nixon's witch-hunts for Communists. Nixon, in the first appellate argument in his life, was starting at the top, and before a tribunal without a single ideological ally. On today's Supreme Court, Nixon could have counted on at least three surefire allies.

Afterwards *The Washington Post* said that the new man provided "one of the better oral arguments of the year." According to insider books about the Supreme Court, the Justices at lunch afterward expressed surprise at Nixon's polished presentation. Abe Fortas called it "one of the best arguments that he had heard since he had been on the Court." Fortas, President Lyndon B. Johnson's confidant and nominee, seemed to be sympathetic to the Hills' case. The Chief Justice seemed to accept Nixon's argument also and implied that the Hills had a case simply because *Life* had not made clear that *The Desperate Hours* was merely reminiscent of the Hills' experience, *not a reenactment*. Nixon explained later that Warren and Fortas were political creatures who understood how brutalizing the press could be.

Strangely, after he returned to Manhattan that night, Nixon dictated a memo to himself that in five, single-spaced pages brilliantly analyzed the oral arguments and outlined what he would have done differently. Among other things, he wrote:

> "What I intended to point out if time permitted was that as distinguished from libel (while it is not a necessary ingredient to the tort it often is present), intent to hurt the plaintiff through the use of falsehood is completely irrelevant in the tort of privacy. *Life* did not intend to hurt the Hills. . . ."

Nixon's memo also critiqued the Court's new concept of the *constitutional* right to privacy, which was not at stake in the *Hill* case. In the months after Justice William O. Douglas' creative language in the 1965 *Griswold* case, this had been developing on a separate track from *tort law* respecting privacy. (This constitutional development is explained in the next chapter.) But Nixon recognized that most lawyers – and perhaps some members of the Supreme Court – were confused by this. In fact, Medina, in his argument, mentioned the *Griswold* brand of privacy and endorsed it. Nixon thought this only muddled the issue before the court in *Time v. Hill*. In his post-mortem memo, Nixon cleared up the confusion in one sentence:

> "Here the question is not the power of the state to infringe on a right but the power of the state to recognize and implement a right."

Nixon understood that *Time v. Hill* was not a case about the extent of the constitutional right to privacy but a case about private individuals protecting their privacy rights against a private entity in such a way so as not to infringe on a publication's broad right to publish without governmental interference. He wrote in his memo to Leonard Garment:

> "I then intended in my opening statement to pursue the subject by pointing out that there was no 'constitutional right to reputation' and that privacy by analogy should be treated the same way."

The old New Dealer Douglas remained silent during Nixon's presentation. You could just imagine him brooding in his mind during the arguments, "I'll be damned if 'Tricky Dick' Nixon is going to subvert my constitutional right to privacy in *Griswold* to get his revenge on the press!" But Nixon was not trying to do that at all. He had hoped, however, to cut down to size Douglas' expansive constitutional right to privacy in hopes that other members of the Court would then have been emboldened to support state laws that provide a right-to-privacy redress, one that does not present the same potential constitutional conflicts that Nixon foresaw in the future for Douglas' constitutional right.

Nixon's post-mortem memo provided a great guideline for a lawyer arguing a privacy tort case before an appellate court. But lawyers don't get a second chance before the Supreme Court on a major case.

Time v. Hill provided an exception. In the following fall the Court announced that it wanted a reargument on the case. The Court does this rarely – only six times in the decade of the 1990s. It asked the lawyers to concentrate on whether New York's privacy statute could be used to deter truthful but intrusive news coverage if it were done by a profit-making enterprise. Was this "misappropriation"?

By the next fall, Nixon was busy touring the country, speaking at one Republican fund-raiser after another, collecting political IOUs for his intended campaign in 1968, two years later. But he took three weeks off for intensive preparation. At the Court, he engaged in an acerbic colloquy with Justice Hugo Black, in which Nixon was able to make his point about *Life*'s coverage: "It was using the Hills as commercial props for the purpose of selling more magazines." This is a theory of the misappropriation tort that a court in California accepted in ruling in favor of actor Clint Eastwood against the tabloid *National Enquirer*. But that was to come in 1982, long after Nixon had argued the *Time v. Hill* appeal, served in the White House, returned to California unhappily, and *again* moved back to New York in search of still another fresh start.

The Court announced the decision in *Time v. Hill* in January 1967, reversing – by a narrow 5-4 vote – the Hills' vindication in the New York State Court of Appeals. Justice William Brennan, for the majority, borrowed principles from libel law, not privacy law, in saying that a court cannot rule against a news publication unless the plaintiff proves that the publication had knowledge of the falsity of what it published or reckless indifference to truth or falsity.[33] (Nixon's point had been that in a privacy case it's the truth that hurts, precisely because it places you in a false light, or discloses private facts, or intrudes upon your solitude, or profits from your personality. A plaintiff in a privacy case ought not have to show that a publication was reckless about the truth.) Still, Justice Brennan brought the issue in the case back to where it belongs, squarely in the tradition of *Roberson*, *Sidis*, and *Spahn*.

Justices Black and Douglas, in accord with their previous holdings, said in their concurrence that the First Amendment provides absolute protection to the press, regardless of motive or accuracy.

Agreeing with Nixon, in dissent, were Fortas, Warren, Clark, and John Marshall Harlan. When Garment telephoned Nixon with the bad news, he grumbled, "I always knew I wouldn't be permitted to win a big appeal against the press. Now, Len, get this absolutely clear: I never want to hear about the *Hill* case again." Without pause, Garment recalled, Nixon turned to some business about the 1968 campaign. Both Nixon and Garment were dogged by the feeling that something – something "inexplicable" – had happened within the Court chambers between the first oral argument and the call for a reargument.

In the beleaguered final weeks in the Nixon White House, Garment, then the President's lawyer, had the satisfaction of reading that the Court, with a Nixon appointee writing the opinion, modified the Court's libel standard by determining that the high "with malice" threshold did not apply to lawsuits brought by *private individuals*, like the Hills, who are not public figures.[34] Under this new standard, the Hills would have won in the U.S. Supreme Court, Garment said, in a 1989 article about his experience, which was published in *The New Yorker. The New Yorker*? Yes, the same magazine that had prevailed in an invasion–of–privacy lawsuit against Billy Sidis 49 years earlier. In fact, in the 1967 *Hill* case, the Supreme Court mentioned the *Sidis* case. In spite of the loss for Sidis, the Supreme Court said in a footnote, his case stands for the proposition that damages are not "foreclosed" where "Revelations may be so intimate and so unwarranted in view of the victim's position as to outrage the community's notions of decency," quoting the U.S. Second Circuit Court of Appeals in the *Sidis* case. At least some part of the "false light" theory had withstood constitutional scrutiny.

In 1985 Nixon, now in retirement, and Garment, practicing law in Washington after eight years on the Nixon and Ford White House staffs, came across an insider book on the Court that they felt confirmed their suspicions that "something happened." The book *The Unpublished Opinions of the Warren Court* by historian Bernard Schwartz said that the original vote within the Court was 6-3 to uphold the judgment for the Hills, in accord with Chief Justice Warren's view that because *Life*'s story was fiction there was no First Amendment issue of censoring newsworthy and factual reporting. Douglas, Black, and Justice Byron White would dissent.

The Chief Justice, as is customary when he is in the majority, assigned another Justice to write the opinion, in this case Justice Fortas.

Fortas, a brash newcomer who had joined the Court only the year before, produced a 16-page draft that irritated Black because of its excoriation of the news media and its advocacy of a broad unconditional right to be let alone. Black didn't like Fortas anyway. Black's hostility and the doubts from elsewhere on the Court about Fortas' proposed opinion persuaded Fortas to agree to the unusual reargument on the case. Over the summer, Black effectively demolished the hyperbole in Fortas' draft, calling it the greatest threat to freedom of the press in the history of the Court, both in tone and substance. Black kept up the pressure and succeeded by the time of reargument to turn the 6-3 sentiment for an endorsement of a limited right to privacy against reckless publishing into a 7-2 straw vote to reverse James and Elizabeth Hill's victory in the New York courts. Now only Chief Justice Warren and Fortas stood foursquare for privacy. After reargument, Harlan and Clark changed their minds, creating the final 4-5 vote. Justice Potter Stewart nearly joined them, too. If he had, the Hills would have won.

Traditionally, if the Chief Justice is not in the majority, the senior member in the majority assigns a judge to write the majority opinion. Justice Brennan apparently assigned himself. According to the opinion that Brennan eventually wrote, the "something that happened" between the first argument and the final decision was not anything inside the Court. It was the decision of the New York Court of Appeals on October 27,1966, in the *Spahn* case discussed earlier in this chapter.

Brennan wrote in the Court's opinion that the New York court in *Spahn* seemed to be saying that a victim did not have to prove reckless falsity by a publication in order to prevail. "We disagree," Brennan wrote for the majority. New York's privacy law must require that a publication is recklessly false before permitting a victim to prevail or the law is an unconstitutional restriction on freedom of the press. *Time v. Hill* was an exceedingly narrow decision, saying only that the instructions to the jury had been defective. The Court declined an invitation from Time, Inc.'s lawyer to declare New York's entire 1903 privacy law unconstitutional.

Black's concurrence and Fortas' dissent included strident language that insiders would have recognized as digs at each other.

Nixon could not have come closer to vindicating the Hills' rights. Just seven years later, the Supreme Court endorsed the "false light" theory in a decision that arguably threatened a free press more than a decision in favor of Mr. and Mrs. Hill would have done.[35]

If Nixon had won, victims of intrusive press coverage in the years that followed would have had an easier time recovering damages. It's even possible that the excessive tabloidism of the 1980s and 1990s would have been mitigated. The Supreme Court's narrow decision provided the leeway for this gossip mongering. But it was not the direct cause. Instead, it was an immigration of British-trained journalists that fueled it, just as their London-trained forebears had done in the Nineteenth Century at the New York *Herald* of Scotsman James Gordon Bennett, the *Sun* of Benjamin Day, and the *World* of Anglophile Joseph Pulitzer.

Did the Twentieth-Century revival of this kind of intrusive journalism begin with Robin Leach, the groveling Australian who introduced to American television his breathless curiosity about "The Lifestyles of the Rich and Famous"? Most of the journalists and publishers who furthered the trend, like Leach, were British or Australian, like the late Robert Maxwell, the Briton who acquired the tabloid *Daily News* in New York, and Australian Rupert Murdoch, who bought the *New York Post*.

The supermarket tabloid *National Enquirer* began to thrive in the early 1990s under publisher Iain Calder, another Scotsman. The area around Lantana, Florida, where the *Enquirer* is based, became an expatriate haven for the top tabloid reporters from London. *National Enquirer*, *Globe*, *Sun*, and *Weekly Word News* – all of these Nineties tabloids set up their headquarters there, all of them written and edited by British journalists.

Traditionally, the mainstream press had kept its distance from the tabloids. But the two forms of journalism merged in the 1990s as the tabloids produced a few legitimate "scoops" and the respectable dailies covered celebrity news more. The merger was complete on October 24, 1994, when *The New York Times*, in connection with the celebrated murder trial of O.J. Simpson, published the following news story:

THE ENQUIRER: REQUIRED READING
IN SIMPSON CASE

With its saccharine stories of celebrities at home (like a 13-photo spread of Vanna White's new baby), its portraits of a waxing and waning Oprah Winfrey, its Rush Limbaugh look-alike contests, its recipes for Chuck Norris's white enchiladas and Toni Tennille's rice creole, its tales of women hooked on Haagen-Dazs or quadriplegics performing miracles or bullets bouncing off dentures or suspenders, *The Enquirer* is still easily ridiculed.

Mainstream reporters may grumble about its checkbook journalism, laugh patronizingly at its hyperbole, talk vaguely about inaccuracies. But always, they look at it.

"I don't think there's a person here who is not reading it religiously," said Christine Spolar of *The Washington Post*.

In a story made for the tabloids, it stands head and shoulders above them all *for aggressiveness and accuracy*.

The British takeover of news gathering in the U.S. was personified by Anthea Disney, a British expatriate who became editor of *TV Guide* in 1992. The influential "bible of television" was a Murdoch property, and Disney was a Murdoch protégée. She said when she got the job that she learned her journalism at *The Daily Sketch*, one of London's gossipy tabloids. "It meant I could ask anybody anything and not be considered rude," she said of her early experience. After *The Daily Sketch*, Disney moved to Murdoch's *Daily News* in New York and then to the Murdoch-owned Fox TV network as a producer. Her assignment: "Current Affair," the first of many shows to bring the London tradition of gossip and sensationalism to television. After transforming *TV Guide* into a more gossip-oriented organ, she became chair of TV Guide, Inc., before leaving in 1999 to develop new Internet-TV hybrid forms of entertainment for Murdoch.

Also in 1992, regular readers of *The New Yorker* were shocked when Tina Brown, who had arrived from England in 1984, was named its new editor. One of the English expatriates had now taken over America's most widely circulated periodical of good taste. Before she had been on the job three months, spy novelist John Le Carre accused the London-trained editor of importing sleazy British journalism habits to New York City. "God protect *The New Yorker* from the English," he exclaimed. In a letter to Brown, Le Carre said, "You have set up a signal that you will import English standards of malice. New York doesn't need them."

Daughter of a British gossip columnist, Brown had earned her reputation by enlivening the upper-class *Tatler* in London and then by "snazzing up" *Vanity Fair* magazine in the U.S. with what one native-born journalist described as "crazed dictators, narcissistic movie stars, philandering politicians and pederastic priests." The owner of *Vanity Fair* and *The New Yorker* and Brown's patron, S. I. Newhouse, Jr., recruited Britons to edit almost all of his 11 well-known magazines, from *Glamour* to *GQ*. In 1998 Brown left *The New Yorker* and – just ahead of fellow expatriate Anthea Disney – led the charge towards a new hybrid style of entertainment, Internet use, and celebrity chasing, as head of a new venture for the Miramax Films Division of the Walt Disney Co. Her first project was a new magazine called *Talk*. In its inaugural issue in the summer of 1999, it revived chatter about the sexual life of President Clinton, which Americans had pretty much moved away from by then.

By the late 1990s, it was not unusual to hear British accents on local television news programs in all parts of the U.S. and in the hallways of the major book publishers in New York City. In 1999 Murdoch's News Corporation continued the infiltration of British and Australian values into American book publishing when HarperCollins, a Murdoch property and then the second largest book publisher in the American market, acquired Avon Books and William Morrow & Company from the company begun by William Randolph Hearst, the aggressive newspaper publisher of the Nineteenth Century.

In 1999, the company that publishes the *National Enquirer* hired mainstream magazine designers and consultants for a make-over of the tabloid and brought them to Lantana. At the time, one of the advertising experts who was brought in, Michael Jeary, offered an accurate portrayal of American journalism at the end of the millennium: "Look at the tabloidization of the news media, with 'Dateline' and '20/20' and Connie Chung and 'Inside Edition.' These shows have taken over the character of the tabloid newspaper. We want people to get back into the habit of considering the *National Enquirer* as the king of the tabloids, not the television shows."

The British journalists came from a different tradition. Their goal seemed to be to provoke; in the U.S. the goal seems to be to uncover abuses, to inform, and to stick up for "the little guy." British reporters had developed an obsession with ferreting out salacious details about their Royal Family – an institution that seems to have been designed to nurture news reporters who are both fawning and snoopy.

British journalists knew very little of the American constitutional protection for freedom of the press. "Great Britain has less freedom of expression than just about any democracy in the world," *Newsweek* observed in 1990. The Official Secrets Act still prevents disclosure of anything the government wants not to reveal; the laws on libel are remarkably restrictive on journalists; and British courts are free to stop the publication of objectionable material before it is published. ("Prior restraint" is extremely rare in American jurisprudence.) It was more than the temperate climates and high salaries around Lantana, Florida, that attracted British journalists to America, although those were the primary draws. It was also the rare (to them) freedom to report and to write. When the British and Australians arrived, schooled as they were in celebrity reporting, they acted like children set free in a candy store. They went wild – unrestricted by governmental censorship. As they gathered stories, they also discovered that Americans are far more willing than Europeans to reveal intimate details – about themselves and their neighbors. Of course, that is exactly what the European visitors in the Eighteenth and Nineteenth Centuries discovered.

**"There is almost no circumstance under which
an American doesn't like to be interviewed,
an observation which I have had a chance to verify
in cracks in the Tunisian rocks under mortar fire.
We are an articulate people, pleased by attention,
covetous of being singled out."**

Journalist A. J. Liebling, 1930s.

Only after the Anglicizing of American journalism was upon them did Americans realize how alien the scare headlines and celebrity fawning were to their own culture. Confidence in the news media declined, according to opinion polls, especially as the strict demarcation between the tabloids and the mainstream press disappeared in the 1990s coverage of the O.J. Simpson murder trial, the death of Princess Diana of England, and the sexual misadventures of Bill Clinton. Two expatriates from England, Mark Hosenball of *Newsweek* and Christopher Hitchens of *Vanity Fair*, especially delved into the salacious aspects of Clinton's behavior relentlessly

"How do they get away with writing that?" shoppers would say upon glancing at a tabloid headline about alien visitors or about the beyond-belief "expose" of a celebrity's love life or about the supposed pregnancy of the First Lady. The Supreme Court's decision in *Time v. Hill* in 1967 was the best place to begin looking for the answer to that question.

Links

To compare the legal development of a constitutional right to privacy – and Richard Nixon's negative impact on that – see the next chapter, on The Constitution.

To understand the legal developments that led to recognition of the privacy tort, review the chapter on Brandeis.

The Constitution

On privacy, the Supreme Court looks to the impetuous liberal Douglas, then to the impetuous conservative Rehnquist, then to the impetuous moderate O'Connor.

A quite different Richard M. Nixon emerges in the story of the constitutional right to privacy, in contrast to privacy protection in tort law. That story begins in the Sixties, just before Nixon's Second Coming into the nation's politics and public policy. It culminates in the Nineties, when his most successful appointee to the Supreme Court – William Rehnquist – could no longer sustain Nixon's and Rehnquist's campaign to chip away at the right to privacy. It was a campaign – ironically, like Nixon's *in favor of privacy* on the tort side of the law – that he and Rehnquist very nearly won.

The constitutional right to privacy is generally regarded as stemming from a Supreme Court decision in 1965 invalidating Connecticut's laws that had made it a crime to use birth control devices or to give information or instructions on their use. (Nixon had no role in this; he was practicing law in New York City, preparing his argument in *Time v. Hill.*) Estelle Griswold, executive director of the Connecticut Planned Parent League, and Dr. C. Lee Buxton, its medical director, were arrested in 1961 for dispensing information about contraceptives to married couples. "The pill" had just come on the market. State courts twice upheld their criminal convictions and $100 fines. They appealed to the U.S. Supreme Court, arguing that the statutes infringed upon a fundamental right to privacy inherent in the marital relationship.

In the Court's majority opinion, Associate Justice William O. Douglas reviewed the previous Supreme Court decisions that had found "peripheral rights" emanating from specific rights in the Constitution, even if they were not specifically mentioned in the Constitution itself. Justice Douglas, then the longest serving member of the Court, had replaced Justice Louis D. Brandeis in 1939 and was as contemptuous of government intrusions into individual rights as Brandeis had been. In the *Griswold* case, Douglas wrote:

"The foregoing cases suggest that specific guarantees in the Bill of Rights have penumbras, formed by emanations from those guarantees that help give them life and substance. Various guarantees create zones of privacy. The right of association contained in the penumbra of the First Amendment. . . . The Third Amendment in its prohibition against the quartering of soldiers 'in any house' in time of peace. . . . The Fourth Amendment explicitly affirms the 'right of the people to be secure in their persons, houses, papers, and effects against unreasonable searches and seizures.' The Fifth Amendment in its Self-Incrimination Clause [protects the right to remain silent]. The Ninth Amendment provides: 'The enumeration in the Constitution, of certain rights, shall not be construed to deny or disparage others retained by the people.'"[1]

Douglas wrote the opinion for a 7-2 majority of the Court, but no other member of the Court fully concurred in his innovative formulation. They simply voted in favor of the outcome, to invalidate Connecticut's anti-contraception laws. The penumbra that Douglas wrote about is the fringe at the edge of a deep shadow created by an object standing in the light.

Three justices who concurred in the result would have rested the decision on the catch-all Ninth Amendment written by James Madison. It says in essence, "If it's not stated in the Constitution, then it's a right reserved by the people." This valuable concurring opinion was researched and drafted by the law clerk to Justice Arthur J. Goldberg, 27-year-old Stephen G. Breyer. Three decades later, Breyer himself would be sitting on the high court. While the Ninth Amendment is a logical place to look for a constitutional right to privacy, or a right to autonomy, or a right of "personhood," it is usually overlooked in legal arguments. Too broad and open-ended for conservative jurists perhaps. Too risky for lawyers trying to get a court to reinforce the constitutional right to privacy. How many of them know that one of the members of the current Supreme Court drafted the most important endorsement of the Ninth Amendment as a protector of individual privacy?

Associate Justice Hugo L. Black, Douglas's liberal friend on the Court, could not see any penumbra, emanating or otherwise, in the Bill of Rights. Nor did he appreciate the value of the Ninth Amendment. He dissented in the *Griswold* case. Nor could he see any prohibition against wiretapping in the Fourth Amendment, as he said in his dissent in the Court's *Katz* decision in 1967. "I like my privacy as well as the next one," Black said, "but I am none-theless compelled to admit that government has a right to invade it unless prohibited by some specific constitutional provision."[2]

The previous cases that Douglas relied on to construct his "penumbra" included *Pierce v. Society of Sisters* in 1926, in which the Court determined that parents' rights to select a religious education for their children is constitutionally protected; *Meyer v. Nebraska* in 1923, finding that the Constitution protects the right of pupils in a private school to learn languages other than English; *NAACP v. Alabama* in 1958, in which the court said that a state's demand for the membership list of the National Association for the Advancement of Colored People would threaten the "freedom to associate and privacy in one's associations"; and *NAACP v. Button* in 1963 in which the Court recognized "the right to express one's attitudes or philosophies by membership in a group."[3]

The Court's recognition of privacy rights predates even those cases. In 1886, before Louis Brandeis or Samuel Warren set pen to paper, the Court in *Boyd v. U.S.*, found that the Fourth Amendment right against unreasonable searches and seizures and the Fifth Amendment right to remain silent

> "apply to all invasions on the part of the government and its employees of the sanctity of a man's home and the privacies of life. It is not the breaking of his doors, and the rummaging of his drawers, that constitutes the essence of the offense; but it is the invasion of his indefeasible right of personal security, personal liberty and private property."

(The *Boyd* case actually involved compelled disclosure of *business* records, not personal papers; "privacy" to Nineteenth-Century courts often meant protecting businesses against governmental intrusions.)

In practice, of course, the Fourth Amendment right against unreasonable searches applies only to citizens confronted with a criminal prosecution, not to all the affairs of one's life. The same is true of the Fifth Amendment right to remain silent, according to a Supreme Court ruling also in 1886.

In 1891, in a case not involving the constitutional right, the Court gave a ringing endorsement to the concept of personal privacy –

> "No right is held more sacred, or is more carefully guarded, by the common law, than the right of every individual to the possession and control of his own person. . . ."

In 1914, in *Weeks v. U.S.*, the Court established that the Constitution would not permit the use of evidence seized in an illegal search or seizure to be used in a federal criminal trial ("the exclusionary rule").[4]

After the *Griswold* decision and the second-guessing from legal scholars that followed it, the Court in 1969 paid homage to the sanctity of one's private residence, in a decision that is commonly grouped with the Court's decisions on obscenity, not those on privacy. Even though it had upheld laws against distributing pornography, the Court took a dim view of a criminal prosecution of a man for *possessing* obscene materials. The Court rejected what it called a state's attempt "to control the moral content of a person's thought." Executing a search warrant for evidence of alleged bookmaking, federal and state agents in Robert Eli Stanley's bedroom had found three reels of dirty movies in a desk drawer in an upstairs bedroom. They took a look at the films with Stanley's home projector, then arrested him. The Court said:

> "The right to receive information and ideas, regardless of their social worth, is fundamental to our free society. Moreover, in the context of this case – a prosecution for mere possession of printed or filmed matter in the privacy of a person's own home – that right takes on an added dimension. For also fundamental is the right to be free, except in very limited circumstances, from unwanted governmental intrusions into one's privacy. . . ."[5]

Although lower courts have embraced the "penumbra" theory for a constitutional right to privacy and Douglas' talk of "emanations," the theory has been severely criticized in subsequent years, notably by Chief Justice William H. Rehnquist and former U.S. Circuit Court of Appeals Judge Robert H. Bork. Despite the strong criticism, the *Griswold* opinion formed the basis for the Supreme Court's later decisions upholding a right to an abortion. In fact, the *Griswold* decision attracts such attacks precisely because it has been the basis for opinions upholding the right of a woman to control her own body.

The *Griswold* ruling was colored by Justice Douglas' proclaimed respect for the institution of marriage – "a right of privacy older than the Bill of Rights." "Marriage is a coming together for better or worse, hopefully enduring, and intimate to the degree of being sacred," wrote Douglas, who himself had troubles making his own first three marriages endure.

Consequently, it wasn't clear to what extent Douglas' constitutional right to privacy protected activities outside of marriage. Then, in 1972, the Court made clear that the right to contraception extended to non-married persons. In *Eisenstadt v. Baird*, it invalidated the conviction in Massachusetts of a birth-control advocate, William Baird, who lectured on contraception to college students and exhibited birth-control products. Relying on the language in *Griswold* and saying that a marriage, after all, is made up of individuals, who are entitled to constitutional rights, the Court said:

> "If the right of privacy means anything, it is the right of the *individual*, married or single, to be free from unwarranted governmental intrusion into matters so fundamentally affecting a person as the decision whether to bear or beget a child."[6]

It was not a great stretch for the Court to conclude that this right to privacy also embraces the right of a pregnant woman, whether married or single, to terminate a pregnancy. And that is exactly what it did one year later in the landmark case of *Roe v. Wade*. Justice Harry A. Blackmun, for the Court, wrote:

> "The Constitution does not explicitly mention any right of privacy. In a line of decisions however, going back perhaps as far as *Union Pacific v. Botsford*, the Court has recognized that a right of personal privacy, or a guarantee of certain areas or zones of privacy, does exist under the Constitution. In varying contexts the Court or individual Justices have indeed found at least the roots of that right in the First Amendment; in the Fourth and Fifth Amendments; in the penumbras of the Bill of Rights; in the Ninth Amendment; or in the concept of liberty guaranteed by the first section of the Fourteenth Amendment. These decisions make clear that only personal rights that can be deemed 'fundamental' or 'implicit in the concept of ordered liberty' are included in this guarantee of personal privacy. They also make it clear that the right has some extension to activities relating to marriage, procreation, contraception, family relationships, and child rearing and education."[7]

This was music to the ears of Justice Douglas, then 75 years old and in his record-breaking thirty-fourth year on the Court. It certainly sounded as if the full Court had endorsed his penumbra theory. Still, the Court seemed to limit the borders of the constitutional right to privacy to getting married or having kids – or aborting kids.

For himself, Douglas could not resist the opportunity to "add a few words" to the *Roe v. Wade* opinion. In his "few words," the always concise Douglas developed a hierarchy of privacy values under the Constitution that serves as a valid guide today:

> "First is the autonomous control over the development and expression of one's intellect, interests, tastes, and personality.
>
> These are rights protected by the First Amendment and in my view they are absolute, permitting of no exceptions. . . .
>
> Second is freedom of choice in the basic decisions of one's life respecting marriage, divorce, procreation, contraception, and the education and upbringing of children.
>
> These ["fundamental"] rights, unlike those protected by the First Amendment, are subject to some control by the police power. . . .
>
> Third is the freedom to care for one's health and person, freedom from bodily restraint or compulsion, freedom to walk, stroll, or loaf.
>
> These rights, though 'fundamental,' are likewise subject to regulation on a showing of 'compelling state interest.' . . ."

Warming up for *Roe v. Wade*, Douglas a year earlier had written another opinion, this time a majority opinion invalidating a vague anti-vagrancy ordinance in Jacksonville, Florida. The ordinance was similar to the strictures in Colonial New England villages; it criminalized "rogues and vagabonds, or dissolute persons who go about begging, common gamblers, persons who use juggling or unlawful games or plays, common drunkards, common night walkers, thieves, pilferers or pickpockets, traders in stolen property, lewd, wanton and lascivious persons, keepers of gambling places, common railers and brawlers, persons wandering or strolling around from place to place without any lawful purpose or object, habitual loafers, disorderly person neglecting all lawful business and habitually spending their time by frequenting houses of ill fame, gaming houses, or places where alcoholic beverages are sold or served, persons able to work but habitually living upon the earnings of their wives or minor children." That kind of local ordinance was no longer permissible under the U.S. Constitution, a unanimous Court said. Speaking of the casual activities of sitting on a park bench or strolling in a city, Justice Douglas wrote:

> "These activities are historically part of the amenities of life as we have known them. They are not mentioned in the Constitution or in the Bill of Rights. These unwritten amenities have been in part responsible for giving our people the feeling of independence and self-confidence, the feeling of creativity. These amenities have dignified the right of dissent and have honored the right to be nonconformists and the right to defy submissiveness. They have encouraged lives of high spirits rather than hushed, suffocating silence.[8]

Much earlier, in a 1967 dissent, Douglas had written:

> "Privacy involves the choice of the individual to disclose or to reveal what he believes, what he thinks, what he possesses. . . . Those who wrote the Bill of Rights believed that every individual needs both to communicate with others and to keep his affairs to himself. That dual aspect of privacy means that the individual should have the freedom to select for himself the time and circumstances when he will share his secrets."[9]

The *Papachristou* case involving the anti-vagrancy ordinance in Jacksonville may have marked a pinnacle in the Court's recognition of an individual's right to exercise "the amenities of life" free from government intrusion.

Six weeks prior to the announcement of the decision, William H. Rehnquist, age 48, had joined the Court. President Richard M. Nixon, when he nominated Rehnquist, had described the conservative Arizonan as his "lawyer's lawyer." Rehnquist was the assistant attorney general who provided the intellectual and legal theorizing to support the Nixon Administration's invasions of privacy in order to subdue or infiltrate dissident political groups in the 1970s. As assistant attorney general, Rehnquist assured the White House that the President could engage in illegal activities, under implied powers in the Constitution. (In an interview in 1977, after he had been driven from office, Nixon said, "When the President does it, that means that it is not illegal."[10]) In fact, Rehnquist chaired a special White House task force on the declassification of sensitive government documents

That declassification task force was comprised, in total, of four men named David R. Young, Jr., Egil Krogh, Jr., G. Gordon Liddy, and E. Howard Hunt, Jr. At the time, in 1971, Hunt and Liddy broke into the office of a Los Angeles psychiatrist to steal the psychiatric records about Daniel Ellsberg, the man who had disclosed the classified Pentagon Papers to the press. The other two, Young and Krogh, were convicted of charges related to the break-in, which was one of the major components of the group of Nixon scandals called "Watergate." Rehnquist's legal theorizing would have justified the break-in under the President's inherent constitutional powers, and it is logical to believe that he had knowledge of it in advance. In fact, in the same month as the Los Angeles burglary but long before it became publicly known, David Young was assigned the task of identifying someone for the President to nominate to a Supreme Court opening. He and his colleague, White House counsel John Dean, selected William Rehnquist.

While his White House task-force colleagues were planning the Los Angeles break-in, Rehnquist testified before Senator Sam Ervin of North Carolina, chair of the Senate Judiciary Subcommittee on Constitutional Rights, to defend the Nixon theory of presidential powers. Rehnquist testified that the President had virtually unlimited powers to investigate private citizens *before* crime happens, under Article IV, Section 4 of the Constitution, which provides, "The United States shall guarantee every State in this Union a Republican form of Government and shall protect each of them against Invasion; and on Application of the Legislature, or of the Executive (when the Legislature cannot be convened) against domestic Violence."

"Does this mean that the government may conduct domestic surveillance where there is no probable cause of criminal activity?" Ervin wanted to know.

Yes, under the government's responsibility to prevent crime as well as punish it, Rehnquist testified. He went on:

> "It would be scarcely surprising if there were not isolated examples of abuse of this investigative function. Such abuse may consist of the collection of information, which is not legitimately related to the statutory or constitutional authority of the executive branch to enforce the laws, or it may consist of the unauthorized dissemination of information which was quite properly collected in the first instance.

I know of no authoritative decision holding that either of these situations amounts to a violation of any particular individual's constitutional rights. I think the courts have been reluctant, and properly so, to enter upon the supervision of the executive's information-gathering activities so long as such information is not made the basis of a proceeding against a particular individual or individuals. But the fact that such isolated executive excesses may not be a violation of constitutional rights does not mean that they are proper, and it does not mean that appropriate steps should not be taken to prevent their recurrence."[11]

Rehnquist may have had an intellectual underpinning for his assertion, but his underestimate of the extent of abuses within the bureaucracy bordered on the naïve. Most of the abuses in 1971 were taking place right under his nose – using his legal memoranda as support!

At the time, it was not the law of the land that the existence of a domestic surveillance operation does not violate civil liberties unless a person is directly affected adversely. The issue had been hotly debated since 1970 when anti-war activists including many Quakers discovered that they were the target of a vast intelligence-gathering effort by the U.S. Army. None of them had been arrested or otherwise overtly affected by the surveillance, but they filed a lawsuit claiming that the whole point of the military's program was to intimidate them and deter them from exercising their rights of political expression. In the process, they said, it violated their privacy. Within a year of Rehnquist's comments before Senator Ervin's subcommittee, the issue reached the Supreme Court. Rehnquist was then a brand-new member of the Court, able to provide the deciding vote. The Court rejected, by a narrow 5-4 margin, arguments that Senator Ervin had made personally to the Court on behalf of religious groups that were the target of the surveillance.[12]

The parties who brought the case to the Court had demanded that Rehnquist disqualify himself from participating, but he refused to do so. And so he cast the deciding vote. Rehnquist's refusal to remove himself from the case was outrageous. He had testified in front of Ervin that, in essence, the dissidents' claim had no merit; he had been the custodian of the evidence in the case at the Department of Justice; *and* he was part of the leadership group at Justice that argued for the continuance of the program when some Army personnel began to have second thoughts about it.[13] All of this happened only a few months before Nixon put Rehnquist on the Court.

A former Army intelligence officer who blew the whistle on the spying, Christopher H. Pyle, pointed out, "Had Rehnquist recused himself, the plaintiffs would have been allowed to conduct pre-trial discovery into the Army's surveillance records – an inquiry which might have uncovered, before the Watergate scandal of 1972, both Rehnquist's role in continuing the surveillance and the Nixon Administration's secret 'Huston Plan' for illegal surveillance operations against opponents of the war in Vietnam."

In his Senate testimony before Ervin, Rehnquist had uttered an expectation that has been quoted ever since by dissident groups victimized by an overkill of government information-gathering:

> "I think it quite likely that self-discipline on the part of the executive branch will provide an answer to virtually all of the legitimate complaints against excesses of information-gathering."

Those words even appear on a coffee mug the groups distributed. Is there any question that President Nixon would want a man like William Rehnquist on the U.S. Supreme Court?

Rehnquist's testimony was on March 9, 1971. To realize how misleading was his faith in the "self-discipline" of the government, consider what happened shortly afterwards:

□ On September 3, 1971, Rehnquist's colleagues on the declassification task force broke into the office of the psychiatrist of former Pentagon staffer Daniel Ellsberg and took documents.

□ That year, the White House ordered wiretaps installed in the offices or homes of 13 government officials and four news reporters.

□ During 1971 a special unit at the Internal Revenue Service was covertly gathering information about American citizens whom the Nixon Administration considered politically distasteful, targeting them for audits and forwarding information about them to other federal agencies.

□ On June 17, 1972, White House operatives supervised a break-in of the offices of the Democratic National Committee in the Watergate Office Building and took documents.

□ Just eight months before Rehnquist spoke, the President had approved a wide-ranging plan by an assistant named Tom Huston to conduct unauthorized wiretaps, mail openings, and infiltrations to keep tabs on unrest among African-American, student, and anti-war dissidents.

Was this the kind of "self-discipline" that Rehnquist had in mind?

Just 48 days after the Ellsberg break-in, President Nixon nominated Rehnquist to the Supreme Court. Shortly after Rehnquist joined the Court (over the objections of 26 of the 100 members of the Senate), it decided to hear a reargument in the challenge it was considering to state prohibitions against abortions. He became one of only two dissenters in the *Roe v. Wade* decision finally announced January 23, 1973. The newest member of the Court wanted no part of penumbras. He wasn't sure any right to privacy existed under the Constitution.

In the same way that Douglas, the Court's senior member, had done, Rehnquist, the youngest member and its "Lone Ranger," now took a special interest in the issue of privacy.

What Rehnquist objected to was the loose use of the word "privacy" to cover a variety of things, such as the right to know what kinds of information are kept about you, or the right to get a job despite a prior arrest that did not result in a conviction; or, especially, the right to control your own body. None of these involve privacy in the true sense, Rehnquist believed.

Outside the courts, what was known as "privacy" was taking on new meaning. In an age of newly asserted individual and group rights, it came to include the right to control your own body and self, as well as the traditional "right to be let alone." Thus, "privacy" was used to justify defiance of codes restricting types of dress and hairstyles – a growing area of conflict now that graduates of the Vietnam War protests and survivors of the permissive Sixties were reaching the workplace.

Furthermore, in an age of computers and sophisticated surveillance devices, "privacy" came to include the right to know what information was kept on you in a databank and the right to correct that information. This notion of "informational privacy" also included an element from the traditional concept of privacy – a right of confidentiality.

Rehnquist wanted no part of this new meaning for privacy. He drafted a "strict constructionist" view of the right to privacy and took it out of town for a try-out.

The place was the University of Kansas Law School in Lawrence, Kansas, in the fall of 1974, a couple of months after President Nixon had been forced from office because of abuses that Rehnquist had sanctioned as assistant attorney general. Rehnquist called his two-part lecture there, "Is an Expanded Right of Privacy Consistent with Fair and Effective Law Enforcement? Or: Privacy, You've Come a Long Way, Baby."[14] Clearly, Rehnquist's answer was that an "expanded right of privacy" *was* inconsistent with fair and effective law enforcement and that privacy had come quite far enough, baby. Rehnquist's whimsical title was based on a slogan in Virginia Slims cigarette advertisements aimed at women.

Announcing himself as a "devil's advocate," because "no thinking person is categorically opposed to 'privacy' in the abstract," the justice spelled out why he felt that "if the balance is struck in favor of 'privacy' some other societal value will suffer."

Some advocates of informational privacy had argued that records of arrests, where the individual had not been convicted, ought not be released by police so that employers, credit grantors, and neighbors could stigmatize an individual. Rehnquist responded in his Kansas lecture by saying, "To speak of an arrest as a private occurrence seems to me to stretch even the broadest definitions of the idea of privacy beyond the breaking point." Rehnquist conceded that this "does not mean an individual has no interest in limiting disclosures or dissemination." But he said even "if the fact of an arrest is by no means conclusive evidence of wrongdoing, it is considered a relevant factor by law enforcement authorities."

Thus, Rehnquist said, he would reject any privacy challenges to a centralized computer file of arrests maintained by the Federal Bureau of Investigation or local police. Instead of limiting disclosure of arrest records (when a conviction had not resulted), why not educate employers not to discriminate on grounds of an arrest, he suggested. Rehnquist actually thought that a personnel officer – once "educated" – would nobly decline to take into account an arrest record concerning an applicant because it may be inaccurate or it may not have resulted in a conviction.

Not only were privacy enthusiasts hampering law enforcement, Rehnquist said, they are sloppy in their thinking. They were including all manner of other interests under William O. Douglas' penumbras. Rehnquist preferred the dictionary meanings of privacy – "the quality or state of being apart from the company or observation of others" and "freedom from unauthorized oversight or observation." To him that sounded like interests that were adequately protected by the Fourth Amendment restriction against unreasonable searches and seizures by the government. And no more.

That was fair enough. But then Rehnquist went on to the flights of fancy that lawyers before the Court have come to expect from him. He said that he did not know what the right to privacy had to do with an abortion since a doctor is present during the procedure and therefore it isn't a total secret.

He asked his audience to imagine the need for the Secret Service to photograph all persons attending political rallies. (The man who shot Presidential candidate George Wallace in 1972, after all, had attended rallies just prior to the shooting.) Citizens attending a political rally have no privacy interest, Rehnquist asserted. What's wrong with the government photographing everyone at a political rally – or photographing everyone doing anything else in public, Rehnquist wondered. Surely he was aware that the Supreme Court had ruled in 1958 that it was unconstitutional for the government to demand a membership list of the NAACP; was he saying that it would be constitutional for the government to photograph everybody at a public NAACP rally and to store the photographs?

After that bold assertion, Rehnquist promised the students and professors more for the next day. He delivered. He complained that "the government is present in the lives of all of us today in a way that would have been inconceivable even 50 years ago." Rather than regulate the personal data collection necessary for government programs, why not discontinue the programs, asked the jurist.

"The applicant [for government benefits] who objects to submitting the information required retains the option to decline participation in the program, although in the real world this may not be a very meaningful option," Rehnquist said. Indeed. And what kind of an option does the individual have to resist providing personal information – or do without the benefit – when filing a government tax return or applying for a driver's license?

Alert constitutional lawyers knew that it was only a matter of time before Rehnquist would have a significant impact on the growth, or more accurately the curtailment, of the constitutional right to privacy.

One civil libertarian who had several police surveillance cases pending before the Supreme Court, Frank Askin of Rutgers Law School, countered with his own lecture at the University of Tennessee Law School 18 days later. The Court had recognized in the past, Askin asserted, "a First Amendment right of privacy – a right to keep government agents from prying into your political activities and associations, even those which appear in a public place." It's important, Askin continued, "for courts and judges to understand what psychologists already know – that the right to control information about oneself is an essential ingredient of a secure personality."[15]

Evidently pleased with the reception to his trial run in Kansas (although the lecture received no notice at all in national news reports), Rehnquist returned to Washington to win over a tougher audience – his eight colleagues, including Douglas, on the U.S. Supreme Court.

They had ceased looking to the senior Douglas for guidance on privacy. He had been alone in dissent in the spring of 1974 when the Court rejected a privacy challenge to the so-called Bank Secrecy Act, which requires banks to keep a copy of the front and back of customers' checks and deposit slips for five years so that government agents may have access to the information later.[16] In November of 1974 – one month after the Kansas road show – Rehnquist joined his colleagues in debating the merits of *U.S. v. Bisceglia*, in which Internal Revenue agents were able to issue a "John Doe" summons (without the name of any target individuals) to rummage through a bank's files to discover the identity of an individual who had deposited an unusual amount of cash and therefore may have incurred an unreported tax obligation.

With only a slight acknowledgment that the privacy concerns were not "trivial," the Nixon-appointed Chief Justice, Warren E. Burger, upheld the intrusion into bank records, with Justice Rehnquist and six others agreeing.[17] Only Justices William J. Brennan and William O. Douglas dissented, finding this "a breathtaking expansion of the summons power." They said, "Any private economic transaction is now fair game for forced disclosure." And they proved to be right. In the years to come the disclosures came in massive loads of computerized data, not just in cumbersome manual records.

On New Year's Eve 1974, William O. Douglas had a debilitating stroke and was forced to retire. Within two years, Justice Rehnquist had his chance to take up Douglas' mantle on privacy issues. At issue before the Court was whether it was a violation of privacy for the police department in Louisville, Kentucky, to circulate a flyer of "active shoplifters." The flyer included the photograph of a young professional named Edward Charles Davis III, who had been arrested on a shoplifting charge that was dismissed shortly thereafter. The words preceding the Court's decision in *Paul v. Davis* were to become more and more familiar at the top of Court opinions in the 1970s about privacy: "Justice Rehnquist delivered the opinion of the Court."[18] (President Gerald Ford's choice to succeed Douglas on the Court, John Paul Stevens, took no part in the consideration of the case, but later in his tenure he proved to be no fan of the constitutional right to privacy.)

Rehnquist now made good on the vow he had made at the University of Kansas Law School in 1974. He shot down Davis' claim that due process had been violated, calling the claim of an invasion of privacy "far afield." He must have relished reciting the "zones of privacy" theory of the late Associate Justice Douglas, and saying that the Court's privacy decisions defy "categorical description." But he credited the "zones of privacy" to the *Roe v. Wade* decision, not the original *Griswold v. Connecticut*. He must have relished even more saying, for a majority of the Court now in 1976, that Davis' case "comes within none of these areas." He could have, of course, found that protecting an innocent man from the stigma of a misleading public police report falls within the area of the Ninth Amendment or the liberty in the Fourteenth Amendment. This argument would have been bolstered by the fact that Davis was among a segment of the population most victimized by records of arrests that are later dismissed – young African-American males. Davis' interest certainly fell within the interests at stake in the *Papachristou* case, the right of innocent persons to walk the streets freely.

That would have been enough of a blow to civil libertarians like Frank Askin had not Rehnquist added what lawyers who dislike the language call "mere dictim." Dictim is language that a judge includes in a decision although it is not essential to a court's ruling in a case. Rehnquist wrote:

> "The activities detailed as being within this definition [of privacy in *Roe v. Wade*] were ones very different from that for which [Davis] claims constitutional protection – matters relating to marriage, procreation, contraception, family relationships and child rearing and education. In these areas it has been held that there are limitations on the states' power to substantially regulate conduct."

Rehnquist had hammered his point. He had completed his coup at the Supreme Court. He had taken the privacy language of *Griswold* and *Roe v. Wade* and frozen it in place. Henceforth, for the next 20 years and more, Rehnquist's "privacy" – and therefore the U.S. Supreme Court's – would be limited to marital sex matters and the subsequent responsibility of raising children. His limits were deliberately drawn. At the same time, the Court was rejecting the view that a state's criminal punishment for acts of sodomy conducted between consenting (straight) adults in private was an unconstitutional invasion of privacy.[19] It was acceptable for a state to impose prison time on a man and woman caught committing sodomy, even in a private place, the Court ruled. Heterosexual, conjugal, non-oral, straight missionary-type sexual matters fall within Rehnquist's definition of privacy, but not private homosexual activity, extramarital activity, or even marital activity that William Rehnquist, but certainly not Alfred Kinsey, would regard as "uncommon."

To be sure we got the message, Justice Rehnquist came back two weeks later with the Court's opinion upholding regulations that prescribe the length of hair that may be worn by police officers in Suffolk County, New York. He again cited the privacy decisions before he was named to the court, and wrote:

> "Each of those cases involved a substantial claim of infringement on the individual's freedom of choice with respect to certain basic matters of procreation, marriage, and family life."[20]

This language further limited Rehnquist's vision of the right to privacy. (What happened to the notions that selecting education for your children and using birth control were included in the right to privacy? Rehnquist left them out.) And the statement conveniently overlooked that the Court's 1972 decision in *Papachristou v. City of Jacksonville* involved a liberty interest unrelated to sex or marriage at all. As *Privacy Journal* newsletter, then in its second year, reported, "Justice Rehnquist had waited a year and a half to get that limited view of privacy into the Court's majority opinions."

Not surprisingly, on April 21, 1976, with Rehnquist in the majority, the Court proclaimed, "We perceive no legitimate 'expectation of privacy'" in a citizen's bank balance, nor in the names of those to whom the customer writes checks, nor in background information about loans and other bank transactions.[21]

In still another case considered in the fall of 1976, members of the

Court seemed to defer to Rehnquist as their expert on privacy. It was Rehnquist who peppered both sides with probing questions about privacy versus the need for effective law enforcement. The others simply listened, as attorneys argued the merits of New York State's law requiring all pharmacists to send to a central computer in Albany a carbon copy of personal prescriptions for certain drugs subject to misuse. "Computers are not unconstitutional machines," said the representative of the State of New York. Simply because you automate a process doesn't make it more threatening, he argued. Picking up on this theme, Rehnquist told the attorney for drug store customers challenging the reporting requirement, "Your argument is that if it's made easier through new technology to enforce a law, then it's unconstitutional." He didn't see any need for the state to justify every new computerized information system to the courts. When the attorney for the challengers objected to the trend towards a mechanized society in which every citizen is numbered, catalogued and compiled, Rehnquist shot back, "What about the requirement that we have a birth certificate?"

Sure enough, before the year had ended, the Court upheld New York's mandatory reporting of retail-drug records. Justice Stevens, President Ford's new appointee to the Court, delivered the unanimous opinion:

> "Disclosures of private medical information to doctors, to hospital personnel, to insurance companies, and to public health agencies are often an essential part of modern medical practice even when the disclosure may reflect unfavorably on the character of the patient. Requiring such disclosures to representatives of the State having responsibility for the health of the community does not automatically amount to an impermissible invasion of privacy."[1]

And so, before the computer revolution had really begun, the Supreme Court had shut off the possibility that electronic data collection by the government, because of its ease and massive volume, could constitute an unconstitutional invasion of personal privacy.

Associate Justice William J. Brennan went along with the new conservative majority on the Court, but added a caution:

> "What is more troubling about this scheme is the central computer storage of the data thus collected. . . . [This] vastly increases the potential for abuse of that information, and I am not prepared to say that future developments will

not demonstrate the necessity of some curb on such technology."

This timid language is the closest the Court or any of its members had come in the intervening two and one-half decades between 1976 and the end of the century to declaring that modern electronic collection of personal information by government agencies *might* raise threats to constitutional rights.

Under Rehnquist's leadership the Court has declined to extend the constitutional right to privacy to extramarital sex, homosexual activity in private, personal financial information in the hands of a third party, or the choice of one's hairstyle.

In 1985, Rehnquist said from the bench, "I don't know why two-way mirrors in a restroom would be a violation of privacy." On the other hand, two years later, he wedged in to one of his dissenting opinions the observation that the right of privacy includes the right to be free of door-to-door solicitors, even if this limits free speech. "To protect citizens' privacy [is a] legitimate government objective," Rehnquist wrote (at a time when his endorsement had absolutely no consequence at all). Go figure! Actually, the way to figure is that William Rehnquist and his conservative colleagues on the Supreme Court can easily find a privacy interest if that is the way to uphold a government regulation or to support the government's attempt to keep information away from public view. The decisions in the past 20 years show that pattern. A good example is one of the few majority opinions ever written by Justice Thomas – and certainly the only one in which Thomas, Rehnquist, and Scalia stood foursquare for personal privacy. The opinion stated that a federal agency may refuse to disclose lists of home addresses of its employees to a labor union seeking to organize them, because of an "interest that individuals have in preventing at least some unsolicited, unwanted mail from reaching them at home."[23] What the conservative jurists were really doing was not defending personal privacy. Each of them believes that no right to privacy provides access to abortions or protects a person reluctant to urinating in front of another person at work – intrusions most of us would find more significant than getting unwanted mail at home. What the trio was doing was defending the prerogative of the government not to disclose certain information in its possession.

Consequently, the Court has created a supreme irony: giving some privacy recognition to personal information that is far less intimate than the areas excluded by the Court. In the Rehnquist years, the

Court has found a privacy interest in the results of personality tests administered in the workplace, in pupil records at school, in arrest information compiled in law enforcement data systems (tell that to unfortunate Edward Davis in Louisville!), and in the home addresses of federal employees.[24]

In 1986, President Ronald Reagan appointed William Rehnquist Chief Justice of the U.S. Supreme Court. During a confirmation hearing by the Senate Judiciary Committee that questioned Rehnquist's suitability (on the grounds of his "reactionary" views on the civil rights of women and minorities), there was not a word of testimony about his constriction of the constitutional right to privacy nor of the support he had provided on and off the bench to the Nixon Administration's massive invasions of privacy.

On the other hand, a refusal to entertain any recognition of a right to privacy in the Constitution – whether in a penumbra or anywhere else – cost one nominee for a Supreme Court seat his opportunity for promotion. The day after the Senate Judiciary Committee in 1987 voted to reject the nomination of Judge Robert Bork to the U.S. Supreme Court, *The New York Times* Court correspondent Linda Greenhouse reported:

> "The issue that jelled for the opposition, surprisingly, was privacy. . . . Indeed, the privacy issue underwent a fascinating transformation during the course of this confirmation debate. Before the hearings began the word 'privacy' in political discourse was widely understood as a metaphor for abortion, a politically dangerous topic that politicians of both parties shied away from. During the hearings privacy became another metaphor entirely. It came to stand for the whole theme of fundamental rights, the concept of an expansive constitution in contrast to Judge Bork's view that the Constitution was limited by its precise language and the intent of its Eighteenth-Century framers."

In the 1980s, Sandra Day O'Connor, then the Court's new youngest member, assumed the Rehnquist role of privacy expert, although she dared not use the term. By now it had been tainted in the minds of many as a code word for the right to abortion. There can be no doubt that since the Court's controversial abortion decisions, Supreme Court justices have avoided the unfettered rhetorical appreciation of personal privacy that their predecessors expressed in their opinions.

Two years after President Reagan appointed O'Connor as an Associate Justice, the Supreme Court considered one of the more unusual appeals it had heard in many years. It involved the simplest "amenity" of life, yet struck at the heart of the freedoms that the founders intended to protect in the Bill of Rights. Justice O'Connor was assigned to write the Court's majority opinion, in which Justice Rehnquist did not join.

A 36-year-old California gentleman brought the case to the U.S. Supreme Court on his own behalf. Edward Lawson simply liked to walk the sidewalks of San Diego, often in the most affluent white neighborhoods. Lawson is an African-American who wears dreadlocks, and so he was frequently arrested or detained for exercising this simple amenity – 15 times in a 22-month period. He was never violating any law. He simply "appeared suspicious," police officers would say. Each time, he refused to comply with a California law that punished a person "who loiters or wanders upon the streets or from place to place without apparent reason or business and who refuses to identify himself and to account for his presence when requested. . . ." Twice he was prosecuted for this misdemeanor; once the charge was dismissed and once he was convicted. By himself, he then sued the police, seeking a declaratory judgment by a federal court that the state law was unconstitutional and should not be used to detain him in the future. The court in California agreed with him, saying that "a person who is stopped on less than probable cause cannot be punished for failing to identify himself." A federal appeals court upheld the trial court's ruling, noting that a California court had ruled earlier that the law requires any person requested by police to produce "credible and reliable" identification.

Because in the U.S. there really is no such thing as "credible and reliable" ID, this places too much discretion in the hands of a police officer on the beat, O'Connor said, for the Supreme Court.[25] In ruling that California's ID requirement was unconstitutional because of its vagueness, the Court mentioned the previously unmentioned *Papachristou* case of 1972 and said:

> "Our Constitution is designed to maximize individual freedom within a framework of ordered liberty. Statutory limitations on those freedoms are examined for substantive authority and content as well as for definiteness or certainty of expression."

Some call it "privacy," others call it "the pursuit of happiness," still others call it "autonomy." O'Connor, like some of her predecessors on the Court, termed this freedom of action "liberty."

(Although O'Connor did not mention this, the Court has affirmed on more than one occasion the existence also of a "right to travel" in the Constitution. In 1958, it stated, "Freedom to travel is, indeed, an important aspect of the citizen's liberty," and in 1964 it said that this right may not be restricted by the government "too broadly and indiscriminately."[26] The Court could have used this right as the basis for ruling in favor of Edward Lawson.)

His courageous challenge in the U.S. Supreme Court won for all Americans the right not to have to present identification upon demand. Exactly ten years after that, Edward Lawson was arrested and spent three nights in jail. His offense? Failure to present a driver's license while he was strolling the streets of Los Angeles.

"If there is any fixed star in our constitutional constellation, it is that no official, high or petty, can prescribe what shall be orthodox. . . . "

Supreme Court Justice Robert H. Jackson, 1943.[27]

Rehnquist's elevation to Chief Justice ironically marked the end of his influence on privacy matters. The turning point was a 5-4 opinion in June 1986 finding no constitutional right to privacy in homosexual acts in one's own home, a decision overruled in 2003.[28] The 1986 case involved the prosecution of Michael Hardwick, whom police found in bed with another man when they entered his home on other business. That the decision was so close, at the height of the AIDS epidemic, was remarkable. The person who cast the deciding vote, Lewis F. Powell, Jr., said that he could easily have gone the other way, and probably would have, had Hardwick argued that prison time for having sodomy in private is cruel and unusual pun-ishment, under the Eighth Amendment to the Constitution. The Court ruled simply that this conduct was outside of its previous perimeters for the right to privacy.

After he retired from the Court, Powell said that he had made a mistake in voting the way he did. On second thought, he confessed, he should have ruled that gay sex was protected by the Constitution. That would have created a 5-4 majority for that view.

Justice Blackmun – who was at the very same time desperately trying to protect his pro-privacy opinion in *Roe v. Wade* – wrote a dissent in the 1986 homosexuality case that made sense of the previous Court rulings on privacy. He saw a duality. The privacy cases protect "decisional" aspects of a person's life, like the right to terminate a pregnancy, and they protect "spatial" interests, like freedom from electronic surveillance and unreasonable searches. Compare this to Rehnquist's view that the privacy cases had been "not particularly helpful" and lacked any unifying principle. Blackmun said that both "decisional" and "spatial" interests were compromised by the police arresting a man in his home for engaging in gay sex in his bedroom.

Eleven days earlier, Blackmun had collected five votes on the Court to continue to protect the right to an abortion and to endorse the constitutional right to privacy. This time Powell was the fifth vote. Rehnquist could no longer count on a majority on the Court to narrow the constitutional right to privacy.

Blackmun had the narrowest of "victories." In his dissent in the gay rights case, he quoted – with great approval, of course – his own language in the pro-abortion majority opinion 11 days earlier:

> "Our cases long have recognized that the Constitution embodies a promise that a certain private sphere of individual liberty will be kept largely beyond the reach of government."[29]

There were more challenges to the right to an abortion coming, and consequently to the constitutional right to privacy that provides its basis. In 1992, Justice O'Connor co-authored the Supreme Court's decision invalidating some and accepting some of Pennsylvania's restrictions on abortions. She appeared to usurp leadership on privacy issues from the Chief Justice, who bitterly dissented. O'Connor did not use the word privacy at all, perhaps to appease the two conservative judges who joined her slim 5-4 opinion in the case of *Planned Parenthood of Southeastern Pennsylvania v. Casey*. She found protected zones of privacy in the Constitution, just as Justices Douglas and Blackmun had, and called them *liberty*. The decision of a married or single person as to whether to have a child and the "private realm of family life" are clearly protected by the Constitution, she wrote with Justices Anthony M. Kennedy and David H. Souter. This opinion was a relief to many Americans who thought that the constitutional right to privacy as well as the right to an abortion would be eliminated by the Court in its decision in the Pennsylvania case. "These matters, involving the most intimate and personal choices a person may make in a lifetime, choices central to personal dignity and autonomy, are central to the liberty protected by the Fourteenth Amendment." The three justices wrote:

> "At the heart of liberty is the right to define one's own concept of existence, of meaning of the universe, and of the mystery of human life. Beliefs about these matters could not define the attributes of personhood were they formed under compulsion of the State."[30]

Griswold was alive and well, O'Connor made clear. But she said further to the anti-*Griswold* doubters among her colleagues, if you don't believe in a constitutional right to privacy, you have to recognize that the original *Roe v. Wade* decision has an "affinity" to prior Court decisions limiting governmental involvement in medical treatments. Here she was surely thinking of one of the very first privacy cases decided by the Court, just a few months after the Warren-Brandeis *Harvard Law Review* article appeared in 1890. In that case, the Court ruled on the appeal of a woman who objected to being compelled to disrobe and submit to a surgical examination without her consent, as a condition of continuing her lawsuit against the Union Pacific Railway to collect damages for a physical injury. The Supreme Court proclaimed,

> "No right is held more sacred, or is more carefully guarded, by the common law, than the right of every individual to the possession and control of his own person, free from all restraint or interference of others, unless by clear and unquestionable authority of law."[31]

Rehnquist did not take on O'Connor on the privacy/liberty issue. But he must have felt burned. Associate Justice Harry Blackmun, the author of *Roe v. Wade* who had fully expected that it would be reversed in 1992, wrote in an opinion concurring with O'Connor (and praising her "personal courage"), "The Chief Justice's criticism of *Roe* follows from his stunted conception of individual liberty [Blackmun's and O'Connor's code word for *privacy*?]. While recognizing that the Due Process Clause [in the Fourteenth Amendment] protects more than simple physical liberty, he then goes on to construe this Court's personal-liberty cases as establishing only a laundry list of particular rights, rather than a principled account of how these particular rights are grounded in a more general right of privacy."

O'Connor seemed to be moving the Court away from Chief Justice Rehnquist's restrictive "laundry list" towards a "more general right to privacy." This gave lawyers in future cases the leeway they needed to widen the Constitutional recognition of privacy. At about the same time, lawyers for gay persons began to expand the notion of *family* so that their claims for privacy protection would fit even within the "laundry list."

Was O'Connor's opinion for a bare 5-4 majority in the *Casey* case an extremely narrow viewpoint of privacy (or liberty), standing only for the proposition that one's belief about abortions is a totally personal decision? (This is a narrow reading, because, after all, it is not a radical thought to say that a person's *beliefs* are protected against government intrusion. That has never been challenged. Nor does it have much to do with the right to an abortion, which involves *acting* on those beliefs.) Or is a more expansive interpretation warranted? Was a slim Supreme Court majority, with O'Connor leading the way, now extending the constitutional right to privacy – a tiny bit – to all of the intimate *attributes of personhood*, including sexuality, family life, personal health care and education, spirituality, intellectual activities, and possibly how one earns and spends one's personal resources? This broader view may be warranted because Justice O'Connor chose to use the world *personhood*, an *expansive*, not limiting, synonym for privacy that only permissive appellate judges and liberal commentators had dared use in the past.[32]

Or, was this language the contribution of Justice Kennedy, who was the teetering deciding vote to uphold the constitutional right to an abortion in 1992? It sounds like him. An insider report by Jeffrey Rosen in *The New Yorker* in 1996 said unequivocally that the words were Kennedy's. After Judge Bork's appointment to the Court was rejected by the Senate, President Reagan had nominated Kennedy, a federal appellate judge from California who seemed a less strident substitute. At his confirmation hearing in 1987, Judge Kennedy said that Americans have a "shared vision" that includes "the idea that each man and woman has the freedom and the capacity to develop to his or her own potential."[33] Since then, Justice Kennedy seems to have disappointed conservatives because he has declined to join the conservative wing of the Court.

Fans of symmetry will notice that the Supreme Court's momentous 1992 decision preserving the right to an abortion *and* the constitutional right to privacy begins and ends with the word *liberty*. Justice Kennedy wrote both sentences and worded them intentionally, according to Rosen's inside report. It is the word that is central to the narrow majority opinion. Is it the new code word among the Court's moderates for *privacy*?

In a subsequent book, Bork has said that he would have voted the other way on the abortion case, refusing to find a right to privacy in the U.S. Constitution. That one vote would have made a huge difference. Thus, the Court's recognition of a constitutional right to privacy was extremely close to dissipating during the years between 1986 and Bill Clinton's election in 1992.

Clinton, as a one-time constitutional law teacher and savvy political candidate for President in 1992, recognized immediately the precariousness of the situation. The day after the Court announced its decision in *Planned Parenthood v. Casey*, Clinton vowed, "I would appoint judges to the Supreme Court with a long history of advocacy for the Bill of Rights, especially the right to privacy." While that turned out to be not totally accurate, Clinton did appoint to the Court two judges who have held the line on this issue.

By the beginning of Clinton's term in office, there could be no doubt that Sandra Day O'Connor had assumed leadership on the Court for privacy issues. It was she who authored an opinion for a splintered Court in 1987 finding that when government employers search employees' desks or offices this "requires balancing the employee's legitimate expectation of privacy against the government's need for supervision, control, and the efficient operation of the workplace." The Court's ruling was equivocal, essentially a 4-4 tie, with Justice Antonin Scalia barely agreeing to make it a 5-4 majority. Without O'Connor's pro-privacy vote and her assertion on this issue, the Court would have required *no consideration* of the worker's privacy interest.[34]

In two opinions in 1995, Justice O'Connor reaffirmed her appreciation of privacy – and she even used the word. In a majority opinion on a very contentious issue within the Court, O'Connor stood up for the interests of aggrieved accident victims who are assaulted by zealous lawyers seeking clients. The Court upheld a Florida rule that lawyers must wait 30 days before soliciting business by advertising directly by mail to an accident victim. Direct advertising by lawyers immediately after an accident was "invasive conduct" and direct mail can create "outrage and irritation" in persons who have stressful or delicate conditions, she wrote, for the Court. She said that a previous decision by the Court that appeared to be contradictory was decided the way that it was only *because the Court did not fully consider the privacy interests* of the targets of the advertising! The earlier decision had ruled *against* regulating lawyers' advertising in grief situations.[35]

It was in dissent five days later that O'Connor reaffirmed her support for the *constitutional* right to privacy that the Court had recognized since the *Griswold* decision. She refused to join the majority of Americans who apparently did not regard urinalysis tests of employees and students as unreasonably intrusive. O'Connor led two moderate colleagues in objecting to the Court's approval of random urinalysis testing for high school athletes. A seventh grader in Oregon named James Acton brought the challenge after he was disqualified from playing football because he declined to submit to mandatory drug testing.[36]

The six-member majority determined that the testing would not be arbitrary because everyone could be subjected to it and because athletes had little expectation of privacy. But O'Connor responded, "In making these policy arguments, of course, the Court sidesteps *powerful, countervailing privacy concerns.*" She pointed out that the Court in 1987 had ruled that blanket searches pose a greater threat to liberty than individualized searches. O'Connor's dissent stated:

> "But whether a blanket search is 'better' than a regime based on individualized suspicion is not a debate in which we should engage. . . . For most of our constitutional history, mass suspicionless searches have been generally considered *per se* unreasonable within the meaning of the Fourth Amendment. And we have allowed exceptions in recent years only where it has been clear that a suspicion-based regime would be ineffectual. [The framers chose to curb the abuses of general warrants not by being evenhanded but by raising the level of suspicion required to conduct a search.] *Protection of privacy, not evenhandedness, was then and is now the touchstone of the Fourth Amendment.*"

In a criminal context, she said, universal searches not based on suspicion are clearly unconstitutional, regardless of how "evenhanded." In a non-criminal context, they are certainly "intrusive."

Sandra Day O'Connor's assertion in the 1992 abortion rights case that any attempt "to define one's own concept of existence" is entitled to constitutional protection remains the current standard for the Supreme Court in this new century. Already the Ninth Circuit

Court of Appeals, the court on which Justice Kennedy formerly sat, has invoked this language to support a finding of a constitutional right to determine the time and manner of one's death. This is an issue that courts will be asked to consider increasingly. Will a new majority of the Court seize on this and expand the constitutional recognition of a right to privacy, especially in a new era in which the government's resources for collecting personal information and checking private conduct have become staggering?

Links

For Justice Brennan's perspective on how the attitudes of the founders should inform citizens today about constitutional rights, see the chapter on Serenity.

To follow the development of "informational privacy" in and out of the courts, see the chapter on Databanks.

Numbers

The six-decade trend towards a national identifying number
for all Americans and attempts to create a national ID document.

From the beginning, most Americans have been vigilant about the dangers of being enumerated by their government. The mounting demands for enumeration since 1936 perhaps prove only that they have not been vigilant enough.

The possibility of a national enumeration[1] system arose seriously for the first time with enactment in August 1935 of a nationwide government pension program, to take effect the next year. This would involve deducting taxes from workers' regular paychecks, depositing the funds in Washington, and then dispersing monthly pension checks to retirees. To make the system work, everybody would have to be issued a number. Or so it was assumed at the time.

Recent immigrants were the ones most concerned; those from Europe were well aware of the latent dangers of a system of enumerating or registering all citizens. The Nazi regime, after all, would soon locate targets of their terror by using various registration systems already in place in the nations they occupied. An Italian immigrant to America told his children, "They are going to require a number for all of us. There goes our family name, it will no longer be important."

"The invention of permanent, inherited patronyms ["last names"] was the last step in establishing the necessary preconditions of modern statecraft. . . . Fearing, with good reason, that an effort to enumerate and register them could be a prelude to some new tax burden or conscription, local officials and the population at large often resisted such campaigns."

Yale University scholar James C. Scott, in *Seeing like a State: How Certain Schemes to Improve the Human Condition Have Failed*," 1998.

In addition, there was simply something in the American spirit that abhorred being known as a number. It was dehumanizing and impersonal, regimented. Many religious fundamentalists feared national registration because of the Biblical threats that pestilence and plague might follow.[2]

The United Mine Workers and the United Steelworkers both expressed a different fear: that Social Security account numbers could be used by companies to blacklist pro-union men and women involved in the labor strife of the time. The unions, in fact, persuaded friendly officials in Franklin D. Roosevelt's New Deal Administration to include in the Social Security Act of 1935 a provision allowing an individual to replace an existing Social Security number with a second one when "showing good reasons for a change," a provision that remains in the law.

The new pension system marked the first time in the United States that a government agency would be required to collect and use personal information from most of the population. This would be unlike the data collection by the Bureau of the Census, which aggregates its individual data once it collects it and makes no decisions based on the information that affect individuals. For the first time, Americans would be asked to register with their government. No wonder there was such unease among the public.

It was unlike previous military conscription programs, as well, which had affected only men in their twenties, and only in wartime. It is true that thousands of rioters in New York City objected to the military draft of 1863 because a man could pay $300 to avoid it or could pay someone to go to war in his place. The bloody riots were a reaction to the unfairness of the system and the racist overtones of the way that it was administered. They were not a reaction to the idea of conscription itself. America's first military registration requirement in "peacetime" was to come in 1940.[3]

In the election year of 1936, Congressional Democrats defended their government-run innovation, and Republicans stressed the disadvantages of the idea – that it would mean lower take-home pay. A week before the election the Republican National Committee flooded employers with millions of official-looking inserts for pay envelopes warning of the deduction to come in the first paycheck of the new year.

But it became clear that the trickiest part of the task of implementing a radical pension program would not be assuring the public about the new payroll deduction, but persuading Americans to register.

And so the bureaucrats never mentioned the word. "The process was called 'assignment of social security account numbers' instead of 'registration,'" recalled Arthur J. Altmeyer, who was FDR's acting chair of the Social Security Board at the time of creation. "The use of the word 'registration' was avoided because it might connote regimentation. An analogy was drawn between the issuance of a social security account card and the issuance of a department store credit card, which was the only form of credit card in common use at the time."[4]

The notion of a government-run registration was so abhorrent that Altmeyer, with Roosevelt's approval, asked the Postmaster General to assume the responsibility of assigning numbers for Social Security purposes. More Americans apparently trusted the local post office than the new Social Security Board. "He agreed to do so and in a few weeks plans were completed for carrying out this gigantic task through the 45,000 post offices, beginning November 16, 1936," Altmeyer recalled in a memoir. "I had urged that the assignment of account numbers should not begin until then in order to avoid becoming involved in the Presidential campaign of that year." In September Republican candidate Alfred M. Landon denounced the "old-age insurance system," saying "To call it 'social security' is a fraud on the working man."

On the day before the election William Randolph Hearst's *New York Journal-American* published a front-page attack on the pension system accompanied by a drawing of a man with his identity masked, stripped to the waist, wearing a dog tag with an identifying number. It was labeled "Snooping and Tagging." The caption stated, "Each worker would be required to have one for the privilege of suffering a pay cut under the Social Security Act, which is branded as a 'cruel hoax.'" (Alf Landon had used that term in his campaign.) The illustration was not far-fetched. The Addressograph Corp. had tried to sell the Social Security Board on the idea of issuing metal nameplates to all registrants. Altmeyer said he kept Addressograph's prototype nametag as a souvenir of these negotiations.

Some press reports said that the new program would require a person's religion, union affiliation, criminal record medical history, and other personal data. The *Boston American* wrote, "Your personal life will be laid bare, your religion and the church you attend will be listed. Your physical defects will go down in black and white. . . . your union affiliation will be stated. . . . Even your divorce, if you have one, will be included."[5] In fact, an applicant needed to provide only name, date of birth, and parents' names. Each file would include only earnings information.

The Social Security Board retaliated against the Republicans' negative envelope stuffers with 50 million leaflets of its own that were distributed at factory gates. The brochures explained the process for *assigning* Social Security numbers (not *registering* for Social Security). One of the government's explanatory films to soothe citizens' fears was run continuously in Times Square on the last day of the election campaign, as well as elsewhere throughout the country.

The 1935 law assigned to the Bureau of Internal Revenue in the Department of Treasury the task of collecting the taxes from both employees and employers. The bureau waited until two days after the election to issue a regulation creating "an account number." Each person was to apply at a post office and be assigned a number and then provide it to his or her employer. The regulation also provided that a person could change his or her number "showing good reason."

Despite misgivings and despite the fact that the Social Security Act had not yet been declared constitutional, most of the 26 million application forms were returned through post offices during the first three weeks of registration. By June of 1937, 30 million persons had applied for numbers. Not bad, in a nation of 50 million employed adults. No one wanted to miss out on a government pension, of course, and there was no need to show any proof of identity in order to register. At the time, there seemed little incentive to get an SSN under an assumed name or to get more than one because that might actually reduce one's later benefits. This remained true so long as the SSN was used for no other purpose. Thus, for many years later, no proof of identity was required to get a Social Security number.

In 1936 the board twice issued statements promising confidentiality and it issued a regulation – Social Security Board Regulation No. 1 dated June 15, 1937 – requiring that no employee "shall disclose to any person or before any tribunal, directly or indirectly" any account information, even in response to a subpoena.

Altmeyer said that this regulation was violated only in a few cases involving persons suspected of espionage and other crimes. But there were other close calls. Every attorney general "at the urging of the Federal Bureau of Investigation," requested access to Social Security information during the 19 years in which Altmeyer was in office. J. Edgar Hoover's persistence paid off, and in 1939, President Roosevelt issued an executive order authorizing FBI access to Social Security files in any criminal investigation.

The information on accounts was intended to stay confidential, but it did not stay that way for long. By 1997, an official publication of the Social Security Administration admitted euphemistically, "The next two decades saw a gentle evolution in SSA's disclosure policies with changes made to respond to changing social needs, additional program responsibilities and other material interests."[6] In other words, in the computer age, the floodgates were opened.

The implied promise that Social Security *numbers* would be used solely for administering the insurance program was a separate issue. That pledge lasted less than a year – and the Social Security Board itself broke it. It directed that the Social Security number also be used in state unemployment insurance programs, which were funded by the 1935 act. This meant that many more employees not covered by the Social Security program – railroad employees, laid-off federal employees, and others – had to get numbers as well. Still, in a time when most families had only one wage earner and when there was little out-of-home employment for women, a majority of Americans still did not have – and did not need – SSNs.

For many years, the 3-by-2-inch Social Security card bearing a person's number had the legend "NOT FOR IDENTIFICATION" printed on its face. This has led many citizens to this day to believe that a law or regulation prohibited the use of the number for purposes other than Social Security. But that was never the case. (Partial restrictions on government agencies *collecting* the numbers were enacted in 1974.) The purpose of the legend, the Social Security officials would say, was merely to notify anyone to whom a card might be presented that it should not be relied upon as evidence of identity. After all, no proof of identity was required then to get a Social Security card. To this day, persons in places of authority nonetheless demand the card and accept it as evidence of identity.

In the first year of the program, the Social Security Board turned to large insurance companies for advice in creating a central record system to keep track of the millions of accounts, in a time of primitive counting machines. The board was shocked to discover that no company had a records system that could serve as a prototype for the massive information collection that the government insurance program would require. The board was building the largest database in the world, and there was no model to emulate. An expert in private-sector data systems told members of the board that it couldn't be done, that the board's only hope of managing the massive amount of data was to create separate regional organizations. This would have required an amendment to the legislation that created the pension system. And it wouldn't work, in a nation where up to a fifth of the citizens move from one community to another in a year.

Instead the board established 12 units organized by geographical regions, but centralized them in the nation's capital and linked them with a single universal index. The index of 30 million names was organized by a phonetic translation of last names, not by numbers, showing that large personal data systems need not be organized by numbers. That was true then and it is true today. The system was good enough to locate a file within a few seconds.

Americans' suspicions of enumeration became clear after World War II when vital statistics officials throughout the country proposed a national Birth Certificate Number, to be affixed to each new birth certificate. This would assign a unique identifying number for a person's lifetime, something the Social Security number was not. Officials in nearly half of the states declined to participate in the program and the idea was dropped.[7]

A number is a number is a number, but Social Security account number 078-05-1120 was one of several numbers that took on lives of their own. It first appeared on a sample Social Security card inserted in wallets sold in 1938. It simply showed a person what the little plastic pocket in the wallet was for. But many purchasers naively assumed that the made-up number was to be their own account number. Thousands of persons had their wages reported under account number 078-05-1120. The year 1943 was the peak, when 5755 wage earners were listed under that number. Even in the 1970s, 39 older persons filed tax returns under 078-05-1120. In the 1970s the Social Security Administration said that it was still processing multiple accounts for persons using what the bureaucrats called "pocket-book numbers."[8]

President Franklin D. Roosevelt signed Executive Order 9397 in 1943 requiring federal agencies to use the Social Security number for identifying individuals in any new "system of accounts." The Civil Service Commission, which managed federal personnel, had asked for the authority. It had decided that it needed a numerical system for keeping track of payroll records of federal civil-service workers, who at that time did not participate in the Social Security program. The order, which is still in effect, directed the Social Society Board to assign an account number to any person required by a federal agency to have one, whether the purpose was for pensions or not. And it directed that, "The Social Security Board and each federal agency shall maintain the confidential character of information relating to individuals obtained pursuant to the provisions of this order." The order also required that the federal agency requiring an account number pay for the enumeration process. The Civil Service Commission always said that it lacked the funds to do this, and so for 18 years civil service employees simply went without SSNs. There was apparently no pressing need for them to have them. Thus, Roosevelt's executive order had no practical impact at all for many years, until federal agencies resurrected it with the coming of computer systems. Executive Order 9397 is an example of a governmental action that profoundly affected citizens' rights but turned out not to be necessary at all at the time.

In 1961, the Civil Service Commission finally decided to issue SSNs to federal employees. As it began to use computer systems for processing tax returns, the Internal Revenue Service decided to use the Social Security number as an individual taxpayer identification number. This was authorized by an amendment to the tax code in 1961.[9] Until the 1980s the IRS was fairly casual about this requirement, imposing only a $5 penalty for failure to comply.

Use of the number as a taxpayer ID opened the floodgates. Soon state tax authorities began to use it. The U.S. Treasury Department began to use it as an identifier for holders of U.S. securities, including savings bonds.

In 1964, the Commissioner of Social Security approved the issuance of Social Security numbers to school pupils in the ninth grade and above, if a school requests this. Pupils in the public schools of Baltimore, where the Social Security Administration was now located, became the leading guinea pigs. Social Security officers set up tables at high schools registering students. Of course, the program was voluntary, but there was no way for pupils *to know* that. Everything done in school seems required.

Issuing SSNs in schools was more cost effective, more orderly, and more convenient than having young people register one by one when they entered the job market. That was one of the stated reasons for issuing them in schools.

There was another purpose, according to the Social Security Administration manual in the 1960s: It was to accommodate requests from school systems "desiring to use the SSN for both automated data processing and control purposes, so that the progress of pupils could be traced throughout their school lives across district, county, and state lines." This was one of the first articulations of the reason behind the many demands for personal information in the Sixties and Seventies: "The computer needs it."

This was a breach of a key principle of privacy protection (one that was not drafted and circulated until a decade later, however). The principle is that information gathered for one purpose ought not to be used for an incompatible purpose without consent of the individual. Pupils thought that they were securing Social Security numbers to make it easier for them when they applied for work. They did not realize that they were also providing a means for school authorities to link records about them.

"The assignment of a number to an individual, I suspect, is going to go out of existence pretty much. The computer can recognize a name as well as a number."

Yale Professor of Economics Richard Ruggles, expert on statistics and computers, in 1968.[10]

And if high school students were being issued Social Security numbers en masse, why shouldn't colleges use them as student ID numbers? This is exactly what happened.

With the coming of the federal Medicare and state Medicaid supplemental health insurance programs in the early Sixties, thousands of Americans who had reached retirement age without ever needing a Social Security number – including many post-World War II newcomers – now had to be issued identifying numbers. If Medicaid and Medicare used SSNs, why not state elderly assistance programs? This is exactly what happened in 1965.

If state elderly programs used SSNs, why not the Indian Health Program? And that is what happened in 1966. In the same year, the Veterans Administration used the numbers for hospital admissions and other accounting purposes. If the Veterans Administration used the numbers, why shouldn't the Pentagon use them as service numbers for all military personnel? And this is what happened in 1967.

A new banking law that Congress passed in 1970 required banks and other financial institutions to get Social Security numbers for all customers, whether the accounts produced taxable income or not.[11] This was an obligation on the bank, not the individual; but most customers did not know this or did not care. Just as we think that most things we are asked to do in school are mandatory, we think that most things we are asked to do in a bank are mandatory. People offered up their Social Security numbers. As a consequence of this requirement, many banks urged customers to have their Social Security numbers printed on the face of their checks, or banks simply went ahead and did so. This, of course, was not required by the law, but it was a natural consequence of it.

There is nothing private about a Social Security number printed on the face of a bank check. Check-out clerks in a grocery store, retail sales personnel, payments processors, the guy who fixes the car, personal friends – everybody gets to see it. Nor is a number printed on an Army dog tag or on thousands of military documents very private.

In fact a prisoner named George Turner at a federal facility in Missouri did well for himself exactly ten years after the military converted to SSNs as service numbers. His job was to sort old Army fatigues from Fort Leonard Wood, the nearby Army training base. It took Turner less than a week – after all, he was serving time for tax fraud – to figure out that he could use the discarded clothing to continue his schemes. On each piece of clothing was a soldier's name and Social Security number. Turner requested blank tax forms by mail and filed phony returns and requests for refunds, using the names and Social Security numbers (which now was *both* taxpayer ID *and* military ID) on the different forms. George Turner generated more than 200 refund checks this way. The Internal Revenue Service after a while detected the fraud, but the Army continued to send discarded clothing to the prison with service member's names and Social Security numbers.[12]

Oddly, while the Social Security number was becoming more and more a public piece of information, as George Turner demonstrated, people in places of authority were treating it as *an authenticator of a person's real identity*, as if it were a secret identifier known only to the individual. This practice had the effect of allowing impostors or perpetrators of fraud to use someone else's Social Security number as a means of "proving identity" with any clerk or bureaucrat in the land.

An advisory committee appointed by the Secretary of Health, Education, and Welfare in 1972 to study the proliferating uses of numerical identifiers and the implications of personal databanks noticed the irony. To attend a weekend meeting in a government building, the members were required to give names and Social Security numbers to a guard at the main entrance. The guard had earlier been given a list of members and their numbers. The committee's final report said:

> "Given the wide dissemination of SSNs, we were impressed by how easily someone could have impersonated any one of us to gain admittance to the building."[13]

This was not a theoretical concern. It was going on all over the country in the 1970s – people enlisting in the Army, applying for a job, getting a birth certificate or driver's license, getting welfare assistance – while using a stranger's Social Security number *to verify their own identities*. This reached epidemic proportions in the Nineties, when it became known as "theft of identity." Still, no one in Congress or the Executive Branch realized the irony and sought to remedy it. There were selected members of Congress who raised concerns about the proliferation of SSN uses, as a dehumanizing trend or threat to privacy, but no one mentioned the misplaced reliance upon the number to authenticate identity.

George Turner, the prisoner in Missouri, was simply ahead of his time. By the 1990s, criminal impostors were victimizing thousands of Americans with schemes similar to Turner's. It was called "identity theft." A stranger would secure the victim's Social Security number – from payroll records, by pretext over the telephone, in trash cans, or at World Wide Web sites – and then pose as that person to get a duplicate birth certificate, driver's license, or job. In a more common variation, the impostor would access the individual's credit report – using the Social Security number to verify identity – and discover the retail credit accounts the person had and the account numbers. Then the stranger would ask the retailers to change the address on the account to the impostor's or to a bogus address set up for this purpose. Or the impostor would simply use the victim's Social Security number to apply for a new account. The victim would be unaware that a stranger was using the accounts to order products and services – dunning notices for over-due accounts would be sent to the impostor's new address, not to the true account holder's address. But notices about the delinquent accounts would be sent regularly to the major credit bureaus. Only when the individual was rejected on a new credit application or had credit cards canceled would he or she become aware of the fraud.

But then reclaiming a clean credit report became impossible. A credit bureau would dutifully erase the bad information as required by the federal Fair Credit Reporting Act of 1971, but in the next 45 days, when retailers and credit-card issuers would make their next automated reports to the credit bureau, the fraud-produced infor-mation would reappear on the victim's credit report. Only after Congress tightened the law in 1996 and the credit bureaus faced several lawsuits did they take partial steps to prevent this from happening over and over. Further, because retailers accepted the losses as a cost of doing business, they didn't bother to change their practices so that the fraud could be curbed. They didn't bother to alter their systems so that Social Security numbers were unnec-essary to retrieve data about an individual.

A prime source of other persons' Social Security numbers is the identifying information at the top of a credit report, what the credit bureaus call "header" or "above-the-line" information, including phone numbers addresses, mother's maiden names, and Social Se-curity numbers. Because most people provide their telephone numbers on credit applications whether or not their numbers are "unlisted," credit bureaus include listed and unlisted phone num-bers "above the line." The Federal Trade Commission, which regulates credit bureaus, ruled in a non-public negotiation in 1993 that credit bureaus are free to rent "header" information all they want.[14] That is when identity fraud became a nationwide epidemic.

This means that "information brokers," which buy personal infor-mation from large vendors and resell it to individuals and small businesses, could easily purchase Social Security numbers and un-listed telephone numbers. Many of these brokers sold the data on their World Wide Web sites.

The Federal Trade Commission has compounded the problem by encouraging credit bureaus to use Social Security numbers to ver-ify the identity of a consumer who seeks to get a copy of his or her credit report, as permitted by law. A Social Security number does not provide much verification of a person's identity if a stranger can get it easily.

A task force created within the Social Security Administration in the early 1970s took a long look at the burgeoning use of the Social Security number. Its study focused on the function of the number as the key component for linking records about a single individual in disparate and remote computer systems.

One reason organizations were collecting Social Security numbers was precisely to link records; they wanted to be able in the future to allow for pooling or merging records about an individual from different systems. Data files were not then linked by telephone or any other telecommunications. Even "batch processing," by which a file or list from one computer file was loaded on to another system to merge data, was just beginning. Data managers, however, certainly anticipated that automated matching and merging of files would soon be routine. If each individual record could be retrieved by a single ID number, then the process of matching files, for whatever reason, would be feasible. Insurance companies, for instance, discovered that if they used separate policy numbers of their own, processing Medicare and Medicaid information was slow and awkward. Using a common number created the possibility of linking records with data systems outside the organization.

The Social Security number was simply a convenient number, one that most people had memorized or had access to. It was widely believed that a common numerical identifier was essential for merging files or even for managing large data systems. The discovery of alternative techniques since that time has made that belief outdated.

The Social Security task force issued a report in 1971 that questioned the desirability of *"any* kind of universal identification system in terms of its psychological impact on the individual citizen."[15] The reason for this "psychological impact" was apparently not the dehumanizing aspect of enumeration, but the loss of control that would come from linking data:

"It is clear that if the SSN became the single number around which all or most of an individual's interactions were structured . . . the individual's opportunity to control the circumstances under which information about himself is collected and disclosed would be greatly circumscribed."

President Nixon's Secretary of Health, Education and Welfare, Elliot L. Richardson, decided to appoint an Advisory Committee on Automated Personal Data Systems to study the larger questions posed by increased use of computers to collect information on individuals. Just a few months after the Social Security Administration task force issued its report, the Secretary's Advisory Committee took a new look at the increasing uses of Social Security numbers.

The HEW committee – the one whose members gave up their Social Security numbers at the front door – issued a well-received report on *Records Computers and the Rights of Citizens* in 1972, saying, "The federal government itself has been in the forefront of expanding the use of the SSN."[16] It concluded:

"We recommend against the adoption of any nationwide, standard, personal identification format, with or without the SSN, that would enhance the likelihood of arbitrary or uncontrolled linkage of records about people, particularly between government or government-supported automated personal data systems."

The committee recommended that use of the number be limited to, first, requirements imposed by federal agencies, and, secondly, only pursuant to authority from Congress. Thirdly, "Congress should be sparing in mandating use of the SSN." Further, "when the SSN is used in instances that do not conform to the three foregoing principles," it should be totally voluntary.

Both the HEW advisory committee and the Social Security Administration task force were created partly in reaction to a standard developed by the American National Standards Institute in 1969 for a uniform identifier for each American, incorporating a person's Social Security number and additional elements. As with the earlier proposal for a mandatory Birth Certificate Number, the public and the press met the idea with immediate opposition. The organization was forced to withdraw the proposed standard.[17]

Congress took the HEW recommendations seriously and in drafting a comprehensive privacy-protection proposal in 1974 moved towards making the recommendations part of the law. Senators Sam J. Ervin, Jr., Charles H. Percy, and Barry M. Goldwater were especially vigorous about this. But support for making the privacy protections apply to private businesses faded in both houses of Congress. What emerged in the late fall was the Privacy Act of 1974, which seeks to protect personal information gathered *by the federal government*, but not information collected by private businesses like banks, credit-card companies, employers, and health-care providers. Congress included in the Privacy Act a modest provision on Social Security numbers that applied to state, local, and federal levels of government only; it did not extend to the private sector. In essence, it authorized current uses of Social Security numbers, but no more. The provision in the Privacy Act says that government benefits may not be denied an individual for declining to provide a Social Security number unless there was an existing federal or state law or regulation specifically authorizing this.[18] (In 1976 Congress amended the law to exempt tax, motor-vehicle, and welfare offices in state government from its limitations. This meant that these agencies could continue to require Social Security numbers.)

Since 1974, agencies at all levels of government have justified their demands for Social Security numbers by pointing to general authorizations in laws predating the Privacy Act that simply allow the agencies to conduct some function or to collect information to conduct their functions. That is not at all what members of Congress had in mind in the fall of 1974, but the practices are only occasionally challenged successfully.

The lasting effect of the HEW report was in its creation of a Code of Fair Information Practice governing computer databases, not in its warnings about Social Security numbers.[19]

Meanwhile, private businesses began insisting on the Social Security number, often using it as a customer or account number. If the Medicare and Medicaid programs used it, why wouldn't it be convenient for insurance companies to use it as a policy number? And that is what many insurance companies began to do. Newspapers sponsoring sweepstakes for their readers often made the Social Security number the basis for entering the contests (although the HEW report strongly condemned this). This only accustomed millions of persons to disclosing their numbers for non-Social Security purposes and non-tax purposes without thinking of the consequences. It also motivated some people to get more than one Social

Security number or to use more than one – to have a better chance of winning.

A man in Cleveland, Ohio, was surprised when his two children, aged seven and five, received notices to pay overdue taxes. Then the father recalled that to enter the children in the *Cleveland Press* sweepstakes in 1976 he had applied for new Social Security numbers for them. The Social Security Administration routinely put the children and their numbers on lists it regularly sends to local tax agencies. The local agency had no record of the two paying taxes and sent the delinquency notices.[20]

A Native American father descended from the Abenaki Tribe had the opposite approach. Stephen J. Roy of Pennsylvania regarded Social Security numbers as part of "a great evil" used by computers to rob people's spirits. This, he said, is what non-Indians would call *dehumanization*. He based his spiritual belief on what he called the legend of Katahdin, the mountain that overlooks a settlement of the Abenaki Tribe in the state of Maine. He did not want his daughter, Little Bird of the Snow, to be enumerated in this way, and insisted that she decide for herself when she was older about having a Social Security number.

But the family received state Aid to Dependent Children, food stamps, and state medical assistance. The state and federal governments insisted that the family provide a Social Security number for four-year-old Little Bird of the Snow. When the state reduced the family's public assistance in the 1980s, the father filed a lawsuit in federal court. He found a sympathetic federal judge. In fact, the judge, Malcolm Muir, said that he himself converts numbers into words as a personal way of remembering digits. The judge nicknamed the chief judge on his court "Phillippino Overpot," for instance, simply as a way of remembering his colleague's telephone number. Using his personal system, the judge figured that the little girl's name would translate into the number 515-94-1802. Would the government accept this number as an alternative? A government witness thought that the bureaucracy could handle this, even if the first three digits would indicate that the number had been issued in Kansas and the judge's fabricated number would be 30,000 numbers ahead of Social Security numbers in use at the time. The Social Security Administration's computers would reject "impossible" account numbers, and so some accommodation would be necessary. Would the father accept it, the judge asked. The father liked the idea a little bit, but was unwilling to accept it as an alternative because it would be a unique identifier.

Only at the end of the trial was it revealed that Little Bird of the Snow had had an SSN assigned to her at birth; the parents had returned it and asked that it be revoked. That was not relevant to Judge Muir. He ruled that the SSN requirements in the welfare and food stamp programs were an unconstitutional infringement on religious beliefs. He enjoined the agencies from denying benefits to the family.

The federal government said that it would appeal the ruling to the U.S. Supreme Court and argue that its inability to get Social Security numbers on everybody would hamper its plans to match computer lists in different state and federal agencies and thereby uncover fraud and "double-dipping."

Department of Justice lawyers were busy that fall with two vexing challenges from individuals concerned about their personal privacy. A woman who wanted to apply for a driver's license without providing a photograph of herself had succeeded in getting the Eighth Circuit Court of Appeals to agree with her argument. Because of the injunction in the Ten Commandments, "Thou shalt not make unto thee any graven image," Frances Quaring did not want to be photographed. Lawyers in the U.S. Department of Justice were preparing to persuade the U.S. Supreme Court to overturn the opinion by the court of appeals that the state of Nebraska had to accommodate the religious objections of Ms. Quaring.

When the Supreme Court heard the Nebraska case, Warren E. Burger, then chief justice of the U.S. and a man renowned for objecting to any and all photographs of himself, immediately asked the attorney for the woman what would happen if press photographers snapped her picture at the Supreme Court. It won't happen, the man responded; she had stayed home on that important day in her life precisely to make sure that it did not happen. Associate Justice Sandra Day O'Connor noted aloud that the Court's decision in the photograph case would surely have an effect on its ruling in the government's anticipated appeal in Little Bird's case.

On June 17, 1985, the Court announced that it was deadlocked 4-4 whether the government had to accommodate a religious objection to providing a photograph. Justice Powell was hospitalized and did not participate. Whenever there is a tie on the high court, the opinion of the lower court stands, meaning that the Eighth Circuit's ruling that a person has a constitutional right not to provide a photograph for a driver's license is the governing law to this day.[21]

On the same day, the court agreed to hear the government's appeal in the case of "Little Bird vs. Big Government."

A few weeks later, the Missouri Supreme Court expressly rejected the Eighth Circuit's decision and ruled that the state *could* deny a driver's license to someone who refused to provide a Social Security number (not a photograph this time) because of that person's "sincerely held" religious belief against being assigned a number.

In contrast to the photograph-drivers' license issue, the Supreme Court had little difficulty on the issue of Social Security numbers and government benefits. In 1986, it voted 8-1 in Little Bird of the Snow's case that the government's demand for a Social Security number does not itself impair a person's freedom to exercise religion, guaranteed in the First Amendment to the Constitution.[22]

"The harm that can be inflicted from the disclosure of a SSN to an unscrupulous individual is alarming and potentially financially ruinous."

U.S. Court of Appeals, Fourth Circuit, 1993.[23]

By the late Eighties, Americans were now being asked for Social Security numbers in order to rent an apartment, to get a fishing license, to order a cable TV connection, to begin telephone service, to donate blood, to make funeral arrangements, to get medical treatment. At different times, people have been asked for Social Security numbers to rent a room at a Holiday Inn, to use credit cards at gasoline stations, and, in Virginia, to register to vote.

The trend towards constant demands for a Social Security number for any transaction, which gave rise to a citizens group in Massachusetts called PANIC, People Against National Identity Cards, was clear – the Social Security number (with all its imperfections)[24] was becoming a de facto national ID number. The nation was inexorably moving towards what had once been unthinkable: requiring every man, woman, and child to have a government-issued identity number and to carry proof of it on one's person at all times.

This was no idle Orwellian fear. The Director of the Passport Office in the Department of State, Frances G. Knight, actually advocated the issuance of an identity card, with fingerprints, to every citizen. This was in 1975.[25] Knight, who held her job for 22 years before retiring in 1977, was the female equivalent of J. Edgar

Hoover, an entrenched, expert bureaucrat whom no politician cared to cross. But on this one, Frances G. Knight stood alone. No one wanted to side with Ms. Knight on a national ID card. By coincidence, at the time, a diverse committee appointed by the Attorney General was studying the use of false IDs to commit crimes. The law enforcement and vital statistics officials on the committee said that they were tempted to recommend creation of a national identity card; they were sure that this would solve all problems related to fraud. But they wouldn't say so publicly, because they were aware that the public reaction would be immediately negative. And so the pro-law enforcement group voted down a proposal to create a national ID number.

Instead in subsequent years, officials and politicians created, one by one, discreet new demands for proof of identity that led in the same direction. But no one else would endorse a national identity card itself.

There was evidence of this in the debates of a Select Commission on Immigration and Refugee Policy established in 1980 to find a way to prevent employers from hiring illegal immigrants and to ration the flow of newcomers to America. The Rev. Theodore M. Hesburgh, then president of the University of Notre Dame, chaired the panel, which included Senators Alan K. Simpson and Edward M. Kennedy, as well as the Secretary of State and Secretary of Labor at the time. Hesburgh could find nothing objectionable about a mandatory ID card in order to hold a job. After returning from Asia, he told the press, "If I can walk into a restaurant in Bangkok and just hand them a card to charge $100, it shouldn't be that difficult to establish some method to establish legal status in the U.S. You wouldn't have to carry it always. If you wanted to use it for other purposes you could do so."

At a meeting in December 1980, after the election of Ronald Reagan as President and a Republican majority in the Senate for the first time in 26 years, Hesburgh asked for a vote on tightening current identity requirements. A majority agreed. Then he asked for a vote on a new "more certain" document that each worker would have to present before getting hired. A slim majority including Kennedy voted *against* that. But Hesburgh said then that he would poll the three members of the panel who were absent. He tried, but the chair could not garner the votes to make such a recommendation.

In the end, the commission's final report avoided recommending a national ID card or a mandatory work card. Instead, Congress tossed around various proposals for requiring existing ID documents for employment, even though none of them, except a passport, verifies citizenship or legal immigrant status. A bipartisan bill in 1982 would have required workers to present one of four different IDs before getting hired. (Strangely, only one of the required documents has a photograph.) The bill also would have required the Reagan Administration to develop a plan for "secure identification" within six months. Congress could not reach agreement on an immigration-reform bill that year, and so the ID proposal died.

A year later, Senator Robert J. Dole convened a three-day hearing on moving towards a national ID scheme. But members of Congress were not willing to endorse such an idea; instead they tossed the issue to the Executive Branch and insisted that it develop a plan for a national identifier.

Witnesses before Dole's committee said that government agencies were relying more and more on the mere presentation of a Social Security number as proof of identity – and also discovering that their files were full of erroneous and duplicate SSNs. The Department of Defense alone found at least 1000 persons in its systems using numbers also being used by others.

The issue was not resolved in the 1980s – nor was the issue of controlling immigration. In 1990 Congress appointed a bipartisan Commission on Immigration Reform to resolve the impasse. In July of 1994, the chair, former Representative Barbara Jordan of Texas, let float a trial balloon. It's the Washington way. She seemed to endorse the idea of a mandatory work card with photograph, or a plastic national ID card, or at least a "tamper-proof" Social Security card.

Because of her advocacy during the nationally televised impeachment hearing about President Nixon in 1974, Jordan enjoyed a reputation as a defender of the Constitution and a liberal. "I would not be a party to any system I felt was an unwarranted intrusion into private lives," she said.

When it came time to testify before a Senate committee the next month, Jordan merely endorsed the idea of a "more secure" worker ID document and a computerized system for employers to verify the identity and citizenship status of any applicant. She seemed to be backing off her original proposal for a national identity card.

Senator Alan K. Simpson of Wyoming, then chair of the immigration subcommittee and primary advocate of the verification system, said:

> "Does this mean we are creating a 'national ID card'? Not at all. I have always provided in my legislation, as the commission has in its recommendation, that no one would be required to carry a card, should one be used, or to present it to law enforcement officials for routine identification purposes. The card, if there is to be one, would be presented *only* at the time of new-hire employment, or at the time of application for federally funded benefits, including health care."[26]

Simpson's proposed card, then, would be required to get a job and to get health care. His insistence that this would not evolve into an all-purpose card was reminiscent of assurances from the Social Security Board in the 1930s. Anyone familiar with the 40-year erosion of the Social Security number as an exclusive, single-purpose identifier would, of course, view Simpson's assurances with great skepticism.

Simpson had disparaged the fear of a national ID number earlier in 1991, at the only Congressional hearing ever held exclusively to study the trend. Representative Andy Jacobs, Jr., of Indiana, convened a hearing of his Ways and Means Subcommittee on Social Security and heard groups representing immigrants discourage use of mandatory identity numbers. Representatives of credit bureaus said for the first time publicly that they were highly dependent on Social Security numbers to keep straight the 450 million credit reports they issue yearly. Robert Ellis Smith, publisher of *Privacy Journal* newsletter, said in his testimony, "It is ironic that less than one year after we Americans rejoiced in the liberation of peoples in Eastern Europe we are seriously considering a means of social control that Eastern Europeans rejected soundly. One year after we rejoiced in the liberation of Nelson Mandela, we are considering a 'domestic passport' similar to that in South Africa."

In the end, Simpson and other immigration reformers settled for a law enacted by the new Republican Congress in 1996 establishing a computerized system of verifying the citizenship status and the accuracy of Social Security numbers of new hires – but only as a pilot project in the immigration-intensive states of California, New York, Texas, Florida, and Illinois.[27] By a vote of 221-191, the House of Representatives narrowly rejected a requirement for a "tamper-proof" Social Security card or a mandatory worker ID document. The law that was passed required the Social Security Administration to evaluate options for a "tamper-proof" card. In a report issued in 1997, the agency said that to issue new cards to every American would cost from $3,898 to $9,231 million. The plan is feasible, the report said, "However, the issuance of an enhanced card raises policy issues about privacy and the potential for the card to be used as a national identification card."[28] In its report, the agency noted with enthusiasm that at least 75 percent of all newborn infants are now being assigned Social Security numbers before they leave the hospital, as part of the Enumeration at Birth program.

"Would government be able to resist the temptation gradually to expand this new system, to track people, or to store more and more information on them? The answer depends on your view of government."

Representative Steve Chabot of Ohio, in debates about creating a database of new hires, in 1995.

It turned out that 1996, not George Orwell's 1984, was the disastrous year for government attempts to monitor individuals by assigning them an ID number. Congress included in the immigration reform law passed that year the following requirement effective October 2000:

> "A federal agency may not accept for any identification-related purposes a driver's license, or other comparable identification document, issued by a state, unless the license or document satisfies the requirements [of displaying the person's Social Security number on the face of the license itself or imbedding it in the document in electronic form]."[29]

Very few people even noticed this new requirement. But when the U.S. Department of Transportation in 1998 proposed regulations to implement the Congressional mandate, thousands of citizens did take notice and registered their objections. Most of the objectors were conservative Americans, many of them reflecting the Biblical injunction against enumeration that had motivated fears among Puritan New Englanders two and one-half centuries earlier. Pushed by a bizarre alliance of the conservative Eagle Forum and the libertarian American Civil Liberties Union, conservative members of Congress took up the cause and successfully repealed the requirement, in a law passed in October 1999. Many Senators and representatives who had voted for the 1996 legislation now voted to repeal it.

But there was more in 1996. The welfare reform law that year created a duplicative National Directory of New Hires, which requires employers to report immediately to Washington the name, Social Security number, and birth date of every person newly hired in the private and public sectors. This time the intention was to catch errant parents who owed child support and should have it deducted from their paychecks. The Department of Labor was assigned to create the system, which would operate nationwide. By contrast, Senator Simpson's immigration system to detect undocumented immigrants seeking employment was created as an experiment involving only five major states.

The solemn assurance from Senator Simpson and others that these two verification systems for screening new hires would be used only for the one discreet purpose of catching illegal immigrants or deadbeat parents was not worth much. After the senator retired from the Senate, members of the House of Representatives in 1999 – oblivious to all the pledges – approved overwhelmingly two new uses for the Department of Labor database: to track down persons who have defaulted on higher education student loans and to catch persons who may be collecting state unemployment compensation and holding a job at the same time.[30] The Senate approved the second use, but not the first.

There is still more. The welfare reform law also required all states to collect Social Security numbers when renewing or issuing licenses *of any kind*, including occupational licenses, marriage licenses, and commercial drivers' licenses. Before enacting this rule in the summer of 1996, Congress deleted non-commercial drivers' licenses from the Social Security number requirement. Later, while interested citizens groups were unaware of what was happening, Congress included *all* drivers' license applications and renewals in the requirement, effective in 2000.

The end result is that each state must now require Social Security numbers to get a driver's license – or a marriage license.

By means of a cruel joke by a Congressional paper-pusher or of an incredible coincidence, the new provision was indexed in the federal statutes as Section 666(a)(13) of Chapter 42! Fundamentalists who believe that the "mark of the beast" condemns anyone who is enumerated see red when they see the number 666. The Book of Revelation in the Bible says that the number 666 *is* the mark of the beast. By another bit of serendipity, the privacy protection organization Electronic Privacy Information Center happened to locate its office in Washington at *666* Pennsylvania Avenue, S.E.

But there is still more. Also in 1996, Congress, in a law allowing employees to transfer their health-insurance benefits, included a provision for "administrative simplification" of payments for health care. In the process, Congress ordered that an identifying number be issued to every doctor and medical facility and *to every patient*, whether or not the patient was paying for the health care himself or herself.[31] It assigned to the federal Department of Health and Human Services the task of deciding whether the health-care identifier should be a person's Social Security number, a totally new number, or a combination of the SSN and additional digits. There was such sharp disagreement within the department over the patient ID number and the objections from the public were so great that Congress in 1998 – mostly the same elected representatives who had approved the original idea – passed a moratorium on this issue as well.

In the previous decade, Congress had required parents to provide their own Social Security numbers on any application for a birth certificate and, beginning in 1997, any application for a Social Security number for a child. Of course parents felt compelled to get Social Security numbers for their newborns, because a 1986 federal law now requires a Social Security number be listed for any dependent child claimed on a federal tax return.[32] The Internal Revenue Service claimed that in the first year after it began requiring Social Security numbers on all dependents, the number of claimed dependents dropped by seven million. The IRS assumed that taxpayers were no longer claiming these seven million persons as dependents because they were not entitled to do so in the first place and feared that they would get caught, through matching of Social Security numbers.

All of this abetted the drift towards a de facto national ID document, as did a secret directive by the Federal Aviation Administration that airlines must ask passengers to present a government-issued photo identification document. The order was issued in 1995 after an anonymous threat to blow up planes at Los Angeles Airport. There was also concern about security at the upcoming

1996 Olympics in Atlanta and concern about the trial of persons suspected of bombing the World Trade Center in New York City. The FAA refused to release the text of the directive. The agency told the public that it did not directly require identification as a condition of boarding an airplane. Airlines were directed to take alternative security precautions if a person declined to present identification.

"From whatever part of the globe a person comes, he may visit all the ports and principal towns of the United States, stay there as long as he pleases, and travel in any part of the country without ever being interrupted by a public officer."

French visitor Francois Andre Michaux, in 1802, marveling at his freedom in the U.S.[33]

Airlines discovered immediately, however, that the government's directive about asking for ID, though it was secret and confusing, allowed them to detect travelers using the return portion of someone else's discounted round-trip ticket, in violation of airline rules. In fact, they could do this *because the directive was kept secret from the traveling public*. Thus, most of the airlines used the directive to deny passage to anyone not presenting an ID. This was for revenue purposes, not for security purposes. After all the connection between assuring the true identification of a passenger and assuring that luggage was free of bombs, weapons, or contraband was tenuous.

At any rate, the directive – combined with the airlines' enthusiasm to interpret it as authority to deny passage to passengers without government-issued ID – served to force most Americans to carry identification whenever they traveled by airplane, without regard to the long-recognized Constitutional right to travel without undue restrictions.[34] Only a few Americans objected, for fear that they would be regarded as callous to airline security.

Americans seemed hardly haunted by the specter of being required to carry identity papers. A national public opinion survey in 1995 asked a cross-section of adults, "Is not having a national government identification number extremely important or not?" In response, 24 percent rated it extremely important, 30 percent said somewhat important, 20 percent said not very important, 20 percent said not at all important. Five percent were not sure. Americans' level of concern was twice as high for getting access to their own credit reports, for having food properly labeled, or for protecting the confidentiality of their personal information. It was three times as high for controlling false advertising, reducing insurance fraud, avoiding excessive debt, or controlling health-care costs.[35]

By the end of the Twentieth Century, the strong coercion to carry photo identification, along with the multiplying demands for Social Security numbers, had created a de facto requirement that every American have his or her "papers in order" at all times. The regimentation anticipated in 1935 was complete.

Links

The era of "informational privacy" is described in the next chapter, on Databanks.

For the origin of the deep-seated religious suspicion of enumeration, go to the chapter on Watchfulness.

Databanks

A Federal Data Center proposal and abuses in credit reporting bring an era of legislative reform.

The collection of Social Security numbers on virtually every adult member of the public in several different contexts in the 1950s and 1960s had a purpose: to make it easier to organize personal information in large automated data files. But the collection of information was Balkanized; each of several federal agencies zealously protected its turf and competed with each other. This resulted in masses of duplicative data. Only the supplier of the equipment was monolithic: the IBM Corp.

A group of economists and federal statisticians under the auspices of the Social Science Research Council met in the early Sixties to make sense of the government's data collection and dissemination. Their chair was a respected professor of economics at Yale University named Richard Ruggles.

The so-called Ruggles Committee issued a report in 1965 expressing concern that information from the Census could not be linked with data at the Social Security Administration and the Internal Revenue Service. It counted more than 600 disparate data systems, none of them linked with each other. The Ruggles Report was the kind of government document that never reaches the consciousness of the public. But one paragraph in it inadvertently changed forever the way Americans view data collection by their government. The committee criticized the decentralized nature of statistics management and recommended consolidation. How to accomplish this?

> "The committee urges that the Bureau of the Budget, in view of its responsibility for the federal statistical program, immediately take steps to establish a Federal Data Center [with] authority to obtain computer tapes and other machine-readable data produced by all federal agencies. It would have the function of providing data and service facilities so that within the proper safeguards concerning the

disclosure of information both federal agencies and users outside of the government would have access to basic data."[1]

Although it suggested a few demographic techniques for disguising the identity of the subject of each bit of data, by and large the report was short on recommending protections for confidentiality. This was because the group anticipated that, while personally identifiable information would be placed in the proposed data center, it would release only cumulative statistics, not the identities of individuals. This nicely got lost in the public outrage that followed news reports of the group's primary recommendation.

The Ruggles group recommended that the data center be part of the Bureau of the Budget. The bureau (later renamed the Office of Management and Budget) manages each year's federal budget, controls the disbursement of funds, and also has wider responsibilities to assure consistency among federal agencies.

Later in 1966 the Bureau of the Budget published a study endorsing the Ruggles idea of a Federal Data Center. The bureau's consultant, economist Edgar Dunn, was widely quoted as saying that the advantages of consolidation outweighed any concern for individual privacy. The immediate public response was negative, although the Bureau of the Budget plan also did not necessarily involve releasing data that would identify specific individuals.

The overtones of a government-run central database with personal information about every man, woman, and child in the U.S. did not escape the American people. After all, many remembered the exhortations in the 1950s of William H. Whyte, Jr., in his popular book *The Organization Man*. He wrote that Americans had lost the sense of individualism and entrepreneurship of the previous 100 years and accepted in its place risk-free but demeaning existences as corporate beings. Drawing on the social analysis in David Reisman's pivotal book earlier in the Fifties, *The Lonely Crowd*, Whyte argued that Americans had become conformist, hardly distinguishable from each other. He told America that the corporate ethic had colored the way Americans are educated, how they are hired, where they live, what they worship, what they think about and what they hope to get out of life. "I am talking about values," the journalist wrote, "a climate which inhibits individual initiative and imagination, and the courage to exercise it against group opinion."[2] Whyte even devoted a chapter to advising "the organization man" how to cheat on personality tests at work.

In response to the negative public reaction to what now was being called a National Data Center, the House Special Subcommittee on Invasion of Privacy reconvened a hearing it had begun the prior year. The House subcommittee and the Senate Judiciary Subcommittee on Administrative Practices under Chair Sam J. Ervin Jr., Democrat of North Carolina, had both focused on various privacy problems in the federal bureaucracy. This time, led by Republican Congressman Frank Horton from New York, the House subcommittee targeted the National Data Center proposal.

Horton began a hearing in the summer of 1966 by asserting that the fragmentation of federal databases was a blessing because it probably protects personal privacy. His colleague, the assertive Cornelius Gallagher of New York, the chair of the subcommittee, said, "We have become a nation of snoopers." The Executive Branch discontinued, for the present, the initiative to consolidate its information collection.

The public's memory of the National Data Center idea was so lasting that eight years later there was outrage again when a hapless bureaucrat proposed a plan to connect all of the federal government's computer systems. He and his colleagues at the General Services Administration called the proposed network FEDNET. Vice President Gerald Ford, who was heading a special White House committee on protection of privacy, intervened and stopped the plan. The bureaucrat, John E. Holt, was demoted. A year later, Holt's daughter appealed to Ford, who was now President, saying that the demotion was unfair. Holt was reinstated and in fact given key responsibility for his agency's privacy-protection office. The public never knew whether Ford himself intervened a second time, this time to restore the dignity of the man who proposed FEDNET.

Congress even wrote into its appropriations legislation for GSA: no procurement of systems like FEDNET without Congressional approval in advance. Two years later, still during Ford's presidency, the same General Services Administration, which is responsible for federal buildings and communications equipment, had not yet learned the hard reality about the public's distaste for any consolidation of government record systems. It proposed a message-switching system with virtually the same purpose as FEDNET. Ford's White House said that it had "violent objections" to the proposal, as did members of Congress. The plan was squelched. This time, GSA named its proposed interconnection Automated Integrated Digital Services – AIDS. That was about a decade before that acronym symbolized a threat much more ominous for Americans.

In 1999 Senator Daniel Patrick Moynihan of New York proposed a commission to study whether the Executive Branch should create a central statistical agency. Hardly anyone noticed.

But in the late 1960s, a lot of people had noticed. In 1968 Congressman Gallagher convened a separate Special Subcommittee on Invasion of Privacy. Echoing William H. Whyte, Gallagher told the subcommittee that a centralized databank "could lead to the creation of what I call the 'Computerized Man'. . . stripped of his individuality and privacy."

And so began a new era of privacy in America. The new focus was on "informational privacy." By contrast, the movement begun by the Warren-Brandeis article in 1880 had focused on physical privacy and on intrusions by the press. The two Boston lawyers were talking about photography and high-speed publishing when they wrote:

> "Numerous mechanical devices threaten to make good the prediction that 'what is whispered in the closet shall be proclaimed from the house-tops.' For years there had been a feeling that the law must afford some remedy."

Their comment could also describe the late Twentieth-Century "mechanical devices" that for the first time allowed rapid and low-cost storage, processing, and dissemination of information about individuals. The devices, of course, are computers. Thus, both the Nineteenth-Century movement about reputational privacy and the Twentieth-Century concern about "informational privacy" were motivated by apprehensions about new technology.

In the days of Brandeis and Warren, the threat seemed to come from privately owned enterprises, not the government. They wrote:

> "Gossip is no longer the resource of the idle and of the vicious, but has become a trade, which is pursued with industry as well as effrontery."

They were referring to the sensationalizing newspapers of the Gilded Age. Their words about commercial gossip could apply as well to the credit bureaus and direct-marketing firms in the computer era.

The first warning in the age of informational privacy came in a popular book by an enterprising journalist named Vance Packard.

Like Rachel Carson's *Silent Spring* in 1962, on environmental concerns, and Ralph Nader's *Unsafe at Any Speed* in 1965, about automobile safety and consumer activism, Packard's *The Naked Society* in 1964 provided Americans with a fresh way of looking at a pressing issue. For the first time, Americans learned about the clandestine gathering of personal information by scores of credit bureaus and consumer-investigating companies. And they were shocked to discover that the information could be erroneous just as likely as it could be correct. Packard revealed outrageous practices in the screening of job applicants, including subjecting them to the "Seventeenth-Century witchcraft" of polygraph tests. Packard earlier had unraveled the mystery of subliminal advertising with his expose *The Hidden Persuaders* in 1957 and later exposed the loss of community in America in his 1972 book *A Nation of Strangers*.

Senator Edward V. Long, Democrat of Missouri, who had convened hearings on wiretapping in the 1960s, added to the public alarm with his 1967 book on electronic snooping, *The Intruders*. "Modern science and technology," he wrote, "seem to have run far ahead of man's ability to handle his new technology wisely."

Alan F. Westin of Columbia University and the American Civil Liberties Union followed the popular books with his two academic studies. First came one on the nature of privacy, *Privacy and Freedom* in 1967, and next came a study of the nature of personal-information handling by large organizations, *Databanks in a Free Society* in 1972. Westin was moderate in his approach, emphasizing that modern changes in American life, as much as computer technology, had caused public and private organizations to try to document every fact about the American people. He shifted the emphasis from identifying the problem to searching for safeguards. Arthur R. Miller, then a professor of law at the University of Michigan and later a Harvard Law School professor who has popularized the legal process on television, popularized privacy issues as well with his 1971 book, *The Assault on Privacy*.

Among the cultural changes after World War II that created the mania for personal-information gathering:

Credit: By 1980 more than half of all retail sales – and virtually all home sales and automobile sales – were made on credit. Retailers needed credit bureaus to report to them on other merchants' experiences with customers.

Mobility: At the same time, more than 35 percent of all Americans no longer lived in the communities where they were born and where they – or at least their families – were known to creditors. One out of five American families was moving each year. The mobility of the American people created a need for *national* credit bureaus. Americans who moved to a new community or traveled away from home came to expect that credit would be extended to them instantly.

Insurance: By the 1980s about eight out of ten Americans depended on insurance to meet soaring medical expenses, far more persons than ever before. It became extremely risky to drive an automobile without insurance coverage, and before long many states began to require it anyway. Consequently, Americans found themselves supplying more and more personal information to satisfy insurance companies that they were insurable – and to verify claims.

Governmental programs: Traditionally, Americans had very little contact with their government. But after World War II it was increasingly unlikely that any American could avoid contact with one government program or another – whether for food subsidies, public assistance, services for disabled persons, medical care, or housing. It was not simply poor people who came to rely on government programs. Middle-class and affluent persons did as well, whether it was student loans, veterans' benefits, farm subsidies, academic grants, pensions, special tax deductions, public education, or simply a driver's license. All of this required government agencies to collect vast amounts of personal data.

Crime: Increased public concern about street crime and the interstate nature of organized crime prompted law enforcement agencies to use computer systems to collect criminal dossiers – long before the systems were well thought-out and before they included safeguards for confidentiality and accuracy.

In short, American institutions found it necessary to gather and process massive amounts of data about individuals at the very same time that new technology permitted these organizations to do so.

By the 1960s, irrespective of computerization, America had become a credentialed society, demanding personal qualifications to receive the coveted benefits of education, employment, health care, licenses, and social services. Westin called the Fifties "the high point of credentialism, of systematically excluding people because of information in their records."[3]

In Europe, by contrast, everybody qualifies for services and for employment merely through their citizenship. In America, we insist upon qualifying only certain individuals based on need or other criteria. That requires sophisticated information collection. In the early years of computing, it was *large organizations* – government bureaucracies, colleges and universities, labor unions, corporate employers, national banks, and insurance companies – that determined who qualified and who did not. This was true because, from the 1950s through the 1980s, only large organizations had the resources to own computer systems.

"The saddest thing of all is reading letters that begin 'Dear Computer, I know there are no humans there.'"

An orders clerk at the 1.5 million Book of the Month Club, in 1973.

It is this huge disparity in size and power between the information collector and the individual that compounds the threat. Nobody worries much when a neighbor or a corner-store merchant invades one's privacy; each of us can protect ourselves against threats from others of equal stature. But when the resources of a large organization are mobilized to collect information about us, or to use it to determine our fate, that becomes a threat of a much larger dimension. Add to that the difficulty of getting persons in large organizations to respond to complaints or to care about the grievances of a single individual and it is possible to understand how threatened Americans were by the new phenomenon of automated data gathering. It was nearly identical to the shock experienced by Americans in the second half of the Nineteenth Century when they felt that their privacy was similarly threatened by rich, monolithic organizations controlling novel technology. In that instance, it was newspapers controlling photography and printing presses; in the Twentieth Century it was insurance companies, credit bureaus, and government agencies controlling computer technology. With that technology, these companies could increase several-fold the amount of personal information they could collect. With that technology, they could manipulate the data in ways that would have been impossible without automation. With that technology, these companies could make crucial decisions about individuals – decisions about whether they participated fully in some of the prerequisites of life in the late Twentieth Century, like housing, employment, credit, schooling, health care. And many of these decisions could be made without the intervention of human beings, certainly without the full knowledge of the individual most affected.

In the years between the proposal for a National Data Center and passage of the Privacy Act of 1974, there were 15 hearings in the House of Representatives, 12 in the Senate, and two joint hearings in Congress on privacy and information collection.[4] While the public was alarmed about intrusive practices in the private sector because of the popular Vance Packard book, politicians in Congress continued to confine their interests largely to governmental abuses.

Finally, public outrage over erroneous and secretive credit reporting reached Congress, and in 1968 the House held two hearings on credit bureaus. In the next year the Senate Committee on Banking chaired by Senator William Proxmire held hearings in earnest on credit reporting. Proxmire, who later created a notorious award for bureaucratic stupidity, had a flare for generating publicity about the issues he cared about. The Wisconsin Democrat knew how to bring to his hearing room credible victims of erroneous credit reporting and disgruntled ex-employees of the credit-reporting services. The Senator did not need to portray the executives of the industry as arrogant and judgmental. They did that for themselves.

The chiefs of the credit-reporting industry were always a myopic bunch, beginning with two brothers who moved to Atlanta in 1899 to establish a reporting service to provide downtown merchants with the payment histories of consumers who had applied for credit. Cator and Guy Woolford called their enterprise Retail Credit Co. Business was slow during the first year, but in 1901 they discovered that life insurance companies were interested in reports on their applicants.

The brothers jumped into that untapped market, in addition to credit reporting. By the middle of the Twentieth Century when both brothers had retired, their company had expanded into a major information company, owning credit bureaus throughout the Southeast United States plus a service that reported derogatory personal information to insurance companies and later to employers. (In 1997, the company spun off its insurance-reporting operation.)

Retail Credit had discovered a fact of life: everybody is glad to have someone else do his or her dirty work. Insurance companies, lending institutions, and employers wanted to know about the drinking and driving habits, the income, the unattractive behavior, and the living conditions of their customers. But they were reluctant to gather this information themselves. This would bring about unsavory reputations and retaliatory lawsuits. Retail Credit Co. undertook the distasteful work. As the insurance industry grew, Retail Credit Co. grew. As credit purchases soared, Retail Credit acquired more and more local credit bureaus.

The old-fashioned standards of the Southern–based company colored its reports. For years, its young, barely trained "investigators" prepared reports for insurance companies that reported the drinking habits of consumers – even the brand of Scotch they preferred – but never mentioned smoking. Countless reports included the fact that a prospective insured was living "without benefit of wedlock" – always with a clearly derogatory tone. Unverified rumors of homosexuality were passed on to insurance companies and employers with hateful epithets. One report about a woman in South Dakota and her daughter said that they practiced "moral standards and habits which may not be accepted standards of society." In 1972, a man in San Francisco discovered that a consumer report about him for a life insurance policy included the comment that he used "his hands in an effeminate manner, also talks in an effeminate manner."

The Atlanta headquarters of Retail Credit was devoid of women in non-clerical positions and of African-Americans anywhere. When Proxmire put its executives in the glare of publicity at a Senate hearing, it became clear that all nine of the good ole boys at the top had been with the company for more than 30 years each. W. Lee Burge, who as president was Proxmire's favored whipping boy, had begun as a mail clerk in 1936. In the 1960s he was only the fourth chief executive at the company since 1899.

More than one former employee testified that supervisors imposed quotas for producing negative information and that staff members were often "zinging it" – simply fabricating information about a consumer based on a glance at a Zip code. One former employee said that his marching orders were, "When in doubt write it down." Even after Proxmire's hearings, the company instructed its employees:

> "If we develop information that there have been arrests, indictments, or convictions, but local police reports are not available for confirmation, WE SHOULD STILL REPORT THE INFORMATION. But when reporting the informa-

tion, put it in the same language as we developed it, such as, 'there is talk in the community that your subject has had police difficulties, but police records are not available locally to verify this information.'"

A Retail Credit consumer report once said that an insurance applicant in Oklahoma was an upstanding citizen, worth several million dollars. Within a year after an insurance company relied on this report and sold a $15 million policy to the man, he turned up bankrupt and dead with a bullet in his head. The Retail Credit man who wrote this report shortly thereafter became head of the company's Seattle operation.

More often – much more often – Retail Credit's shortcomings in accuracy resulted in normally insurable persons being victimized by erroneous or misleading *negative* information. This of course would cost the person an insurance policy or a job. But there was no way at all for the victim to discover exactly what was in the file.

**"We are dealing with a new technology, whose applications
are just beginning to be perceived and whose capacity
to deprive us of our privacy simply cannot be measured
in terms of existing systems or assumptions
about the immutability of the technology."**

**Harvard Law Professor Arthur R. Miller,
then of the University of Michigan, in 1968.**[5]

Obviously, the credit-reporting businesses and the retailers wanted the public to understand as little as possible about this activity. Most local credit bureaus were not even listed in local phone directories, or they used company names that disguised their real purpose. Many were also debt collection agencies, adding to the confusion. Consumers who sought to see what kind of information existed on them in the local credit bureau, possibly to clear up misinformation, were simply sent away.

Automation changed the business radically. The small cooperatives originally set up by local department stores couldn't finance computerization. At the time, they kept each consumer's data on a 3-by-5 card. It cost about $1 per record to convert this data into an automated file. Each credit bureau had thousands of cards. The large credit-reporting companies like Retail Credit Co., Chilton Corp., TRW (whose parent company was a defense contractor), and Trans Union began to buy up the local bureaus and automate them, with pre-packaged computer systems. This satisfied the growing number of national credit grantors like gasoline companies, car-rental companies, and travel services, which no longer had to query hundreds of Mom-and-Pop credit bureaus before approving applications from an increasingly mobile population.

In 1965, Retail Credit Co. owned 35 local credit bureaus, few of them computerized. By 1969, when Proxmire was drafting a law to regulate them, the company owned more than any other company, 61. It had its eye on the thriving credit bureau in the nation's capital, the Credit Bureau of D.C. Immediately after CBDC bought out its competition in 1969, Retail Credit paid $3 million for the newly expanded credit bureau and its files of two million active shoppers in Washington, D.C. That and other acquisitions in 1970 gave Retail Credit 116 credit bureaus and made it the largest private depository of personal information in the nation. (Later, the Federal Trade Commission ruled that this acquisition, plus one in Portland, Oregon, were done in such a way as to discourage or eliminate competition in the local markets.) Still, consumers who were a part of the company's vast files had never even heard of Retail Credit Co.

In 1971 a federal court barred it from buying up any more credit bureaus, but that did not stop the acquisitions.

Retail Credit Co. was a hybrid, because it sold both credit reports, which include ledger-type information on a consumer's payment history, and consumer investigative reports, which are subjective narrative reports describing a person's lifestyle. These latter reports are prepared for insurance companies and, to a lesser extent, employers. Since the Woolford Brothers got Retail Credit into the consumer investigative field, it has controlled at least 90 percent of the market. To this day, the company's credit-reporting competitors do not prepare investigative reports.[6]

Because the company's name included the word *credit* and because it had always been involved in both businesses, the distinction between credit reports and investigative consumer reports was lost. The confusion remains today. For years, consumers have complained that the company includes "lifestyle" information in its credit reports, and the company has predictably responded that credit reports include only bill-payments information.

In 1969, Proxmire secured a unanimous vote in the Senate on a bill to regulate both credit bureaus and consumer investigative companies. Proxmire's bill represented a major breakthrough. It would be the first law ever to limit the use of personal information, the first ever to require the erasure of outdated negative information, the first ever to require a private company to tell citizens what information it stores on them, the first ever to require a private company to correct information in its possession. In fact, it would be the first law ever to limit the dissemination of information by private businesses. Because it regulated both credit bureaus and consumer investigating firms, the proposal that was to become the Fair Credit Reporting Act also perpetuated the confusion about the two entities.

Proxmire's provisions requiring more openness in their operations and an obligation to make corrections shocked credit bureau executives. But they were generally comfortable with the rest of the regulatory scheme. After all, the Houston-based trade association, Associated Credit Bureaus, Inc. (which itself owned several credit bureaus in competition with Retail Credit Co.), boasted that it drafted many parts of the bill.

Burge of Retail Credit felt that giving a consumer a copy of his or her own report would cut into company profits because a consumer would simply show that credit report to a credit grantor the next time he or she applied for credit. And so Proxmire agreed that a credit bureau could comply with the new law by merely describing "the nature and substance" of what was in the file.[7]

Also, the credit bureau executives correctly feared that consumers outraged by the inaccuracies and slurs in their files would want to sue for damages. Thus, they got the Senate to agree to write into the bill a huge gift: Consumers would be *barred from suing a credit bureau or consumer investigating company for libel or invasion of privacy over inaccuracies they discover in their files.* This provision remains in the law today.[8]

When the Senate bill reached Missouri Representative Leonor K. Sullivan of the Subcommittee on Consumer Affairs, she had her own ideas about appropriate legislation. Sullivan had a reputation in Washington as a consistent defender of consumer rights. She toughened up many of its provisions but was unable to get her subcommittee to report a bill to the full House. Then, as Congress moved to adjourn for 1970, Proxmire used the long-established Congressional technique of attaching a rider to legislation previously approved by one house. He attached his bill to an unrelated banking bill that had been approved by both houses. Sullivan had only an eleventh-hour opportunity to include a few of her pro-consumer provisions in the final bill, but only a few. On October 26, 1970, President Richard M. Nixon signed into law an imperfect Fair Credit Reporting Act of 1971, the world's first information-privacy law.

The law had been on the books barely two-and-a half years when the Federal Trade Commission accused the Retail Credit Co. of violating it. The commission, which enforces the FCRA, cited the consumer investigative operation for a long list of violations: mis-representing itself to consumers and to sources, continuing to re-port obsolete adverse information, pressuring its staff to produce negative information, hassling consumers who sought to know what was in their files, and failing to reinvestigate the accuracy of information challenged by consumers, as required by the new law. Several employees testified in a commission hearing that they were pressured to produce a certain quota of negative information. They said that it was customary for them to identify themselves as repre-senting an insurance company, not Retail Credit Co., when they collected information. A federal court upheld the charges against the company. The company was required in 1982 to circulate the court's order among its employees for guidance. Evidence uncov-ered in 1991 in one of the continual consumer lawsuits against credit bureaus and consumer investigative companies showed that the company had not done so. "Order? What order?" said one em-ployee questioned in the lawsuit.

The reputation of Retail Credit Co. took such a beating from the Senate Banking Committee and the Federal Trade Commission that in 1975 the company paid a handsome fee for consultants to find it a new name. The first choice was a flop, "Infax." Another company already owned the rights to that name. Once back to the drawing boards, the consultants invented "Equifax," to convey a feeling of equitable dealings and factual information.

In a totally separate action, the Federal Trade Commission also cited the credit-reporting side of the business for swallowing its competition in violation of anti-trust laws. This occurred in 1978, when Equifax owned 120 regional credit bureaus throughout the South, the New York City area, and the Pacific Northwest.

The commission initiated another investigation in the mid-1990s and again cited Equifax for having inadequate procedures for as-suring the accuracy of its credit reports, failing to reinvestigate promptly consumer complaints of inaccuracies, ignoring consum-ers' documentation of corrections, allowing incorrect information to reappear in credit reports once it has been "corrected," and furnishing credit reports to organizations without a permissible purpose under the 1971 law. Under a settlement in August 1995, the company is required to discontinue these violations and to file periodic reports with the federal government documenting its progress towards improving its accuracy rate.[9]

From the time of the passage of the Fair Credit Reporting Act to the end of the century, the majority of consumer complaints received by the Federal Trade Commission in Washington involved credit bureaus – more than those concerning debt collectors, funeral directors, or used care salesmen.

In 1988, Equifax Inc., was earning close to $700 million per year in sales from credit reports – issuing 120 million a year to retail stores, credit-card companies, and financial institutions. It was also selling insurance reports, physical measurements on insurance applicants, motor vehicle reports from state databases, marketing surveys, real estate records, and reports that monitored patterns of credit-card use by shoppers. But the company seemed mired in its Old South culture. It called in a hot-shot from IBM Corp., C.B. "Jack" Rogers, Jr., to drag the company into the high-tech, privacy-conscious Nineties. One of the first things Rogers did was to hire Alan F. Westin, the long-time privacy expert, as a paid consultant. Westin nudged Equifax towards some consumer-oriented reforms and persuaded the company to sponsor regular public-opinion surveys on attitudes about privacy and information collection. With Westin, Equifax acquired the added advantage of having a noted "privacy expert" vouch for its good faith. Often Westin was quoted in press reports saying that the credit bureaus were improving their performances. The reports rarely mentioned that he was on the payroll of one of the bureaus. The inaccuracy rate of credit reports coming out of Equifax and its competitors did not improve. According to figures from the companies themselves in the early 1990s, from 21 to 33 percent of their reports continue to have erroneous information in them.

The story of Equifax's major competitor in the "information business" is even more curious. In the 1950s, a biophysicist in Detroit named Harry C. Jordan inherited a local credit bureau. He saw the potential of the coming computer revolution for a business keeping track of millions of bits of account information. Jordan persuaded banks in California to finance the automation of his credit files – and in the process persuaded the same banks to buy his reports on credit applicants.

Dr. Jordan's Credit Data Corporation then established a New York City computer facility and hooked in Buffalo, Syracuse, Chicago, and Detroit. In 1968, an aerospace and electronics contractor based in Cleveland named TRW Inc. (shortened from Thompson-Ramo-Woolridge Corp.) paid the biophysicist handsomely for his automated credit bureaus. Thus, the new entity, TRW-Credit Data Corporation, had a big head start in automation over the tradition-bound folks at Retail Credit Co. in Atlanta, who were more obsessed with blackballing mothers living out of wedlock than with spinning magnetic computer tapes.

Basing its credit operation in Southern California, TRW bought up local credit bureaus on the West Coast, in the Great Lakes area, and in the Northeast. Retail Credit Co. wrapped up the South. Chilton Corporation's credit bureaus were scattered in the Boston, New Orleans, and Denver areas. The privately held Trans Union Corporation, formerly Union Tank Car Corporation and later acquired by the billionaire Pritzker family of Chicago, went after the middle of the nation. Associated Credit Services, Inc., had most of the action in Texas. TRW eventually bought up Chilton, and Equifax bought up ACS. And thus, by 1990, there were just three national credit bureaus.

If a biophysicist could build a credit bureau into a regional automated information company, an engineer could take it into the computerized 1990s. TRW assigned a veteran engineer, Richard D.C. Whilden, to head its Information Systems Group in 1984. He and his colleagues, with their advantage in automation, sensed that the company could exploit the personal information it had in its possession, not limiting its use to credit approvals. After all, once a person reaches middle age, he or she may not apply for credit much any more. How to turn that dormant data into a profit center?

TRW found a way. In the late 1980s, it began exploiting the emerging concept of "target marketing" or "database marketing." TRW realized that advertisers were beginning to question the wisdom of devoting billions of dollars to mass-media messages that would inevitably reach millions of consumers uninterested in the products. "Seventy percent of it falls on deaf ears," said one advertiser. Instead, according to the new concept, modern sellers should target their messages to consumers *known to be interested.* This meant compiling the addresses and telephone numbers of persons likely to be buyers, and directing a commercial message directly to them. To make that direct marketing effective, marketers now needed to know about consumer lifestyles, their prior spending habits, their neighborhoods, and their demographics. Sophisticated computerization made that possible. TRW could put its hands on some of that data from its own credit files. It soon created a target-marketing division to do precisely that, to extract from credit files the raw materials for targeted marketing lists.

"Everything revolves around buying and selling, promoting and advertising. This logic leads ultimately to the gangsterization of culture – the collapse of moral fabric and the shunning of personal responsibility in both vanilla suburbs and chocolate cities."

Cornel West, professor of divinity at Harvard University, in 1994.

Traditionalists in direct marketing were awed by the new practices. A lobbyist for the Direct Marketing Association said that the trade association of mailers was "mind-boggled" over TRW's intrusion into the mailers' turf. An executive of The Kleid Co., Inc., a major list provider, said at the time, "The public may not appreciate the fact that we now have their incomes, ages, number of children, credit data, and the like."

Stoking the target-marketing engine, of course, was data from the Bureau of the Census. The bureau was not releasing information that could be tied to identified individuals. The law prohibits that. But it was aggressively supplying marketing companies with "Census block" data. That includes the demographic characteristics – race, religion, income levels, vehicle ownership, home property values – of groups of 200 persons or so, a "Census block."

TRW could "overlay" this cumulative Census data on its address lists showing credit limits and frequency of credit use. Then it merged this data with lists from magazine and catalog publishers to produce "enhanced lists" grouped by consumers' likely purchasing habits.

Marketing pros began glibly referring to their segmented "clusters" as, "Pools & Patios" (affluent Caucasian empty-nest couples), "Soccer & Braces" (families with elementary-school youngsters), "Blue Blood Estates" (very wealthy), "Shotguns & Pickups" (rural good ole boys), "Black Enterprise" (upwardly mobile African-Americans), even "Grumpies" (grim, ruthless, upwardly mobile professionals – who use lots of credit cards and use them frequently).

By the mid 1990s, computers had allowed marketers to move light years away from the times when Benjamin Franklin in the 1740s sold books by mail with a money-back guarantee, or when Aaron Montgomery in 1872 initiated the first direct-mail catalog, or when Mr. L.L. Bean with $400 in 1912 began an obsessive effort to build the world's most effective mailing list, or when ladies working the telephones at Sears, Roebuck and Co., prior to World War II kept customer records in shoe boxes.[10]

Target marketing was the new wave of the 1990s, inducing list compilers to learn all they could about consumers. "The future of marketing is based on *actual* household purchases," said one jubilant practitioner of the art. "We turn birds of a feather into sitting ducks," said another. All of this created an upsurge in advertising mail. It now reached 37 billion pieces a year, more than a tenth of the total mail delivered by the Postal Service. There were simultaneous retail trends in the 1990s. Consumers used credit cards for more and more over-the-counter purchases, thus creating a paper trail of what they had taken home. (Nonetheless, there still is no law effectively preventing credit-card companies from selling that data). In addition, most large food stores, using the bar code affixed to products, began to track the purchases of customers who used a frequent buyer card or check-cashing card. The stores did this so that they could market directly to the customers in the future – based, as the man says, "on actual household purchases." In addition, most manufacturers of products were automatically capturing telephone numbers of persons who call corporate toll-free numbers for product information. Magazine publishers could alter the advertising content based on the demographics of the recipient's nine-digit Zip codes. Cable TV providers could do the same. This meant that people were exposed to different advertising content depending on where they lived. It was *targeted* at them as members of a particular demographic group. By combining the ability of cable television to *narrowcast* and food markets' ability to harvest data about an individual shopper's choices, some marketers went even further. They could alter the commercials on cable television to match the known demographics and buying habits of a household *and* measure the impact of those messages in food stores directly afterwards.

Thus, at the beginning of this century, the traditional assumption that anyone could make purchases anonymously was pretty much lost, unless a person took special precautions.

TRW and its Target Marketing Services division were on a roll. But then, in 1991, the Federal Trade Commission ordered the company to cease using credit information in its target-marketing operation. In a settlement filed with a federal court in Dallas, TRW agreed to abide by this ruling. Equifax agreed voluntarily to cease the practice, but Trans Union challenged the FTC's ruling in court.[11] At the same time, the attorney general of Texas accused TRW Credit Data and its two major competitors of violating the Texas Deceptive Trade Practices Act. Attorneys general in 17 other states joined the lawsuit, adding the other two major credit bureaus to the case and alleging systemic violations of consumer rights. All three companies settled the charges, essentially agreeing to the reforms that the attorneys general had sought.[12] Also during the 1990s, there were continual lawsuits from consumers who claimed that TRW, Trans Union, and Equifax did not adequately correct inaccurate information in their files. A typical case involved a couple in Indiana who said that TRW and Trans Union did nothing after the couple challenged the accuracy of their credit reports, which showed $60,000 in bad debts. Actually the debts belonged to someone else with a similar name. One year after Trans Union said that it had corrected the information, it provided a credit report to TRW with the bad information in it. TRW passed the inaccurate report on to a mortgage lender, which for the second time rejected the couple's application. Because of the hassle, both husband and wife lost their jobs, as well as the financing on their new home. Keith and Phyllis Mirocha successfully sued the two credit bureaus.[13]

The Federal Trade Commission's enforcement action against TRW actually resulted in a precedent that blind-sided consumers and benefited credit bureaus engaged in the target-marketing business. In the settlement agreement filed with the court in Dallas, the commission reversed its existing interpretation of the Fair Credit Reporting Act and let TRW extract consumer-identifying information *from the top of a credit report* and exploit it commercially, without any safeguards for the consumer. Credit bureaus call this "above the line information" or "header information," and it generally includes a person's address, telephone number (whether it is listed or unlisted), mother's maiden name, and Social Security number. The agreement with TRW meant that the credit bureaus, even if they could not use information about a consumer's actual credit history to build target-marketing lists, still could use the identifying information at the top of a credit report. (Trans Union insisted that it could use actual credit information in its list operation, and that is why it challenged the Federal Trade Commission on this issue for the balance of the 1990s.)

TRW, like Retail Credit, moved to shed its corporate name of the bad publicity, unhappy consumers, Congressional hearings, and lawsuits that were inherent in credit reporting. It sold an 84-percent interest in TRW Information Systems to two Boston speculators for roughly $1.01 billion in February 1996. The new company hired the same corporate makeover firm that invented "Exxon" and "Xerox." The consultants, who apparently favor Xs, suggested the new name of "Experian" – to suggest "experience and expertise." In December of 1996, the venture capitalists flipped Experian for $1.7 billion to GUS, Great Universal Stores, the British retail giant that makes Burberry coats. This meant that credit files on 170 million Americans were now in the hands of a foreign business, which in turn possesses 708 million credit reports in 40 other nations. In 1998, Great Universal completed the merger of credit reporting and target marketing by acquiring Metromail, Inc., the leading direct-marketing company in the U.S. Bringing Metromail into the Experian corporate family gave Experian a huge advantage. It could now apply its sophisticated techniques for developing demographic categories and credit predictability to Metromail's massive lists of virtually every household in the U.S. Metromail starts early in the process; it even badgers child-birthing coaches to give it the names of expectant parents so that it can add to its database of 4.1 million infants born each year in the U.S. (Trans Union, Experian's major competitor, bought a minority interest in the other major direct-mail list compiler in the U.S., Acxiom of Conway, Arkansas. Acxiom claims to have demographic and lifestyle information on more than 95 percent of the households in the nation. It is the company that provides the 100 million home addresses and phone numbers that different search services on the Web provide to users seeking to locate people.)

The passage of the Fair Credit Reporting Act of 1971 began a two-decade parade of federal and state legislation purporting to protect personal privacy in discreet sectors of the economy. This Era of Regulation really began in earnest with the formation of a study committee by U.S. Health, Education and Welfare Secretary Elliott L. Richardson in 1972. The committee's 25 members, including Chair Willis H. Ware of The Rand Corp., produced the first portrait of information gathering and its impact on personal privacy ever provided by the U.S. government.

In forming the committee, the department undertook one of the first genuine efforts to find a diverse membership; it selected a black man from Philadelphia, a teenager from Minneapolis, a bureaucrat from Puerto Rico, a total of nine women, at least six persons conversant with computer data systems, as well as law professors Arthur R. Miller and Layman E. Allen and a recognized expert in computer technology, Joseph Weizenbaum of MIT. The executive director was David B.H. Martin, a confidant of Richardson's from Massachusetts and a devoted public-policy wonk. He was assisted by Carole W. Parsons, who later directed the Privacy Protection Study Commission, which would be created by the Privacy Act of 1974. The committee's lasting contribution was development of a Code of Fair Information Practice, five principles for managing automated personal data systems. It recommended that the federal government apply the code to all of its data gathering on individuals.

Martin, the executive director, said that the principal members of the committee did not want to recommend a rule of absolute confidentiality – a rule that would be unenforceable and counterproductive. For a federal agency to refuse under any circumstances to disclose personal information may actually not always be in a person's best interest, Martin recalled.[14] On the other hand, a federal agency should not be able to disclose personal information for any purpose whatsoever. What Martin and the committee members were seeking was *fairness* in information handling, not necessarily secrecy.

After ten months of hearing testimony, the group began brainstorming at one of its weekend sessions on December 16, 1972. Martin listed on a chalkboard all of the entitlements the members thought were important for a citizen who found himself or herself listed in a computer databank. The list grew, especially after the chair and the director left the room for a break. By the time that they had returned, the chalkboard showed about a dozen items. The members then dashed off to catch airplanes, leaving David Martin and Willis Ware behind. "Dave and I both realized that a dozen restrictions would be too complex, and somehow we winnowed the list down to the few principles that are now the code," Ware recalled 25 years later. "We did that 'off-line' and simply presented it to the committee as a *fait accompli* at its next meeting, March 1, 1973. Some proposals fell away simply because of the cost of implementation."

After a draft report had been prepared, Ware recalled, "Dave, Carole, and I were sitting around musing out loud what to call this thing we had invented. Somebody, an attorney whose name I cannot identify, walked into the room, listened to our story, and said just offhandedly, 'Oh, that's just like the Code of Fair Labor Practice.' Bingo. Out of that interaction came the name, Code of Fair Information Practice."[15]

In July 1973, Casper Weinberger, who had succeeded Richardson as Secretary of Health, Education, and Welfare, released the 346-page report on *Records Computers and the Rights of Citizens* of the Secretary's Advisory Committee on Automated Personal Data Systems. Information managers clamoring for guidance on "this privacy thing" finally had it. The report included a five-point Code of Fair Information Practice:

☐ There must be no personal data record-keeping systems whose very existence is secret.

☐ There must be a way for an individual to find out what information about him is in a record and how it is used.

☐ There must be a way for an individual to prevent information about him that was obtained for one purpose from being used or made available for other purposes without his consent.

☐ There must be way for an individual to correct or amend a record of identifiable information about him.

☐ Any organization creating, maintaining, using, or disseminating records of identifiable personal data must assure the reliability of the data for their intended use and must take precautions to prevent misuse of the data.[16]

The most notable principle – and the most difficult for many data managers to grasp – was the third, the principle of secondary use.[17] It requires an organization to articulate to an individual the purpose for requesting personal information and then to use that information – either inside or outside the organization – only for that stated purpose. Any incompatible use would require the consent of the individual.

Edward J. Bloustein, the privacy scholar at Rutgers University who later became president of the university, presaged the notion of secondary use with his observation in 1964 that there is "an assumption that information given for one purpose will not be used for another."[18]Alan F. Westin did the same in his ground-breaking treatise on the new "informational privacy," *Privacy and Freedom*, in 1967:

> "Consent to reveal information to a particular person or agency, for a particular purpose, is not consent for that information to be circulated to all or used for other purposes."[19]

There was general acceptance of the HEW code from the start – from IBM Corp. after it conducted its own study, from the Business Roundtable of major corporate executives, within Congressional committees, among the emerging cadre of privacy advocates, and from academics here and in Europe. Many tried to improve on it, but no one did.

Swedish officials, working independently to draft the world's first national law on data protection, incorporated the same elements of the HEW code in the Swedish Data Act, which was enacted July 1, 1973. In turn, "the Swedish model of data protection had an enormous and direct influence on the development of data protection in Western European countries," according to a study of the world's privacy laws by David H. Flaherty.[20]

The world's first data protection law anywhere was drafted by Spiros Simitis, now a professor of law at University of Frankfurt in Germany and at Yale University. The state of Hesse in central Germany enacted it in 1970. Only after it was amended in the 1980s did it incorporate elements of the code first developed by HEW. Since then, like most European laws, it has said:

> "Personal data may in principle be further processed only for the purposes for which they have been collected or stored."

After the HEW report was issued, Senator Ervin led a Congressional effort to draft a law applying the principles to government and private organizations that collect information about people.

An ironic result of the ultimate invasion-of-privacy calamity – the Watergate scandal of 1972 – was that it accelerated enactment of the federal Privacy Act of 1974, which limits disclosure of federal agencies' files. At the same time that he was leading the Senate investigation into the abuses of the Nixon Administration, Ervin had been attempting to get the Senate to pass laws protecting the privacy, first, of government employees and, secondly, of all Americans who found themselves in databanks. His interest in these issues was one key reason that Senate leaders designated him to lead the Watergate investigation. Ervin's interest in privacy actually transformed him from the South's intellectual apologist for segregation in the 1950s to a national hero on restricting intrusions by federal authorities. When Ervin was asked to explain his apparent inconsistency, he replied, in 1971: "The stronger the government is, the less freedom the individual has."

But his proposals weren't going anywhere, mainly because it was fashionable during the Nixon Administration to oppose further regulation of private businesses and to oppose expansions of the federal bureaucracy. Representatives Edward I. Koch, a liberal Democrat who later became mayor of New York City, and Barry M. Goldwater Jr., a conservative Republican from Southern California and son of the 1964 Republican candidate for President, teamed up in the House of Representatives to draft a joint proposal to create a federal privacy board and require "fair information practices" in all entities collecting personal information. But their omnibus privacy bill wasn't moving at all either.

In 1973, William Safire, Nixon's loyal speechwriter and policy planner, left the White House to become a columnist for *The New York Times*. Safire had discovered in 1973 that he had been one of the 13 current or former government employees whom Nixon had ordered wiretapped by the FBI. As a columnist Safire became a passionate crusader for personal privacy. He also remained concerned about Nixon's welfare, as the President's stature – and mental health – weakened in the Watergate siege of 1973. "The time has never been so ripe for a reassertion of the right to privacy, and if the President can use the current mood to increase the sum of personal freedom, he would make the desperate hours of 1973 worthwhile," Safire wrote. He suggested that the beleaguered President could save himself by becoming identified as a defender of personal privacy. (Safire recalled Nixon's participation in the landmark *Time v. Hill* case before the Supreme Court eight years earlier.[21])

Nixon's few remaining aides at the White House accepted Safire's intriguing idea. They inserted a ringing endorsement of privacy-protection legislation in what was to be Nixon's final State of the Union address in January 1974, when the President's approval ratings in the polls had dipped to 25 percent. The speech focused renewed national attention on the issue and helped Ervin collect votes in the Senate for his proposal. A month later, on February 21, Nixon issued a comprehensive message on privacy and called for a serious study of the issue under Vice President Ford. By the fall, Ervin, Goldwater Jr., and Koch had gathered enough support to pass their privacy proposal, but at a significant cost. They were forced to delete all references to the private sector. Instead, the bill established a Privacy Protection Study Commission, to study privacy threats in the private sector. Koch and Barry Goldwater, Jr., eventually became members. In July of 1977 it produced more than 100 recommendations for fine-tuning information management in the private sector. But there was no sentiment in Congress then to enact any of them.

"Privacy advocates know they have Richard Nixon and the plumbers to thank for passage of the Privacy Act of 1974."

Privacy expert Alan F. Westin, in 1979.

Congress passed the Privacy Act of 1974 four months after Nixon had left office. His successor, Ford, had found it necessary to proclaim, in his first week in office, "There will be no illegal tapings, eavesdropping, buggings, or break-ins in my administration." Ford took the issue seriously. In his ten months as vice president, he had been assigned leadership of a White House policy committee on privacy. He brought his closest political associate to Washington to direct it. Fittingly, it was Gerald Ford who signed the Privacy Act into law; he had actively encouraged it when he was vice president. The new law required all federal agencies to comply with the Code of Fair Information Practice drafted by the HEW advisory committee in 1973. The law also required them to list publicly all of their databanks storing personal information. The first inventory published in July 1976 reported 6,723 systems maintained by 85 agencies with entries on a total of 3.8 billion named individuals.

The Privacy Act began a succession of federal and state laws that purported to protect personal information in large data systems. In the following years, Congress enacted:

Family Educational Rights and Privacy Act of 1974 (the "Buckley Amendment" or FERPA) – requires federally funded school systems and universities to protect student data and to provide parents of young pupils or college students themselves rights of access and correction.

Right to Financial Privacy Act of 1978 – requires federal investigators to provide a formal written request before getting access to a customer record at a bank or credit-card company, in which case the customer will get advance notice of the request.

Cable Communications Policy Act of 1984 – requires cable-television providers to inform subscribers of the kinds of information kept on them and their rights to review it and correct it.

Computer Matching and Privacy Protection Act of 1988 – formalizes the process by which federal agencies match records from different computer lists to detect fraud and duplication.

Employee Polygraph Protection Act of 1988 – virtually eliminates the use of polygraph machines (sometimes called "lie detectors") for employment purposes.

Video Privacy Protection Act of 1988 – prohibits video rental stores from disclosing customers' names and addresses and the titles of videos rented.

Telemarketing Abuse Prevention Act of 1994, as amended in 2003 – requires telephone sales callers to abide by a federal do-not-call list.

Driver's Privacy Protection Act of 1994 – in essence requires each state motor vehicle department to provide an opportunity for persons to "opt-out" of the rental of their names and addresses by the motor vehicle department.[22]

Health Insurance Portability and Accountability Act of 1996 (or HIPPA) – created regulations to give a patient a right to see one's own medical records and to require that medical providers keep records confidential, with exceptions.

Identity Theft and Assumption Deterrence Act of 1998 – makes theft of a person's identity a federal crime and requires the Federal Trade Commission to assist victims.

Financial Modernization Act of 1999 – limits disclosures by banks of customer account information for non-banking purposes.

Between 1974 and 1978, nine states led by Minnesota (which on April 11, 1974, beat Congress by nine months) enacted laws similar to the Privacy Act.

In each instance when it enacted "privacy-protection" legislation, Congress played tricks on the American people. You have to examine the small print in the laws to find them. For example:

□ In the initial months of the Carter Administration, government lawyers ruled that the Privacy Act – despite its language – permits agencies to match computer lists among different state, federal, and private agencies to catch welfare cheats, deadbeat Dads, and other villains of the moment. They were not about to let a privacy law slow down efforts to winnow out fraud among welfare recipients.

☐ The law on student records gives no rights directly to students or parents; a complainant's only recourse is to persuade an office in the U.S. Department of Education to cut off *all* federal funds to an institution, a highly unlikely occurrence that has in fact never occurred.

☐ The law on financial records doesn't limit state investigators nor private investigators at all. It does not prevent financial institutions from voluntarily disclosing information for commercial purposes.

☐ Cable television hasn't become the interactive medium that Congress anticipated, and so cable providers don't store the kind of sensitive personal information anyone cares about protecting or correcting. However, as cable lines begin to provide Internet access and interactive services, the 1984 law may become relevant to cable TV subscribers in the way that Congress intended.

☐ The law on computer matching still allows state and federal agencies, for instance, to cut off benefits from someone whose private bank account appears to show a hefty balance.

☐ The video privacy law, in fact, permits rental shops to disclose names and addresses of customers, with the *category* of films rented (like "dirty adult movies"), if not the actual titles. Disclosure of this information can be as damaging as releasing specific names of titles. Also, the 1988 law does not protect the confidentiality of individual records held by libraries or bookstores, which for most people, if not members of Congress, are far more sensitive. Americans were surprised to discover the lack of protection for customer records at bookstores when the independent counsel investigating President Clinton successfully compelled two bookstores in Washington, D.C. to identify the titles of books purchased by Monica Lewinsky. The counsel, Kenneth Starr, wanted evidence that she had purchased some books to give to the President.

☐ When it passed the Driver's Privacy Protection Act, Congress led Americans to believe that the law would give citizens a right to chose not to have their names, addresses, and identifying information sold or otherwise disclosed by state motor vehicle departments. It was passed in response to stalkers and anti-abortion activists getting the home addresses of their targets from state motor vehicle records. In 1999, the American people discovered that the law included a huge loophole. It still allowed the sale of Social Security numbers or drivers' photographs, until it was amended later.

Only the anti-polygraph law and the telemarketing law have really worked as intended.

During this time, when Congress and state legislatures were enacting protections, there was an extensive effort to assure that the criminal histories loaded into the Federal Bureau of Investigation computer system were accurate and were used only for legitimate law enforcement purposes. There was an identical problem at the state level, where there were 50 counterparts to the FBI's national network being created. What was true of the raw files in the early computer systems of credit bureaus and other private businesses was true of the automated records of law enforcement. They were, said federal Judge Gerhard Gesell, "out of effective control. . . incomplete and hence often inaccurate. . . no procedure exists to enable individuals to obtain, to correct, or to supplant the record."[23]

In 1973, the Governor of Massachusetts, Francis Sargent, decided to take a bold action. He refused to provide his state's criminal records to the FBI, because the system was "poorly secured and loosely controlled." Although he was confident that the state would ultimately prevail in its defiance, Sargent was surprised that the move increased his popularity. "Frankly, I thought we could get creamed," he recalled. "I questioned how a mere governor would fare against Efram Zimbalist, Jr., the myth of J. Edgar Hoover (not to mention his 'private' files), and hordes of 'G-men.' Would the cry go out that our action was interfering with the 'war on crime'?" But there turned out to be a strong untapped constituency for protecting privacy, even in criminal records.[24] This was true not only in Massachusetts, but also in several other states.

The bureau sued Governor Sargent, then backed off. Facilitating the settlement was former Massachusetts politician Elliott Richardson, who by now was Attorney General of the United States. Later, the federal court in the District of Columbia told the FBI three times that it had an affirmative obligation to keep an accurate database. The bureau had contended that, in creating a national database of state criminal histories for the use of police departments everywhere, it was a mere neutral repository of arrest information. It had no obligation to correct the data or control its dissemination, it claimed. The federal court in Washington rejected this defense.[25] The FBI is not like a librarian, who of course does not vouch for the materials he or she makes available. The FBI has an obligation to make sure that information it disseminates, even if it comes from state agencies, is accurate and up to date.

In the years since 1970, the public-opinion polling firm of Louis Harris & Associates has asked a representative sample of the American people, "How concerned are you about threats to your personal privacy in America today – very concerned, somewhat concerned, only a little concerned, or not concerned at all?" The answers provide a consistent measure of the increasing concern over the years. Ironically, Equifax, Inc., sponsored the Louis Harris surveys for many years. The credit-reporting conglomerate is the company that had created a lot of the public concern about the collection of personal information in computer systems. Here are the results of the Louis Harris polls: [26]

1970	34 percent concerned
1977	47 percent concerned (including 25 percent very concerned)
1978	64 percent concerned (31 percent very concerned)
1983	77 percent concerned (48 percent very concerned)
1990	79 percent concerned (46 percent very concerned)
1991	79 percent concerned (48 percent very concerned)
1992	78 percent concerned (47 percent very concerned)
1993	83 percent concerned (53 percent very concerned)
1995	82 percent concerned (47 percent very concerned)
1997	92 percent concerned (64 percent very concerned)
1998	88 percent concerned (55 percent very concerned)

A look at other survey responses gathered by Louis Harris & Associates shows the reason for the significant jumps in concern between 1992 and 1997. Americans had discovered the Internet. If large faceless data systems caused them concern about their personal privacy, what about the distribution of that information throughout the much more vast domain called cyberspace? Were there any controls at all in this new environment? Once again, as they had in the 1890s and the 1970s, applications of new technology brought with them renewed interest in protecting privacy.

\Links

To discover the impact of the Internet on personal privacy, go on to the next chapter, on Cyberspace.

To read about the FBI's alteration of the phone system for surveillance purposes during the 1990s, go back to the end of the chapter on <u>Wiretapping</u>.

To read about the return of sensational journalism in the 1990s, go to the end of the chapter on <u>Torts</u>.

Cyberspace

Personal computers and the World Wide Web bring renewed concern about protecting privacy.

A survey by Louis Harris & Associates in 1994 showed that a third of all respondents had heard or read nothing about the on-line world. When told about it, more than three out of five respondents expressed concern about threats to their personal privacy on-line, and three out of five cited this as their number-one concern about using the Internet.[1]

Of computer users surveyed by Harris in 1997, a third now said that they were using an Internet service provider, like America On-Line, Prodigy, CompuServe, or one of the smaller companies; half of those not currently using the Internet planned to start within the year. In the interim, between 1994 and 1997, the number of Internet sites had more than doubled. There seemed to be more than 120,000 at that point, but no one knew for sure. An estimated 30 million users in the U.S. now had access to the Internet, the global "network of networks." But significantly, of those who told Harris poll takers that they did not plan to join the stampede to the Internet, 52 percent said that they would be more likely to do so if their personal information and communications could be protected. Half of those not subscribing to an on-line service said that they would be more likely to do so if there were privacy safeguards.[2]

It would not have been surprising if ordinary Americans had been reluctant in 1997 to admit that privacy was a concern in using the Internet. *Time* magazine had published an alarming cover story on July 3, 1995, about what it called "cyberporn," saying that it was popular, pervasive and surprisingly perverse." The magazine relied on fraudulent surveying data by an undergraduate student at Carnegie-Mellon University, which vastly overestimated the presence of pornography on-line and its popularity. *Time* repeated the student's claim that more than 80 percent of the images on the Internet were sexually-oriented. The magazine later retracted many of its assertions and admitted "damaging flaws" in its story. By now the damage had been done. The "Nightline" news program on

ABC television picked up *Time*'s story, and members of Congress introduced legislation based on the assumption that Time's portrayal of the Internet had been accurate. This and other news accounts shaped perceptions of the 'net as primarily a place for sleaze. In January of the same year, *Newsweek* published a cover story on "shame," arguing that this was a beneficial value – to keep our individualism in check, to conform our behavior to the moral code of the majority. In such a climate, it would not have been unusual for anybody to express a concern about confidentiality and security on-line for fear of being perceived as a consumer of pornography.

As Internet users began to visit the World Wide Web to shop or to download helpful information, this perception decreased. By 1998, browsing on the Web was a common activity for a wide assortment of reasons. Thus, expressing concern about the confidentiality of personal information on-line no longer raised an immediate suspicion that a person was solely interested in keeping secrets about visiting sexually oriented sites.

Whether the perceived threats to privacy on-line were real or imagined, the Internet exposed millions of Americans firsthand to the capabilities of computers, especially computers storing information about people. In fact, the potential threats to privacy were real enough. They could be grouped in six categories:

Lack of communications confidentiality – With the ability to send and receive electronic mail messages becoming widespread in the 1980s, early users of computers with telephone modems immediately wanted to find a way to scramble their messages for security. They were no different than Thomas Jefferson, James Madison, George Washington, or Alexander Hamilton, all regular users of codes in their correspondence.

The FBI, already befuddled by the cleverness of computer hackers, became alarmed that sophisticated computer users could encrypt their communications on-line and keep them secret from law enforcement in the event of a criminal investigation. Perverts, pederasts, pornographers, and criminal syndicates could hide their activities by encrypting their words and images. The intelligence agencies – the National Security Agency, the Central Intelligence Agency, and others – had long attempted to keep cryptography out of the hands of civilians. The law-enforcement and intelligence people persuaded the newcomers in the Clinton Administration in the spring of 1993 to join them in actively discouraging the development and use of encryption. Vice President Al Gore, who as a member of the House and the Senate had developed a solid understanding of modern technology, led the effort.

The law enforcement and intelligence agencies would have liked to have made possession of scrambling technology a crime, but the courts were wary of that. There were, instead, two weapons for federal authorities. First, they resorted to the International Traffic in Arms Regulations to declare that exporting encryption software was illegal. Because the Internet was developing as a global medium, this deterred many individuals and companies from making encryption products available on-line, for sale or for free, because disseminating scramblers overseas on the 'net, might be considered a federal crime.

In fact, between the years of 1993 and 1996, federal prosecutors dangled the Damocles sword of a criminal indictment over an encryption entrepreneur from Boulder, Colorado, named Philip Zimmermann. He had developed the first readily available software for encryption and made it available for free on the Internet in 1991. Borrowing an idea from Garrison Keillor's bogus advertisement for "Ralph's Pretty Good Groceries" on his *Prairie Home Companion* radio program, Zimmermann called his product PGP – for Pretty Good Privacy. Obviously, once it was available on-line, there was no way to keep it from falling into the hands of foreigners – or more accurately into their computers. For three years, the U.S. attorney in San Jose, California, considered indicting Zimmermann for violation of the export laws. Until the federal government officially terminated its investigation, many computer users came to believe erroneously that using encryption may be a crime.

There was a second result of using export controls. University of Miami cyber-law expert A. Michael Froomkin wrote in 1996,

> "Largely because of the ban on export of strong cryptography, there is today no strong mass-market standard cryptographic product within the U.S. even though a considerable mathematical and programming base is fully capable of creating one."[3]

One federal court invalidated the export controls as governmental limits on instrumentalities of free speech. But by then, export policy had effectively deterred American companies from developing encryption products because the products could not be marketed abroad as well as in the U.S. Many of the popular electronic-mail programs manufactured in the U.S. were sold with no encrypting element, for instance.

Secondly, to control the use of scrambling techniques, the federal government looked to its role of developing standards to promote compatibility among new products. The National Security Agency encouraged the standards-setting agency, the National Institute of Standards and Technology, to coordinate an effort to develop a federally sanctioned standard for encryption products. Thus, the agency that was created to establish uniformity in electric sockets and flame-retardant materials became the locus for an intense debate about protecting the confidentiality of personal communications while at the same time permitting law enforcement and intelligence gatherers to do their jobs. The intent of the NSA and the FBI was to incorporate within the encryption standard a means for allowing the government to have access to encrypted communications.

In 1994 NIST unveiled its proposed Escrowed Encryption Standard known as the "Clipper chip." It was intended for use on telephones. For assuring secure electronic mail and computer files, it proposed a standard known as the Capstone Chip-based Fortezza PCMCIA card. Use of the chips was voluntary. But computer users knew immediately that they didn't want them, for they were equipped with a trap. There were few complaints about the level of encryption; both chips used a sophisticated 80-bit formula. The problem was, according to those wanting to use effective computer encryption, that the two standards were designed on the assumption that a government agency would keep a copy of the two digital keys necessary to decrypt messages. This allowed the government to retain the ability to unscramble any message sent using the chip. Nobody wanted to buy products with this escrow element in it, and the proposed standard died under its own weight. By the fall of 1999, the White House had pretty much given up its campaign to prevent the American public from using cryptography to protect their communications.

Loss of Anonymity – Just as patriots in the 1770s and computer users in the 1990s relied on cryptography, they both relied on anonymity as well.[4] But was it possible to preserve anonymity on the Internet? If you selected a pseudonym for yourself or filtered your messages through so-called "anonymous remailers," you could achieve some degree of protection in on-line correspondence. But the vast number of individuals using Internet service providers had no assurance of anonymity. The ISPs have policies of disclosing the identity of users to law enforcement agencies when they demanded it with the proper legal paperwork. The operators of Web sites were not hesitant to disclose the identities of persons who had registered on them.

And what about shopping on the Internet? Electronic commerce became widely available about five years after a physicist in England named Tim Berners-Lee in 1989 developed a simple and uniform interface that permitted access to almost any resource linked to the Internet. This platform was named the World Wide Web. Prior to that, there was no assurance that a user could download information in a format understandable to his or her computer software or could search through another computer system with ease. Now individual users could browse through colorful and animated on-line "catalogues." They could get sound and graphics. They could purchase products with a credit card. They could also gain entry to fee-based Web sites. But users also discovered belatedly that whenever they visited a World Wide Web site, the site would send to their computers a token of gratitude. It is called a "cookie," a hidden indicator that the user has visited the site, to which pages within the site, and on which dates. This is meant to make the person's next visit to the site rapid – because much of the Web-site information need not be downloaded onto the user's computer all over again. Most cookies have expiration dates encoded in them, so that they are automatically erased from a computer. The Web site chooses the expiration date, of course, not the user. Through cookies, the Web site can direct a return visitor to portions of the Web site that will be of particular interest, based on the cookie's record of previous visits. Through cookies, one Web site can pick up the credit-card and address information previously provided to another Web site earlier. But virtually all customers – including very savvy 'net users – did not realize this. They had to discover that they could disable cookies or erase them or change the expiration dates.

Netscape, the maker of browser software that originated the use of cookies, said that these little gems were called cookies "for no compelling reason." Others say that computer geeks first developing the capability saw the potential for Web sites to gobble up endless amounts of information and thought of the Cookie Monster on the "Sesame Street" children's television program.

For a brief time in 1999 there were indications that some disreputable pornography sites, most of them located overseas, were using cookies to "lock in" a visitor so that the home page would appear and reappear each time the user made a move on his or her keyboard. The only way to stop this was to shut down one's computer and restart it.

A further danger was that a new breed of Internet advertising intermediaries could exploit the cookies placed on a user's computer by Web sites that he or she had visited previously. They could amass several indicators of that person's likes and dislikes – at least on-line – and then alter the content of the banner ads that their clients would aim at each individual. This allowed these on-line advertising specialists, notably a company called DoubleClick, to customize the content of their clients' commercial Web sites to fit the known consumer tastes of each individual user. DoubleClick pioneered the use of cookies to track the number of times users see banners displayed on the sites of all of the company's clients. Now DoubleClick can assure that a user most likely will see slightly different commercial Web pages than would his or her neighbor across the street, or his or her spouse in the next room. And none of them would realize this. Kevin O'Connor, DoubleClick's chairman, boasted, "There's a lot of data out there on the Web, but not all of it's useful, because the only useful data is that which predicts future behavior, like knowing what someone has bought in the past." The company's Eastern sales manager could not contain his enthusiasm. "On the Web and only on the Web can the promise of an integrated marketing campaign that is targetable, measurable, and accountable truly exist," he exclaimed. "The Web fulfills the promise that ad agencies have been making to their clients for years."

This so-called "on-line profiling" had an additional dimension. It meant that for the first time *advertisers,* and even advertising service agencies like DoubleClick, would be collecting personal information. In the past, retailers, credit grantors, and even wholesalers collected personal information about customers, but not advertisers and advertising agencies.

DoubleClick also has the capability to capture electronic-mail addresses. When in 1999 DoubleClick acquired a company named Abacus Direct that possesses millions of physical addresses, telephone numbers, and known consumer preferences, alarms sounded for many privacy activists. "Now they can combine data about on-line purchasing with personal data gathered off-line and bombard us with customized e-mail and telephone sales calls!" they complained. Indeed, the newly merged company said that that is exactly what it can now do.

With the popularity of the World Wide Web, it was possible for the first time to keep a log not only of purchases made by a shopper but also of mere window-shopping. If on-line purchasing caught on, shoppers could no longer assume, as they can in the real shopping world, that they remain totally anonymous whenever they merely "feel the merchandise" or even when making a purchase (so long as they use cash).

"In cyberspace, everyone will be anonymous for 15 minutes."

Graham Greenleaf
of the New South Wales Privacy Committee
in Australia, 1990s.

Anonymity on the Internet would be a double-edged sword, of course. While it would preserve the status quo with regard to shopping, it would also provide safe havens for strangers who sought to harass others on-line or to send slanderous or salacious electronic mail or chat-room missives.

To meet the demand for anonymity on-line, high-tech companies in Europe developed software – and even on-line banks – for processing payments anonymously, much like an electronic traveler's check. With this technique, the seller needs only to determine that real or electronic signatures match; the seller does not need to know anything more about the identity of the buyer. These techniques proved that anonymity in electronic commerce was feasible. But American companies selling products on-line showed a lack of interest in these "digicash" possibilities. One reason may have been that the major credit-card companies had no interest at all in having on-line merchants accept alternatives to credit cards.

Cookies are a limited threat to individuals who are the only ones using their own computers, especially if they know how to disable cookies or can resist subliminal advertising created directly for them. But if an individual has access to the World Wide Web through a computer that is used by a few other persons – at work, at a school or a university, or even at home, then cookies might create embarrassment. They create a history of every site visited on the Web, including those that a person may have intended to visit without the knowledge of others.

Lack of security – The possibilities in the on-line world were exciting, but securing this new network – open to millions of unsophisticated users worldwide – got very little attention, not even as an afterthought. Electronic vandals called "hackers" infiltrated, altered, and often disabled major Web sites, including those operated by *The New York Times*, the Pentagon, the U.S. Department of Justice, the U.S. Senate, and the FBI itself. A 19-year-old hacker admitted in 1999 that he was able to infiltrate the Web site of the White House and alter its content. When Eric Burns pleaded guilty to another offense, altering the Web site of the United States Information Agency, a federal judge ordered him not to touch a computer for three years after he served his sentence.

In addition, computer users everywhere in the 1990s received warnings of free-floating self-replicating codes that could corrupt an individual's software. This affected even computer users who were not yet on-line, for at first these "viruses" were introduced into a personal computer or major system through pirated or amateur compact discs. Soon, mischievous strangers were sending them through electronic mail. Further, it was possible in the late 1990s for malicious hackers to "spoof" someone else, by entering his or her personal computer and sending electronic mail in the name of the victim.

Even the most up-to-date Web sites of large companies were not secure enough. For instance:

□ In 1999 an error in designing hallmark.com allowed anyone to search the Web site for texts of private love notes and the senders' identities. At the site a sender posts a private greeting, then generates an e-mail message to the intended recipient telling how the message can be accessed at Hallmark's site with a password. Until the error was corrected, anyone could search the site by key words and find intimate messages intended for Valentine's Day. The response of the company: "We certainly are committed to providing privacy. The new system has, built in, a new standard to ensure this kind of thing doesn't happen again."

□ Visitors to the site of one of the world's largest toy retailers, F.A.O. Schwarz, for a brief time in February 1999 were able to print out other customers' ordering information, including home phone numbers (but not credit-card numbers). The response of the company's vice president for public relations: "We would take any breach of security very seriously. We are going to make a lot of changes."

□ At the same time, a man using a search engine stumbled upon the names, e-mail addresses, home addresses, and phone numbers of hundreds of entrants in contests at the home page of CBS Sportsline. A CBS executive's response: "We take security very seriously." He promised that the problem has been fixed forever.

□ In Toronto a visitor to the home page of Air Miles, which offers travel rewards for frequent purchases, stumbled upon the names, account numbers, home phone numbers, e-mail addresses, and home or business addresses of 30,000 Air Miles members. The response of the company president: "We are concerned, particularly in view of our commitment to protecting the privacy of members' information."

□ When it began making information on individuals available on its Web site in March 1997, the Social Security Administration required a user to provide name, Social Security number, date of birth, state of birth, and mother's maiden name to get access to his or her entire career earnings record to date and the person's anticipated benefits. But four out of five of the authenticating elements requested at the Web site are not difficult for a stranger to ascertain about an individual. People are sensitive about their incomes. The public reaction was immediately negative, and the agency was forced to shut down the service for nearly a year. Before it began offering this service, the agency had tested its procedures at five locations. It had even asked the systems security team at the highly sensitive Los Alamos National Laboratory to provide advice. Still it had not anticipated that the public would object to the ease with which strangers could get information on them. When it reopened, the Web site (1) no longer included earnings information, (2) loaded personal data on its site only once there was a request for it; and (3) delivered benefits information to the individual through e-mail, not on its Web site.[5]

□ Experian, the credit bureau formerly known as TRW, proudly unveiled a service on its Web site August 13, 1997, providing a copy of one's own credit report for inspection to anyone who provided a name, Social Security number, and a small fee by credit card. Everything worked fine for a day or two, and even privacy critics of the company praised the effort. On Friday, August 15, when 2000 requests arrived all at once, the volume triggered a software glitch that misdirected 200 credit reports (including Social Security numbers, account numbers and balances) to the wrong persons. Experian shut down the Web service to fix the problem.

Digital photographs – The technology available to homebound users with relatively modest personal computers progressed so rapidly that before the end of the decade they were routinely sending photographs to each other on-line. On their own Web sites, school systems began posting pictures of students. Businesses posted pictures of employees without consent. They failed to realize how digital photos can be altered, cut and pasted, placed out of context, and downloaded by anyone anywhere. None of this is possible to do with 8x10-inch hard-copy glossies, but it's possible with digital images. A popular hobby for some amateur *webmeisters* was to attach the face of a celebrity to nude bodies from other illustrations. The mischief was not limited to celebrities. College friends and former spouses also found their images disseminated globally in illicit settings, beyond their control.

Third-party records – The threat to privacy on the World Wide Web affecting the most people was the buying and selling of personal information through Web sites. Yet, this was the threat getting the least attention from government agencies and private-sector watchdogs. Here the individual could exercise no control. The person probably never even knew about the exchanges and certainly never did business with the on-line "information brokers" making the sales.

For example in 1993 an entity named Digital Detective dispatched electronic-mail advertisements all over the Internet saying that for a price it would provide lots of personal information on anyone you wish. The ad said, "You provide an SSN. I will advise you of all the names which have been used with this SSN" or "You provide a name. Any name okay, but very common names will render a useless list. You'll receive new address if they moved, telephone number, residence type, length of residence, gender, date of birth, up to four household members and their dates of birth. Also can provide up to ten neighbors, their addresses, phone numbers, and residence types." "Digital Detective" also offered to sell a credit report to anyone who asked, whether he or she identified oneself or not, so long as the requester provided "a signed statement that your request is for bona fide, legal reasons." This was an attempt to comply with the requirement in the Fair Credit Reporting Act that companies regularly selling information about consumers to third parties assure themselves that the information will be used only for credit, employment, insurance, or some other transaction initiated by the consumer.

In 1996, a rapidly growing "information broker" on the West Coast called CDB Infotek advertised in e-mail messages that its "Missing Links" allows customers to "search through 542 million credit bureau header files with only an individual's name to uncover: full name and a/k/a's, current and previous addresses, Social Security number, date of birth, phone number, demographic information, neighbors, and much more!" It also offered access to the Postal Service's National Change of Address computer lists, Social Security records, data about ownership of real estate, lists of registered voters (in violation of some state laws), and files on assets. Seven months after this ad appeared, Equifax, Inc., the national credit-reporting company in Atlanta, acquired CDB Infotek.[6]

At the end of a decade in which credit reports, Social Security numbers, unlisted telephone numbers, and even medical data were being bought and sold on-line, there were still no meaningful legal protections for medical and financial information, whether disseminated electronically or the old-fashioned way. An example of the tragedy that can occur happened in 1999 in New Hampshire, where a 21-year-old man downloaded information from on-line research services to track down a high school classmate whom he was stalking. He discovered the location of her workplace and went there and killed her and himself. In a cruel legacy left on his own Web site, the man wrote, using his own misspelling, "It's actually obsene what you can find out about people on the Internet."

Commercial exploitation – Computer users linked to the Internet found themselves receiving lots of unsolicited advertisements by electronic mail. Marketers could send this "spam" mail in different ways. They could merely piggyback on someone else's message to several recipients, or send a message to all the subscribers of a certain Internet service provider, or harvest all the addresses of persons participating in "newsgroups" or "chat rooms." Such bulk e-mail, which became known as "spam," is inexpensive to transmit.

Where did the label "spam" come from? "The genesis can be found in a Monty Python's Flying Circus sketch in which a customer in a restaurant asks what's on the menu," according to Simson Garfinkel, cyber-columnist for *The Boston Globe*, and computer-medicine expert Alan Schwartz. "The waitress tells him, 'Well, there's egg and bacon; egg, sausage, and bacon; egg and Spam; egg, bacon, sausage, Spam; and Spam (and so on).' Then a chorus of Vikings begins chanting, 'Spam, Spam, Spam, Spam.'"

Spam was then and is now a processed luncheon meat in a can. Some word experts will tell you, therefore, that during the 1940s the term "spam" was used to describe anything that is commonplace. But Garfinkel and Schwartz said, "The Internet use of the word originated in chat rooms and on multiplayer Internet adventure games called MUDS (multiuser dungeons). . . . A few delinquents would `say' the same message again and again in a chat room, filing the screen in the process, and other people would call these messages `spam.' It was just like the Monty Python skit – senseless repetition."[7]

The science fiction writer Isaac Asimov anticipated spam, although he seemed to think that it would have benign applications. He wrote,

> "We can be reasonably sure that almost all [direct-mail advertising] could be transmitted electronically over long distances. A master copy can be transmitted at one postal-electronic station and copies can be reproduced at various receiving points, in the desired numbers, and each with an appropriate address printed out from the mail listing obtained from the central computer."

That was in *1973*. Asimov's crystal ball was cloudy in one aspect; he anticipated that the final delivery would be by hand. But he must be credited with anticipating the ease and low-cost of electronic mail: "The communications satellite is distance insensitive. A beam of radiation sent out to a satellite can be amplified and relayed to any point on earth (via one or two other satellites, if necessary). A message can be sent as quickly and as cheaply from New York to Los Angeles via satellite as from New York to Hoboken."[8]

Even if it was kept secure, electronic mail raised an additional threat to the sanctity of people's personal correspondence, by the very nature of the medium. It was somehow both intimate and public at the same time. A divorce lawyer who uses e-mail files as evidence in his cases pointed out the novel attributes of e-mail. "It combines the casualness of speech with the permanence of writing. It's got a lot of potential for embarrassing the other side," he said.

There is a second method for commercial exploitation when using the World Wide Web. That is the use of personal information that individual "window shoppers" leave at a commercial Web site. For instance, many sites ask a person to provide an electronic mail address and demographic information in order to get access to all or parts of a site. When ordering a product for delivery, of course, an on-line shopper must provide a physical address and a credit-card account number. This information is voluntarily disclosed by a person, in contrast to the consumer data gleaned from "cookies."

An early prototype of on-line gathering of consumer choices was a joint venture by IBM Corp. and Sears called Prodigy. In the early Nineties, it offered a service called videotext to a quarter of a million subscribers. They would respond to advertising text by providing personal responses to all sorts of inquiries from advertisers. Prodigy had no policy restricting its use or disclosure of the information. In fact, users discovered later that Prodigy had the capability of lifting selected data from a user's computer hard drive – kind of a reverse cookie. Videotext was supplanted in the early 1990s by the appealing graphics and animation made possible by the new platform known as the World Wide Web.

In the years that followed, policy makers in Washington showed special concern about home pages appealing mainly to children. After hearing several witnesses in a hearing in June 1996, the Federal Trade Commission staff concluded:

> "Young children sitting at a computer terminal can easily disclose significant amounts of information about themselves and their families, or establish an ongoing relationship with someone thousands of miles away without a parent's knowledge."[9]

The staff found, for instance, that the home page of Batman Forever asks children to provide information about their families. Kellogg's Web site asks what kinds of cereal they like and whether their parents let them pick their own cereal. The site of disney.com asks for e-mail and home addresses of children. *Discover* magazine takes kids' home addresses for new subscriptions and then says it is not responsible for protecting credit-card information that has been provided. The CBS Web sites for children announce to users that any information disclosed there "is ours to use without restriction." These practices led Congress in 1998 to enact the Children's On-Line Privacy Protection Act, which requires the consent of parents before Web sites aimed at children 13 or younger may collect information about kids on-line.[10]

This became virtually the federal government's sole priority – alerting the public to the capture of personal information left at a Web site and its subsequent use or disclosure. At FTC workshops, White House conferences, policy meetings at the U.S. Department of Commerce, concern about privacy in the Internet age was confined to this one discreet aspect. There was no discussion at all of communications security, anonymity, leaky Web sites, digital photographs, or third-party records in the 'net.

This was the result of the myopia of a Friend of Bill – Bill Clinton – named Ira Magaziner. Clinton's policy advisor arrived at the White House, ironically, with a reputation as a visionary futurist. In 1997 Magaziner was assigned the task of shaping federal policy towards what was then called the National Information Infrastructure or – for a few years – "the information highway." (These are actually much broader terms, encompassing the computerized "network of networks" known as the Internet *and* interactive television, electronic payments systems, dedicated networks, and specialized on-line data services. The Internet is the main artery of all of this. The World Wide Web is the platform for making access to all of the connected databases easy.)

Magaziner had been traumatized by the bitter and unsuccessful effort with Hillary Clinton to reform the nation's health-care apparatus in Bill Clinton's first term. Fresh in his mind was the limit of government's capability to direct a loose collection of private entities. This is especially difficult in an industry in its developmental stage, like the one scrambling to make money on the Internet. Besides, much of the strength of the Internet from 1990 to 1994 was its lack of inhibitions and regulations. It truly was an electronic frontier, more like a Western cowboy town than the electronic strip mall it became after 1994. For these reasons, Magaziner calculated that an attainable goal was to persuade American businesses to adopt privacy policies on their Web sites. More meaningful privacy protections were left for another day.

And so the chastened Magaziner approached his friend, the President of the United States, and urged that the White House stress voluntary "self regulation" in the development of the National Information Infrastructure – which, U.S. bureaucrats had to learn, was already in fact a *global* infrastructure (even if the U.S. had invented it). It was an unusual strategy for an interventionist Democratic administration – especially one that in all other aspects of high-tech policy pursued governmental regulation – in areas of copyright and cryptography for instance. But the President agreed with this approach. What President would not have? This was undoubtedly astute, considering that this old friend had gotten the administration into so much political hot water over interventionist health-care policy in its first term. This was also an approach that pleased the executives of West Coast high-tech companies who had made big donations to Clinton's reelection campaign.

"Self regulation" became a sacred mantra, at least in the area of personal privacy. Magaziner won new friends for the White House among the privacy-intensive businesses – the credit bureaus, the direct mailers, the information brokers, and the mainstream corporations that saw the Internet, or information highway or information infrastructure or whatever it was, as no more than an opportunity to target more consumers for their products. When he left the White House at the end of 1998, they even gave him a plaque for his efforts.

And so from 1994 to 1999, businesses and high-level members of the Clinton Administration, when they thought about personal privacy in the Internet age, thought only of voluntary efforts on corporate home pages to disclose to consumers what might become of the personal information they entrusted the companies with on-line.

Consequently, the underlying issues of inadequate security and inadequate recognition of personal privacy on-line were allowed to fester in cyberspace. They were left for a subsequent administration and Congress to face, much as the issue of injustice towards African-Americans was allowed to fester in the Eisenhower Administration after the *Brown v. Board of Education* school-desegregation court decision in 1954. The problem was left for a successor administration to attempt to solve.

The Internet is, in many respects, much like a real city – truly a global village. It has a highly efficient postal system – much better than any one nation's – although we must remember that the on-line system does not provide a level of security even close to that of a first-class letter. E-mail has a level of confidentiality closer to that of a postcard.

In this virtual village are libraries, and bookstores, and art galleries, small shops and huge superstores. There are places to stop and chat, and places to find long-lost friends. There are also back alleys, sleazy streets, and dangerous neighborhoods where you venture at your own risk. Moreover, in contrast to exploring a real city, you can easily wander into these dark corners of the on-line world inadvertently, and from the supposed safety of your own home.[11]

Not surprisingly, the Internet – and especially the ease of the World Wide Web – ushered in a third era of privacy concern much like the concern in 1890 that motivated the landmark article on privacy by Louis Brandeis and Samuel Warren and much like the response to the National Data Center in the 1970s. In all three instances, the new consciousness was a direct response to new technological applications. This was indeed true in the late 1990s, but there was more at work here.

For years, computer miscues and abuse of personal information had occurred *within* corporations and government agencies. Many computer errors were patched up without the public ever knowing. For instance, it was common practice for organizations to cover up computer-related crimes, and often not to have them prosecuted at all, when they discovered that they had been victimized. Once companies began to display their wares on the World Wide Web, the snafus became instantly public. In fact, on the Web, it was usually members of the public who discovered the flaws.

Upon a closer look, Americans might see that life in this virtual city would require a reassessment of many aspects of American life that had left them exposed to commercial and governmental abuses of their personal information and of their personal autonomy. As more and more Americans came to know the Internet, they would be forced to reevaluate their relationships with large organizations – government agencies and businesses. They would be forced to question their own willingness to provide strangers with all sorts of personal details, their intense addiction to knowing personal details about others, their repeated acceptance of claims that new technology would inevitably be benign, and their willingness to sacrifice personal dignity as the cost for preserving security in their communities. If they looked, Americans would find much in their nation's history to illuminate that reevaluation.

Ben Franklin's Web Site: An Epilogue

Common-sense from the Eighteenth Century for the Twenty-first Century

Just two years after he was married and a year after creating America's first public library, Benjamin Franklin began publishing a handbook of both practical advice and philosophical homilies. That was in 1792 when the publisher and writer was 26 years old. He called it *Poor Richard's Almanack*. Its combination of useful suggestions and good humor made it a popular publication for the next 25 years.

The *Almanack* is the source for such lasting aphorisms like "God helps those who help themselves," "Never leave til tomorrow that which you can do today," "A word to the wise is enough," "Lost time is never found again," "Eat to live and not live to eat," "Early to bed, and early to rise, etc.," and of course "Three may keep a secret if two of them are dead." For Eighteenth-Century devotees, it was also a source of recipes and personal-hygiene tips and for determining times of sunrise and sunset, high and low tides and planting and harvesting. Franklin chose to publish the handbook under a pseudonym, the fictitious name of Richard Saunders.

If technology had kept up with him or if he had lived in our own times, Ben Franklin would certainly have disseminated his collection of advice and information on his own World Wide Web site. Franklin would have loved the World Wide Web – the fascination of the technology, the possibilities of reaching a diverse and vast number of people, the merger of graphics and text, the accommodation to short attention spans, the informality and irreverence of the prose, the chance to hear back from readers instantly, the opportunities for easily exerting influence on public officials and private businesses, and the egalitarian environment of it all. The capability to link to different Web sites allows for the kind of rambling intellectual treasure hunt that Ben Franklin seemed to value. The eclectic nature of his writings and his use of a pseudonym bring to mind the several Web sites on privacy and "cyberrights" that suddenly began to appear in the last three years of the Twentieth Century. Many of them have been produced by individuals who choose to keep their anonymity – or at least their pseudonymity – and who do not confine their Web sites to any one subject matter.

There would be one key difference if Ben Franklin operated his own Web site today. He would not give away his advice and information for free, like so many contemporary pamphleteers of the Web. In fact, Franklin wrote in *Poor Richard's Almanack* that he knew that he could not fool his readers if he claimed to be publishing the handbooks to enlighten the public. "Men are now adays too wise to be deceived by pretences." No, wrote Franklin, "the plain truth of the matter" is that his new wife threatened to burn all of his books and "rattle traps" if he did not begin to earn some real money for the family.

If we can judge from the value he placed on tranquillity and solitude, as expressed in his *Autobiography*, and the importance he placed on technological advancement and successful commerce and communications, Ben Franklin's Web site would offer advice on protecting one's own privacy tempered with pragmatism. As an entrepreneur, Franklin would first offer guidance to businesses that must guard the personal information they possess. Next, as a patriot, Franklin would offer advice to his fellow citizens, to protect their privacy. In the Age of the Internet, Ben Franklin's Web site would offer advice along the following lines:

Corporate Policies

An organization establishing privacy policies should incorporate the elements of the widely accepted Code of Fair Information Practice. This code appears in the chapter on Databanks.

An organization must make sure that other entities handling personal information in behalf of the first organization are bound by these same principles.

An organization must conduct periodic risk assessments, balancing the possibility or probability of unauthorized access or disclosure against the cost of security precautions and the expected effectiveness of the precautions.

Organizations must take special precautions in collecting and using personal information about children, both those 13 or younger and those 18 or younger.

An organization should openly disclose its policies and practices with regard to electronic surveillance of its employees' and customers' telephone calls, electronic mail, Internet usage, changing rooms, and rest rooms. It should articulate in advance the reasons for the surveillance and discontinue it once the rationale disappears.

An organization should designate an individual or office (whether full-time or part-time) to manage privacy issues. This individual or office should (a) act as an ombudsman for customers and employees, (b) assess the privacy impact of new undertakings, (c) assure that the organization complies with all laws and trade-association standards; and (d) inform the organization of the latest technology and policies that affect the privacy of customers or employees.

An organization should train employees periodically to respect confidentiality and to abide by company policies.

If it utilizes "opt-out" for customers to stay out of certain uses of their information, an organization should make exercising "opt-out" totally easy. A person ought to be able to check a box on a bill or click a box on a Web site.

Individuals' Privacy

Be discreet when filling out application forms, whether on-line or in paper form. Often, you can provide general instead of specific information and still complete the transaction (for example, responding "over 18" or "younger than 65" when asked for age). Try to determine what information on an application or warranty form is for marketing purposes and not necessary for completing the transaction. When you are asked to sign authorizations to disclose your personal information, date the form or add an expiration date and cross out language that makes the authorization too broad or general. Revoke the authorization in writing if you reconsider later.

Protect the confidentiality of your Social Security number. Just say no. Social Security numbers are really not necessary when applying for credit or insurance. There are legal limits when *government agencies* ask for Social Security numbers (explained in the chapter on Numbers). Any request for your number when the transaction has tax consequences – like getting a job or opening a bank account or buying a house – is legitimate. In other cases, ask for a random number you select or, if you must, try providing only the last four digits.

Attach conditions to sensitive information that you feel you have to provide. Ask that it not be further disclosed outside the organization or that it be destroyed after a certain period. Ask to inspect it in the future. This creates a binding contract with the organization. If it refuses to accept your conditions, that tells you about its information practices.

Never provide sensitive information over the telephone or Internet to someone you don't know – including your Social Security number, home address or phone number, bank-account or insurance-policy numbers, bank balance, mother's maiden name, or medical information. If you want, call back the company and keep a record of its phone number.

Phrase your demand so that it elicits a positive response, not a negative one. Don't say, "I refuse. . . ." Say, "Because I'm concerned about my privacy, I chose to keep that information to myself. . . ." Assume that most clerks, as individuals, will identify with your concerns, and you will discover that many of them do. Be persistent. Be prepared to try three or four times before the organization caves in.

Ask to inspect and correct files about yourself where federal law permits this – credit reports, consumer investigations, school records, federal-agency files, cable TV providers, and criminal records. A dozen states provide these rights for insurance files and 15 states have these rights for personal information stored by state agencies. Almost half the states and a federal policy require this for medical records

Ask the post office not to disclose your new address to commercial mailers when you file a change-of-address form. Better still, make your change of address *temporary* not permanent. A temporary forwarding instruction is good for one year, and the Postal Service does not forward temporary change-of-address information to commercial list users and direct marketers. Ben Franklin, custodian of the mails in the Colonial period, would like this suggestion.

Ask to inspect your own medical file and to add information to it if necessary. A federal regulation as well as laws in about 20 states give you this right, although there is no right by law to amend or add to your record.

Organize your telephone service for your own convenience.
Have your telephone number listed without an address in the directory. This will provide much of the same protection that you seek from an unlisted number – and for no charge – because marketers are not interested in collecting phone numbers without addresses. This will keep you out of the address and telephone directories on the World Wide Web. For a small monthly fee, phone companies will provide you a second phone number that will ring with a distinctive sound. You can make this your "public number" that you provide to businesses and government agencies. Reserve your original telephone number for friends and relatives, and then you will know when they are calling. In addition, ask the major mailers to delete you from their telephone and mailing lists.

Remember that cellular, mobile, and cordless phones are not secure. Neither is electronic mail; regard it as you would a postcard. Remember that a recipient of your e-mail can pass it on to the whole world, inadvertently or intentionally. You have to respond to e-mail carefully to avoid sending responses to persons you did not intend to receive it. Some states require e-mail advertising to be labeled in the subject line. Don't ever use telephones and computers at work for sensitive or embarrassing communications. Federal law permits employers to monitor phones, e-mail, and Internet use.

Add your cell and home telephone numbers to the Federal Trade Commission's do-not-call list. By federal law, commercial telemarketers must abide by that list. The same law prohibits recorded advertisements and fax advertisements into your home unless you consent. Call 800/382-1222 from the phone that you wish to register or go to www.donotcall.gov. Charities and polling organizations are still able to call, as are companies that you have done business with.

Learn all you can about new technologies that affect your privacy – automated telephone devices, the Internet, genetic tests, electronic mail, bar codes, automated highway toll collection, skin implants for identification, two-way cable television, airport-screening devices, and biometric Identification like hand scans and eye scans. Know how they work – what they can do and can't do.

Protect against theft of identity. This crime is the impersonation of you by a stranger to get identity documents or use your credit accounts. The main vehicle for it is the circulation of your Social

Security number or carelessness with it by organizations. Keep your SSN out of general circulation as much as you can. Keep it off your driver's license and your personal checks.

Think of Noah's Ark. To protect your privacy, think in twos. Rip in half any documents with vital personal information on them, including Social Security numbers, bank account information, or credit-card numbers. Deposit them in separate side-by-side trash containers. Empty each trash can at alternating times, so that these sensitive documents can not be reconstructed after you dispose of them. Or use a paper shredder. Use two phone numbers at home. Use a personal mailing address and a "public" mailing address, which can be a post office box, a commercial mail-receiving firm, an office address, or a landlord's address. This second address will not disclose your physical whereabouts, or that of your children. Have two Internet service providers and electronic mail providers, one for sensitive uses and the other for "public" uses. Have two credit cards, one for customary use and one for on-line use. If something goes wrong on-line, you can promptly cancel that credit card with no inconvenience. Use two doctors to disguise certain sensitive treatments, if necessary.

Zealously protect the identities and addresses of your children. Avoid having them enumerated until they reach an age when they are seeking employment. This will keep them out of dangerous databanks and locator services. Take advantage of tax credits and deductions without providing SSNs for your children, if you can; otherwise be willing to do without the tax benefits. Keep them off mailing lists by using an adult's name on magazine lists and direct-mail purchases. Don't provide their names on any applications that parents submit. Do not permit them to provide family information – or information about their physical whereabouts – on the Internet.

Resist surveillance in the community. Make it clear to law enforcement and businesses what you think of the presence of camera surveillance everywhere. Demand that they prove that it is effective. Point out its cumulative effect on the culture and the community.

Take time to devise in your mind a strategy for dealing with the press if you should be suddenly thrust into a newsworthy situation. Select in your mind a trusted friend you would call upon, to advise you, to be a liaison between you and news reporters, and to assure that you disclose to the public exactly what you want to and keep private exactly what you want to.

Shop ahead. When you seek insurance, a mortgage, retail credit, a bank account, or other important transaction, be prepared to dicker. Provide the least amount of personal information possible to get the transaction. Be prepared to be asked for more. Provide a little more, if you wish, and be prepared to be asked again to provide more information. Shop around for a transaction you really don't need, simply to practice your technique of negotiating for the least amount of privacy sacrifice. Most important, be fully prepared to do without the transaction or to shop elsewhere if you believe that you are being asked for too much personal information. If you are dealing with a dominant business or a monopoly, be prepared to complain to the state agency that regulates the business. It may have guidelines that help you or it may be willing to intervene on your behalf.

Shop Around. The new century has brought a few new products and services that actually enhance your privacy – e-mail forwarding services that protect your anonymity, encryption software, innovative telephone-answering machines, mail receivers. Seek them out.

It is going to cost you. In the information age, privacy comes with a cost. You can expect to pay slightly more for some of the duplicative services you need, and you may pay a premium for dealing with an organization that respects your personal information. You may have to do without some of the enticing discounts that require you to agree to be bombarded by commercial messages in the future. The rewards for paying these additional costs are immense. They bring an increased sense of control and dignity to your life. In addition, you will find that you can accomplish a whole lot more or have more leisure time after you take precautions to ration the interruptions and intrusions into your life. One of the richest men in America, Paul Mellon, once said, "The idea of power never appealed to me. What has appealed to me is privacy. To me, privacy is the most valuable asset that money can buy."

Choose your battles. Not every collection of personal information or every intrusion is worth expending your energy. Decide which information is most sensitive to you and which moments in your life are most important to protect. However, you should err on the side of protectiveness, because you cannot anticipate which information about you will become crucial in the future. Remember that nearly all of the personal information that businesses and government agencies collect concerns *how we spend our money*. Work hard to limit it to that. "In things of moment, on thy self depend," Ben Franklin would say on his Web site.

For most of us, organizations have not yet been able to intrude into the really important aspects of our lives – our spirituality, our beliefs, our sexuality, our home life, our creativity, our fantasies, our sorrows, and our joys. Using laws where they exist and common sense and determination where they do not, we must preserve our right to privacy for ourselves, our neighbors, and those still to come.

Benjamin Franklin

Notes

To the Reader

[1] The term "the silences of traditional history" is from D. Michael Quinn.

Watchfulness, pages 8-27

[1] Williston Walker, *The Creeds and Platforms of Congregationalism* (Boston: The Pilgrim Press, 1960).

[2] David H. Flaherty, *Privacy in Colonial New England* (Charlottesville: University Press of Virginia, 1972), p. 151.

[3] James H. Cassedy, *Demography in Early America, 1600-1800* (Cambridge: Harvard University Press, 1969), p. 56.

[4] Mederic Louis Elie Moreau de Saint-Mery, *Voyage to the United States of America*, excerpts reprinted by Oscar Handlin, *This Was America* (New York: Harper & Row, 1949), p. 100.

[5] Fischer, p. 72.

[6] Flaherty, p. 189.

[7] Harriet Beecher Stowe, *Oldtown Folks*, quoted by David Hackett Fischer, *Albion's Seed: Four British Folkways in America* (New York: Oxford University Press, 1989), p. 69.

[8] Flaherty, p. 193.

[9] Cassedy, p.5.

[10] Cassedy p. 29.

[11] Cassedy p. 236.

[12] Cassedy p. 63.

[13] Flaherty, p. 196-7.

[14] Flaherty, p. 151.

[15] Flaherty, p.169.

[16] Flaherty, p. 218.

[17] Flaherty, p. 237.

[18] David M. O'Brien, *Privacy, Law, and Public Policy* (New York: Praeger, 1979), p. 37.

[19] Flaherty, p. 10.

[20] Edward Corbyn Obert Beatty, *William Penn as Social Philosopher* (New York: Columbia University Press, 1939), first page, chapter VII.

[21] Richard D. Brown, *Knowledge is Power, The Diffusion of Information in Early America, 1700-1865* (New York: Oxford University Press, 1989), p. 47.

[22] Flaherty, p.28.

[23] Flaherty, p.26.

[24] Fischer, p. 68.

[25] Christopher Bram.

[26] Philippe Aries and Georges Duby, editors, *A History of Private Life: Passions of the Renaissance*, Vol. III (Cambridge, Massachusetts, Harvard University Press, 1989).

[27] See John Demos, editor, *Remarkable Providences 1600-1760* (New York: George Braziller, 1972), p. 48.

[28] Flaherty, p. 49.

[29] Fischer, p. 71.

[30] Flaherty, p. 77, and Fischer, p. 278.

[31] Flaherty, p. 77.

[32] Janna Malamud Smith, *Private Matters* (Reading, Massachusetts: Addison-Wesley Publishing Company, Inc., 1997), p. 60.

[33] Aries and Duby, p. 507.

[34] Quoted by Richard C. Turkington, George C. Trubow, and Anita L. Allen in *Privacy Cases and Materials* (Houston: The John Marshall Publishing Company, 1992), p.5.

[35] Flaherty, p. 127.

[36] "What Shelter From Arbitrary Power? A Reply to [James Wilson's Speech in 1787] : 'A Democratic Federalist,'" *Pennsylvania Herald*, Philadelphia, October 17, 1787, in *The Debate on the Constitution, Federalist and Antifederalist Speeches* (New York: The Library of America, 1993), p. 74

[37] *Votes and Proceedings of the Freeholders and other Inhabitants of the Town of Boston*, p. 16-17, quoted by Nelson B. Lasson in *The History and Development of the Fourth Amendment to the U.S. Constitution* (Baltimore: Johns Hopkins University, 1937).

[38] Brown, p. 177.

[39] Flaherty, p. 118.

[40] For more on the Twentieth-Century debate on encryption, see the chapter on Cyberspace.

[41] William Bradford, *Of Plimouth Plantation*, p. 149-153, quoted by Thomas H. O'Connor, "The Right to Privacy in Historical Perspective," 53 *Mass. Law Quarterly* 101 (June 1968).

[42] Brown, p. 147.

Serenity, pages 28-48

[1] The Adams quotations are from David H. Flaherty, *Privacy in Colonial New England* (Charlottesville: University Press of Virginia, 1972), p. 4-5.

[2] *Benjamin Franklin Autobiography* (New York, The Modern Library, 1950), p. 93-94).

[3] James T. Flexner, *Washington, The Indispensable Man* (Boston: Little, Brown and Company, 1974), p. 180.

[4] Flexner, p 229.

[5] Philippe Aries and Georges Duby, editors, *A History of Private Life: Passions of the Renaissance*, Vol. III (Cambridge, Massachusetts, Harvard University Press, 1989), p. 134.

[6] David Hackett Fischer, *Albion's Seed: Four British Folkways in America* (New York: Oxford University Press, 1989), p. 581.

[7] The quotations from Franklin and Hamilton are from Flaherty, p. 108-9; the quotation about being too much an American is from Henry Steele Commager, Introduction to *Benjamin Franklin Autobiography*; and the quotation from the Penn family is from David Freeman Hawke, *Franklin* (New York: Harper & Row, 1976), p. 191.

[8] This occurrence sheds light on the necessity of using middle names, mentioned in reference to John Quincy Adams in the chapter on Mistrust.

[9] Henry Adams, *The United States in 1800* (Ithaca, Great Seal Books, 1958), p. 103.

[10] Isaac Weld, Jr., *Travels Through the States of North America* (London: 1799), p. 123-4, quoted by David J. Seipp in his first version of "The Right to Privacy in American History" (Cambridge: Harvard University Program on Information Resources Policy, 1976), p. 112. Seipp has distributed three versions of his monograph, of which the third, Working Paper W-77-5 (Cambridge: Harvard University Program on Information Resources Policy, 1977), is most commonly available. In the footnotes here, the references are to Seipp I, Seipp II, or Seipp III (the final version).

[11] Henry Adams p. 32.

[12] James H. Cassedy, *Demography in Early America, 1600-1800* (Cambridge: Harvard University Press, 1969), p. 209.

[13] Cassedy, p. 70. The quotation from Governor Hunter is from the same source. For the impact of this Biblical passage on the concerns of fundamentalist Christians about Social Security numbers, see the chapter on Numbers.

[14] Quoted in Seipp II, p. 29.

[15] Seipp II, p. 29.

[16] Robert C. Davis, "Confidentiality and the Census, 1790-1929," in *Records, Computers and the Rights of Citizens, Report of the Secretary's Advisory Committee on Automated Personal Data Systems, U.S. Department of Health, Education and Welfare* (Washington: U.S. Government Printing Office, 1973). Also published by The MIT Press, Cambridge, Massachusetts, 1973.

[17] Bureau of the Census, 1990 and Arthur R. Miller, *The Assault on Privacy* (Ann Arbor, Michigan: The University of Michigan Press, 1971), p. 131.

[18] Davis, in HEW report, p. 182.

[19] Seipp I, p. 62.

[20] In a 1995 opinion upholding anonymous pamphleteering free of government regulation, the U.S. Supreme Court reiterated that, as a Constitutional right, "The freedom to publish extends beyond the literary realm." *McIntyre v. Ohio Elections Commission*, 514 U.S. 334 (1995).

[21] Alan F. Westin: *Privacy and Freedom* (New York: Atheneum, 1967), p. 331. See also "The Constitutional Right to Anonymity: Free Speech, Disclosure and the Devil," 70 *Yale Law Journal* 1084 (1961).

[22] *The Debate on the Constitution, Federalist and Antifederalist Papers*, Part

Two (New York, Literary Classics of the United States, Inc., 1993), p. 1139 and following.

[23] Richard D. Brown, *Knowledge is Power, The Diffusion of Information in Early America, 1700-1865* (New York: Oxford University Press, 1989), p. 180.

[24] Christy Millard Nadalin, "The Last Years of the Rhode Island Slave Trade" in 54 *Rhode Island History* 2, 1996 (Providence: The Rhode Island Historical Society). It was said that Walt Whitman did much the same thing in the Nineteenth Century, writing rave reviews of his own work under pseudonyms.

[25] Brown p. 177.

[26] From *The Papers of James Madison*, quoted in U.S. Congress, Office of Technology Assessment (no longer existing), *Defending Secrets, Sharing Data: New Locks and Keys for Electronic Information* (Washington: U.S. Government Printing Office: 1987), p. 14.

[27] John Locke, *A Letter on Toleration*, quoted by Edward Keenness, *Liberty, Property, and Privacy: toward a Jurisprudence of Substantive Due Process*, (University Park, Pennsylvania: The University of Pennsylvania Press, 1996), p. 9. The concepts of privacy and "personhood" related to Locke's formulation are described in the chapter on The Constitution.

[28] Albert H. Cantril and Susan Davis Cantril, *Live and Let Live: American Public Opinion About Privacy at Home and at Work* (New York: American Civil Liberties Union, April 1994).

[29] David A.J. Richard's, *Toleration and the Constitution* (New York, Oxford University Press, 1986), p. 41, note 81. The quotations from Madison are from the same source, p. 113 and 115.

[30] William J. Brennan, Jr., "The Constitution of the United States: Contemporary Ratification," a speech October 12, 1985, at Georgetown University Law Center, Washington, D.C., reprinted in *Georgetown Law*, Fall 1985, p.4.

[31] *Kelley v. Johnston*, 425 US 238 (1976) (Marshall dissenting).

[32] John Deering, *Arkansas Democrat-Gazette*, October 1998.

[33] Westin, p. 330.

[34] John Shattuck, "Privacy and the Constitution," remarks to the Georgia Commission on the Bicentennial of the U.S. Constitution, October 17, 1987, reprinted in unpublished manuscript "Privacy: Cases, Materials and Questions" by Christopher H. Pyle and John Shattuck.

Mistrust, page 49-72

[1] David J. Seipp, "The Right to Privacy in American History," (Cambridge: Harvard University Program on Information Resources Policy, 1976), Seipp I, p. 10. See note 10 in the previous chapter.

[2] Seipp I, Chapter 1 introduction.

[3] Seipp I, p. 13, note 55.

[4] G. Robert Blakey, concurrence in *Electronic Surveillance, Report of the National Commission for the Review of Federal and State Laws Relating to Wire-*

tapping and Electronic Surveillance (Washington: U.S. Government Printing Office, 1976), p. 187.

[5] Seipp I, p. 18.

[6] *Denis v. Leclerc*, 1 Martin (O.S.) 297 (La. 1811).

[7] The law remains in effect. 42 U.S. Code 1702.

[8] Joseph Story, *Commentaries on Equity Jurisprudence, Second Edition* (Boston: 1830), p. 221, quoted in Seipp III, p. 15.

[9] Seipp I, p. 15.

[10] *Congressional Record*, 1876-77 (44th Congress, 2nd Session, part I, December 21, 1876), p.350, quoted by Seipp I, p. 17.

[11] Seipp I, p. 18.

[12] Alan F. Westin: *Privacy and Freedom* (New York: Atheneum, 1967), p. 336.

[13] Seipp I, p, 19.

[14] Seipp I, p. 22.

[15] Seipp I, p. 15-16.

[16] Seipp I, p. 20.

[17] *The New York Times*, March 1, 1986.

[18] Seipp I, p. 20.

[19] Seipp I, p. 11.

[20] Seipp III, p 13.

[21] Davis, p. 185. Information in the next paragraph comes from the same source.

[22] James C. Scott, *Seeing like a State: How Certain Schemes to Improve the Human Condition Have Failed* (New Haven: Yale University Press, 1998).

[23] Development of Social Security numbers is described in the chapter on Numbers.

[24] Davis, p. 187.

[25] Seipp I, p. 30.

[26] Miller, p. 131.

[27] Davis, p. 190.

[28] Seipp I, p. 31, Davis, p. 191.

[29] Erik Larson, *The Naked Consumer* (New York, Henry Holt and Company, Inc., 1992), p. 33.

[30] Larson, p. 53. See also David Burnham, *The Rise of the Computer State* (New York, Random House, Inc., 1983), p. 23-26.

[31] Seipp I, p. 75.

[32] *The New York Times*, July 19, 1875, p. 4, col. 4. Boston *Globe*, May 25, 1890, p. 1.

[33] Seipp III, p. 46.

[34] Seipp I, p. 77.

[35] Larson, p. 34.

[36] Seipp III, p. 52.

[37] See Seipp I, p. 46.

[38] Seipp I, p. 29.

[39] *The New York Times*, December 31, 1866, p. 4.

[40] *Henisler v. Freedman*, 2 Pars. Equity and Law 274 (Pa., 1851). Much of this history of the telegraph company comes from David Seipp's research.

[41] See references earlier in this chapter, at note 11.

[42] Seipp III, p. 33.

[43] Seipp I, p. 33.

[44] *Ex parte Brown*, 72 Mo. 83 (1880).

[45] David Samuels, "The Confidence Man," in *The New Yorker*, April 26 & May 3, 1999, p. 150. The other descriptions of Gould come from Seipp's research. David H. Flaherty suggested the comparison to Bill Gates.

[46] Seipp III, p. 66. In Greek mythology Dionysius is identified with raucus revelry.

[47] Seipp I, p. 146.

Space, pages 73-101

[1] Quoted by Oscar Handlin, *This Was America* (New York: Harper & Row, 1949), p. 322.

[2] George Orwell, "Riding Down From Bangor," in the socialist weekly publication in London in the 1940s, *Tribune*, November 22,1946, quoted by T. R. Fyvel, *George Orwell: A Personal Memoir* (New York: Macmillan, 1982), p. 144. Also in Sonia Orwell and Ian Angus, ed., *Collected Essays, Journalism and Letters of George Orwell* (London: Secker & Warburg, 1968).

[3] Paul Leicester Ford, *The Writings of Thomas Jefferson* (New York: G.P. Putnam's Sons, 1894), p. 180, quoted by James H. Cassedy, *Demography in Early America, 1600-1800* (Cambridge: Harvard University Press, 1969), p. 229.

[4] Handlin, p. 94.

[5] Quoted by David S. Reynolds, *Walt Whitman's America* (New York: Random House, 1995), p. 107.

[6] Quoted by Richard Reeves, *American Journey: Traveling With DeTocqueville in Search of Democracy in America* (New York: Simon & Schuster, 1982), p. 98.

[7] Thomas H. O'Connor, "The Right to Privacy in Historical Perspective," 53 *Mass. Law Quarterly* 101 (June 1968), p. 103.

[8] David J. Seipp in his second version of "The Right to Privacy in American History" (Cambridge: Harvard University Program on Information Resources Policy, 1976), p. 4. (See note 10 in the chapter on Serenity.)

[9] Seipp II, p. 6.

[10] Quoted by Handlin, p. 118.

[11] W.J. Cash, *The Mind of the South* (New York: Alfred A. Knopf, Inc., 1941), p. 57.

[12] Franny Trollope, *Domestic Manners of the Americans* (New York: Penquin Books, 1832), p. 43.

[13] Quoted in *Life in Utah: Centennial Selections from BYU Studies* (Provo, Utah: Brigham Young University BYU Studies, 1996), p. 107.

[14] Robert F. Copple, "Privacy and the Frontier Thesis: An American Intersection of Self and Society," 34 *American Journal of Jurisprudence* 94 (1989). Compare Turner's observation with that of an editor of *Scribner's* magazine in 1890 that the quest for privacy is compatible with both individualism and democracy, quoted in the chapter on Brandeis.

[15] David Hackett Fischer, *Albion's Seed: Four British Folkways in America* (New York: Oxford University Press, 1989), p. 655 and p. 660.

[16] D. Michael Quinn, *Same-Sex Dynamics among Nineteenth-Century Americans* (Urbana: University of Illinois Press, 1996), p. 88.

[17] Henry Adams, p. 30.

[18] Leslie Howard Owens, *This Species of Property: Slave Life and the Culture of the Old South* (New York: Oxford University Press, 1976), p. 24.

[19] Frederick Law Olmsted, *The Cotton Kingdom: A Traveller's Observation on Cotton and Slavery in the American Slave States*, edited by Arthur M. Schlesinger, Sr. (New York: Alfred A. Knopf, 1953), p. 31 et seq., quoted by John Michael Vlach, *Back of the Big House* (Chapel Hill: The University of North Carolina Press, 1993), p. 153.

[20] Harriet A. Jacobs, *Incidents in the Life of a Slave Girl* (1861), edited by Jean Fagan Yellin (Cambridge, Massachusetts, Harvard University Press, 1987), p. 10.

[21] Quoted by C. Vann Woodward, *Mary Chesnut's Civil War* (New Haven, Yale University Press, 1981), p. 28 and cited by Fischer, p. 304.

[22] Anita L. Allen, "Surrogacy, Slavery, and the Ownership of Life," 13 *Harvard Journal of Law & Public Policy* at 141.

[23] Owens.

[24] "An Interview with Ralph Ellison," *Harper's*, May 1967, p. 84, quoted by Vlach, p. 168.

[25] Quoted by Robert Ellis Smith, *Privacy: How to Protect What's Left of It* (New York: Doubleday, 1979), p. 327.

[26] Vlach, p. 16.

[27] John R. Stilgoe, *Borderland: Origins of the American Suburb, 1820-1939* (New Haven: Yale University Press, 1989), p. 204.

[28] Stilgoe, p. 31.

[29] Stilgoe, p. 189.

[30] Charlotte Perkins Gilman, *Women and Economics: A Study of the Economic Relation Between Men and Women as a Factor in Social Evolution* (1898). Reprint (New York: Harper & Row, 1966), quoted by Allen.

[31] Barbara Welter, "The Cult of True Womanhood," 18 *American Quarterly* 1511 (1956).

[32] Quinn, p. 92.

[33] Reynolds, p 563.

[34] Quoted by Robert V. Remini, *Daniel Webster: The Man and His Times* (New York: W.W. Norton & Co. 1997), p. 308. Hammond's beliefs paralleled those of Henry Ward Beecher four decades later, as recounted in the chapter on Sex.

Hammond's assessment of Webster seemed accurate, as Webster is described in the previous chapter on Curiosity.

[35] Henry David Thoreau, *Walden* (New York: Rinehart Co., Inc., 1959), p. 112, quoted by Robert Ellis Smith, *Workrights* (New York: E.P. Dutton, Inc., 1983), p. 13.

[36] Quoted by Smith, *Workrights*, p. 11-12.

[37] "Criticizing Public Men," *The New York Times*, January 15, 1874, p. 4.

[38] Allan Nevins, *Ford: The Times, the Man, The Company* (New York: Scribner's, 1954), p. 554.

[39] Andrew Sullivan in *The New York Times Magazine*, February 28, 1999.

[40] Seipp III, p. 99.

[41] Thoreau, p. 106 and following. The final paragraph quoted here, which the author wishes to emphasize, actually appears ahead of the other text in the original.

Curiosity, pages 102-120

[1] Charles William Janson, *The Stranger in America, 1793-1806* (London: J. Cundee, 1807). Reprint (New York: Press of the Pioneers, 1935), p. 20, quoted by David J. Seipp, *The Right to Privacy in American History* (Cambridge: Harvard University Center for Information Policy Research, 1981). See note 10 in the chapter on Serenity. Seipp II, p. 7 and Seipp I, p. 112.

[2] Henry Adams, *The United States in 1800* (New York, 1899). Reprint (Ithaca, N.Y.: Great Seal Books, 1958), p. 39-40.

[3] Quoted by Oscar Handlin, ed., *This Was America* (New York: Harper & Row, 1949), p. 118.

[4] Paul Blouet and Jack Allyn, *Jonathan and His Continent: Rambles Through American Society* (New York: 1889), p. 226-227, quoted by Seipp I, p. 114.

[5] Attributed to cultural anthropologist Edward Hall, who wrote in the 1950s and 1960s, by Alan F. Westin, *Privacy and Freedom* (New York: Atheneum, 1967), p. 29.

[6] Richard D. Brown, *Knowledge is Power, The Diffusion of Information in Early America, 1700-1865* (New York: Oxford University Press, 1989), p. 45.

[7] Seipp I, p. 8.

[8] Catherine Drinker Bowen, *Miracle at Philadelphia* (Boston: Little, Brown and Company, 1986), p. 157.

[9] Alexis de Tocqueville, *Democracy in America*, translated by Henry Reeve. Reprint (New York: 1945), vol. 2., p. 179.

[10] Brown, p. 47.

[11] Frank Luther Mott, *American Journalism* (New York: The MacMillan Co., 1962), p. 223.

[12] Marc Osgoode Smith in "'God Protect *The New Yorker* from the English': Sensationalism and the Anglicizing of the American Media," monograph (Wooster, Ohio: College of Wooster Department of History, 1993), p. 42.

[13] Except possibly for *La Presse* in Paris, which claimed more. Mott, p. 225

[14] David S. Reynolds, *Walt Whitman's America* (New York, Random House, 1995), p 81.

[15] Charles Frederick Wingate, ed., *Views and Interviews on Journalism* (New York: F.B. Patterson, 1875), p.92.

[16] William Grosvenor Bleyer, *Main Currents in the History of Journalism* (Boston: Houghton Mifflin Company, 1927), p. 181

[17] Patricia Cline Cohen, *The Murder of Helen Jewett: The Life and Death of a Prostitute in Nineteenth-Century New York* (New York: Alfred A. Knopf, 1998), p. 291-320.

[18] These accounts of press coverage of Daniel Webster come from Robert V. Remini, *Daniel Webster, The Man and His Time* (New York: W.W. Norton & Co., 1997), p. 308-309, 490, 568-569.

[19] Marc Smith, p. 65.

[20] Arthur M. Schlesinger, Sr., *The Rise of the City* (New York: Macmillan, 1933), p. 189.

[21] Simon Michael Bessie, *Jazz Journalism: The Story of the Tabloid Newspapers* (New York, E.P. Dutton & Co., 1938), p. 55.

[22] Hearst's riches built the ornate castle at San Simeon, California, where the publisher entertained international visitors, including, in 1933, his "personal friend," the Irish playwright George Bernard Shaw. After his visit, Shaw arrived by boat in New York City. He was forced to slip out of his stateroom and hide out in Manhattan to avoid hordes of news reporters. In a major speech broadcast nationally by radio from the Metropolitan Opera House, the 77-year-old curmudgeon told the audience, "An American has no sense of privacy. He does not know what it means. There is no such thing in the country." He entitled his speech "The Political Madhouse in America and Nearer Home." What is surprising is that Shaw began his long-anticipated trip to America by spending four days at San Simeon, which, more than any other structure in America, was financed by gossip.

[23] Charles Dudley Warner, "Newspapers and the Public," *Forum*, April 1890.

[24] According to Seipp I, p. 139. See also Seipp, "The Right to Privacy in Nineteenth Century America," 94 *Harvard Law Review* 1892 (1981).

[25] M.J. Savage, "A Profane View of the Sanctum," *North American Review*, 141 (August 1885).

[26] Allan Nevins, *Grover Cleveland: A Study in Courage* (New York: Dodd, Mead & Company, 1932), p 305.

[27] Quoted by Seipp I, p. 132.

[28] Seipp I, p. 150.

[29] Herbert Spencer Hadley, "Can the Publication of a Libel Be Enjoined?," 4 *Northwestern Law Review* 145 (January 1896). (The speech was given in 1895.)

[30] Schlesinger, p. 193.

[31] *Saturday Evening Gazette*, March 22, 1890, p. 3, and June 7, 1890. The Boston *Globe* in its June 8 edition published a similar 23-word mention of the reception.

[32] James H. Barron, "Warren and Brandeis, The Right to Privacy, 4 *Har. L. Rev.* 193 (1890): Demystifying a Landmark Citation," 8 *Suffolk University Law Review* 875 (1979), p. 898.

[33] Barron, p. 900.

[34] Barron, p. 901.

[35] *Saturday Evening Gazette*, January 25, 1890.

Brandeis, pages 121-152

[1] "Warren and Brandeis, The Right to Privacy, 4 Har. L. Rev. 193 (1890): Demystifying a Landmark Citation" by James H. Barron, 8 *Suffolk University Law Review* 875 (1979), p. 906.

[2] Samuel D. Warren and Louis D. Brandeis, "The Right to Privacy," 4 *Harvard Law Review* 193 (1890), December 15, 1890.

[3] Arthur M. Schlesinger, Sr., *The Rise of the City* (New York: Macmillian, 1933), p. 197.

[4] David J. Seipp in his first version of "The Right to Privacy in American History" (Cambridge: Harvard University Program on Information Resources Policy, 1976), p. 165.

[5] *The New York Times*, June 15, 18, and 21, 1890, cited in Brandeis-Warren article, p. 195. See also Dorothy Glancy, "Privacy and the Other Miss M," 10 *Northern Illinois Law Review* 401 (1990).

[6] Thomas McIntyre Cooley, *A Treatise on the Law of Torts, 2d edition* (Chicago, Callaghan & Co., 1888), p. 29.

[7] Cooley, *A Treatise on the Constitutional Limitations* (Boston: Little, Brown & Co., 1868), p. 306.

[8] E.L. Godkin, "The Rights of the Citizen, IV – To His Own Reputation," 8 *Scribner's*, p. 65.

[9] *Scribner's*, 1889.

[10] James Fitzjames Stephens, *Liberty, Equality and Fraternity* (London: Smith, Elder & Co., 1873), quoted by Richard C. Turkington, George B. Trubow, and Anita L. Allen in *Privacy: Cases and Materials* (Houston: The John Marshall Publishing Company, 1992), p. 32.

[11] *De May v. Roberts*, 46 Mich. 160, 9 N.W. 146 (1881).

[12] *Union Pacific Railway v. Botsford*, 141 U.S. 250 (1891). Dissenting – and thus finding no right to privacy in this case – was Associate Justice Henry B. Brown, who later complained about press invasions of privacy, in the 1890 article cited in note 9 of this chapter.

[13] Letter from Brandeis to Warren (April 8, 1905), reprinted in *Letters of Louis D. Brandeis (1870-1907): Urban Reformer 302-02* (Melvin I. Urofsky and David W. Levy, eds., Albany: State University of New York Press, 1971), quoted by Barron p. 888.

[14] Barron, p. 913. For Brandeis' ambivalence, see also A. T. Mason, *Brandeis: A Free Man's Life* (New York: Viking Press, 1946), p. 70, and Lewis J. Paper, *Brandeis* (Englewood Cliffs, N.J.: Prentice-Hall, Inc., 1983), p. 36.

[15] Paper, p. 36.

[16] Charlotte Perkins Gilman, *Women and Economics: A Study of the Economic Relation Between Men and Women as a Factor in Social Evolution* (1898). Reprint (New York: Harper & Row, 1966).

[17] William L. Prosser, "Privacy," 48 *California Law Review* 383 (1960).

[18] Barron, p. 893.

[19] Godkin, "The Right to Privacy," *The Nation* (December 25, 1890), p. 496.

[20] *Schuyer v. Curtis*, 147 N.Y. 434, 42 N.E. 22 (1895).

[21] Alan F. Westin: *Privacy and Freedom* (New York: Atheneum, 1967), p. 348.

[22] Robert F. Copple, "Privacy and the Frontier Thesis: An American Intersection of Self and Society," 34 *American Journal of Jurisprudence* 94 (1989), p. 97.

[23] "Law and Privacy," *Scribner's* (February 1891), p. 261. The unnamed editor here seems to be paralleling the egalitarian sentiments of Frederick Jackson Turner mentioned in the chapter on Space.

[24] Alexis de Tocqueville, *Democracy in America*, translated by Henry Reeve (1835). Reprint (New York: A.A. Knopf, 1945), vol. II, p. 104.

[25] Copple, p. 105.

[26] *Roberson v. Rochester Folding Box Co.*, 171 N.Y. 538, 64 N.E. 442 (1902).

[27] "An Actionable Right of Privacy?," 12 *Yale Law Journal* 34-38 (1902-3), quoted by Hillel Schwartz, *The Culture of the Copy* (New York: Zone Books, 1996), p. 327.

[28] Denis O'Brien, "The Right to Privacy," 2 *Columbia Law Review* 486 (1902). This is the same Justice O'Brien who dissented in the 1895 *Schuyler* case mentioned earlier; in that case he took the pro-privacy position.

[29] Quoted in *Publishers Weekly*, July 18, 1980, also quoted by Robert Ellis Smith, *The Law of Privacy Explained* (Providence, R.I.: Privacy Journal, 1993), p. 4.

[30] Schwartz, p. 327.

[31] "How Privacy Got Its Gender," 10 *Northwestern Illinois University Law Review* 441 (1990).

[32] *The New York Times*, August 23, 1902.

[33] Robert J. Shores, in 1914 in *Forum*, quoted by John R. Stilgoe, *Borderland: Origins of the American Suburb, 1820-1939* (New Haven: Yale University Press, 1989), p. 198.

[34] *Pavesich v. New England Life Insurance Co.*, 122 Ga. 190, 50 S.E. 68 (1905).

[35] Barron, p. 910.

[36] Mason, p. 61, and Paper, p. 34.

[37] Philippa Strum, *Louis D. Brandeis, Justice for the People* (Cambridge: Harvard University Press, 1984), p. 326.

[38] Frank J. Donner, *The Age of Surveillance* (New York: Random House, 1981), p. 35-37.

[39] Strum, p. 326.

[40] Paper, p. 310.

[41] *Whitney v. California*, 274 U.S. 375 (1927).

[42] Paper, p. 311.

[43] Walter F. Murphy, *Wiretapping on Trial: A Case Study of the Judicial Process* (New York: Random House, 1965), p. 124.
[44] *Olmstead v. U.S.*, 277 U.S. 438 (1928).

Wiretaps, pages 153-192

[1] Samuel Dash, Richard E. Schwartz, and Robert E. Knowlton, *The Eavesdroppers* (New Brunswick, N.J.: Rutgers University Press, 1959), p. 30.
[2] This chronology appeared in Dash's book and some of it reappeared in *Berger v. N.Y.*, 388 U.S. at 46 (1966).
[3] George P. Oslin, *Prelude to Modern Communications* (Macon, Ga.: Mercer University Press, 1992), p. 251.
[4] *Los Angeles Times*, June 18, 1976.
[5] *Scientific American*, 106 (March 30, 1912), p. 284.
[6] "Police Espionage in a Democracy," *Outlook*, May 31, 1916, p. 235. On the same page, *The Outlook* magazine announced, "The Senate Judiciary Committee on Wednesday of last week reported, by a strict party vote of 10 to 8, a recommendation that the nomination of Mr. Louis D. Brandeis as a Justice of the United States Supreme Court be confirmed.
[7] *Berger* at 46.
[8] *Wiretapping in Law Enforcement, Hearings before the House Committee on Expenditures*, 71st Cong., 3d Sess., 1931, p. 26.
[9] This important case is discussed in the previous chapter.
[10] Brief cited in *Olmstead v. U.S.*, 277 U.S. at 452 (1928).
[11] *Nardone v. U.S.*, 302 U.S. 379 (1937). *Nardone v. U.S.*, 308 U.S. 338 (1939).
[12] *Weiss v. U.S.*, 308 U.S. 321 (1939). For details, see James G. Carr, *The Law of Electronic Surveillance* (New York: Clark Boardman Company, 1997), National Lawyers Guild, *Raising and Litigating Electronic Surveillance Claims* (San Francisco: Lake Law Books, 1977), and Alan F. Westin, "The Wiretapping Problem: An Analysis and a Legislative Approach," 52 *Columbia Law Review* 165 (February 1952).
[13] National Lawyers Guild, p. 1-8, and Walter F. Murphy, *Wiretapping on Trial: A Case Study of the Judicial Process* (New York: Random House, 1965).
[14] Athan Theoharis, *Spying on Americans* (Philadelphia: Temple University Press, 1978), p. 67.
[15] *Goldman v. U.S.*, 316 U.S. 129 (1942).
[16] *Silverman v. U.S.*, 365 U.S. 505 (1961), the "spike mike" case, and *Clinton v. Virginia*, 377 U.S. 158 (1964), the "thumbtack" case.
[17] Theoharis, p. 106 and 125.
[18] Theoharis, p. 102.
[19] *Irvine v. California*, 347 U.S. 128 (1954).
[20] Theoharis, p. 108.
[21] National Lawyers Guild, p. 1-8.
[22] Patricia Holt, *The Bug in the Martini Olive*, (Boston: Little, Brown and Company, 1991).

[23] *The New York Times*, December 12, 1997, p. C20.

[24] From *Surveillance and Espionage in a Free Society*, a report by the planning group on intelligence and security to the Policy Council of the Democratic National Committee. Edited by Richard H. Blum (New York: Praeger Publishers, 1972), p. 100.

[25] *U.S. v. Lopez*, 373 U.S. 427 (1963).

[26] *Berger v. New York*, 388 U.S. 41 (1967).

[27] *Katz v. U.S.*, 389 U.S. 347 (1967).

[28] Edith J. Lapidus, *Eavesdropping on Trial* (Rochelle Park, N.J.: Hayden Book Co., 1973).

[29] Arthur R. Miller, *The Assault on Privacy* (Ann Arbor, Michigan: The University of Michigan Press, 1971), p. 101.

[30] Department of Justice data compiled by David Burnham, Trac Inc., Washington, D.C.

[31] *Hearings Before the Subcommittee on Administrative Practice and Procedure, Committee on the Judiciary*, U.S. Senate, 90th Cong., 1st Sess. ("Senator Long hearings"), March, April, May 1967, p. 262.

[32] Senator Long hearings, p. 15

[33] Lapidus, p. 11.

[34] *Electronic Surveillance, Report of the National Commission for the Review of Federal and State Laws Relating to Wiretapping and Electronic Surveillance* ("Wiretap Commission Report") (Washington: U.S. Government Printing Office, 1976), p. 203.

[35] Senator Long hearings, Book II, p. 48. See also Wiretap Commission Report, p. 188 and following.

[36] National Lawyers Guild, p. 1-6.

[37] *Lee v. Florida*, 391 U.S. 378 (1968).

[38] Public Law 90-351, 18 U.S. Code 2510. The 2001 anti-terrorism law altered procedural matters in this law but none of the aspects discussed in this chapter.

[39] *U.S. v. White*, 401 U.S. 745 (1971).

[40] Miller, p. 161.

[41] Gerald Gunther and Noel T. Dowling, *Constitutional Law* (Mineola, N.Y.: The Foundation Press, Inc., 1970), p. 891.

[42] Lapidus, p. 40, and Wiretap Commission Report, p. 188.

[43] *Intelligence Activities and the Rights of Americans, Hearing Before the Senate Select Committee to Study Governmental Operations with Respect to Intelligence Activities*, 94th Cong. 2d Sess. Rep. No. 94-755, testimony of Attorney General Edward H. Levi, November 6, 1975.

[44] Wiretap Commission Report, p. 207.

[45] Lapidus, p. 7.

[46] *U.S. v. U.S. District Court*, 407 U.S. 297 (1972).

[47] *Zweibon v. Mitchell*, 363 F.Supp. 936 (D.C. 1973), 516 F 2d 594 (D.C. Cir., 1975).

[48] *Federal Data Banks, Computers and the Bill of Rights Before the Subcommittee on Constitutional Rights of the Committee on the Judiciary*, U.S. Senate, 92d

Cong., 1st Sess. (1971), p. 602.

[49] This is recounted in the chapter on the Constitution.

[50] Wiretap Commission Report, p. 213.

[51] Holt, p. 62.

[52] *U.S. v. Torres*, 751 F.2d 875 (7th Cir., 1984).

[53] *Privacy Journal*, February 1979, p. 3.

[54] 50 U.S. Code 1801.

[55] Public Law 99-508, amending 18 U.S. Code 2510.

[56] 18 U.S. Code 2522.

Sex, pages 193-223

[1] J. Edgar Hoover with Courtney Ryley Cooper, "Camps of Crime," *American Magazine*, February 1940, p.14.

[2] Increase Mather, *Wo to Drunkards*, p. 29, quoted by David H. Flaherty, *Privacy in Colonial New England* (Charlottesville: University Press of Virginia, 1972), p. 189.

[3] Paul Lancaster, "The Great American Motel," *American Heritage*, June/July 1982, p. 106.

[4] Warren James Belasco, *Americans on the Road: From Autocamp to Motel, 1910-1945* (Cambridge, Mass.: The MIT Press, 1979), p. 168. Belasco says, "Hotel men led the campaign."

[5] *Hotel Management*, October 1929, cited by Belasco, p. 205.

[6] Hooker, Elbert L., "The Urban Tourist Camps," *Studies in Sociology*, Vol. 1, No. 1, Summer 1936 (Dallas: Southern Methodist University), p. 12-22.

[7] Belasco, p. 161.

[8] James H. Jones, *Alfred C. Kinsey: A Public/Private Life* (New York: W.W. Norton, 1997), p. 574. Also in *The New Yorker*, Aug. 25-Sept. 1 1997, p. 99.

[9] Jones, p. 631. *The New Yorker*, p. 100.

[10] Compare this with the Nineteenth-Century diarist, mentioned in the chapter on Space, who wrote that "the very greatest men that have lived have been addicted to indulgences with women," and with Henry Ward Beecher's assertion, discussed later in this chapter, that the public can never judge the "hidden self" of great men.

[11] In *The New Yorker*, Aug. 25-Sept. 1, 1997, p. 114.

[12] This and much of the following material come from James R. Petersen, "*Playboy*'s History of the Sexual Revolution," *Playboy*, February 1996 and following, published as *The Century of Sex: Playboy's History of the Sexual Revolution: 1900-1999* (New York: Grove Press, 1999), p. 201 and p. 228.

[13] *Roth v. U.S.*, 354 U.S. 77 (1957).

[14] Edward J. Bloustein, "Group Privacy: The Right to Huddle," 8 *Rutgers Camden Law Journal* 219 (1977).

[15] Quoted by Richard Reeves, *American Journey: Traveling with DeTocqueville in Search of Democracy in America* (New York: Simon & Schuster, 1982), p. 197.

[16] Albert H. Cantril and Susan Davis Cantril, *Live and Let Live: American Public Opinion About Privacy at Home and at Work* (New York: American Civil Liberties Union, April 1994).

[17] When Senator Hoey died in 1954, he was succeeded by a quite different product of North Carolina, Sam J. Ervin, Jr., who campaigned tirelessly for privacy protections while he served in the Senate for the next 20 years. (See the chapters on Wiretaps and on Databanks.)

[18] David S. Reynolds, *Walt Whitman's America* (New York, Random House, 1995), p. 195. Comstock's impact on mail confidentiality is mentioned in the chapter on Mistrust.

[19] Reynolds, p. 394-5.

[20] D. Michael Quinn, *Same-Sex Dynamics among Nineteenth-Century Americans: A Mormon Example*, (Urbana: University of Illinois Press, 1996), p. 33-35.

[21] For an account of the press coverage of Webster's relations with women, see the chapter on Curiosity.

[22] Reynolds, p. 198.

[23] Reynolds, p. 1 and p. 198.

[24] Quinn, p. 91.

[25] Reynolds, p. 461.

[26] Still, many states outlawed abortions towards the second half of the Nineteenth Century to protect women from unsafe procedures. More than 30 states had laws against abortions when the Fourteenth Amendment was enacted in 1868, according to Stephen M. Krason and William B. Hollberg, "The Law and History of Abortion: The Supreme Court Refuted," in *Abortion, Medicine, and the Law*, edited by J. Douglas Butler and David F. Walbert (New York: Facts on File Publications, 1986).

[27] H.L. Mencken, "Puritanism as a Literary Force" in *A Book of Prefaces* (New York: A.A. Knopf, 1924), p. 233-234.

[28] Altina L. Waller, *Reverend Beecher and Mrs. Tilton – Sex and Class in Victorian America* (Amherst, Mass.: University of Massachusetts Press, 1982), p. 114 and following.

[29] There is more about Anthony Comstock in the chapter on Mistrust.

[30] Robert Shaplen, *Free Love and Heavenly Sinners: The Story of the Great Henry Ward Beecher Scandal* (New York: Knopf, 1954), p. 163. This book provides a reliable account of the whole Beecher-Tilton scandal.

[31] Shaplen, p. 199.

[32] Waller, p 132.

Torts, pages 224-256

[1] Amy Wallace, *The Prodigy* (New York: E.P. Dutton, 1986), p. 55.

[2] The *Roberson* case is discussed in the chapter on Brandeis.

[3] *Sidis v. F-R Publishing Corp.*, 113 F. 2d 806 (1940), cert. denied, 311 U.S. 711 (1940).

[4] This use of the word *unwarranted* in 1940 may be the source of language in the federal Freedom of Information Act of 1966 that exempts certain government documents from mandatory public disclosure including "personnel and medical files and similar files the disclosure of which would constitute a clearly *unwarranted* invasion of personal privacy."

[5] *Melvin v. Reid*, 112 Cal. App. 285, 297 P. 91 (1931).

[6] *Wolston v. Reader's Digest*, 443 U.S. 257 (1979).

[7] *Briscoe v. Reader's Digest*, 4 Cal. 3d 529, 483 P. 2d 34 (1971).

[8] The *Pavesich* case is discussed in the chapter on Brandeis.

[9] "How Privacy Got Its Gender," 10 *Northwestern Illinois University Law Review* 441 (1990).

[10] *Lake v. Wal-Mart*, 582 N.W. 2d 231 (Minn., 1998)

[11] *Zacchini v. Scripps-Howard Broadcasting Co.*, 433 U.S. 562 (1977). The U.S. Supreme Court agreed that Zacchini's "privacy" interest was violated by the broadcast.

[12] William L. Prosser, "Privacy," 48 *California Law Review* 383 (1960). The reference to "Judge Cooley" is Thomas M. Cooley, whose 1888 article on the "right to be let alone" is quoted in the chapter on Brandeis.

[13] Edward J. Bloustein, "Privacy as an Aspect of Human Dignity: An Answer to Dean Prosser," 39 *New York University Law Review* at 1003 (1964).

[14] Robert Ellis Smith, *The Law of Privacy Explained* (Providence, R.I.: Privacy Journal, 1993), p.16-24.

[15] *Swidler & Berlin v. U.S.*, 524 U.S. 399 (1998).

[16] Edward J. Bloustein, "Privacy as an Aspect of Human Dignity: An Answer to Dean Prosser," 39 *New York University Law Review* at 981 (1964).

[17] *Reed v. Real Detective Pub. Co.*, 162 P. 2d 133 (1945).

[18] *Galella v. Onassis*, 487 F. 2d 986 (2d Cir. 1973). Caroline Kennedy's co-author is Ellen Alderman. *The Right to Privacy* (New York: Alfred A. Knopf, 1995).

[19] *Nader v. General Motors Corp.*, 25 N.Y. 2d 560, 307 N.Y.S. 2d 647, 255 N.E. 2d 765 (N.Y. 1970).

[20] *Spahn v. Julian Messenger, Inc.*, 18 N.Y. 2d 324, 221 N.E. 2d 543, reaffirmed 21 N.Y. 2d 124, 233 N.E. 2d 840 (1967).

[21] *Haelan Laboratories, Inc. v. Topps Chewing Gum, Inc.*, 202 F 2d 866 (2nd Cir., 1953).

[22] *Carson v. Here's Johnny Portable Toilets, Inc.*, 698 F. 2d 831 (6th Cir. 1983). *Namath v. Sports Illustrated*, 48 A.D. 2d 487, 371 N.Y.S. 2d 10 (1975). *Booth v. Curtis Publishing Co.*, 15 A.D. 2d 343, 223 N.Y.S. 2d 737 (1962). *Koussevitzky v. Allen, Towne & Health, Inc.*, 68 N.Y.S. 2d 779 (Sup. Ct., 1947). *Ann-Margret v. High Society Magazine, Inc.*, 498 F. Supp. 401 (S.D.N.Y., 1980). *Friedan v. Friedan*, 414 F. Supp. 77 (S.D. N.Y., 1976). *Hirsch v. SC Johnson & Son*, 90 Wis. 2d 379, 280 N.W. 2d 129 (1979).

[23] *Cher v. Forum, Ltd.*, 692 F. 2d 634 (9th Cir. 1982).

[24] *Eastwood v. Superior Court for Los Angeles County*, 198 Cal. Rptr. 342, 149 Cal. App. 3d 409 (Cal. App. 2 Dist. 1983).

[25] *Selleck v. National Enquirer, Inc.*, CA C 441-180 (Cal. Super. Ct., 1983).

[26] *Virgil v. Time, Inc.*, 527 F. 2d 1122 (9th Cir. 1975), on remand superseded by 424 F. Supp. 1286 (S.D. Cal, 1976).

[27] *Florida v. B.L.F.*, 491 U.S. 524 (1989).

[28] *U.S. Department of Justice vs. Reporters Committee for Freedom of the Press*, 489 U.S. 749 (1989).

[29] Chief Justice Rehnquist joined in this decision. But look in the next chapter at what he said about the lack of a privacy interest in arrest and conviction information, in a lecture in 1974.

[30] In 1999, the U.S. Supreme Court reiterated this distinction, ruling that California could deny commercial use of automated criminal data provided by the police even though another state law makes individual arrest information public. *LAPD v. United Reporting Publishing Co.*, 98-678.

[31] Leonard Garment, *Crazy Rhythm: My Journey from Brooklyn, Jazz, and Wall Street to Nixon's White House, Watergate, and Beyond* (New York: Times Books, 1997), p. 79-97. The *Time v. Hill* episode was originally published as "Annals of Law: The Hill Case," *The New Yorker*, April 17, 1989.

[32] The *Roberson* case is discussed in the chapter on Brandeis.

[33] *Time v. Hill*, 385 U.S. 372 (1967).

[34] *Gertz v. Robert Welch, Inc.* 418 U.S. 323 (1974).

[35] *Cantrell v. Forest Publishing Co.*, 419 U.S. 245 (1974).

The Constitution, pages 257-283

[1] *Griswold v. Connecticut*, 381 U.S. 479 (1965).

[2] *Katz v. U.S.*, 389 U.S. 347 (1967), (Black dissenting).

[3] *Pierce v. Society of Sisters*, 268 U.S. 510 (1925); *Meyer v. Nebraska*, 262 U.S. 390 (1923); *NAACP v. Alabama*, 377 U.S. 288 (1958); *NAACP v. Button*, 371 U.S. 415 (1963). See also *Gilbert v. Minnesota*, 254 U.S. 325(1920), saying that parents are free to teach pacifism in the home.

[4] *Boyd v. U.S.*, 116 U.S. 616 (1886). *Union Pacific Railway Co. v. Botsford*, 141 U.S. 250 (1891) (discussed in the chapter on Brandeis). *Weeks v. U.S.*, 232 U.S. 383 (1914).

[5] *Stanley v. Georgia*, 394 U.S. 557 (1969).

[6] *Eisenstadt v. Baird*, 405 U.S. 438 (1972).

[7] *Roe v. Wade*, 410 U.S. 113 (1973). (The names of cases cited in the opinion have been deleted.)

[8] *Papachristou v. City of Jacksonville*, 405 U.S. 156 (1972).

[9] *Warden v. Hayden*, 387 U.S. 294 (1967)(Douglas dissenting).

[10] Quoted by Frank J. Donner, *The Age of Surveillance* (New York: Random House, 1981), p. 243.

[11] *Federal Data Banks, Computers and the Bill of Rights Before the Subcommittee on Constitutional Rights of the Committee on the Judiciary*, U.S. Senate, 92 Cong., 1st Sess. (1971), p. 602.

[12] *Laird v. Tatum*, 402 U.S. 1 (1972).

[13] Christopher H. Pyle and John Shattuck, unpublished manuscript "Privacy: Cases, Materials and Questions." Pyle first revealed this spying by the Army, in *The Washington Monthly*, January 1970. Rehnquist, however, did recuse himself from an important case that same year on the President's authority to order wiretaps for collecting foreign intelligence; this is discussed in the chapter on Wiretapping.

[14] William H. Rehnquist, Stephens Lectures, University of Kansas Law School, 1974. This was chronicled by Robert Ellis Smith, "The Court Pulls Back on Privacy," *The Washington Star*, November 28, 1976.

[15] Quoted by Smith, in *The Washington Star*.

[16] *California Bankers Association v. Shultz*, 416 U.S. 21 (1974).

[17] *U.S. v. Bisceglia*, 420 U.S. 141 (1974).

[18] *Paul v. Davis*, 424 U.S. 714 (1976).

[19] *Doe v. Commonwealth's Attorney*, 403 F. Supp. 1199 (E.D. Va., 1975), aff'd 425 U.S. 901 (1976). Later, the Court rejected a challenge to Georgia's punishment of homosexual sodomy, *Bowers v. Hardwick*, 478 U.S. 186 (1986).

[20] *Kelley v. Johnson*, 425 U.S. 238 (1976).

[21] *U.S. v. Miller*, 425 U.S. 435 (1976).

[22] *Whelan v. Roe*, 429 U.S. 589 (1976).

[23] *Department of Defense v. FLRA*, 510 U.S. 487 (1994).

[24] Employment testing, *Detroit Edison Co. v. NLRB*, 440 U.S. 301 (1979). Pupil records, *Doe v. McMillian*, 412 U.S. 306 (1973). Law enforcement data systems, *Department of Justice v. Reporters Committee for Freedom of the Press*, 489 U.S. 749 (1989). Federal employees' home addresses, *Department of Defense v. FLRA*, 510 U.S. 487 (1994). At the same time, the Court has recognized the confidentiality necessary between patients and psychotherapists. *Jaffee v. Redmond*, 518 U.S. 1 (1996).

[25] *Kolender v. Lawson*, 461 U.S. 352 (1983).

[26] *Kent v. Dulles*, 357 U.S. 116 (1958), "[Travel] may be as close to the heart of the individual as the choice of what he eats, or wears, or reads. Freedom of movement is basic in our scheme of values." And *Aptheker v. Secretary of State*, 378 U.S. 500 (1964).

[27] *West Virginia State Board of Education v. Barnette*, 319 U.S. 624 (1943).

[28] *Bowers v. Hardwick*, 478 U.S. 186 (1986). *Lawrence v. Texas*, 02-102 (2003).

[29] *Thornburgh v. American College of Obstetrics & Gynecology*, 476 U.S. 747 (1986).

[30] *Planned Parenthood of Southeastern Pennsylvania et al v. Casey*, 505 U.S. 833 (1992).

[31] *Union Pacific Railway v. Botsford*, 141 U.S. 250 (1891). This case is placed in context in the chapter on Brandeis.

[32] J. Braxton Craven, "Personhood: The Right to be Let Alone," 1976 *Duke Law Journal* 699, and Laurence H. Tribe, *American Constitutional Law* (2d Ed. 1988), sec 15-1, at p. 1302.4. Tribe, a Harvard Law School professor, has been an advisor to Justice Kennedy, according to the Jeffrey Rosen report mentioned

in the text; if so, the presence of Tribe's term "personhood" in the *Casey* opinion lends credence to the idea that Kennedy wrote that section of the opinion.

[33] Jeffrey Rosen, "The Agonizer," *The New Yorker*, November 11, 1996, p. 86.

[34] *O'Connor v. Ortega*, 480 U.S. 709 (1987).

[35] *Florida Bar v. Went for It*, 515 U.S. 618 (1995).

[36] *Acton v. Vernonia School District*, 515 U.S. 646 (1995). In 1989, the Court had ruled that urinalysis tests required in workplaces are not unconstitutional. *National Treasury Employees Union v. von Raab*, 489 U.S. 656 (1989) and *Skinner v. Railway Labor Executives' Association*, 489 U.S. 602 (1989).

Numbers, pages 284-308

[1] I use the term *enumeration* in this chapter, for lack of a better word, in its second dictionary sense, that is, "issuing a number to everyone," not in the first sense of merely counting them. *Enumeration* in the chapter on Mistrust, however, refers to counting the population.

[2] These fears were present in Colonial times, as recounted in the chapter on Serenity. Revelation 13:16-17 and 14.9-10 in the Bible speaks of a great beast that resembles Satan: "And he causeth all, both small and great, rich and poor, free and bond, to receive a mark, or the name of the beast, or the number of his name. And that no man might buy or sell, save that he had the mark, or the name of the beast, or the number of his name. . . . And the third angel followed them, saying with a loud voice, If any man worship the beast and his image, and receive *his* mark in his forehead, on in his hand, the same shall drink of the wine of the wrath of God, . . . and he shall be tormented with fire and brimstone." This has been the source of fear of enumeration by many fundamentalist Christians.

[3] Mandatory registration for the Selective Service System continued even after World War II, but Congress did not enact President Harry S. Truman's proposal in 1948 to make military training universal for all males. During the War in Vietnam a lottery system for enlisting military personnel was instituted in 1969. Congress and President Richard M. Nixon permitted the selective service law to expire in 1973, but mandatory registration for males at their eighteenth birthdays was reinstated in 1980. Still, the requirement that young men enlist in the armed services, as opposed to merely register for a possible draft, has not reoccurred since the Vietnam war years.

[4] Arthur J. Altmeyer, *The Formative Years in Social Security* (Madison: University of Wisconsin Press, 1966), p. 68-71.

[5] Social Security Administration, "Privacy and Customer Service in the Electronic Age" (November 1997).

[6] "Privacy and Customer Service in the Electronic Age."

[7] Alan F. Westin, *Privacy and Freedom* (New York: Atheneum, 1967), p. 304.

[8] *Records, Computers and the Rights of Citizens, Report of the Secretary's Advisory Committee on Automated Personal Data Systems, U.S. Department of Health, Education and Welfare* ("HEW report") (Washington: U.S. Government

Printing Office, 1973), p. 112. Also published by The MIT Press, Cambridge, Massachusetts, 1973.

[9] Public Law 87-397, 26 U.S. Code 6109.

[10] Richard Ruggles, "On the Need and Values of Data Banks, in *Ethics and Data Banks, Symposium of the Graduate School of Business Administration*, May 2, 1968 (Minneapolis: University of Minnesota, 1968), p. 233.

[11] Bank Secrecy Act, 31 U.S. Code 1051.

[12] Omaha *World-Telegram*, November 18, 1981, p. 34, *Chicago Sun Times* News Service), quoted by Robert Ellis Smith, *Report on the Collection and Use of Social Security Numbers* (Providence, R.I.: Privacy Journal, 1990), p. 3.

[13] HEW report, p. 131.

[14] This issue is further discussed in the chapter on Databanks.

[15] Social Security Administration, "Social Security Number Task Force Report to the Commissioner" (May 1971).

[16] HEW report, p. 121.

[17] HEW report, p. 122, note.

[18] 5 U.S. Code 552a (note). The Privacy Act covers the federal government only, except for this provision on Social Security numbers, which applies to all levels of government.

[19] For a discussion of the recommendation in the HEW report for a Code of Fair Information Practice, see the next chapter, on Databanks.

[20] *Computerworld*, October 4, 1976, quoted in Smith report on SSNs.

[21] *Jensen v. Quaring*, 472 US 478 (1985), 728 F 2d 1121 (8th Cir. 1984).

[22] *Bowen v. Roy*, 476 U.S. 693 (1986). Judge Muir's intriguing decision is at 590 F Supp 600 (1984). The details about the trial are recounted in the Jurisdictional Statement by the Department of Justice before the U.S. Supreme Court.

[23] *Greidinger v. Davis*, 988 F. 2d 1344 (4th Cir. 1993).

[24] Many national ID numbers in Scandinavia, Israel, and elsewhere are issued sequentially at birth and can identify an individual for life, unlike our Social Security number, which has an imperfect numbering system based on the state of issuance and, roughly, the time of issuance. Strictly speaking, it is not required of every citizen (yet). There are persons with more than one number and there are numbers being used by more than one person.

[25] *Privacy Journal*, April 1975, p. 3.

[26] Alan Simpson, "U.S. Needs System to Verify Eligibility for Employment," *The Plain Dealer*, Cleveland, *Dallas Morning News*, and other newspapers, August 14, 1994. See also Robert Ellis Smith, "The True Terror is in the Card," *The New York Times Magazine*, September 8, 1996, p. 58.

[27] Sec 656(b) of the Immigration Responsibility Act 1996, 42 U.S. Code 653(j).

[28] Social Security Administration, *Report to Congress on Options for Enhancing the Social Security Card*, September 1997.

[29] 5 U.S. Code 301 (note). The repeal was included in the 1999 Department of Transportation appropriations bill, Public Law 106-69.

[30] The authorization to use the database for additional purposes was included in HR 3073 in 1999; it was not enacted.

[31] 42 U.S. Code 1320 d-2(b).

[32] Birth certificates, 42 U.S. Code 1305, 42 U.S. Code 607, 42 U.S. Code 602. Applications for a minor's Social Security number, 42 U.S. Code 405(c)(2). Minor dependents on a tax return, 26 U.S. Code 6109(note).

[33] Quoted by Oscar Handlin, *This Was America* (New York: Harper & Row, 1949), p. 118-119.

[34] The Supreme Court cases are cited in the chapter on The Constitution.

[35] Louis Harris and Associates, *Equifax-Harris Mid-Decade Consumer Privacy Survey 1995* (New York, N.Y.: Louis Harris and Associates 1995).

Databanks, pages 309-337

[1] "Report of the Committee on the Preservation and Use of Economic Data to the Social Science Research Council," March 1965, monograph of the Social Science Research Council, Washington, D.C., p. 18-22.

[2] William H. Whyte, Jr., *The Organization Man* (New York: Doubleday & Co., 1956), p. 439.

[3] Quoted by Katherine Davis Fishman, *The Computer Establishment* (New York: McGraw-Hill, 1981), p. 418.

[4] James Rule, Douglas McAdam, Linda Stearns, and David Uglow, *The Politics of Privacy* (New York: The New American Library, 1980), Appendix.

[5] Arthur R. Miller, "On Proposals and Requirements for Solutions, in *Ethics and Data Banks, Symposium of the Graduate School of Business Administration*, May 2, 1968 (Minneapolis: University of Minnesota, 1968), p. 227.

[6] In 1996, the company spun off its Insurance Services Group as a separate company called ChoicePoint.

[7] The law was amended in 1996 to require disclosure of "all information" in a credit report to a consumer who asks, and in 2003 to make this without charge.

[8] Consequently, victims of inaccurate credit reports sue credit bureaus for violating the section of the law that requires bureaus to correct errors promptly and to "follow reasonable procedures to assure maximum possible accuracy of the information." 15 U.S. Code 1681.

[9] Federal Trade Commission Docket Number C-3611, File Number 902 3149, approved August 18, 1995.

[10] Nat Ross, "A History of Direct Marketing" (New York: Direct Marketing Association, 1992). Benjamin Franklin provided this guarantee: "Those persons who live remote, by sending their orders and money to said B. Franklin, may depend on the same justice as if present."

[11] A federal appeals court ordered the agency to provide more evidence about Trans Union's practices. *Trans Union Corp. v. Federal Trade Commission*, 81 Fed 3d 228 (D.C. Cir. 1996).

[12] *Alabama et al v. Trans Union Corp.*, 92C 7101 (N.D. Ill, 1992).

[13] *Privacy Journal*, May 1993, *Mirocha v. TRW et al*, 805 F. Supp 663 (S.D. Ind., 1992).

[14] Interview with the author, 1974.

[15] Letter to the author, March 30, 1999.

[16] *Records, Computers and the Rights of Citizens, Report of the Secretary's Advisory Committee on Automated Personal Data Systems, U.S. Department of Health, Education and Welfare* ("HEW report")(Washington: U.S. Government Printing Office, 1973), p. xx. Also published by The MIT Press, Cambridge, Massachusetts, 1973.

[17] For early articulations of the principle of secondary use, see the chapter on Mistrust.

[18] Edward J. Bloustein, "Privacy as An Aspect of Human Dignity: An Answer to Dean Prosser," 39 *New York University Law Review* at 1003 (1964).

[19] Alan F. Westin: *Privacy and Freedom* (New York: Atheneum, 1967), p. 375.

[20] David H. Flaherty, *Protecting Privacy in Surveillance Societies* (Chapel Hill: University of North Carolina Press, 1989), p. 94.

[21] Richard Nixon's role in the case of *Time v. Hill* is described in the chapter on Torts.

[22] This law was amended in 1999 to require the consent of a person, not merely an opportunity to "opt out," before names could be included in the lists that state motor-vehicle agencies rent.

[23] *Menard v. Mitchell*, 328 F. Supp. 718 (D.D.C. 1970).

[24] Francis W. Sargent, "Politics of Privacy: The View from Massachusetts," *Privacy Journal*, April 1975.

[25] *Menard v. Saxbe*, 498 F. 2d 1017 (D.C. Cir. 1974). *Tarlton v. Saxbe*, 507 F. 2d 1116 (D.C. Cir. 1974). In 1973, Congress passed a law permitting a person to review and correct arrest information, at least in systems created with federal funds, 42 U.S. Code 3771.

[26] *Privacy Journal*, October 1993, citing Louis Harris & Associates, *Harris-Equifax Consumer Privacy Surveys*, also *Privacy Concerns & Consumer Choices* New York: Louis Harris & Associates, 1998). The question in 1970 was not identical to the one quoted in the text here. See also Alan F. Westin, *Databanks in a Free Society* (New York Quadrangle Books, 1972), p. 466.

Cyberspace, pages 338-353

[1] Louis Harris & Associates, *Interactive Services, Consumers, and Privacy: A National Survey* (New York: Louis Harris & Associates, 1994).

[2] Louis Harris & Associates and Alan F. Westin, *Commerce, Communication, and Privacy Online, A National Survey of Computer Users* (New York: Louis Harris & Associates, 1997).

[3] A. Michael Froomkin, "It Came From Planet Clipper: The Battle over Cryptographic Key 'Escrow,'" 1996 *The University of Chicago Legal Forum* 15.

[4] See the Chapters on Watchfulness and on Serenity.

[5] Social Security Administration: "Privacy and Customer Service in the Electronic Age" (Washington, D.C., 1997). Other references to Web sites are from *Privacy Journal*, April 1999).

[6] In 1997 Equifax spun off its insurance-reporting operation including CDB Infotek and formed a closely-affiliated company called ChoicePoint. The chair of Equifax, Inc., during the 1990s, C.B. Rogers, Jr., for instance, is chair of the Executive Committee of ChoicePoint's Board of Directors; ChoicePoint's president was executive vice president of Equifax.

[7] Simson Garfinkel and Alan Schwartz, *Stopping Spam* (Sebastopol, Calif.: O'Reilly & Associates, 1998).

[8] Isaac Asimov, "The Individualism to Come," in an advertisement supplement to *The New York Times*, Section 11, January 7, 1973.

[9] Federal Trade Commission, "Public Workshop on Consumer Privacy on the Global Information Infrastructure, Staff Report" (Washington, D.C., 1996), p. 33.

[10] Public Law 105-277, 15 U.S. Code 6501-6505. The law is separate from the Child's On-line Protection Act, 47 U.S.Code 231, passed at about the same time, which seeks to shield children from sexually oriented materials on the World Wide Web.

[11] Some of this language is borrowed with permission from Laurence Kearley of the Immigration and Refugee Board, Government of Canada, in "The Protection of Privacy on the Internet," a monograph (Ottawa, 1995)

Index

Fort Leonard Wood, 292
Fortas, Abe, 247
Fortezza PCMCIA card, 341
Forum, 239
Fountain pen, 123
Fourteenth Amendment, 45, 88, 89, 261, 271, 279
Fourth Amendment, 4, 47, 53, 147, 161-163, 168, 169, 170, 171, 183, 258, 259, 269, 282; "protects people, not places," 170-171; see also Searches
Fowles, John, 18
Fox TV, 253
Frankfurt, University of, 330
Frankfurter, Felix, 144, 145, 146, 152, 162
Franklin, Benjamin, 19, 22, 30, 33-34, 37, 81, 107, 116, 118, 152, 325, 354, 355, 361; as Postmaster, 43, 49, 50, 357; see also *Autobiography*; Richard Saunders
Franklin, John, 50
Franklin, Peter, 50
Franklin Mills Flour, 138
Free Love, 215, 216
Free speech, 25, 47; see also First Amendment
Freedom of Information, 127, 133
Freeh, Louis, 189
French, 2, 10, 19, 26, 36, 50, 75, 78, 103, 104, 105, 118, 307
Freud, Sigmund, 212, 224
Friday, Nancy, 204
Friedan, Betty, 238
Friendly, Henry, 147, 149
Frontier, American, 71, 75, 77, 78, 80, 85, 91, 92, 101, 107, 210, 351
Froomkin, A. Michael, 340
"Fruit of the poisonous tree," 160
Fruits of Solitude, 17
Fuller, Buckminster, 225
Fuller, Margaret, 99
Funeral directors, 322

Galbraith, John Kenneth, 29
Galella, Ronald, 234-235, 246
Gallagher, Cornelius, 311, 312
Gambling, 54, 70, 160, 170, 262
Garfield, James, 62, 69
Garfinkel, Simson, 348
Garment, Leonard, 244, 248

Gates, Bill, 70
Gates, Henry Louis, 202
General Motors Corp., 235-236, 246
General Services Administration (GSA), 311
Genetic tests, 358
Georgetown University Law Center, 142
Germans, 36, 105
Germany, 330
Gesell, Gerhard, 335
Gilded Age, 70, 222, 312
Gilman, Charlotte Perkins, 94, 95, 133
Glamour, 254
Global village, 77, 352
Globe, 252
Goddard, Henry W., 227
Godkin, E.L., 106, 128-137, 212
Goldberg, Arthur J., 258
Goldberg, Lucianne, 222
Goldwater, Barry M., 297
Goldwater, Jr., Barry M., 331
Gone with the Wind, 200
Goodale, James C., 133
Gore, Al, 189, 340
Gossip, 10, 68, 78, 102, 104, 106, 115, 118, 119, 123, 127, 130, 135, 142, 252, 253, 312
Gould, Jay, 70-71, 114
GQ, 254
Grant, Ulysses S., 117
Graven image, 299
Gray, John Clinton, 139
Great Universal Stores, 327
Greeley, Horace, 112, 217
Greenhouse, Linda, 275
Greenleaf, Graham, 344
Greenwich Village, 207
Griswold, Estelle, 257

Haagen-Dazs, 253
Hackers, 339, 345
Hadley, Herbert Spencer, 118
Hamilton, Alexander, 34, 40, 41, 42, 50, 339
Hammond, James H., 96
Hardwick, Michael, 1
Harlan, John Marshall, 171, 250, 251
HarperCollins, 254
Harris, Nick, 156
Harrison, Benjamin, 71
Hartford Courant, 115

Meiklejohn, Alexander, 247
Mellon, Paul, 360
Men, 10, 24, 40, 63, 85, 93-96, 97, 133,
    141, 156, 202-204, 206, 207, 209-
    211, 219, 230, 275, 288, 317, 328
Mencken, H.L., 213
Mental distress, see Emotional distress
Merchants, 23, 75, 107, 108, 313, 316,
    344
Metromail, Inc., 327
Miami, University of, 340
Michaux, Francois Andre, 78, 103, 307
Michigan, 130, 313, 318
Microphone, 123, 155, 156, 159, 162,
    163, 164, 165
Microsoft, Inc., 5, 70
Midler, Bette, 233
Military, 61, 64, 88, 113, 175, 207,
    265-266, 292, 293
Miller, Arthur R., 132, 170, 313, 318,
    328
Miller, Warren, 229
Milwaukee Braves, 237
Mind of the South, The, 78
Minnesota, 230, 231, 333
Miracle at Philadelphia, The, 106
Miramax Films, 254
Mirocha, Keith and Phyllis, 326
Mirrors, 124, 274
Missing Links, 347
Missouri, 70, 155, 164, 199, 292, 293,
    300, 313, 320
Mitchell, John N., 179, 182
Mobile phone, 358
Mobility (moving residences), 75-76,
    319
Models, 140
Monitoring, 9, 87, 98, 154, 156, 159,
    173, 178
Montgomery, Aaron, 325
Monty Python's Flying Circus, 348-349
Moon Hoax, 110
"Morbid and sensational prying," 241,
    242
Moreau de Saint-Mery, Mederic, 75
Mormons, 79, 80, 81, 82, 209, 210
Morning Herald, 108
Morse, Samuel F.B., 66, 71, 123, 154
Morse, Wayne, 173
Morton, Nathaniel, 17
Motels and motor courts, 18, 56,
    193-200

Moulton, Frank, 215, 218, 222
Moynihan, Daniel Patrick, 200, 312
MTV, 207
MUDS (multiuser dungeons), 349
Mugwumps, 136, 221
Muir, Malcolm, 298, 299
Murdoch, Rupert, 252
Murphy, Frank, 162
My Secret Garden, 204

Nabokov, Vladimir, 199
Nader, Ralph, 235, 236, 237, 313
Naked Society, The, 313
Namath, Joe, 238
Names, 58, 284, 298
Nardone, Frank Carmine, 160
Nation, The, 128, 134
Nation of Strangers, A, 313
National Association for the
    Advancement of Colored People
    (NAACP), 259, 269
National Change of Address, 348
National Data Center, 146, 309, 310,
    311, 316, 353
National Directory of New Hires, 302-
    305
National Enquirer, 239, 240, 249, 252,
    253, 254
National identification card, see
    Identifier, universal
National Information Infrastructure, 351
National Institute of Standards and
    Technology (NIST), 341
National Institute on Alcohol Abuse,
    190
National security, 53, 164, 173, 175,
    179, 181, 182, 183, 184, 185; 1978
    law, 187; see also Wiretapping
National Security Agency, 339
Native Americans (Indians), 12, 15, 16,
    18, 39, 87, 125, 298
Nature, 19, 99-101
"Nature and substance (of a credit
    report)," 320
Nazi regime, 284
Nebraska, 259, 299
Netscape, 342
New England Life Insurance Co., 143
New Hampshire, 25, 26, 34, 39, 178,
    348
New Haven, 21
New Jersey, 38, 117

Table of Cases Mentioned

About the Author

Robert Ellis Smith has edited and published the monthly newsletter *Privacy Journal* since 1974. A journalist and an attorney, Smith has long been recognized as an advocate for more privacy protection. He has testified frequently before Congressional committees, regulatory bodies, and state legislative bodies and has appeared on the major network television programs. A graduate of Harvard College, he began his career as a news reporter for daily newspapers including the *Detroit Free Press* and *Newsday*. After that, he was assistant director of the Office for Civil Rights in the U.S. Department of Health, Education and Welfare. He is a graduate of Georgetown University Law Center. Twice he has been asked to write the definition of privacy for *The World Book Encyclopedia*. Smith's first book, *Privacy: How to Protect What's Left of It*, was nominated for an American Book Award in 1980. Since then he has written *Workrights, Our Vanishing Privacy*, and a series of privacy reference books. *Privacy Journal* was established in Washington, D.C., and is now based in Providence, Rhode Island.